SCOTTISH CASTLES

SCOTTISH CASTLES

Adrian Pettifer

THE BOYDELL PRESS

© Adrian Pettifer 2024

All Rights Reserved. Except as permitted under current legislation
no part of this work may be photocopied, stored in a retrieval system,
published, performed in public, adapted, broadcast,
transmitted, recorded or reproduced in any form or by any means,
without the prior permission of the copyright owner

The right of Adrian Pettifer to be identified as
the author of this work has been asserted in accordance with
sections 77 and 78 of the Copyright, Designs and Patents Act 1988

First published 2024
The Boydell Press, Woodbridge

ISBN 978 1 83765 204 4

The Boydell Press is an imprint of Boydell & Brewer Ltd
PO Box 9, Woodbridge, Suffolk IP12 3DF, UK
and of Boydell & Brewer Inc.
668 Mt Hope Avenue, Rochester, NY 14620–2731, USA
website: www.boydellandbrewer.com

A CIP catalogue record for this book is available
from the British Library

The publisher has no responsibility for the continued existence or accuracy
of URLs for external or third-party internet websites referred to in this book,
and does not guarantee that any content on such websites is, or will remain,
accurate or appropriate

Printed and bound in Great Britain by
TJ Books Limited, Padstow, Cornwall

CONTENTS

List of Illustrations	vii
Acknowledgements	ix
Preface	xi
List of Abbreviations	xv
Introduction	1
Aberdeenshire	13
Angus	43
Argyll: Islands	58
Argyll: Mainland	63
Ayrshire	79
Banffshire	99
Berwickshire	108
Bute County	113
Caithness	118
Clackmannanshire and Kinross-shire	125
Dumfriesshire	133
Dunbartonshire	146
East Lothian	149
Fife	163
Inverness-shire	184
Kincardineshire	193
Kirkcudbrightshire	200

Lanarkshire	209
Midlothian	221
Moray and Nairnshire	238
Orkney	249
Peeblesshire	254
Perthshire	258
Renfrewshire	274
Ross	278
Roxburghshire	284
Selkirkshire	295
Shetland	299
Skye	302
Stirlingshire	306
Sutherland	315
Western Isles	319
West Lothian	321
Wigtownshire	329
Glossary	335
Bibliography	365
Index of Sites	367

ILLUSTRATIONS

Plates

All photographs are the author's own.

Craigievar Castle, Aberdeenshire	21
Fyvie Castle, Aberdeenshire	27
Claypotts Castle, Angus	47
Duart Castle, Argyll Islands	60
Castle Stalker, Argyll Mainland	67
Dunstaffnage Castle, Argyll Mainland	70
Balvenie Castle, Banffshire	101
Castle Sinclair Girnigoe, Caithness	121
Old Keiss Castle, Caithness	124
Lochleven Castle, Kinross-shire	130
Caerlaverock Castle, Dumfriesshire	136
Comlongon Castle, Dumfriesshire	138
Dirleton Castle, East Lothian	151
St Andrews Castle, Fife	179
Urquhart Castle, Inverness-shire	190
Dunnottar Castle, Kincardineshire	196
Threave Castle, Kirkcudbrightshire	207
Craignethan Castle, Lanarkshire	215
Borthwick Castle, Midlothian	222
Crichton Castle, Midlothian	227

Cawdor Castle, Nairnshire	241
Duffus Castle, Moray	244
Kirkwall Palace, Orkney	251
Huntingtower Castle, Perthshire	268
Eilean Donan Castle, Ross	280
Hermitage Castle, Roxburghshire	289
Smailholm Tower, Roxburghshire	293
Dunvegan Castle, Skye	305
Stirling Castle, Stirlingshire	310
Linlithgow Palace, West Lothian	325

Plans

An oblong tower house: Comlongon	359
An L-plan tower house: Crathes	360
A Z-plan tower house: Claypotts	361

ACKNOWLEDGEMENTS

My thanks to Caroline and everyone at Boydell & Brewer for their efforts in getting this into print. Also to Cath D'Alton for drawing the plans.

PREFACE

This book completes my British Castles trilogy. Following the form of the others in the series (*English Castles* and *Welsh Castles*, both published by Boydell), it aims to provide a short account of every Scottish castle that survives in a reasonable state of preservation. As in the previous volumes, castles are defined as the defensive, lordly residences of the Middle Ages – although in Scotland, this must be extended into the early modern period. The definition excludes ancient fortifications and many more recent mansions that have appropriated the title. Admittedly, the term is stretched rather thin to cover the quasi-fortified houses of James VI's long reign. This was a period of transition, so some sifting has been necessary to select buildings with modest defensive credentials as opposed to the many turreted lairds' houses, no matter how lovable.

Even when we have whittled down the list to the more plausible contenders, the sheer number remaining is still daunting. This is because of the many tower houses that dot the landscape, most of them rarely, if ever, open to the public. Often, they are not even closely visible without encroaching on private property, so some pruning on the grounds of visitability seemed appropriate this time around. Castles deemed to be of especial importance are included as main entries regardless. The remainder are accorded a full entry if they are open for more than the occasional afternoon, or if their exteriors can at least be viewed reasonably close-up from roads or public footpaths. Those that do not satisfy these modest criteria are summarised very briefly.

Castles that do not merit even a short entry in a book of this length are relegated to an Other Sites section at the end of each county. They are mostly late tower houses, whether much altered and embedded in private houses, or shattered ruins, generally on farmland. Castles of particular interest that have disappeared are also mentioned there. A handful of sites that might have been dismissed as too meagre for inclusion have been reprieved owing to their historical importance or breathtaking locations. In line with the other two books, Scotland's few town defences and ecclesiastical fortifications are also included.

Only about a fifth of the castles in this book preserve substantial remains of courtyard defences or residential buildings. Most Scottish castles are wholly or primarily tower houses. The visitor may find the preponderance of the tower house a little repetitive, compared with the multi-towered enclosures of Wales or the sheer variety in England. However, the intricacies of each one are a pleasure to examine, where it is possible to do so. The permutations in shape are described in the glossary but, as a visitor experience, there are four basic types: Among the most visited are those that form the core of later stately homes. Typically, they are authentic externally but transformed within, except for the ubiquitous barrel-vaulted undercroft. Next comes the modest free-standing tower, with original features lovingly preserved. Then there is the maintained ruin, which can be very instructive despite its incomplete state. Finally, there is the blight of the neglected and crumbling ruin, on which more will follow.

I have given a broad indication of accessibility at the end of each entry, ranging from 'freely accessible' to 'private'. Specific opening times are avoided because they tend to change over time (up-to-date details can usually be found on the internet). Check beforehand for unexpected closures if you are travelling any distance, particularly as many properties rely on private functions nowadays for much-needed additional revenue.

The state-run agency Historic Environment Scotland maintains many of the earlier castles, along with a representative sample of the later ones. It is well worth joining this organisation for an annual season ticket (there are reciprocal arrangements for members of English Heritage and Cadw). Most of their staffed sites are open daily in the summer months and some, to a lesser extent, during the winter. Unstaffed sites are freely accessible, occasionally with recourse to a local key keeper. The National Trust for Scotland has surprisingly few genuine castles in its care, but they include some absolute gems. Local authorities are poorly represented on the whole.

All other castles opening their doors belong to individuals or private trusts. Many of them are members of the Historic Houses Association, which also provides a yearly pass for a reasonable fee. The continuing accessibility of privately run castles cannot be taken for granted. Although some have remained open for decades, others have failed to make a living in the precarious tourist industry. The dedicated castle hunter will have to plan trips to coincide with some quite limited opening times. An increasing number serve exclusively as wedding venues, conference centres or holiday accommodation and are thus denied to a wider public. I have treated these as inaccessible unless they fulfil the criteria already given. The small number of castles that are now hotels usually welcome non-residents to their bars and dining rooms, so there is scope for a limited inspection.

The most vexing category is the uncared-for ruin, slowly crumbling away in a field or an uninviting farmyard. There are still far too many of these and determining accessibility is much less clear cut. Although the Scottish Outdoor Access Code gives greater leeway to the responsible walker than in England, agricultural land should not be trampled on when crops are growing and many visitors will understandably be deterred by the bulkier forms of livestock. I have classed such ruins as inaccessible unless there appears to be a well-established right of way. In any case, great caution is required owing to the danger these buildings pose to life and limb. A growing number are ineffectually cordoned off because of their hazardous condition. They seem condemned to slow disintegration.

There are a few ways to alleviate the frustration of inaccessible castles. The Scottish Castles Association organises periodic members' tours to places not usually open. Doors Open Days, taking place in different regions throughout September, provide a rare opportunity to visit a handful of castles (the catalogue changes over time). Even if no opening arrangements are given, it is worth making enquiries if you are interested in a particular site. Changing ownership or usage may cause changes in accessibility, so my advice in the text should not be taken to override conditions encountered on the day. It hardly needs adding that, without personal transport, many castles will require an awful lot of footwork. Some do even with a car, since considerate parking may not be possible close by.

The gazetteer is divided into geographical sections for the convenience of the visitor. They mainly correspond to the historic (pre-1975) counties, though small, adjacent counties have been amalgamated and it seemed practical to treat the island groups as separate entities. The current administrative divisions are a confusing jumble and quite unsuitable for a gazetteer. I have followed the most commonly used place names but there are often several variants. The same applies in applying the designation 'castle', 'tower' or 'house'.

Scottish castles are unevenly distributed. Some do indeed overlook mountain-fringed lochs but they are thinly spread over the Highlands and islands. The greatest concentrations are found in the Lowlands – the eastern coastal plains, the rolling south west and the sporadically urban landscape of central Scotland. Finding sites (except for the minority of signposted ones) can be difficult. Many are out of town, off the beaten track and camouflaged by vegetation. The index provides Ordnance Survey grid references for each entry, while Google Maps are invaluable where the monument has been correctly tagged.

ABBREVIATIONS

BoS	Buildings of Scotland
HES	Historic Environment Scotland
HHA	Historic Houses Association
LA	Local Authority
NTS	National Trust for Scotland
PSAS	Proceedings of the Society of Antiquaries of Scotland
RCAHMS	Royal Commission on the Ancient and Historical Monuments of Scotland

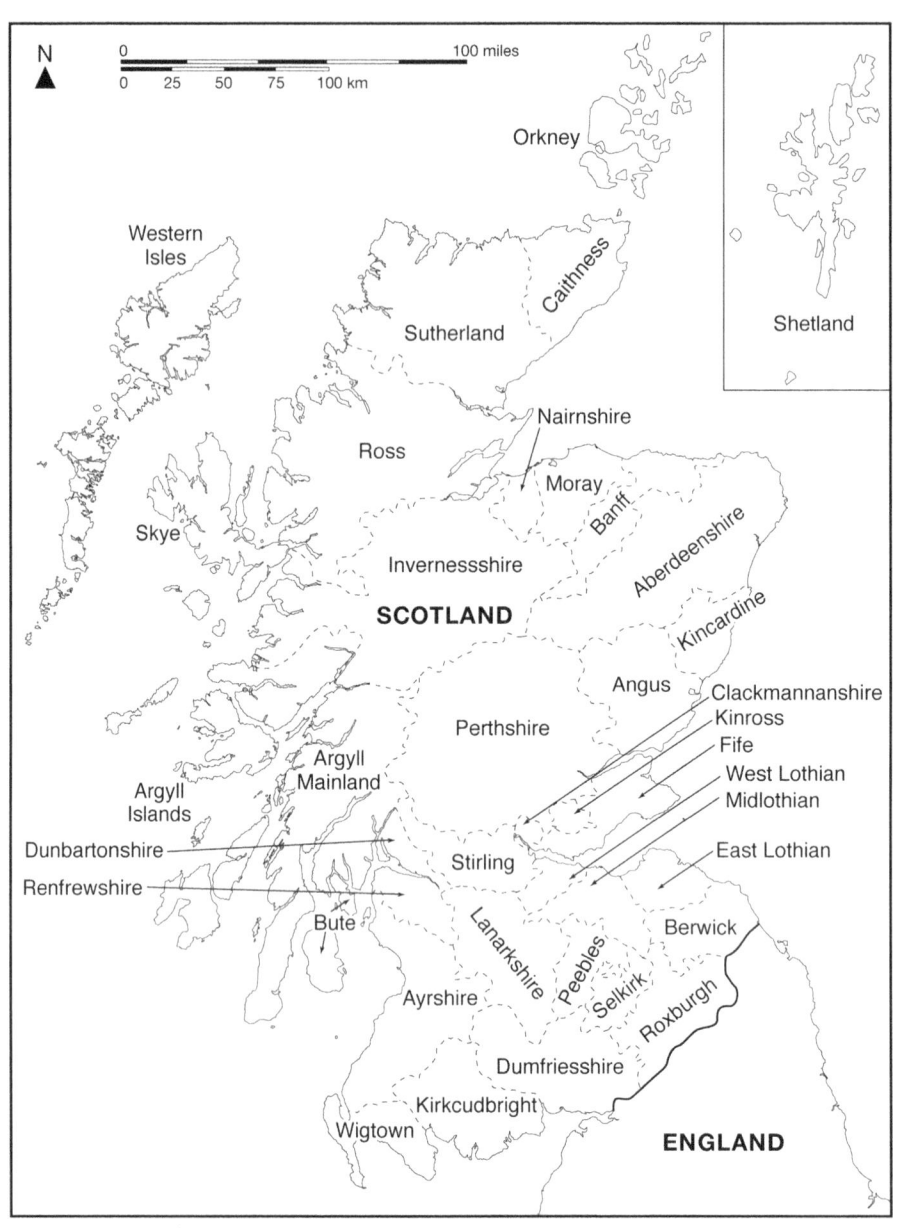

The counties of Scotland as used in this volume

INTRODUCTION

The castles of Scotland form a large and distinctive group, differing in many ways from their English counterparts. Here, the age of the castle falls later than in the rest of Britain. It begins with the arrival of Anglo-Norman settlers, invited by David I in the twelfth century, and ends – admittedly in a very diluted form – sometime after James VI had taken the road south in 1603. In the earlier period English developments (largely imported from Europe) were followed, from motte-and-bailey earthworks to multi-towered curtain walls, though Scotland has virtually none of the square keeps characteristic of Norman England. The Wars of Independence marked a change, with many castles being destroyed by the Scots themselves to make them untenable for the English invaders. Afterwards, most new castles centred upon the latter-day keeps known as tower houses. Such towers were built in ever-increasing numbers from the fourteenth century onwards, when serious castle building was coming to an end in England. They evolved from austere, oblong boxes to a variety of elaborate layouts, defence moving away from an embattled parapet to gunports at ground level. The last generation of castle building was a transitional period, the climax of a castellated style increasingly divorced from its fortified roots but still retaining token defensive features.

Origins

There are curious precursors of the tower houses that would later dominate so much of Scotland in the remarkable brochs found mostly in the Highlands and Islands. These tapering, circular towers date from the late Iron Age. The few that survive in a recognisable state, notably Mousa Broch in Shetland, show an unexpected sophistication at the edge of the known world. The tribes who occupied northern Britain did not succumb to Roman occupation, though their resistance was aided by the difficult terrain. Despite efforts by the governor Julius Agricola and the emperor Septimius Severus, Caledonia was never successfully incorporated into Roman Britannia. For most of its existence the province was bounded by Hadrian's Wall. A second-century advance to the Antonine Wall, between the Forth and the Clyde, proved short-lived.

Scotland as we know it emerged as a result of the slow unification of its four main peoples – Scots in the north-west, Picts in the north-east, Britons in the south-west and Angles in the south-east. Although the Anglian sector from the Tweed to the Forth had long formed part of the Kingdom of Northumbria, its annexation by Scotland was confirmed by the Battle of Carham in 1018. With the Norman seizure of Cumberland in 1092, the Anglo-Scottish Border was almost permanently defined, though much of the north and west remained nominally under the rule of Norway.

Castles – the fortified homes of feudal lords – originated in northern Europe during the decline of the Carolingian empire. Scotland, like the rest of Britain, did not yet embrace the new trend. There had long been duns – hillforts defended by ramparts of earth or vitrified stone – but these were communal fortifications. The strong natural situations and strategic locations of some, like Edinburgh and Dumbarton, destined them to become castles in the accepted sense later.

Norman Infiltration

Castles first appeared in England with the Norman Conquest. They spread to Wales as a result of piecemeal Norman penetration, but there was no similar attempt to colonise Scotland. William the Conqueror's incursion of 1072 resulted in the customary declaration of allegiance by the Scots' king, Malcolm III (Canmore). Malcolm launched raids into England several times, until his defeat and death at Alnwick in 1093, but hostilities were comparatively rare for the next two centuries. Malcolm's three sons, who reigned in turn, appreciated the advantages of the feudal system for extending their grip on a fragmented realm. This was most marked during the long reign of the youngest son, David I – an English baron as well as the Scottish king – who turned Scotland into a feudal realm on the Anglo-Norman pattern. Although there was no Norman conquest of Scotland, there was nevertheless an influx of Norman and Flemish settlers attracted by offers of land. Personally bound to the king, these settlers formed allies in David's struggle to control the semi-independent regions of Moravia in the north and Galloway in the south-west. The great families of Bruce, Comyn, Gordon and Stewart were all of Norman ancestry.

These settlers found themselves as vulnerable to local hostility as the Norman conquerors of England, so they brought the concept of the castle with them. Like elsewhere in Britain, the first castles were the artificial mounds or scarped, natural hillocks known as mottes, usually accompanied by an earthwork enclosure (bailey) defended by ramparts and ditches. Timber palisades topped the ramparts, while a wooden 'keep' was often placed on the summit of the motte. Scottish lords quickly adopted this new style of fortification, so not all mottes are evidence of Norman settlement. Many are now insignificant mounds, but the Mote of Urr and the Bass of Inverurie are among the most impressive motte-and-bailey earthworks in Britain.

Although some ambitious stone churches were already rising, the kingdom did not yet follow the growing English trend for masonry castles. The only stone building in any castle of that age is a chapel: St Margaret's in Edinburgh Castle. David I took advantage of England's paralysis in the civil wars known as the Anarchy to extend his rule to the Tees; it has been suggested that the oblong keeps at Carlisle and Bamburgh are actually his work. If so, the greatest Scottish castles of the century are actually south of the Border. Once Henry II had restored order to England, he quickly coerced Malcolm IV back beyond the Tweed.

The almost total absence of castle masonry in the twelfth century does not extend to the territories then beyond Scottish rule. In fact, the oldest stone castles in Scotland were built in lands occupied by the Norse, rather than Normans. It should be pointed out that they were Christian settlers, so no longer quite the fearsome Viking raiders of former days. The construction of Cubbie Roo's Castle, on a small island in the Orkneys, took place in 1145 according to the *Orkneyinga Saga*. The Castle of Old Wick on the Caithness coast may have followed before the century was over (its date is disputed). They are both simple, square-plan towers, dimly inspired by Norman keeps in England. The Bishop's Palace in Kirkwall has a stone hall undercroft of twelfth-century date, close to the great Romanesque cathedral. Another early castle is the simple walled enclosure of Castle Sween in Argyll.

David I's grandson, William I (the Lion), also sought to take advantage of English vulnerability during Prince Henry's revolt in 1174. His invasion led to his defeat and capture – again at Alnwick – in 1174. One of the conditions imposed by Henry II of England for his release was that the castles of Edinburgh, Stirling, Berwick, Jedburgh and Roxburgh should be held by English garrisons. These strategically important castles were presumably royal establishments, but little is known of their original forms. Richard the Lionheart sold them back to William to help finance his participation in the Third Crusade. William himself raised several castles to consolidate his grip on the north, though the only likely remnant is the motte at Auldearn.

The Golden Age

Most of the thirteenth century is taken up with the long reigns of the two kings Alexander (II and III), who made energetic efforts to impose royal control over the more distant parts of their realm. It is called the Golden Age, though only in comparison with the horrors that followed. Norse attempts to assert their authority over the Hebrides were repulsed. In 1263 the King of Norway's fleet appeared in the Firth of Clyde. Despite the inconclusive Battle of Largs, these islands were formally purchased by the Crown three years later. Until 1296 the century was remarkably free of strife with England, except for a brief invasion by Alexander II in support of the Magna Carta barons. The new

Gothic style caught on quickly in cathedrals and abbeys which, though fewer in number, are nearly as ambitious as their English counterparts.

In the first half of the century the Scots began to build castles in stone. Oblong-plan keeps at Hailes and Aberdour are a rarity, perhaps because they were already falling out of favour in England. Simple curtain walls around compact courtyards are more common. These early castles of enclosure lacked the towers and complex entrance defences that were becoming standard in England. Alexander II himself appears to have built stone castles of this type, still represented in a denuded form at Banff and Kinclaven. Even the ambitious enclosures at Kildrummy and Rothesay were towerless originally, and castles of this type would continue to be built in the latter half of the century and beyond.

Nevertheless, Scotland was emerging from the shadows, and this became more apparent after the accession of Alexander III in 1249. Masons were catching up with the rest of Europe and some fine stone castles arose. One of the earliest examples is Dirleton, which in its surviving portion admirably displays the new confidence in construction: a thick and well-built curtain with towers projecting at close intervals, enabling bowmen to overwhelm attackers with flanking fire from arrow slits. These towers are semi-circular towards the field to deter undermining and provide an all-round view from the parapet.

Although Scotland had largely bypassed the phase of castles dominated by lumbering square keeps, there are several examples of the cylindrical donjons that enjoyed a brief popularity in England and were especially common in France. By far the most impressive to survive is William de Moravia's mutilated keep at Bothwell, intended as the hub of an extensive castle of which little else was actually built at the time. Kildrummy, on the other hand, has lost its keep but retains much of its towered curtain. Other walled enclosures with round corner towers – such as Dunstaffnage, Old Inverlochy and Lochindorb – show familiarity with 'Edwardian' principles of defence that were reaching perfection in conquered Wales. The twin-towered gatehouse with a long gate passage also appeared, notably at Caerlaverock. On a simpler level were defensive hall houses.

Some of these castles were far from complete when Scotland's fortunes took a dramatic turn. Alexander III accidentally rode over a cliff's edge one dark night in 1286. His granddaughter, the young Queen Margaret of Norway, perished *en route* to Scotland four years later, leaving several candidates competing for the vacant throne. Edward I of England adjudicated at the Scots' request but it became clear that he regarded his nominee, John Balliol, as a puppet ruler who was there to do his bidding. When King John refused to send troops to serve in France, Edward declared him deposed and invaded in 1296. This unleashed a lengthy period of total war followed by centuries of mistrust and hostility. It also explains the relative dearth of early stone castles, since a scorched earth policy resulted in many being razed to the ground by the Scots themselves.

Wars of Independence

Following the sack of Berwick there was little resistance to the English advance. However, if Edward I thought that Scotland could be conquered and held down like Wales, he was to be disillusioned. The early rising of Andrew Moray and William Wallace was soon crushed but English misrule awakened Scottish patriotism. In Robert the Bruce, they found a king whose ruthlessness would match Edward's own. The turning point came in 1307, when Edward – 'Hammer of the Scots' – died leading another invasion. His son, Edward II, showed much less aptitude for warfare. While he dithered, Robert was able to unite the Scots by crushing his rivals for the throne, especially the Comyns. In 1314 the Battle of Bannockburn demonstrated the might of the Scottish schiltron against mounted English knights. From then on the Scots raided northern England with impunity, though an attempt by Robert's brother to conquer Ireland ended disastrously. They won a diplomatic victory with the Declaration of Arbroath, finally gaining recognition as an independent nation with the Treaty of Edinburgh-Northampton in 1328. Robert died soon after.

The tables might have turned yet again from 1332, when a bellicose Edward III supported John Balliol's son Edward against Robert's son David II. Soon only five castles remained loyal to the exiled boy king but, from 1337, the English had bigger fish to fry. Scotland was saved by the outbreak of the Hundred Years' War, though David rashly invaded England in 1346 in support of the French and was captured at the Battle of Neville's Cross. He spent the next eleven years a captive until his release under the terms of the Treaty of Berwick. Subsequent wars with England were frequent but usually brief, the Scots offering the potential threat of a second front as a consequence of their Auld Alliance with France. Additionally, there were private feuds among the great Border families. One such spat between the Douglases and the Percys culminated in the moonlit Battle of Otterburn in 1388.

For medieval sieges there is no period more intense than the two long Wars of Independence. Castles were taken, re-taken, torn down, patched up and torn down again. Bannockburn itself was triggered by an English attempt to relieve Stirling Castle from a long encirclement. Some individual castles held out heroically on both sides, but Robert the Bruce concluded that castles occupied by English garrisons were a liability. As castles were recaptured they were usually destroyed to forestall any future reoccupation by the enemy. Owners of newly built castles had to raze them, which must have been a terrible sacrifice, and royal castles were no exception. That the destruction was usually quite thorough is attested by the scarcity of early stone castles in much of Scotland, even where (as at Dundonald) a later castle was built on the same site and might have been expected to utilise more of the older structure had it survived. Where the destruction was less than total it was still quite severe. While one half of the keep at Bothwell stands proudly, the other half was ruthlessly torn down. Only in the north and west do more early castles survive, because here the Bruce had the upper hand and garrisoned them against populations who were sympathetic to his exiled rivals.

The wars impoverished Scotland, purged the aristocracy of those elements not unconditionally loyal to the Bruces and left a landscape of misery and destruction. Recovery would be slow. As confidence returned gradually, so did the castle as a lordly residence. However, Scotland would no longer follow England, which in the fourteenth century was producing castles of some architectural distinction. Caerlaverock and Bothwell were rebuilt in something like their originally intended forms. The Earl of Douglas would raise an old-style castle with a strong curtain wall and flanking towers at Tantallon, while towards the end of the century the Duke of Albany built an unusual, gatehouse-dominated castle at Doune. Elsewhere, the Scots went back to basics, erecting mighty stone boxes of scant ostentation and remarkable grimness. The earliest, such as Duffus and Drum, actually rose while the Wars of Independence were still raging. In many ways they are a throwback to the oblong keeps of Norman England but here they are called tower houses. The tower house in its various permutations would become the norm for the next three centuries. It contained the principal accommodation and, while a courtyard or 'barmkin' was still needed for the many ancillary buildings, its surrounding wall was generally quite subsidiary to the great tower itself.

A fourteenth-century date is claimed for many tower houses. However, documentary evidence is usually lacking and those that are demonstrably so early are relatively few. They are massive, thick-walled structures with few windows, barrel-vaulted ceilings and entrances at first-floor level or even higher up, originally reached by a flight of removable wooden steps. The royal examples at Lochleven and Dundonald, along with the Earl of Douglas' effort at Threave, show that they were the chosen type of residence for even the greatest in the land. One variant started early. David II gave the (now buried) tower house at Edinburgh Castle a short wing or 'jamb' projecting from one side. This was copied at Dunnottar, Neidpath and elsewhere by the end of the century, so the 'L-plan' tower house was born.

David II died in 1371 and his nephew inherited the throne as Robert II. Thus began Scotland's long-lasting if ill-fated Stewart (later Stuart) dynasty. Despite all the minorities and exiles, the Scots remained remarkably faithful to this dysfunctional family, though not to individual monarchs.

The Age of the Tower House

From 1406 until 1625, with one interruption, Scotland was ruled by a succession of six kings called James (murdered, blown up, murdered, killed in battle, died prematurely, emigrated). James I had been captured by pirates and was a prisoner in England when his reign began; he would not be released for another eighteen years. This deterred Scotland from honouring the Auld Alliance when Henry V of England re-ignited the Hundred Years' War in 1415, though many Scottish volunteers stiffened the ranks of the French army. Although hostilities flared up from time to time, the fifteenth century saw relatively little open conflict with England, preoccupied as it was first with losing France and then with dynastic strife. The Scots took advantage of the Wars of the Roses to recover Roxburgh and Berwick, though Berwick was later wrested back again. There was periodic internal discord, notably a showdown between the Crown and the Black Douglases. This entailed a lengthy bombardment of Threave Castle in 1455 by the royal artillery. The Red Douglases in their turn would prove almost as vexing, resulting in another protracted siege at Tantallon in 1491.

Before the siege, Threave's tower house had been reinforced by a towered curtain with small slits for defence by early cannon. These may be the first gunports in Scotland, identifiable by the little roundels giving a dumbbell or inverted keyhole shape to the whole. They herald the arrival of a weapon that would ultimately sound the castle's death knell. James II built up an artillery train, including the famous cannon Mons Meg. Ironically, one of them would be his undoing, when a bolt flew out and struck him at the siege of Roxburgh in 1460. James himself began Ravenscraig Castle in Fife, which consists mainly of a massive screen wall cutting off a coastal promontory. It represents one of very few attempts to design a castle with walling thick enough to withstand the growing power of artillery.

Elsewhere the dominant theme of the previous century continued. During the fifteenth century there appears to have been a fourfold increase in the number of tower houses built (there is still scant evidence for dating and much disagreement). Many were erected by the lower rungs of the aristocracy. This is the century in which the building of genuinely fortified homes all but came to an end in England, despite its internal discord. The fact that castle building actually escalated in Scotland has been interpreted traditionally as evidence of greater insecurity. Nevertheless, the ability to invest long term in costly and impressive stone structures is, on the whole, more an indication of stability than anarchy. The tower house was a symbol of lordly domination as much as defensive intent. This is one reason why it was seldom adapted to the squatter profile required in an age of artillery.

Although the great oblong box remained the norm there were more L-plan tower houses, with the entrance brought down to ground level where it could be flanked by the wall at right angles to it. Tower houses vary tremendously in size, depending on the resources and status of their builders. The most impressive of them all is Borthwick, raised by Sir William Borthwick in the 1430s, with an unusual a pair of jambs projecting from the same front. It is followed in scale by Comlongon, the date of which is less clear. Both towers are honeycombed with mural chambers and crowned by machicolated parapets (few other towers were accorded such a distinction). Balgonie, Cardoness, Castle Campbell, Newark (Selkirkshire) and Spynie are good representatives of the dozens that have survived largely true to their original form.

Some of the examples already cited are accompanied by courtyard buildings. The older tower houses at Threave and Craigmillar were augmented by curtain walls with round corner towers; the latter (uniquely) is machicolated all the way around. Already some lords were migrating out of tower houses into more spacious accommodation in a walled courtyard, as at Balgonie, Dean and Crichton, where a great hall and other residential buildings abutted the curtain. This was also the century when the royal palace complexes at Edinburgh, Linlithgow and Stirling began to take shape.

The House of Fence

In 1513 James IV invaded England, fulfilling the terms of the Auld Alliance when the English once again made war in France. Intercepted just over the Border at Flodden by the Earl of Surrey's army, he was hacked down along with many of his nobles. This disaster heralded another turbulent period for Anglo-Scottish relations. The English, thrown out of France and reconciled under the Tudor dynasty, were able to kick sand in Scots' faces. There was no longer any serious attempt at conquest but Henry VIII, with his usual ruthlessness, was determined to enforce a dynastic match between his son Edward and the young Mary Queen of Scots. The Rough Wooing (1543–51), though comparatively brief, saw a return to the total warfare of the fourteenth century, the Scots suffering further defeats at Solway Moss and Pinkie. Fortunately for them, a French expeditionary force arrived to even out the contest, the English withdrawing under the terms of the Treaty of Boulogne. Relations gradually improved after the Reformation, particularly when it became clear that James VI would succeed Elizabeth I on the English throne. However, this did nothing to quell the endless feuding between reiver families on either side of the Border.

The tower house of 1500 barely differed from one built 100 years earlier. The windows might be a little larger or more frequent, the walls a little thinner, the doorway at ground level even if there was no jamb to protect it. By 1600, however, the tower house had been transformed into the 'house of fence' that is still a common sight across much of Scotland. Walls got thinner and windows considerably larger. Even though they were protected by iron grilles, it is clear that light and comfort had triumphed over genuine fortification. The main trappings of defence included a stout iron gate called a 'yett' barring the entrance, along with gunports and shot holes in the walls. The wide-mouthed gunport – basically a horizontal slot allowing a wider field of fire – replaced the early keyhole type. A handful at ground level sufficed to cover every approach. Defence from the wall-head was outmoded – in many cases the parapet was eliminated, with a gabled attic taking its place. Attics were generally added within the parapets of older towers to increase the accommodation. Ornate rows of parapet corbelling and corner bartizans enlivened the skyline. The architectural forms eschewed England and derived from the French chateau, though the overall effect is distinctively Scottish.

At least three times as many tower houses were raised during the sixteenth century, compared to the number that already existed. An Act of Parliament of 1535 demanded the building of towers and barmkins as a form of civil defence. The last few decades of the century were particularly busy, and many older towers were embellished in the new style. Even quite lowly lairds, enriched after the Reformation in 1560, participated in the building boom. They often belonged to minor branches of the great aristocratic families so were distinguished by their place of origin or residence, such as Forbes of Tolquhon. Most counties exhibit a variety of families building tower houses, though one or two names tend to predominate.

Hence, in terms of numbers, the sixteenth century is the dominant one for Scottish castles, though many of the new tower houses are relatively modest affairs. While the simple oblong and L-plan types remained common, some evolved in a series of permutations. A stair turret was often placed in the re-entrant angle to create a 'stepped' L-plan. By now the jamb often projected in two directions, flanking two walls of the main block. A logical step, first realised around the middle of the century, was to add a second jamb or tower at the corner diagonally opposite, so that all four walls could be raked by gunfire. These ingenious 'Z-plan' tower houses are mainly confined to the north-eastern counties. They were defensively efficient while providing extra accommodation in the flanking towers. Claypotts is a picturesque example, while Noltland in the Orkneys is an unusually formidable one, bristling with gunports. Other variants, such as the T- and E-plans (the latter without the central bar), are much less common. By now it is possible to date many of these tower houses and identify their builders, owing to surviving documentation and inscribed panels on the buildings themselves.

Despite the glut of new tower houses there was still migration towards residential buildings outside its confines. At castles such as Edzell, Huntly, Rowallan and Tolquhon the old tower house became secondary to a great hall and other accommodation erected around a barmkin. The royal palace quadrangles at Edinburgh and Stirling were safely within the defensive perimeter. Attempts to erect castles capable of withstanding artillery, as opposed to the mere provision of gunports, are confined to no more than a handful of surviving examples: Dunbar with its gun battery and the thick screen walls of Blackness and Craignethan – the latter two both erected by the innovative Master of the King's Works, James Hamilton of Finnart. Serious defences erected during the Rough Wooing, like the artillery fort at Eyemouth, were purely garrison posts with arrow-head bastions of the kind recently invented in Italy. It is significant that no castle adopted this drastic approach, though the massive Half Moon Battery at Edinburgh Castle was erected after its predecessor had been blasted down in the great siege of 1568–73.

Opinion is divided as to whether the Scots continued to erect semi-fortified homes out of necessity, or whether they created a unique brand of Renaissance mansion in which the 'defences' are pure theatre. At best they were intended only to provide a secure place for the family treasure and to keep rival lairds at bay. Feuding between families was endemic, particularly in the more remote parts, and the glitter of courtly life was often tarnished with bloodshed. The out-of-control nobility was accustomed to the free-for-all of long minorities. Six years' rule reduced Mary Queen of Scots to a traumatised state at the tender age of twenty-four, while conditions remained volatile well into James VI's long reign. In such an environment lairds understandably felt a good measure of insecurity.

Scottish Baronial

In 1603 James VI rode south to become James I of England. This union of the Crowns put an end to hostilities between the two countries, for the time being at least. Henceforth, James would rule Scotland with his pen; he returned only once, in 1617. He left with the Scottish Baronial style of bartizans, dormer windows, caphouses and crow-stepped gables about to reach its zenith, as the skylines of Craigievar, Crathes and Glamis testify. In each case, these were embellishments to older towers and done purely for effect. James died in 1625 and the Scottish castle more or less died with him. As the seventeenth century progresses it becomes difficult to regard most new lairds' houses as defensible even in the most diluted sense, though there was no drastic change in their layout or architecture. Some tower houses for which a later origin was assumed, such as Coxton and Nisbet, have been plausibly reinterpreted. That leaves just a handful of honourable exceptions, going down to Leslie as late as 1661.

One might wonder why castle building ended when it did. It continued for longer in Ireland owing to the Plantations. Scotland was about to be convulsed by a century of chaos – first, the Civil Wars, then successive Jacobite uprisings. However, these conflicts were decided on the battlefield. Old castles were attacked only if they got in the way and their resistance was generally brief. Apart from Dunnottar (1651), there is a surprising lack of the drawn-out sieges that characterised the Civil Wars in England. There was no consistent policy of 'slighting' castles to make them untenable but some were destroyed in the Jacobite period – Bonnie Prince Charlie himself had Inverness Castle blown up. Blair in Perthshire was the last in Britain to withstand a short siege, by retreating Jacobites in 1746. The Jacobite threat saw Edinburgh, Stirling and Dumbarton castles turned into garrison posts ringed by artillery defences. New, purely military fortifications were also established, notably Fort George on the Moray Firth.

Recent Times

Those Hanoverian fortresses remained garrisoned until quite recently. Owing to their absence in most county towns (a legacy of the Wars of Independence), few Scottish castles degenerated into courthouses and prisons like their English counterparts. Some genuine tower houses were expanded into mansions and transformed internally to keep up with prevailing fashions. In many cases the later accretions have since been demolished, leaving the tower alone again. Far more old castles were abandoned for more up-to-date residences. Subsequent occupation by tenants or servants has resulted in a small number of towers (such as Amisfield and Claypotts) surviving in a remarkably unspoilt condition. However, the vast majority were left to decay. The great five-volume survey of castellated architecture, published in 1887–94 by the architects MacGibbon and Ross, documents much of what then remained. Their detailed drawings are fascinating for comparison with today.

Some of the best-known Scottish 'castles' are entirely, or very largely, later mansions built when the castellated style enjoyed a romantic revival. Inveraray and Culzean are notable Georgian examples, while Balmoral and Dunrobin are splendid instances of Scottish Baronial as revived by the Victorians. Since Victorian times some decaying castles have been given a new lease of life: strongholds such as Kisimul and Eilean Donan were restored (or well-nigh rebuilt) by determined individuals, often descendants of the original builders. More recently dozens of ruined tower houses have been reoccupied and this trend continues, though suitable candidates are becoming fewer. Janet Brennan-Inglis, who rescued Barholm Tower, describes in her book the heroic battles waged – against planners, neighbours, bankruptcy and the elements – by restorers, many of whom were not persons of great substance (see bibliography). There are even some entirely modern tower house replicas.

These initiatives have usually been for private occupation or commercial profit. Thankfully the growing appreciation of ancient monuments had already resulted in a fine cross-section of castles being consolidated and made accessible by the state and other organisations (this is another largely unsung achievement). Alas, many others continue to crumble and there have been some regrettable demolitions of unstable structures – even Elphinstone Tower in East Lothian, which was one of the finest fifteenth-century tower houses. Clearly many castles face future oblivion but there is still time to save some of the more deserving, if the will and the money can ever be found.

Scottish Monarchs

The list runs from Canmore to the Act of Union, with royal castles to which each monarch (in some cases probably) contributed surviving works:

Malcolm III 'Canmore' (1058–93)
Donald III 'Bane' (1093–97)
Edgar (1097–1107)
Alexander I (1107–24)
David I (1124–53): *Edinburgh*
Malcolm IV 'the Maiden' (1153–65)
William I 'the Lion' (1165–1214): *Auldearn*
Alexander II (1214–49): *Banff, Kinclaven*
Alexander III (1249–86): *Tarbert*
Margaret 'the Maid of Norway' (1286–90)
John Balliol (1292–96)
Interregnum (1296–1306)
Robert I 'the Bruce' (1306–29): *Tarbert*
David II (1329–71): *Edinburgh, Lochleven*
Robert II (1371–90): *Dumbarton, Dundonald, Edinburgh, Kindrochit, Stirling*
Robert III (1390–1406)
James I (1406–37): *Linlithgow*
James II (1437–60): *Ravenscraig (Fife), Stirling*
James III (1460–88): *Linlithgow, Ravenscraig (Fife)*
James IV (1488–1513): *Dumbarton, Dunbar, Edinburgh, Falkland, Holyrood, Linlithgow, Rothesay, Stirling, Tarbert*
James V (1513–42): *Blackness, Dunbar, Edinburgh, Falkland, Holyrood, Linlithgow, Stirling, Tantallon*
Mary I 'Queen of Scots' (1542–67): *Edinburgh*
James VI (1567–1625): *Doune, Edinburgh, Linlithgow, Stirling*
Charles I (1625–49)
Interregnum (1649–60)
Charles II (1660–85): *Blackness, Dumbarton, Edinburgh, Holyrood*
James VII (1685–88)
William II 'of Orange' (1688–1702) and Mary II (1688–94): *Blackness*
Anne (1702–14): *Stirling*

ABERDEENSHIRE

This large north-eastern county is renowned for its abundance of castles. The vast majority are late tower houses, with the defensive limitations typical of that era, but there are some interesting survivals from earlier periods. The Bass of Inverurie and the Doune of Invernochty are impressive earthworks of the motte-and-bailey kind. The Wars of Independence have robbed the county of some thirteenth-century stone castles but the seat of the earls of Mar at Kildrummy – which suffered a bitter siege during that conflict – is a fine example of a multi-towered enclosure, despite its ruinous state. Early tower houses survive at Hallforest and Drum, the latter in perfect condition. Moving into the fifteenth century there are more oblong tower houses, such as Cairnbulg and Pitsligo, along with the first L-plan in the county at Ravenscraig. Fyvie, unusually, retains one side of an ambitious courtyard castle with angle towers.

Nevertheless, it is in the latter part of the sixteenth century that the county comes into its own, producing some of the most memorable examples of the Scottish Baronial style. They were created by master masons such as John Bell and Thomas Leiper for a host of families, of whom the many cadet branches of the all-powerful Gordon earls of Huntly are predominant. Despite the allure of their residences they were often at each other's throats, so some trappings of defence were a necessary precaution as well as an indication of status. The norm in Aberdeenshire is a picture-perfect (though often quite restored) tower house, whether oblong, L-plan or Z-plan. Some have later been extended into mansions set in large country estates. Many are not routinely open but a few of the best examples are happily maintained by the National Trust for Scotland, while some others can be visited or at least viewed externally. At the lower end of the scale come battered ruins such as Corse and Gight, as well as towers later put to utilitarian purposes at Corgarff and Kinnaird Head. Craig, Delgatie, Glenbuchat and Pitfichie are handsome towers, but top ranking must go to Castle Fraser, Midmar and – above all – to William Forbes' soaring masterpiece at Craigievar. There is also outstanding work in the courtyard castles at Huntly and Tolquhon, along with the gatehouse added at Fyvie.

The decorative upper works on some of these towers were only achieved early in the seventeenth century, but as that century progressed the flood becomes a trickle. Craigston and Braemar are notable tower houses belonging to the early part of the century, while Leslie is a curious revival of the genre from 1661.

County reference: BoS *Aberdeenshire: North and Moray*; BoS *Aberdeenshire: South and Aberdeen.*

ABERGELDIE CASTLE occupies an estate beside the River Dee, two miles east of Balmoral. This harled, oblong tower house, with a round stair turret at one corner, is attributed to Alexander Gordon of Abergeldie in the 1550s. It was nearly washed away by flooding in 2016.
Access: Visible from the north bank of the river (off the A93).

ARNAGE CASTLE lies in secluded grounds three miles west of Arthrath. This Victorian mansion incorporates a modest late sixteenth-century Z-plan tower house with square flanking towers. Built by Thomas Leiper for the Cheynes of Arnage, it retains some triple shot holes.
Access: Private.

AUCHANACHIE CASTLE stands on a farm half a mile west of Ruthven. It consists of a small oblong tower house with a half-round stair turret projecting from one side. A contemporary domestic range is attached. It was held by the Gordons of Avochie and bears the year 1594.
Access: Private.

BALFLUIG CASTLE rises prominently half a mile south-east of Alford. This gabled L-plan tower house features a jamb that projects in two directions and is taller than the rest. The austere tower belonged to the Forbeses of Corsindae and bears the year 1556 above the entrance.
Access: Visible from the road.

BASS OF INVERURIE, a classic motte-and-bailey earthwork, is a surprising sight in the middle of Inverurie Cemetery, off Keithhall Road on the south-east outskirts of the royal burgh. The tall, conical motte with a flat top is, as so often in Scotland, an adaptation of a natural hill. To the east is a tree-covered bailey that is also above the surrounding ground level. The apparent ditch between them was only cut in the nineteenth century. On the north the earthwork is afforded the protection of the River Urie, before its confluence with the Don. The rest of the perimeter was surrounded by a ditch but that has long been filled in. This prodigious earthwork may have been raised by the Leslies sometime in the twelfth century but seems more likely to be the work of Prince David, who founded the burgh around 1195. David, Earl of Garioch and Huntingdon, was William the Lion's brother. This may be where Robert the Bruce lay seriously ill in 1308, before defeating the Comyns at the first Battle of Inverurie (the second was a Jacobite victory in 1745). Wooden

palisades no doubt crowned the steep banks but there is no indication that they were ever replaced by masonry. A group of Pictish symbol stones in a protective case has been placed at the foot of the motte.
Access: Freely accessible (LA).
Relations: Motte-and-baileys such as the Doune of Invernochty, the Peel Ring of Lumphanan and the Mote of Urr.

BELDORNEY CASTLE occupies an estate two miles south of Haugh of Glass. This somewhat altered, Z-plan tower house has a large round flanking tower and a smaller square one. It was built by George Gordon of Beldorney before his death in 1575. Later side wings project in front.
Access: Private.

BRAEMAR CASTLE overlooks the Old Military Road (A93) in rugged terrain a mile north of Braemar village. Originally known as Mar Castle, this tower house was begun in 1628 by John Erskine, second Earl of Mar, supplanting nearby Kindrochit Castle. Built as a hunting lodge, the comparatively late date of the tower may be explained by the lawlessness that still persisted in this upland area. The tower follows the conventional L-plan but shows the influence of contemporary lairds' houses in its symmetry. Instead of a main block with a subsidiary jamb, it consists of two tall wings of equal size at right angles. Round corner bartizans are corbelled out halfway up. A circular turret projects in the re-entrant angle between the two wings, containing a broad spiral staircase. Iron grilles still bar the original window openings here, while the entrance in the stair turret retains its yett. Conventional barrel vaults crown the three ground-floor undercrofts, one of them a kitchen, while a grate covers the entrance to a pit prison as inhospitable as any.

Owing to its strategic position, the tower did not survive unscathed for long. William of Orange's troops were driven out in 1689 by the Jacobite John Farquharson, who burnt the tower. The sixth Earl of Mar signalled the beginning of the Old Pretender's uprising by raising his standard here in 1715; he fled into exile on its collapse. In 1748, after the Young Pretender's abortive rising, Braemar and Corgarff were converted into fortlets for Hanoverian garrisons controlling the new military road to Inverness. The stair turret and bartizans received embattled tops to serve as look-out posts. As at Corgarff, a concentric wall pierced by musket ports was built closely around the tower house. It has pointed bastions projecting from the middle of its four sides. Unlike Corgarff, a utilitarian atmosphere no longer pervades inside. In 1797 the Farquharsons of Invercauld regained possession. In the ensuing century they transformed the four storeys above the undercrofts into a little mansion. Opulent rooms belie the gaunt, harled exterior, though the garrison's presence is still attested by graffiti in several window embrasures.
Access: Open regularly in summer.

Reference: Guidebook (Pilgrim Press).
Relations: Corgarff and Kindrochit. Alloa and Mar's Wark (Stirling) are older seats of the Erskine earls.

CAIRNBULG CASTLE is a forbidding, grey-harled mass on a country estate two and a half miles south-east of Fraserburgh, off the B9033. The Black Comyns had a castle here and the low mound on which it stands, originally surrounded by marshland, may be their truncated motte. The earliest masonry visible is the tower house that dominates the rest. Four storeys tall to the embattled parapet, it may have been begun after Sir Alexander Fraser acquired the lands by marriage in 1375. However, at least the upper part is probably of the fifteenth century, along with the staircase jamb that turned it into an L-plan tower. The jamb flanked the original entrance and is crowned by a gabled caphouse. Unusual pointed vaults cover the two lower storeys of the main block. As usual, the first floor formed the hall, with mural chambers and window seats. The embattled parapet, with diminutive corner bartizans, projects on corbels. Recessed within is a gabled attic, wholly Victorian but no doubt recreating an older addition.

Most of the Frasers of Philorth (the original name) were called Alexander, and one of them added an oblong residential block to the east in the latter part of the sixteenth century. It is only attached to the older tower house by the jamb. At the south-east corner of this block a circular flanking tower was built, also of four storeys though modest in size when compared with the older tower house. A lopsided version of the Z-plan was thus contrived. The upper crown, recessed within the parapet of the round tower, is an imaginative Victorian enhancement. The Frasers sold Cairnbulg in 1703 and the castle slowly drifted into ruin. From 1896 Sir John Duthie restored it for occupation, largely rebuilding the residential block that had collapsed.

Access: Open by appointment only (HHA).
Reference: *PSAS* (83).
Relations: Kinnaird Head and the Castle of Pittulie are later works of the Frasers of Philorth.

CASTLE FRASER, in spacious grounds four miles south-east of Monymusk, was known as Muchall-in-Mar until 1695. It is now a fine example of a Z-plan tower house, but the two flanking towers were added to the opposite corners of an older oblong block. This tower was probably built by Thomas Fraser, who received the barony in 1454. His descendant, Michael Fraser, employed the master mason Thomas Leiper to transform the building from 1576. He extended the original tower house a little to the west and added the flanking towers – square on the north-west and circular on the south-east. The layout was probably inspired by nearby Midmar Castle. Triple shot holes pierce the flanking towers at ground level.

Michael's son Andrew embellished the skyline in Scottish Baronial style. A panel high up displays the royal arms and the name 'I Bel', showing that the master mason John Bell was responsible for these upper works. The free corners of the main block and the square flanking tower are adorned by round bartizans with conical roofs. Cannon spouts and dormer windows (one of them bearing the year 1618) enliven the attics, while the tall round tower is crowned by a balustrade. Dormers and turrets also enrich the two low wings that Andrew, now Lord Fraser, added to the north of the tower house in the 1630s, on the site of the original barmkin. Most of the windows of the tower house are sash enlargements but otherwise the exterior has changed little.

A blocked archway on the north side was the original entrance, leading directly into the hall at first-floor level. Thomas Leiper replaced it with a ground-floor doorway in his north-west tower, flanked by the main block. In 1795 the present entrance was cut through on the south. It leads into the barrel-vaulted undercroft. At this level the square flanking tower contains the kitchen with a wide fireplace. A spiral staircase ascends to the hall. This lofty room is also covered by a barrel vault, showing the junction between Thomas Fraser's building and the later extension. The original blocked entrance can be seen. There is a grand fireplace at the dais end, its long lintel supported on columns.

The Frasers remained in occupation until 1921 and the changing tastes of later generations have transformed the three storeys (including the attic) above the hall. Little corner alcoves in the attic denote the bartizans. Each floor of the square flanking tower is divided into two chambers. One of them, a small room level with the hall vault, is said to have been used as a Catholic chapel, though a strongroom for valuables seems more likely. Most of the rooms in the circular tower are square for greater domestic convenience. At seven storeys this tower dominates the rest.

Access: Open regularly in summer (NTS).
Reference: Guidebook by M. Ash.
Relations: Midmar. Thomas Leiper also worked on Arnage, Tolquhon and the House of Schivas.

CASTLE OF PITTULIE, now a decaying ruin, is attributed to Alexander Fraser of Philorth (who also built Kinnaird Head Castle) in the 1590s. It stands in the middle of a field a short distance east of Pitsligo Castle. It is basically an oblong laird's house but a tall jamb projects at one end.

Access: Visible from the road.

CORGARFF CASTLE, reached from the A939 at Cock Bridge, stands amid dramatic Grampian scenery at the head of Strathdon. This oblong tower house was probably built by John Forbes of Towie, who leased the lands around 1550. In 1571 Adam Gordon of Auchindoun set fire to the new tower while John and his retainers were away. His wife and twenty-six others were consumed by the flames. Alexander Forbes attacked with a band of Highland raiders in 1607, while the Jacobites burnt the tower again during the 1689 rising. After the failure of the Young Pretender's revolt, Corgarff and Braemar were adapted in 1748 to house Hanoverian garrisons guarding the new military road leading to Inverness. Although the Jacobite threat soon faded, the small garrison remained until 1831.

Despite this stormy history, the austere tower house survives intact on the outside, if much altered internally. The harled walls gleam white against the surrounding hillsides. The gabled roof, lacking a parapet, no doubt reflects the original arrangement. A caphouse at one corner marks the top of the vanished spiral staircase. Steps ascend to the first-floor entrance – a late instance of such extra security – overlooked high up by machicolation corbels. Twin vaulted undercrofts remain at ground level, but the upper floors were transformed in 1748 to house the garrison. A once-lofty hall was divided into two floors and its crowning vault was removed. Above it, the former solar and the spartan attic were also converted into barracks. As at Braemar, the whole has been closely surrounded by an eight-pointed wall pierced by numerous musket ports.

Access: Open daily in summer (HES).
Reference: Guidebook by C. Tabraham. *PSAS* (61).
Relations: Braemar.

CORSE CASTLE is signposted from the B9119, a mile west of the Crossroads Hotel on the A980. A short way along the road this attractive ruin comes into view among the trees, overlooking the Corse Burn. Two-and-a-half sides of the L-plan tower house stand to the wall-head, including the jamb with its gable flanked by the bases of bartizans. They show a main block rising four storeys high, including the attic. A round stair turret projects from the middle of the south wall. However, the rest of the tower has collapsed to its foundations, along with another stair turret that projected at the north-west corner. The position of the two stair turrets suggests a Z-plan building, to which a jamb was subsequently added, but there is no apparent join in the masonry. The lintel over the doorway, in the side of the jamb, bears the year 1581 and the initials of William Forbes of Corse. His previous residence was destroyed by brigands, and he determined to 'build me such a house as thieves will need to knock at ere they enter'. The building is understandably well equipped with shot holes.

Access: Freely accessible with caution.
Relations: Forbes' son went on to embellish nearby Craigievar.

COULL CASTLE   Three miles north of Aboyne, a sideroad leaves the B9094. Beyond the Tarland Burn, a footpath at a bend in the road runs past Coull Church, then through a field towards the scanty remains of this castle.

The ditch cutting off the approach is still deep, but the masonry is reduced to fragments and footings. Nevertheless, it is of interest as the remains of a stone castle destroyed during the Wars of Independence. This was a thirteenth-century walled enclosure with round flanking towers. The base of what might be taken as a small round keep is quite distinct, along with the hall block at the rear of the courtyard, overlooking the burn. The castle was entered through a twin-towered gatehouse, now barely discernible. This and the overall layout made it reminiscent of Kildrummy on a smaller scale. The castle was established around 1228 by Sir Alan Durward, Alexander II's son-in-law and justiciar. His surname derives from the hereditary office of royal door ward. However, the towers and gatehouse must have been added by a descendant later in the century. The castle was then ruthlessly torn down, presumably by Robert the Bruce during his campaign against the Comyns in 1307.

Access: Freely accessible with caution.

Relations: Kildrummy. Durward also raised the Peel Ring of Lumphanan and the first Urquhart Castle.

CRAIG CASTLE is perched above the Burn of Craig in a wooded estate off the B9002, three miles south-west of Rhynie. It was the seat of the Gordons of Craig until 1892. The original tower house now dominates a cluster of later buildings around a small courtyard, denoting the original barmkin. It is entered through an imposing gateway of 1726. The harled, L-plan tower is magnificently severe, with little window space in its five main storeys and two rows of unusually large, wide-mouthed gunports. Apart from the gunports, the tower house could be taken for a building of the fifteenth century or early sixteenth century, but there are marked similarities with a few others erected around 1570. The entrance, flanked by the jamb as usual, leads into a barrel-vaulted undercroft. Crossing the entrance passage is a mural passage, leading past two more vaulted storerooms to the spiral staircase, as at Gight and Towie Barclay. Over the intersection between the two passages is a delicate ribbed vault, as at Gight and Delgatie. (Delgatie and Towie Barclay also have rib-vaulted halls but that is not the case here.)

If this tower dates from the 1570s then its builder was William Gordon, though he saw fit to place the arms of his father and grandfather on either side of the royal arms in the three re-gilded heraldic panels over the entrance. The doorway retains its yett and there is an original grille over the window above. The kitchen occupies the jamb at ground level, but the upper floors have been subdivided and modernised. Although there is no parapet, a mural passage around the top floor forms a sentry gallery, with openings behind the windows to light what was presumably the garrison's quarters. The roof line is quite severe apart from the crow-stepped attic gables, one stretch of elaborate corbelling high up and a single round corner bartizan.

Access: Private.

Reference: *PSAS* (64).
Relations: Delgatie, Gight and Towie Barclay. There is also a Craig House in Angus and a Castle Craig in Ross.

CRAIGIEVAR CASTLE is the perfect example of a later Scottish tower house. It combines a fairytale Scottish Baronial skyline and a splendid Jacobean interior with (by the standards of the time) a reasonably defensible exterior. For most of its considerable height the tower is quite plain. Its pink-harled walls are softened by rounded corners. The windows are small, except for those lighting the hall. Such severity may be due to the fact that the tower was begun by the Mortimers of Craigievar in the late sixteenth century. However, in 1610 debts forced them to sell the unfinished tower to William Forbes of Menie. 'Danzig Willie' made his fortune trading in the Baltic, and he spared no ornament in embellishing the building as a symbol of his prosperity.

The top two storeys project slightly on an ornate corbel table. Most of the corner bartizans begin at this level, their round drums capped by conical roofs. Two stair turrets project from the first floor upwards, one of them crowned by a caphouse. Chimneys rise above the main gables, while balustrades crowning the entrance tower and the other stair turret show the arrival of the Renaissance. Several dormer windows complete the picturesque profile. These upper levels are attributed on stylistic grounds to the master mason John Bell.

Craigievar is a classic example of the stepped L-plan. A slender tower (at seven storeys the tallest part) projects in the re-entrant angle between the main body of the tower house and its jamb. This tower has the entrance archway at its base, flanked by a shot hole in the jamb, but unusually it does not contain the staircase. The yett is made as usual from interleaving iron bars. Three ground-floor undercrofts, one of them the kitchen, are covered by the customary barrel vaults.

Between the kitchen and the jamb undercroft, a straight staircase ascends to the magnificent first floor. At this level the main body of the tower house is filled by the hall, twice as high as the other storeys. Such an arrangement is traditional enough, but the barrel vault of the hall is covered by Renaissance plasterwork of great delicacy. Note the pendants and the medallions of Classical heroes. Above the fireplace are the royal arms, also in plaster, with lion and unicorn supporters. William Forbes' arms can be seen on the ceiling, along with the year 1626. Lower down the hall is lined with Renaissance panelling, returning to form a screen with a musicians' gallery above. There are two corresponding storeys in the jamb, both with fine plaster ceilings, one of them bearing the year 1625. The lower of these private chambers formed the solar. It preserves its original panelling and leads to the laird's study in the entrance tower. William Forbes is among the portraits in the bedchamber above. These rooms are largely furnished with seventeenth-century items.

Craigievar Castle, Aberdeenshire

Two spiral staircases ascend to the upper storeys. Here the main body of the tower house is divided into two unequal parts by a cross-wall. Along with the rooms in the jamb and the entrance tower, there was ample accommodation for the Forbes household. The main bedchamber, above the hall, has another splendid plaster ceiling. In the more modernised rooms on the third floor, the bartizans provide tiny turret chambers with ornamental shot holes. A long gallery is contrived in the attic.

Craigievar was just complete when William Forbes died in 1627. His son, another William, was a prominent Covenanter during the Civil War but the tower house avoided attack. It escaped drastic alteration in the nineteenth century owing to the advice of Lord Sempill's architect, who recognised it as 'one of the finest specimens in the country'. And so it remains, one of the few tower houses that is neither sadly ruined nor transformed by later fashion. A leaning stretch of wall survives of the barmkin, with a simple gateway and a round corner turret. The tower house stands on a wooded hillside close to the A980, five miles south of Alford.

Access: Open regularly in summer (NTS).
Reference: Guidebook by M. Ellington.
Relations: John Bell's work at Castle Fraser, Lickleyhead and Tillycairn. Contemporary plaster ceilings at Glamis, Thirlestane and Muchalls.

CRAIGSTON CASTLE stands within a country estate half a mile north-east of Fintry. It is reached via a long drive starting at a bend in the B9105. This commanding tower house was built by John Urquhart of Craigfintry, whose arms are depicted on a panel near the bottom of the north jamb. A matching panel on the narrower south jamb contains the inscription, 'This vark foundit ye fourtine of March ane thousand sex hounder four zeiris and endit ye 8 of Decembr 1607'. So, it was built over the period 1604–07 and features one of the most arresting tower house facades in Scotland.

The building is a rare example of the so-called E-plan, with twin jambs facing west – a form that ultimately goes back to Borthwick. Near the top the two jambs are united by what can only be described as a triumphal arch, no doubt inspired by the recent gatehouse at Fyvie and probably designed by the same master mason. The underside is painted to resemble a ribbed vault. Above this arch projects an ornate balcony, adorned with the carved figures of a piper and four armed warriors. A balustraded caphouse crowns the arch. The other fronts are plain but dignified, revealing an elevation of four storeys, including the attic (the jambs, though no higher, contain five storeys). High up on the outer corners are lengths of ornate corbelling, as if to support square bartizans that were never built. Unusually, none of the gables are crow-stepped. The long stones at the corners and around the window openings have been omitted from the modern re-harling. On either side the tower house is flanked by much lower wings, added in 1733 by another John Urquhart, who made his fortune as a privateer.

As might be expected at so late a date, this is a tower designed more for effect than defence. There are no shot holes and the regular rows of windows, even at ground level, cannot have offered much security even when iron grilles covered them. A little porch has been added, filling the recess between the jambs at ground level. The inner entrance, between the jambs, leads into the ground floor, which is divided into several vaulted compartments, including the kitchen. A straight staircase ascends to the first-floor hall (now the drawing room). Numerous carved Renaissance panels depicting kings, mythical heroes and biblical figures have been incorporated into later doors and window shutters. From here two narrow spiral stairs within the thickness of the walls lead to the upper storeys, which reflect continuous occupation by later generations of the Urquhart family. The attic originally formed a long gallery but has been subdivided.

Access: Primarily a functions venue but there are limited opening times.
Reference: *PSAS* (108).
Relations: Fyvie. The E-plan tower houses at Borthwick, Castle Kennedy and Castle Stuart (Inverness-shire).

DELGATIE CASTLE dominates a country estate two miles east of Turriff. Robert the Bruce granted the lands to the Hay family, who were created earls of Erroll in 1453. Mary Queen of Scots visited George Hay, the seventh earl, after her victory at Corrichie in 1562. He began the existing tower house soon afterwards – the hall fireplace bears the year 1570. To begin with, it was an oblong tower, the ribbed vaulting suggesting the same team of masons who built the towers at Balbegno and Towie Barclay. An older origin has been claimed for the narrow wing with thinner walls appended on the west side, which gives the ensemble the appearance of an L-plan tower. However, it looks more like an addition of the early seventeenth century. In 1594 Francis Hay, the ninth earl, joined the Catholic Uprising and the tower house was battered by James VI's cannon. The Hays lost possession for their involvement in successive Jacobite risings. Captain John Hay purchased Delgatie back in the 1950s and restored it from dereliction.

The original tower rises five storeys to its corbelled-out parapet, with cannon spouts and modest bartizans. A low attic is recessed within. By contrast the later wing has a plain, gabled roof line; its six storeys with enlarged windows do not align with the other portion. The grey harling conceals the junction between them, while a discordant eighteenth-century block fills the re-entrant angle. The ground-floor entrance into the wing is covered by a Victorian porch. Then comes the rib-vaulted entrance passage to the original tower, containing at this level a barrel-vaulted kitchen with a huge fireplace. A broad spiral staircase in one corner leads up to the hall on the first floor, with its remarkable (and rather archaic) ribbed vault. In addition to the year, the fireplace bears the inscription 'my hoyp is in ye Lord'. The stair continues up to the top, passing a succession of rooms with original beamed ceilings. Most notable is the one on the second floor, painted with bizarre allegorical figures. There are mural chambers within the considerable thickness of the walls. The staircase also serves the wing, where the decor reflects more recent centuries of occupation.

Access: Open daily.
Reference: *PSAS* (44).
Relations: Towie Barclay and Balbegno. Painted ceilings at Earlshall, Crathes and Huntingtower.

DOUNE OF INVERNOCHTY An impressive earthwork rises beside the A944, just south-west of Bellabeg in the hilly terrain of Strathdon. Although largely a natural mound, it has been scarped and shaped to form a steep-sided, roughly oval motte with a flat top. Surrounding it is a ditch that was fed with water from an adjacent stream, which flows into the River Don beyond. To the south-west are the denuded ramparts of the bailey. Excavations revealed a curtain wall around the perimeter of the motte and – oddly – a chapel rather than a tower on the summit. The earthwork was probably raised in the mid-twelfth century by Morgrund, mormaer of Mar, but abandoned in the thirteenth for Kildrummy Castle. The chapel lasted several centuries longer as Strathdon's parish church, until a new one was built across the river. A defensive role returned briefly in World War Two, when an observation post was set up on the summit.

Access: Freely accessible.
Reference: *PSAS* (53).
Relations: Kildrummy. Motte-and-bailey castles like the Bass of Inverurie and the Peel Ring of Lumphanan.

DRUM CASTLE stands amid fine gardens off the A93, midway between Aberdeen and Banchory. This is a castle of two parts: a picturesque Jacobean mansion and an early tower house dominating the rest. In 1323 Robert the Bruce granted lands in the forest of Drum to his loyal armour-bearer, William de Irwin, but the unspoilt tower house may already have been built. It has been suggested that it was erected as a hunting lodge for Alexander III by his master mason, the appropriately named Richard Cementarius. Given the turmoil into which the Crown plunged following Alexander's death, it is possible that the tower remained incomplete until William de Irwin came along, but it seems more likely to have been wholly built by William. In either case, it may be regarded as one of the earliest Scottish tower houses.

The tower is divided vertically into three barrel-vaulted compartments. Defence was paramount here and the windows (except for a couple of later insertions) are tiny. A row of corbels supports the embattled parapet – a prototype of the corbelled-out parapets that would become so common. Rounded corners, more difficult to hack with a pick, compensate for the tower's oblong shape. A modern staircase leads to the original first-floor entrance passage through the massive thickness of the wall. The doorway at the end is blocked and the hall can now only be reached through the later house. From this passage a straight mural stair descends to the gloomy undercroft, containing a well in a recess. Returning the same way, an adjacent spiral stair ascends in one corner to the top compartment. This formed the solar, once surmounted by an unlit sleeping loft in the vault, as the rows of corbels demonstrate. A wooden ladder now leads to the parapet. Original drains cross the wall walk and a latrine is provided for the guard, while the recesses on the inside of the parapet gave archers more space to deploy.

William de Irwin was the ancestor of the Irvine of Drum family, most of whom bore the name Alexander. They conducted a long-running feud with the Keith earls Marischal. One of them fought a mutually fatal duel with Hector MacLean of Duart at the Battle of Harlaw (1411). The thirteenth Alexander Irvine added the new mansion that abuts the tower house – one of the dormer windows bears the year 1619 upside down. This picturesque, harled range shows some adherence to traditional defensive forms in the square, gabled towers that clasp the outer corners, the row of vaulted undercrofts linked by a corridor and the strong yett still on display near the entrance. Nevertheless, the thinly walled barmkin and the little gatehouse on the north show scant regard for defence. Except for a brief expulsion in the Civil War, when Drum was captured by the Covenanters, the Irvines remained here until 1975. Their long occupation is reflected in the state rooms on the main floor of the house, which now have a Georgian and Victorian appearance. They end in the barrel-vaulted hall on the first floor of the tower house, converted into a library in the 1840s.

Access: Open regularly (NTS).
Reference: Guidebook by O. Thompson. *PSAS* (134).
Relations: The early tower houses at Hallforest, Lochleven and Duffus.

DRUMINNOR CASTLE, on an estate two miles south-east of Rhynie, has lost the tower house for which James, Lord Forbes, obtained a licence to crenellate in 1457. The sixteenth-century residential block that adjoined the tower does survive. It formed part of a courtyard complex.

Access: Private.

DUNNIDEER CASTLE crowns a precipitous hill a mile west of Insch. A footpath ascends to it from Western Road. The summit is surrounded by the double rampart and ditch of an Iron Age hillfort. The inner rampart was in fact a wall of vitrified stones but this is only apparent where they peep out of the grassy bank. Within the enclosure are the remains of a square tower that reused some of these stones. Most of the structure is reduced to footings but one chunky wall stands high. A gaping hole marks the position of a sizeable window that lit the hall at first-floor level. The tower is tentatively attributed to Joscelin de Balliol, brother of the great magnate John Balliol, who is recorded as being in possession in 1260. It would thus be a late Norman-style keep, or alternatively a very early tower house. This inhospitable site does not seem to have been reoccupied for long.

Access: Freely accessible (uphill walk).
Reference: *PSAS* (69).
Relations: Joscelin's brother's castle at Buittle.

ESSLEMONT CASTLE is a ruined L-plan tower house in a clump of trees beside the A920, two miles south-west of Ellon. Excavations have shown that an earlier and more massive L-plan tower stood close by, in the middle of a five-sided curtain wall with flanking towers. This was burnt in 1493, during a feud between the Cheynes of Esslemont and the Earl of Erroll. Henry Cheyne obtained a licence to crenellate in 1500, though it is unclear if he carried out anything more than repairs. Mary Queen of Scots was entertained here while suppressing the fourth Earl of Huntly's rebellion in 1562. As a reward she made Patrick Cheyne a baron and the form of the present tower house suggests that it was built after that ennoblement. Modest in scale, it occupied one angle of the vanished enclosure. The re-entrant angle is filled largely by a square tower containing a generous spiral stair. The salient feature is a round corner tower projecting at the rear of the tower house. It incorporates one of the older flanking towers and now carries the remains of a square caphouse supported on corbelling. The main body of the tower house was three storeys high, no doubt with a vanished attic above, but the plain window openings are later enlargements. Abandoned since 1625, the building stands to nearly its full height apart from the collapsed gable end of the jamb.

Access: Freely accessible with caution.
Reference: *PSAS* (78).
Relations: There were other Cheynes at Arnage and Duffus.

FYVIE CASTLE has one of the most magnificent castellated facades in Scotland. It is set in a large country estate by the River Ythan, a mile north of Fyvie village. The harled south front, with its square corner towers and central gatehouse, is a startling contrast to the tower houses and barmkins more typical of later Scottish castles. William the Lion had a royal hunting lodge here, which Edward I visited during his invasion of 1296, but nothing now visible is that old. In 1390 Robert II granted the manor to Sir Henry Preston, in exchange for the ransom of a Percy knight captured at the Battle of Otterburn. Tradition asserts that the Preston Tower, at the east end of the facade, is his tower house. On Henry's death in 1433 the castle passed by marriage to Alexander Meldrum. He is credited with the south curtain wall and the Meldrum Tower to the west. As the two towers are very similar, it is more likely that the whole front (except for the gatehouse) was built in one operation. Both towers have stair turrets aligned with the curtain. Clearly an ambitious quadrangular castle on the English pattern was intended.

In 1596 the castle was purchased by Sir Alexander Seton, later Lord Chancellor and first Earl of Dunfermline. In the middle of the south front he inserted the gatehouse with its semi-circular flanking towers, a complex known as the Seton Tower. It bears the year 1599. A crowning arch unites the flanking towers high up, the top floors of the gatehouse being corbelled out to form an oblong top. Dormer windows and bartizans with conical roofs create a Scottish Baronial skyline, not only on the new gatehouse but also on the older corner towers. Gabled attics replaced the older parapets, giving these three structures five storeys in all. The gatehouse towers show some regard for defence, with wide-mouthed gunports guarding the approach. However, this ambitious entrance – a throwback to the twin-towered gatehouses of old – must have been primarily for display.

A Renaissance doorway leads into the gate passage, later blocked at the inner end. Seton also built the long residential block forming the west range. Internally, the only vestige of his work is the remarkable staircase – a traditional

Fyvie Castle, Aberdeenshire

spiral of wide treads but vaulted in a series of rising compartments supported on arches. A seventeenth-century plaster ceiling covers the great hall, now called the Morning Room. Otherwise, the interiors of the west range and the narrow south range, behind the show front, reflect the changing tastes of the Gordons of Fyvie, who transformed the castle into a stately home.

Fyvie is now reduced to these two ranges, as the other two sides of the courtyard were demolished in the eighteenth century. The Gordon Tower at the north end of the west range dates only from the 1790s, while the large adjunct known as the Leith Tower was added by the industrialist Alexander Leith, who purchased the castle in 1889. These towers maintain Fyvie's supposed tradition of being named after the families that built them.

Access: Open regularly in summer (NTS).
Reference: Guidebook by C. Hartley. *PSAS* (73).
Relations: Seton's mansion at Pinkie. Late twin-towered gatehouses at Tolquhon, Dudhope and Boyne. Fyvie's gatehouse probably inspired the triumphal arch of Craigston.

GIGHT CASTLE   A mile south-east of Cottown of Gight, on the B9005, is a small car park signposted 'Braes of Gight Wood'. From here a footpath leads through the woods to this overgrown ruin. Pronounced 'Gecht' with a hard 'ch', it is alternatively known as Formantine Castle. It belonged to the Gordons of Gight, a family notorious for feuding with their neighbours. One of its last occupants was Catherine Gordon, whose son Lord Byron visited as a child. Afterwards it was abandoned and continues to decay.

This truncated L-plan tower house stands close to a cliff above the River Ythan. The entrance passage, through the thickness of the wall, is crossed by a mural passage linking the three vaulted storerooms in the main block and the kitchen in the jamb. The passage ends at a fallen spiral staircase that led upwards. This arrangement, instead of the customary corridor, is also found at Craig and Towie Barclay, while the little ribbed vault over the intersection of the two passages occurs at Craig and Delgatie. It is therefore believed that all four tower houses were built by the same team of masons (Delgatie bears the year 1570). The unusual thickness of the walls for that period is another feature in common. Delgatie and Towie Barclay are noted for their rib-vaulted halls, but the first-floor hall here is very ruinous and nothing remains of the storeys above. The low wing attached was added in the seventeenth century.

Access: Exterior only.
Relations: Craig, Delgatie and Towie Barclay.

GLENBUCHAT CASTLE can be found off the A97, six miles south-west of Kildrummy. It overlooks that picturesque stretch of the River Don valley known as Strathdon. This tower house was built by John Gordon of Cairnburrow following his marriage to Helen Carnegie. A worn inscription above the entrance bore their names and the year 1590, along with the motto 'No thing on earth remanis bot faime'. Four years later royal troops seized Glenbuchat during the Catholic Uprising. It was sold in 1738 by a later John Gordon, the staunch Jacobite 'Old Glenbucket', whose reputation is said to have given George II nightmares. Although long abandoned, the tower house lacks little more that its roof and floors.

Glenbuchat is a good example of a Z-plan tower house, with square flanking towers at diagonally opposite corners of the main block. The south-west tower contains the entrance doorway, flanked by the main block. Slits for handguns command the approach, but large windows in the upper storeys show the defensive compromises of the late sixteenth century, even if they were once barred by iron grilles. The main block contained only two floors plus the attic stage, though an extra storey was contrived in both of the towers. From the entrance a corridor leads past two storage undercrofts into the kitchen, with an arched fireplace in the end wall. These ground-level rooms are barrel-vaulted as usual. A curious staircase in the south-west tower curves upwards to the first-floor hall, later divided into two chambers by a cross-wall. Twin spiral stairs ascended to the upper floors. They are housed in re-entrant angle turrets that rise unusually from arches instead of the more usual corbelling. The tower house has the jagged skyline typical of its period. Prominent chimneys crown the gable ends, while bartizans clasp the angles of the flanking towers.

Access: Exterior only (HES).
Reference: Guidebook (includes Kildrummy) by C. Tabraham.
Relations: Z-plan tower houses such as Castle Fraser, Midmar and the Wallace Tower.

HALLFOREST CASTLE stands in a field about a mile south-west of Kintore. It is reached by taking a drive running north-east from the B994, then a footpath to the north. This sadly neglected ruin is one of the oldest tower house in Scotland. According to tradition it was built by Robert the Bruce as a hunting lodge. However, it is more likely to have been raised by his staunch supporter Sir Robert Keith, the Great Marischal, to whom Robert granted these lands in 1309. It was still a seat of the earls Marischal when Mary Queen of Scots visited in 1562. There are shadowy accounts of damage inflicted during the Civil War, after which it was abandoned.

The tower is a massive oblong with thick walls and the remains of barrel vaulting at two levels. Both compartments were divided into two storeys by wooden floors, serving from the ground upwards as storeroom, kitchen, hall and solar. Enough remains to show that at least one more floor existed above the second vault. Ragged holes at hall level on the second floor denote sizeable windows, showing that even an early tower house could make concessions for comfort. One of these apertures may have been the entrance, reached via an external staircase or perhaps just a ladder. About a quarter of the tower has succumbed to a deep breach. If a spiral staircase linked each floor, it must have been in this fallen corner. Another corner survives as a precarious finger pointing upwards. Nothing remains of the barmkin that presumably accompanied the tower.

Access: Well seen from the footpath.

Relations: The early tower houses at Drum and Duffus. Later castles of the Keith earls at Inverugie, Ackergill and Dunnottar.

HARTHILL CASTLE, in extensive grounds a mile east of Oyne, belonged to the Leiths of Harthill. It is dated 1601. This lofty, well-restored Z-plan tower house has one round and one square flanking tower. A stretch of barmkin wall and a picturesque gateway also survive.

Access: Private.

HOUSE OF SCHIVAS   A turreted L-plan structure, on an estate two miles north of Ythanbank, was built by Thomas Leiper for George Gray of Schivas in the 1580s. Though basically a laird's house, it has an array of ornamental shot holes and a diminutive gatehouse.

Access: A functions venue with occasional open days.

HUNTLY CASTLE originated as a motte-and-bailey earthwork, probably raised late in the twelfth century by Duncan, Earl of Fife. Until 1506 it was called Strathbogie. Robert the Bruce recovered from an illness here in 1307, during his campaign to drive out his Comyn rivals. The lands passed to the Gordons, who hailed from the Borders but soon emerged as the most powerful family in the north east. Alexander Seton inherited by marriage in 1408 but his successors adopted the prestigious Gordon name.

Alexander was created first Earl of Huntly, taking the title from the Gordons' original lordship in Berwickshire. In 1452 the Earl of Moray sacked the castle in Alexander's absence. George Gordon, fourth Earl of Huntly, became Lord Chancellor and lavishly entertained Queen Mary of Guise here. However, after losing the earldom of Moray he rebelled against Mary Queen of Scots in 1562. The corpulent earl collapsed and died after the Battle of Corrichie and the castle was ransacked by Mary's troops. More serious damage was inflicted in 1594, after the sixth earl (another George) joined the Catholic Uprising against James VI. Although exiled, he returned to favour and was elevated to the rank of first Marquis of Huntly. In 1647 the castle endured its only protracted siege, on behalf of the king. The Covenanters under General David Leslie brutally hanged the garrison after its fall.

The tree-lined approach from Castle Street recalls its days as an aristocratic mansion, but most of the castle is very much a ruin. It occupies the bailey of the earthwork castle, overlooking the River Deveron. To the west is the conical motte, long devoid of buildings. The main defence was a massive L-plan tower house of the early fifteenth century on the north side of the courtyard. It was blown up by order of James VI in 1594 but the foundations have been exposed. Sixteenth-century and seventeenth-century buildings, mainly of a purely domestic character, formed a loose quadrangle around the courtyard. They reflect the confidence of the Gordons, despite their chequered history. Most of these buildings are reduced to fragments and footings, except for the vaulted bakehouse and brewhouse beside the tower house. An earth ravelin to the east is a relic of the Civil War siege.

Huntly would be a meagre ruin indeed were it not for the palace block on the south side of the courtyard, now an empty shell but otherwise virtually intact. Supplanting the older tower house as the Gordons' main residence, it was also quite defensible originally. Alexander, the first earl, began building after the sack of 1452. He determined the layout – an oblong block with a cylindrical tower projecting boldly at the south-west corner. However, only the stage below courtyard level appears to be his work. It consists of three barrel-vaulted cellars linked by a corridor, with a sinister prison in the base of the tower. Keyhole gunports pierce the outer wall. Evidently building was left unfinished because the existing superstructure dates from the time of the ill-fated fourth earl. It bears the year 1553 on the gable. Above a second row of vaulted undercrofts there are two residential floors, comprising a hall and solar in the main block and a bedchamber within the tower. They provided separate suites for the earl and countess.

On his return from exile the first marquis embellished the top storey with oriel windows and a monumental inscription at the wall-head: 'George Gordoun First Marquis of Huntlie: Henriette Stewart Marquesse of Huntlie: 1602'. The ornate fireplaces also date from his time, along with the magnificent display of heraldry on the stair turret known as the Frontispiece, which stands

at the north-east corner in a faint echo of the Z-plan. These additions make Huntly one of the best examples of the Scottish Baronial style.
Access: Open daily in summer and regularly in winter (HES).
Reference: Guidebook by A. Rutherford. *PSAS* (56 and 67).
Relations: The fourth earl's castle at Gordon. There is also a Castle Huntly in Perthshire.

INVERALLOCHY CASTLE, in a field a mile west of St Combs, is rare for retaining much of its barmkin wall, along with the jagged gable end of an oblong tower house at one corner. They were built by William Comyn of Inverallochy around 1504 but are now slowly decaying.
Access: Visible from the road.

INVERUGIE CASTLE Two and a half miles north-west of Peterhead, a turning off the A90 leads to this sorry ruin, just north of Inverugie village. The River Urie flows just behind. When MacGibbon and Ross sketched this unusual tower house it stood virtually intact. However, soon afterwards part of it collapsed in a gale; it was then blown up in an abortive attempt to clear the site. The tower house was a four-storey oblong block with twin round towers projecting at the eastern corners. It is thus akin to that handful of E-plan tower houses with square jambs at either end of one front. Now the decaying walls stand at most to half their original height and the north-east tower has collapsed. The building was erected towards the end of the sixteenth century by George Keith, the fifth Earl Marischal. At right angles is a purely residential range of around 1670, with an arched gateway to the barmkin attached. In a field to the north is the motte of an earlier stronghold.
Access: Well seen from the road.
Relations: The fifth earl built the quadrangle within Dunnottar Castle.

KILDRUMMY CASTLE, despite its ruinous condition, is one of the most impressive of Scotland's earlier strongholds. Justly called 'the noblest of northern castles', it stands in the Don valley about a mile south-west of Kildrummy village, off the A97. Its initial construction is attributed to William, Earl of Mar, in the mid-thirteenth century. It was an ambitious walled enclosure for its date, but the flanking towers were probably added to the curtain wall towards the end of the century by his son, Donald. Only Bothwell was conceived on a grander scale but, unlike that ambitious castle, Kildrummy was largely completed to its original plan.

Like most Scottish castles, it put up no resistance when the English first invaded in 1296. When Robert the Bruce declared himself king in 1306, he sent his family here for safe keeping. His queen and daughter escaped on the approach of an English army, nominally led by the Prince of Wales, who – as Edward II – would not be noted for his military aptitude. Robert's brother Neil stayed behind to offer a staunch resistance. Assaults with siege engines failed to have any effect. According to John Barbour's poem *The Brus*, written in the 1370s, the castle was eventually betrayed from within. Osbourn the blacksmith set fire to the great hall, where the corn was temporarily stored, depriving the castle of its food supply. Neil Bruce was executed at Berwick. The castle was later recovered but it escaped King Robert's demolition strategy. In 1335 Kildrummy was one of only five castles still loyal to the exiled David II. It was again besieged, this time by Scots supporting the English puppet king, Edward Balliol. Lady Christian Bruce (Robert's sister) defended it until her husband, Sir Andrew Murray, arrived with a relieving force.

David II wrested the castle from the Earl of Mar in 1363 and installed a royal garrison. It was later granted to the Elphinstone family, the earls of Mar only regaining possession in 1626 after a long legal dispute. Kildrummy met its end in the Jacobite wars. Retreating rebels set fire to the domestic buildings in 1690. John Erskine, sixth Earl of Mar, organised the abortive 1715 uprising from here. The castle appears to have been slighted after its failure.

The castle comprises a large and roughly D-shaped enclosure, its straight north-west curtain overlooking the steep drop to a ravine which is now a rock garden. Elsewhere the castle was surrounded by a broad ditch, much of it surviving. There are clearly two thirteenth-century building phases, because the original rubble curtain is interrupted by four inserted towers of ashlar masonry. On the south-east, at the apex of the 'D', stood a mighty gatehouse, sadly reduced to its footings. Two round-fronted towers flank the entrance to a long gate passage. With its rearward projection into the cobbled courtyard, the plan resembles the Edwardian gatehouses of Wales. Following a visit to Kildrummy in 1303, Edward I paid his master mason, James of St George, £100 for unspecified works somewhere. It has been suggested that the gatehouse was an addition by that celebrated architect, though the sum seems hardly adequate and Scottish builders were quite capable of such a structure by the late thirteenth century. In front of the gatehouse is the base of a later barbican with a drawbridge pit.

From the gatehouse the curtain curves back in straight sections. Halfway along on either side are U-shaped flanking towers with tall arrow slits, both now quite ruinous. The north angle of the enclosure is occupied by the circular Warden's Tower, rising nearly to full height and now the best-preserved part of the castle. Two residential chambers, probably for the constable, surmounted a ground-floor prison. At the west angle stood the larger Snow Tower, one of Scotland's few cylindrical keeps. It rose through seven storeys, some of them vaulted, and would thus have outshone the round keep at Bothwell in height, though not in girth. Unfortunately, the keep proved too heavy for its own good. It collapsed in 1805 and only the consolidated base remains.

Against the north-west curtain lay the domestic buildings, also reduced to little more than foundations. In the centre was the great hall, permitted the luxury of windows through the curtain on this comparatively secure side overlooking the ravine. The adjoining solar was built up into an oblong tower house – the Elphinstone Tower – in the sixteenth century. Perhaps the older keep was showing signs of instability. Only one side survives to full height, but it shows the usual gabled profile. Otherwise, there is just the east wall of the chapel, forming a shallow projection from the curtain near the Warden's Tower. Its three lancet windows compromise the defensive integrity of the circuit, though the foundations of another half-round tower in front show at least an intention to remedy that weakness.

Access: Open regularly in summer (HES).
Reference: Guidebook (includes Glenbuchat) by C. Tabraham. *The Castle of Kildrummy* by W. D. Simpson. *PSAS* (96).
Relations: Bothwell and other mature castles of enclosure such as Dunstaffnage, Caerlaverock and Old Inverlochy. Later earls of Mar built Braemar and Mar's Wark (Stirling).

KINDROCHIT CASTLE is now in the middle of the pleasant village of Braemar, off Balnellan Road. The remains, overlooking the Clunie Water, are meagre but well maintained. It began as a hunting lodge of the first Stewart king, Robert II, who came here frequently. It originally formed a hall house with square corner turrets, but only the very ruinous undercroft remains. After Robert's death, his brother-in-law Sir Malcolm Drummond was granted a licence to crenellate in 1390. He appended an oblong tower house on the north, jutting awkwardly into the older hall block. This was one of the largest tower houses in Scotland but is reduced to turf-covered footings. In 1402, while still under construction, Malcolm was abducted and killed by Highland raiders. Two years later Alexander Stewart, illegitimate son of the notorious Wolf of Badenoch, stormed Kindrochit. He forced Malcolm's widow to marry him and thus obtained the earldom of Mar. It was long abandoned by the time Braemar Castle was built a mile to the north.

Access: Freely accessible (LA).
Reference: *PSAS* (57).
Relations: Braemar. Other work of Robert II at Dundonald, Edinburgh and Stirling.

KINNAIRD HEAD CASTLE, overlooking a headland at the northern tip of Fraserburgh, is an oblong tower house, begun in 1570 by Sir Alexander Fraser of Philorth. He founded the fishing port around the same time. Apart from some enlarged windows the tower is authentic externally, white-harled and rising three storeys to a corbelled-out parapet that rounds into bartizans at the corners. However, this is a tower house with a difference, because the lantern of a later lighthouse rises from the top. Positioned at the entrance to the Moray Firth, the tower was first adapted in 1787. The engineer Robert

Stevenson, urged not to demolish the tower, erected the cylindrical structure within in the 1820s. It fills one half of the interior. The rest was transformed into the keeper's quarters, though a barrel vault still covers the truncated first-floor hall. It remained in use until 1991.

The barmkin has been supplanted by ancillary buildings, though a small oblong tower from the perimeter survives on the rocks to the east. It is called the Wine Tower from the tradition that it served as the laird's wine store. Externally it is quite austere. A modern staircase leads to the original entrance, placed at second-floor level for extra security, and into a chamber with seven pendants hanging from the plain barrel vault. They bear the arms of the Frasers and associated families. This room may have served as a Catholic chapel. There is no built-in staircase so the two lower floors must have been reached by internal ladders through hatches in the vaults.

Access: The tower house is open regularly in summer (HES). The interior of the Wine Tower is open occasionally.

Relations: Sir Alexander built the Castle of Pittulie. There is also a Kinnaird Castle in Perthshire.

KNOCK CASTLE can be found two miles west of the bridge over the Dee at Ballater. An unsignposted track, at a bend on the B976, ascends north-west though the woods to this oblong tower house on a rocky knoll. Though now a shell it is structurally complete. Modest in scale, the tower is four storeys high including the attic gables. A gabled caphouse surmounts the corner that contained the spiral stair, while round bartizans are corbelled out high up at two other corners. The simple entrance leads into a gutted interior that has lost its ground floor vault. Beneath the upper floor windows are groups of three shot holes pointing downwards, each angled in a different direction. According to tradition Henry Gordon of Knock lost his seven sons, all ambushed and beheaded by their Forbes enemies in 1591. When informed of this disaster he plummeted down the staircase to his death. Unfortunately this tragic tale cannot be linked to the current structure, but rather to a previous tower that stood close by. It appears to have been destroyed during the inevitable feud that followed. Henry's brother Alexander, who hanged the Forbes perpetrator, is credited with the existing tower.

Access: Freely accessible (HES – uphill walk).

KNOCKHALL CASTLE A mile north of Newburgh via a minor road is the virtually intact shell of an L-plan tower house. Four storeys high including the attic gables, the ground-floor rooms (including a kitchen in the jamb) are both vaulted as usual. They are separated by a passage leading to the fallen spiral stair in a square projecting turret. There are wide-mouthed gunports low down. The tower bears the year 1565 over the walled-up doorway, which is situated as usual in the re-entrant angle. It was built by William, Lord Sinclair, but damaged by Covenantors under the Earl Marischal in 1639. The regular rows of enlarged windows date from a restoration afterwards. The tower was abandoned after a fire in 1734.

Access: Well seen from the road.

LESLIE CASTLE rises in its own grounds two miles west of Auchleven. It very much appears to be a conventional, stepped L-plan tower house, four storeys high including the attic, but a stone on the re-entrant stair turret reads 'Funded [i.e. founded] Jun 17 1661'. That is late indeed! It would be curious to know the motives of its builder, Sir William Forbes, Baronet of Monymusk, in resurrecting a type of building more typical of his grandfathers' generation. His arms and initials are carved on the hall fireplace at first-floor level. In fact, the 'last fortified house in Scotland' may not even quite be that, since there are the remains of another tower bearing the year 1666 at Cluny Crichton. Perhaps these lairds hankered for tradition after the restoration of the monarchy. In many ways the tower is a faithful tribute to its forebears. The vaulted ground-floor rooms include a kitchen with a deep fireplace, round bartizans are corbelled out high up at the corners, and there is even a decent array of shot holes. The tower is more regularly laid out than previous examples, with three main rooms on each floor, while the square turret in the re-entrant angle has a staircase rising in straight sections all the way up. Novelty is displayed by the gables, which are no longer crow-stepped, and the Jacobean-style chimneys crowning them.

Even more surprisingly, the tower house stood in one corner of a walled barmkin with a square gate tower, now vanished. William Forbes sold his new tower to the Leiths in 1671. It was abandoned in 1820 and was a roofless shell in a precarious state by 1979. In that year it was purchased by the architect David Leslie, who embarked on a comprehensive ten-year restoration to make it habitable again. He rebuilt the top part of the stair turret, making it the dominant feature once again, and reinstated the conical roofs of the bartizans. Covered in a coat of white harling, the tower house looks decidedly new once more.

Access: A functions venue. Visible from the road and open by appointment.
Relations: Cluny Crichton. Monymusk was the chief seat of the Forbeses of Monymusk.

LICKLEYHEAD CASTLE occupies a wooded estate half a mile south of Auchleven. This gabled L-plan tower house has a taller jamb that projects in two directions. It was built for the Leiths of Lickleyhead, probably by the master mason John Bell late in the sixteenth century.

Access: Private (now a holiday let).

MIDMAR CASTLE, previously known as Ballogie, is one of the most attractive of the later tower houses and a fine example of the Z-plan. Two miles west of Echt, a sideroad runs south from the B9119 towards the building, which is concealed in wooded grounds. Its layout is partly obscured by later additions, but the square-plan central block has diagonally opposite flanking towers, one square and one circular. The circular tower is almost as big as the main block and rises six storeys to an embattled parapet. The main block and the square tower both have four storeys beneath their gabled attics. High up there are round bartizans with conical roofs at the three free corners of the square tower, along with gabled turrets at the two free corners of the main block. The entrance, in the side of the square tower, leads to a generous staircase ascending in straight sections to the first floor. From there it transfers to a turret spiral stair corbelled out in the re-entrant angle. Another turret stair leads all the way up in a re-entrant angle of the circular tower. A passage skirts around the barrel-vaulted ground floor of the main block to connect the two flanking towers.

Alexander Gordon of Abergeldie and Midmar was dispossessed in 1562, following his role in the fourth Earl of Huntly's revolt against Mary Queen of Scots. Restored to his lands two years later, when Gordon support was needed against new rebels, he appears to have built the existing tower house over the ensuing decade. He employed the master mason George Bell, work continuing until the latter's death in 1575. Midmar probably formed the inspiration for Castle Fraser, which was remodelled from the following year. Like Castle Fraser, it is possible that the main block incorporates an older tower. The low eighteenth-century wings in front are now another feature in common. Midmar suffered damage during the Catholic Uprising of 1594. The interior has some simple plaster ceilings and much eighteenth-century panelling. It was restored and re-harled from a state of dereliction in 1977–80. Cunningar Motte recalls a previous fortification in a field half a mile to the north-west.

Access: Private.
Reference: *PSAS* (113).
Relations: Castle Fraser and other masterpieces of the Scottish Baronial at Craigievar, Glamis and Crathes. Alexander also built Abergeldie.

MONYMUSK HOUSE   From Monymusk's priory church a drive runs north-east to this mansion by the River Don. It is dominated by an altered L-plan tower house, built by William Forbes of Monymusk in the 1580s. The first-floor hall retains a painted ceiling and a heraldic overmantel.

Access: A functions venue but visible from the drive.

PEEL RING OF LUMPHANAN   The name recalls the wooden palisade that must have crowned the perimeter of this large motte. A heightening of a natural mound, it is roughly oval in shape – a modern pathway cut into the side of the

steep slope allows an easy ascent. The motte is surrounded by a concentric rampart bank. The broad moat between them, now dry, was originally fed by the adjacent Lumphanan Burn. A second moat beyond is no longer apparent and there is no sign of any accompanying bailey. The tradition that it was raised by Macbeth has no basis in fact, though he was beheaded nearby in 1057 after his defeat at the Battle of Lumphanan. Excavations indicated an early thirteenth-century date, making this a relatively late example. It appears to have supported a hunting lodge of Alexander II's son-in-law, Sir Alan Durward. Edward I came here in 1296 to receive homage from Sir John de Melville. Foundations of a fifteenth-century hall can be discerned in the turf in one quadrant. The site lies a mile south-west of Lumphanan village, off the road to Dess.
Access: Freely accessible (HES).
Reference: *PSAS* (128).
Relations: Durward's main seat was Coull. He also raised the original Urquhart Castle.

PITCAPLE CASTLE stands on an estate half a mile north-east of Pitcaple. This mansion is dominated by a Z-plan tower house, built by the Leslies of Pitcaple in the late sixteenth century. It has twin round flanking towers with conical roofs; tall bartizans mark the other two corners.
Access: Private.

PITFICHIE CASTLE is an oblong tower house of four storeys, including the gabled attic. At the south corner a prominent round tower takes the place of the more customary jamb. The entrance, immediately beside the main block in the flanking tower, is guarded by wide-mouthed gunports. In the other re-entrant angle, a stair turret is corbelled out from the first floor upwards, while a square caphouse crowns another spiral stair at the west corner of the main block. The ground floor contains two barrel-vaulted compartments, one of them the kitchen, connected by a corridor. The tower house was built by the Urrie family of Pitfichie, apparently in the 1560s, though the master mason David Bell was at work here in 1607. By 1796 it was a roofless ruin. Two sides of the main block collapsed in 1936 and the rest narrowly avoided demolition. They were rebuilt when the tower house was restored and re-harled from 1978. The conical roof of the tower reflects the original arrangement, as does the rebuilt caphouse squeezed in beside it at the top of the stair turret. A fragment of barmkin wall survives. Pitfichie overlooks the River Don, a mile north-west of Monymusk.
Access: Well seen from the road.
Reference: *PSAS* (55).
Relations: Other members of the Bell family worked at Castle Fraser, Craigievar, Lickleyhead, Midmar and Tillycairn.

PITSLIGO CASTLE, though more ruined, resembles Tolquhon in its quadrangular layout and the retention of an older tower house. This tower house occupies most of the south side of the castle. It is a massive oblong, almost windowless, though presumably there was more lighting in the fallen east wall, which contains the entrance. Barrel vaults cover both the undercroft and the seemingly lofty hall above, but both were divided into two storeys by wooden floors. The tower would have dominated still more before the removal of its top storey. It is attributed to Sir William Forbes of Pitsligo, who obtained the lands by marriage in 1424.

Unlike Tolquhon, the courtyard appears to be the work of several building phases. Panels above the gateways and on the stair turret bear the years 1577, 1603, 1633 and 1656, though some of these appear to commemorate family events. The surrounding curtain, with a single round tower projecting at the north-east angle, is probably contemporary with Tolquhon, but work on the internal buildings continued well into the seventeenth century. There are ranges of buildings on all four sides but they are mostly quite ruinous. Best preserved is the west range, pierced by the entrance passage. A row of upper-floor windows overlooking the courtyard is reduced to jagged holes. Above the gate arch a panel bears the Forbes arms. A square stair turret projects into the north-east corner of the courtyard. Beyond is the vaulted undercroft of the flanking tower, with wide-mouthed gunports. The castle is fronted by a lightly walled outer enclosure. Its round-headed entrance, with another armorial panel, is capped by a pediment.

In 1633 Alexander Forbes was ennobled as Lord Pitsligo. The fourth lord, a Jacobite, fled after the Battle of Culloden and the castle was ransacked by Hanoverian troops. It then fell into a sad state of decay but is gradually being consolidated by the Pitsligo Castle Trust. Castle Street ascends from Rosehearty to the remains.

Access: Freely accessible with caution.
Reference: *PSAS* (88).
Relations: Tolquhon.

RAVENSCRAIG CASTLE   Although the castle of the same name in Fife is better known, in its prime this tower house was one of the largest and strongest in Scotland, an impression it still manages to convey despite its ruined and badly neglected state. Unfortunately it has decayed badly since it was sketched by MacGibbon and Ross. Back then it was clearly discernible as an L-plan structure, four storeys high and dominated by a tall, round stair turret in the re-entrant angle. Since then, much of the main block has fallen in, burying the collapsed vaults under a pile of grass-covered rubble, while the whole is thickly swathed in foliage. The jamb is still largely complete but the windows are torn into ragged holes and the stair turret has fallen. The entrance, in the ground floor of the main block, is flanked by the jamb as usual. The thick walls and relatively low profile seem designed to compensate for the growing power of artillery – an affinity with its Fife namesake – and the walls are well provided with keyhole gunports that have unusual cross-slits for better sighting.

A licence to crenellate the 'Craig of Inverugie' was granted in 1491 but the recipient is not specified – it seems that the Keiths of Inverugie were lairds at that time. James VI attended a wedding here in 1589. The tower occupies a knoll above the River Ugie, a little upstream from Inverugie Castle, and is surrounded by the ditches of a triangular enclosure. A mile north of Inverugie, starting at a sharp bend in the road, a rough track alongside the riverbank leads to the remains.

Access: Exterior only.
Reference: *Transactions of the Glasgow Archaeological Society* (8).
Relations: Ravenscraig (Fife).

TERPERSIE CASTLE stands on a farm a mile north-west of Tullynessle. Built around 1561 by William Gordon of Terpersie, this Z-plan tower house was burnt by Covenantors in 1645. Well restored from ruin, it has twin round flanking towers embracing the modest main block.

Access: Private.

TILLYCAIRN CASTLE   This restored, L-plan tower house near Ordhead resembles Craigievar, though less elaborate. Matthew Lumsden of Tillycairn appears to have built it in the 1540s but the bartizaned skyline is a later embellishment attributed to the architect John Bell.

Access: Private.

TOLQUHON CASTLE   The ambitious courtyard mansion of a relatively minor laird lies west of the Pitmedden-Tarves road (B999). A plaque high up to the right of the gatehouse is very specific about the period of construction: 'Al this warke excep the auld tour was begun be William Forbes 15 Aprile 1584 and endit be him 20 October 1589'. The 'auld tour' is Preston's Tower, at the north corner of the quadrangle. It may have been built by Sir John Forbes, who married the Preston heiress in 1420. Although more massive than the later buildings, this oblong tower house is now very ruinous. Two sides have collapsed but most of the barrel-vaulted undercroft remains. From the ground-floor entrance a mural stair ascended to the hall, with the imprint of a torn-out fireplace. Most of the two upper storeys have fallen. A well in the courtyard is the sole relic of the original barmkin.

The present mansion, masterpiece of the master mason Thomas Leiper, forms a quadrangle with ranges on all sides. Most important was the south-east range, opposite the gatehouse. Though now roofless, it survives intact to its crow-stepped gables. In the middle of the courtyard front a half-round stair turret rises to a square caphouse, though the main entrance occupies a side jamb. Despite the secure positioning of the entrance, along with the shot holes high up in the stair turret, this is clearly a residential block rather than a new tower house. A grand staircase in the jamb ascends to the great hall, with hexagonal paving slabs, large windows and a grand fireplace. Beyond is the solar, surmounted by the main bedchamber. The lower south-west range is filled by a long gallery, showing the arrival in Scotland of Elizabethan trends. Opposite is the more ruinous north-east range, which probably housed the laird's retainers. Barrel-vaulted undercrofts underlie each range, those below the south-east range being linked by a corridor. Beneath the solar is the kitchen, with the usual wide-arched fireplace.

Tolquhon (pronounced 'Tolhoon') shows some attention towards defence on the outside. Towers project at diagonally opposite corners of the enclosure, echoing the Z-plan tower houses of the period (Preston's Tower does not project at all). The square tower at the east corner contains a pit prison at its base. Its counterpart on the west is round externally but contains square chambers for domestic convenience. Beside Preston's Tower on the north-west front is the charming little gatehouse. Its semi-circular flanking turrets bristle with wide-mouthed gunports, while lower down are triple shot holes of ornamental appearance. The twin windows near the top preserve their protective iron grilles, while two panels above the arch to the vaulted gate passage depict the arms of William Forbes and his king. The walled outer enclosure has little defensive value, though its gate arch is flanked by more shot holes.

James VI visited the castle soon after its completion. William Forbes of Tolquhon, who seems to have been an unusually benevolent laird, died in 1596. His ornate tomb at Tarves has survived the demolition of the church that contained it. In 1718 the impoverished last Forbes owner was evicted. The castle continued to serve as a farmhouse but gradually fell into ruins.

Access: Open regularly in summer (HES).
Reference: Guidebook by C. Tabraham and K. Owen. *PSAS* (72).
Relations: Leiper's work at Arnage, Castle Fraser and the House of Schivas. The late gatehouses at Fyvie, Dudhope and Boyne.

TOWIE BARCLAY CASTLE, in its own grounds a mile south of Birkenhills, is a squat L-plan tower house with a shallow jamb. The ribbed vault of the hall suggests that the Barclays of Towie employed the same team of masons who worked at Delgatie and Balbegno in the 1570s.

Access: Private.

UDNY CASTLE, in spacious grounds just north of Udny Green, is an oblong tower house of the Udny family, with rounded angles and corner bartizans. An offset in the masonry halfway up suggests that the upper part was added to an older structure in the late sixteenth century.

Access: Private.

WALLACE TOWER   The Wallace Tower, or Benholm's Lodge, is a small and picturesque Z-plan tower house, four storeys high including the attic. It has shot holes and crow-stepped gables, while the twin round flanking turrets are capped by conical roofs. A crudely carved figure in a niche probably represents Sir Robert Keith, the tempestuous younger brother of the Earl Marischal. He built the tower around 1610 as a town house – it originally stood on Netherkirkgate in Aberdeen. Redevelopment in 1963 saw the tower taken down stone by stone by the city council and re-erected a mile and a half away. It now overlooks the River Don in Seaton Park off Tillydrone Avenue, a short distance west of the medieval cathedral in Old Aberdeen. The so-called Motte of Tillydrone close by is actually a Bronze Age burial mound.

Access: Exterior only. There are plans to renovate and open.
Relations: Loch Doon Castle has also been moved.

WESTHALL CASTLE, on an estate north of Oyne, is mostly a Victorian mansion. However, one corner is formed by a late sixteenth-century tower house of the Gordons of Westhall. This odd variant of the E-plan has two towers – one square and one round – flanking adjacent corners.

Access: The gardens are open occasionally.

OTHER SITES   *Aberdeen*'s royal castle, rebuilt in stone by Alexander III, was recovered from the English by Robert the Bruce in 1308 and destroyed. Two tower blocks on Castlehill mark the site, overlooking the harbour. The Black Comyn castle of *Dundarg* (near New Aberdour), also destroyed after Sir Andrew Murray wrested it from English hands in 1334, is reduced to a later fragment on a precipitous rock above the sea. The so-called *Castle of King Edward*, on a promontory near Danshillock, comprises a few fragments of early curtain wall. Mottes include *Auchindoir*, the *Castle of Rattray* (near Blackhill) and the *Peel of Fichlie* (near Glenkindle).

A gabled gateway and other fragments on a coastal promontory attest the barmkin of *Boddam Castle*. *Balmoral Castle*, Queen Victoria's Highland retreat near Crathie (gardens open), occupies the site of an earlier tower house. *Barra Castle* (near Oldmeldrum) in its present form is an attractive laird's house of the seventeenth century, but the ground-floor vaults of the main block survive from an older tower. Some other tower houses are badly ruined, much altered or largely rebuilt:

Aboyne Castle
Asloun Castle (ruin, near Alford)
Balquhain Castle (ruin, near Chapel of Garioch)
Birse Castle
Cluny Castle (near Monymusk)
Colquhonnie Castle (ruin, near Forbestown)
Corsindae House

Ellon Castle (ruin)
Fedderate Castle (ruin, near Maud)
Old Slains Castle (ruin, near Kirktown of Slains)
Skene House (near Lyne of Skene)
Slains Castle (ruin, near Cruden Bay)

ANGUS

The early castles of Angus perished in the Wars of Independence. The oldest masonry still visible is a stretch of curtain wall at Red Castle, followed by the rare monastic fortifications of Arbroath Abbey. That is virtually all before the fifteenth century, but there follows a sequence of courtyard castles surviving in varying degrees of preservation, the best being Edzell with its ruined domestic buildings and the compact barmkin of Mains. Then there is the remarkable late sixteenth-century 'chateau' overlooking the Tay at Dudhope. Edzell also has by far the finest of the walled gardens that were once a common amenity beyond the barmkin.

The county abounds in tower houses, though visitability is limited by the number on private estates. Some are simple oblongs like Broughty and Invermark. Affleck and Glamis are two contrasting fifteenth-century L-plan tower houses, the former little altered but the latter now the core of a great aristocratic mansion. The L-plan is followed in the next century at Edzell, while the tower at Melgund just formed the chamber block for a contemporary hall range attached to it. The Z-plan is best represented by the archetypal example at Claypotts with its picturesque caphouses. Only the turreted skyline of Glamis can compete with the best Scottish Baronial work in neighbouring Aberdeenshire. Angus castles are primarily concentrated in the coastal plain and the Tay valley, with several now in suburban Dundee. However, there are some further inland – Forter and Invermark are relatively remote. The Lindsays and the Ogilvys – often consumed by bitter rivalry – stand out among the various families who raised these towers.

County reference: BoS *Dundee and Angus*.

AFFLECK CASTLE, originally known as Auchinleck, stands concealed in wooded grounds north-west of Monikie, off Hillhead Road. Though not large, it is one of the best-preserved fifteenth-century tower houses in Scotland. In 1471 the Earl of Crawford restored the lands to his armour-bearers, the Auchinleck family, who probably built the tower soon afterwards. It passed to the Reids in the seventeenth century. They retained possession despite their involvement in the Young Pretender's rising. In 1760 they built Affleck House alongside, but the tower was preserved scarcely altered as service accommodation.

Externally the tower house is quite severe, its small windows – some covered by their original iron grilles – regularly spaced. Gunports of the inverted keyhole type peep out at ground level. The plain parapet, mounted on a row of corbels, rounds into tiny bartizans at the corners. This is an L-plan tower, but the jamb is just a small projection, containing a spiral staircase up to second-floor level. It is crowned by a recessed little caphouse, while another caphouse marks the position of the other staircase that continues from the second floor to the top. The entrance doorway, flanked by the jamb, has a niche for a statue above. It leads into two unvaulted undercrofts. The spiral stair ascends to the retainers' hall – the only barrel-vaulted level. Above that is the finer laird's hall, where the staircase ends. Steps ascend to a small chamber in the jamb, with a spy-hole overlooking the hall from the adjacent latrine. The other spiral stair climbs from the hall to the remarkable solar, its fireplace supported on shafted columns. This room has three tiny mural chambers. An archway beside the fireplace leads into a vaulted oratory in the jamb, with a carved piscina and ornate brackets for candles. The gabled attic, recessed within the parapet, is the only later addition.

Access: Formerly in state care but now private.
Reference: *Affleck Castle* by W. D. Simpson.
Relations: Fifteenth-century tower houses such as Castle Campbell, Balgonie, Cardoness and Newark (Selkirkshire). There are tower house oratories at Dean, Lochleven, Comlongon and Borthwick.

AIRLIE CASTLE occupies a promontory above the River Isla, on an estate two miles west of Kirkton of Airlie. The present house is eighteenth century but in front is a stretch of curtain wall and a slender gate tower. They date from Sir Walter Ogilvy's licence to crenellate in 1432.

Access: A functions venue.

ARBROATH ABBEY   Founded for Tironensian monks by William the Lion in 1178, this was one of the largest monasteries in Scotland. Here in 1320 the nobles assembled to sign the Declaration of Arbroath, which eventually persuaded the Pope to recognise Robert the Bruce as their legitimate king. Just outside the gates in 1446 the Lindsays and the Ogilvys fought a bloody battle for possession of the abbey's lucrative court. Despoiled after the Reformation, the massive ruins of the early Gothic abbey church lie at the north end of the High Street of this old royal burgh, some way inland from the coast and harbour.

Arbroath was one of Scotland's few semi-fortified ecclesiastical establishments. Running westwards from the church is a high stretch of wall, with the shell of a large gatehouse in the middle and the oblong Regality Tower at the end. This is a portion of the abbey's precinct wall, which once enclosed a large rectangle with a tower at each corner. Although the gatehouse is typically monastic in character, its wide outer archway was barred by a portcullis as the surviving grooves show, while below the stepped gable are the corbels of a machicolated parapet. The Regality Tower rises intact to four storeys, the lower two vaulted, with more machicolation corbels at the wall-head. It probably formed a tower house for the 'bailie', the official of the courthouse that stood against the wall alongside. Both the precinct wall and the gatehouse were built around 1300, though the upper floors of the Regality Tower date from the fifteenth century. Despite its defensive characteristics, the precinct wall must primarily have been a status symbol. It did not save the abbey from a sacking by English sea raiders in 1350. The abbey church formed the north side of the circuit, as at St Andrews, and its imposing but very accessible west front could hardly have deterred intruders.

Access: Open daily (HES).
Reference: Guidebook by R. Fawcett.
Relations: Crossraguel has another monastic tower house, while Pittenweem and St Andrews had other fortified monasteries.

BALFOUR CASTLE   A sideroad, heading south from the B951 at Kirkton of Kingoldrum, soon passes this striking circular tower. Narrow and slightly tapering, with a curious sloping roof line, this six-storey edifice is an unusually tall flanking tower and appears to have guarded the south-west corner of a vanished barmkin, as indicted by the stubs of curtain wall projecting from it. Nothing else is known about the site. It is attributed to Walter Ogilvy of Balfour, the brother of Cardinal Beaton's mistress, in the mid-sixteenth century. The tower is now attached to a nineteenth-century farmhouse.

Access: Well seen from the road.
Relations: The Ogilvy branches at Airlie, Cortachy, Forter and Inverquharity.

BALLINSHOE CASTLE is the diminutive but attractive ruin of an oblong tower house, just three storeys high, including an attic stage that has mostly disappeared. None of the floors were vaulted. There are shot holes below the small windows. A vanished round stair turret projected at one corner, while the base of a bartizan survives diagonally opposite. Though tolerably complete the structure is cracked and slowly decaying. The seat of the Lindsays of Ballinshoe, it probably dates from the late sixteenth century. The remains are reached off the A926, two miles south-east of Kirriemuir.

Access: Exterior only.
Relations: Branches of the Lindsays at Edzell, Vayne, Lordscairnie and Pitcruvie.

BALLUMBIE CASTLE   Although it is possible to get close up, in the summer you can see little of this ramshackle ruin for the trees. All is extremely overgrown, but it is possible to make out a small walled quadrangle. The seat of the Lovells of Ballumbie, the castle is presumed to date from the 1540s but could be much older. Certainly the courtyard form, with no evidence of a tower house, goes better with the castles of enclosure raised before the Wars of Independence, although nearby Dudhope is another late instance. The two eastern angles have round flanking towers which, like the linking curtain wall, stand intact apart from their parapets. The towers are pierced by wide-mouthed gunports concealed beneath the ivy. These will be later insertions if the masonry is indeed older than the usually accepted date. The curtain continues on the south but the whole of the west and north sides of the enclosure, including the square corner towers, date from 1810 when the abandoned castle was converted into a stable block for nearby Ballumbie House. On the north there is a steep drop to the Fithie Burn. The remains stand on Elm Rise in the Ballumbie Castle housing estate, on the north-eastern outskirts of Dundee.

Access: Exterior only.
Relations: Dudhope.

BRAIKIE CASTLE stands in a field at Wester Braikie, two miles north-east of Kinnell. It is the gabled shell of an L-plan tower house, with a wide spiral stair rising to hall level in the jamb. A plaque over the entrance bears the initials of Thomas Fraser of Kinnell and the year 1581.

Access: Visible from the road.

BROUGHTY CASTLE, jutting into the Firth of Tay, dominates the waterfront of Broughty Ferry. The tower house results from a licence to crenellate, granted in 1490 to Andrew, Lord Gray of Fowlis. Entered at ground level, it has four storeys below the renewed, corbelled-out parapet. The ground floor is divided into two vaulted storerooms. The strategic position of the castle resulted in a busy military history. In 1547 it was handed over to the invading Duke of Somerset. For two years the English garrison, reinforced by artillery-proof earthworks on the landward side, defied all attempts to recapture it. They finally surrendered after bombardment from the French expeditionary force. The gabled attic and the corner caphouse at the top of the spiral stair were probably added soon after, though these features were rebuilt during the nineteenth-century restoration. In 1571 Broughty briefly fell into the hands of Mary Queen of Scots' supporters. It was captured by General Monck in 1651.

In 1860 the site became part of Lord Palmerston's vast network of coastal fortifications, prompted by fears of a French invasion. A stone-lined rampart with gun emplacements replaced the older barmkin wall but the decaying tower house was restored to accommodate the garrison. Although done in an antiquarian spirit, the restoration was heavy-handed and most of the architectural features are Victorian. The projecting corner jamb with mock gunports is entirely an addition of that time, converting an oblong tower into a retro L-plan (the jamb is left un-harled to contrast with the rest). Though criticised at the time for its military inadequacy, the place was garrisoned in both world wars. It now houses the Castle Museum of maritime and local history.

Access: Open daily in summer and regularly in winter (HES).

Relations: Fowlis and Castle Huntly were other seats of the Grays of Fowlis. Blackness was also converted into a coastal fort.

CLAYPOTTS CASTLE, though comparatively small, is the perfect example of a Z-plan tower house. Now engulfed in the suburbs between Dundee and Broughty Ferry, just off the A92 on Claypotts Road, it was built by John Strachan of Claypotts. Two stones high up in the flanking tower gables are inscribed with the years 1569 and 1588. They may commemorate the start and end of construction – a long period showing the financial constraints of its builder. The main block is flanked by round towers at diagonally opposite corners, both with a shallow staircase turrets in the re-entrant angle. Both towers are surmounted by square caphouses. Their crow-stepped gables face different directions, enhancing the picturesque skyline. These caphouses were adorned by dormer windows but only one now survives. As usual by this period there is no wall walk, except for short stretches on the gable ends of the main block. By contrast, everything is grim severity lower down, despite some

Claypotts Castle, Angus

sash windows inserted later. Twelve wide-mouthed gunports pierce the walls near ground level, comprehensively covering all approaches. A groove cut into the adjacent staircase projection allows one gunport a wider field of fire.

Another gunport, in the stair turret adjoining the south-west tower, commands the only entrance. A blank panel that would have contained the Strachan arms surmounts the doorway. It opens into two barrel-vaulted undercrofts in the main body of the tower house. A mural passage leads to the kitchen, also vaulted, in the south-west flanking tower. Both the main staircase beside the entrance and a service stair in the further undercroft ascend to the hall. This room is now bare but structurally little altered, with a large fireplace. Smaller fireplaces at each end of the floor above show that it was partitioned into two chambers, while the attic preserves its original timber roof – something of a rarity in Scotland. The flanking towers provide five storeys of additional chambers, including those in the caphouses. Despite their round exteriors these towers contain square rooms for greater domestic convenience, with the exception of the undercroft of the north-east tower.

John Strachan died in 1593 and the lands were later purchased by the Grahams of Claverhouse. John Graham, the celebrated Viscount Dundee, lived nearby at Dudhope Castle and by his time Claypotts was leased to tenant farmers. Their occupancy, too modest to keep up with the latest fashions, has preserved its unspoilt appearance. (See plan on page 361).

Access: Exterior at any time (HES). There are occasional open days.
Reference: Guidebook by M. R. Apted. *PSAS* (88).
Relations: Good Z-plan tower houses such as Hatton, Noltland, Drochil and Castle Menzies.

COLLISTON CASTLE, on an estate two miles south of Leysmill, is a large Z-plan tower house with round flanking towers, one of them crowned by a square caphouse. It was built around 1553 by John Guthrie, though it has been somewhat altered and extended in later centuries.

Access: Private (now a holiday let).

CORTACHY CASTLE occupies an estate beside the River South Esk, just outside the village. This largely Victorian mansion incorporates a long L-plan block with round towers flanking the two outer corners. It was probably built in the sixteenth century by the Ogilvy lords of Airlie.

Access: Private.

CRAIG HOUSE, in secluded grounds west of Ferryden, was built in 1637 but retains one side of a fifteenth-century barmkin wall of the Wood family. At each end is a non-projecting square corner tower with a corbelled-out parapet. There are also remains of an outer courtyard wall.

Access: Private.

DUDHOPE CASTLE stands on a ridge overlooking the Firth of Tay in Dudhope Park, half a mile north-west of Dundee city centre. It was long the seat of the Scrymgeour family, hereditary constables of that town. A window above the gateway bears the year 1600 and the late sixteenth century seems right for the present complex, putting its construction during the long tenure of James Scrymgeour. It doesn't appear to incorporate any older work. James VI was entertained here during his return to Scotland in 1617. John Graham of Claverhouse, Bonnie Dundee, later purchased the castle. He lived here until he was fatally wounded leading the Jacobites to victory at Killiecrankie in 1689. The castle has been much altered through later use as a barracks, then offices. It narrowly escaped demolition in 1958 but has since been restored by the city council to something resembling its original appearance.

For Scotland this is the comparatively rare sight of a quadrangular castle with corner towers – or rather half a castle, as only the south and east ranges stand. It is clearly inspired by the chateaux of the Loire but the defences are largely illusory. The two ranges are not quite at right angles to each other and there was only a barmkin wall on the north and west. Slender round towers with conical roofs project at three angles, while the gate passage through the east range is flanked by semi-circular turrets. The courtyard layout and the form of the gatehouse are thus akin to Fyvie and Tolquhon, which are both contemporary. A vaulted gate passage leads into the former courtyard. Owing to the sloping ground the east range is now of four storeys and the south range of five, but both have been heightened by one floor, making them slightly higher than the flanking towers. Uniform rows of enlarged windows, both inside and out, exude a starkness only partly relieved by the white harling. Internally the accommodation has been transformed, though the south range preserves a row of barrel-vaulted cellars linked by a corridor, culminating in a kitchen with a large fireplace. Two of the towers contain spiral stairs.

Access: Exterior only (LA).
Relations: Fyvie and Tolquhon.

EDZELL CASTLE   This charming ruin lies in the shadow of the Angus Hills, a mile west of the picturesque village of Edzell. A mutilated motte to the south of the present complex attests its Norman predecessor. In 1358 the Lindsays inherited the manor. During the course of the sixteenth century their castle developed from a solitary tower house into a courtyard mansion.

The tower house, now occupying the south-west corner of the quadrangle, may be the work of Walter Lindsay of Edzell, who died in 1513. Though lacking its roof and floors, it is structurally intact. Its external austerity is relieved only by a double row of corbels at parapet level, bulging at the corners and in the middle of each side to form the bases of vanished bartizans. It is an L-plan tower house, though the jamb is a modest projection containing the spiral staircase. A keyhole gunport in the jamb commands the adjacent entrance to the tower house, while the wide-mouthed gunports at the base of the tower are later insertions. The ground floor is divided into two vaulted storerooms, one of them linked to the hall on the floor above by a mural service stair. Joist holes show that a minstrels' gallery surmounted the vanished screen in the hall. Two upper storeys were partitioned into private chambers, while attic gables rise above the parapet.

Larger windows were inserted in the tower house by Walter's son David, who became ninth Earl of Crawford. Before his death in 1558 he embarked on the expansion of the castle, building a west range alongside. This range has a gate passage in the centre, flanked by a barrel-vaulted kitchen and storerooms. Above the round-arched entrance four blank panels once contained heraldry. Large windows on the upper floor show the defensive limitations of this entrance front, though they were originally barred by iron grilles.

In 1562 David's young son of the same name (who did not inherit the earldom) played host to Mary Queen of Scots. After reaching maturity he continued the expansion with a gabled great hall on the north side of the courtyard. Its courtyard front has collapsed but the other walls stand high. A cylindrical tower projecting at the north-west angle balances the tower house at the other end of the west front. Wide-mouthed gunports in this tower command the adjacent stretches of wall. The other two sides of the courtyard show only foundations against the surrounding curtain wall.

Later in life Sir David Lindsay turned his attention to the walled garden that is Edzell's chief claim to fame. This formal garden has been recreated in the Jacobean style, but the remarkable surrounding wall is original. A gateway bears David's arms and the year 1604. Each side preserves a set of nine sculpted reliefs. On the east wall are the Planetary Deities, on the south the Liberal Arts, on the west the Cardinal Virtues – Renaissance art expressed with crude northern vitality. The garden enclosure was hardly defensive despite the shot holes in the little summerhouse projecting at the south-east corner. This charming structure is the only part of the castle still roofed. Sir David's expenditure left the Lindsays impoverished when he died in 1610. A succession of absentee landlords allowed the castle to decay into its present condition.

Access: Open daily in summer (HES).
Reference: Guidebook by W. D. Simpson and C. Tabraham. *PSAS* (65).
Relations: Castles of the Lindsay earls at Finavon, Invermark and Lordscairnie. The reconstructed Jacobean garden at Drummond.

ETHIE CASTLE, in its own grounds three miles south-east of Inverkeilor, is a courtyard mansion of various periods, including a much-altered L-plan tower house raised in the sixteenth century by the Carnegies of Ethie. The complex also incorporates a round barmkin turret.

Access: Private (now a guesthouse).

FARNELL CASTLE, in secluded grounds west of the village, originated as a modest L-plan tower house with an unusual semi-circular jamb crowned by a caphouse. Built early in the sixteenth century by the Bishop of Brechin, it was later extended into a longer range.
Access: Private.

FINAVON OLD CASTLE, south of Milton of Finavon, is a lofty ruin in the grounds of the present Finavon Castle, a Victorian mansion. Probably built in the late sixteenth century by David Lindsay, eleventh Earl of Crawford, only two sides of this L-plan tower house stand high.
Access: On private land.

FORTER CASTLE is reached by a sideroad off the B951, in hilly terrain midway between Clackavoid and Bridge of Brewlands. It stands near the head of Glen Isla. This is a simple L-plan tower house with the jamb projecting on two sides. The entrance, in the side of the jamb, leads to a staircase ascending in straight flights to the first floor, after which the stair transfers to a turret corbelled out in the re-entrant angle. There are two further storeys, including the gabled attic. Forter was built around 1560 by James Ogilvy, lord of Airlie, on land that had previously belonged to Coupar Abbey. The Earl of Airlie's refusal to sign the National Covenant resulted in the Earl of Argyll burning the building in 1640. This incident spawned the ballad 'The Bonnie House of Airlie'. It survived surprisingly well as an empty shell until being restored for habitation from 1988. The top floor of the main block is largely a reconstruction, along with the corner bartizans. The wrecked interior was subject to a painstaking restoration, including the reconstruction of the ground-floor vaults. In the first-floor hall is a modern beamed ceiling, painted in the traditional manner.
Access: A functions venue but well seen from the road.
Relations: Other seats of the Ogilvys of Airlie at Airlie and Cortachy.

FOWLIS CASTLE is set in its own grounds at Fowlis Easter, near the fifteenth-century parish church. This oblong tower house has a projecting stair turret and a prominent chimney stack. A date stone, reset nearby, suggests it may have been built as late as 1640 by Andrew, Lord Gray.
Access: Visible from a public footpath.

GARDYNE CASTLE, on an estate a mile south of Pitmuies, incorporates an L-plan tower house with prominent corner bartizans. The jamb is semi-circular and surmounted by a square caphouse. Built by the Gardynes of Leys around 1568, the main block has since been extended.
Access: Private.

GLAMIS CASTLE is reached from the village by a mile-long, tree-lined avenue through the landscaped park. A large tower house dominates this celebrated mansion. The elaborate skyline makes Glamis (pronounced 'Glarms') one of the best examples of the Scottish Baronial style, but the picturesque gables and round bartizans crown a much older tower. Its association with Macbeth may be spurious but Glamis was a royal hunting lodge from early times. In 1372 Robert II granted the lordship to Sir John Lyon. He married the king's daughter and became Lord Chancellor, only to be murdered in his bed in 1382. If Sir John built the tower house, as tradition asserts, it would be the one of the oldest examples of the L-plan. The original first-floor doorway (now a window) may support an early date, since in mature L-plan tower houses the entrance invariably came down to ground level. However, it has been suggested that the jamb was added by his grandson Patrick, who became Lord Glamis in 1445. Except for a temporary forfeiture under James V, the castle has belonged to their descendants ever since.

Closer dating is impossible because of the embellishments wrought by another Patrick Lyon. He was created first Earl of Kinghorne in 1606, the year inscribed above his new ground-floor entrance. This is located in a rounded stair turret, added by the earl in the re-entrant angle of the tower house. Patrick's bartizans are surmounted by conical roofs. He added an attic above the older four storeys, eradicating the former parapet. Lower residential wings project symmetrically from the jamb and the opposite gable end, as if to mimic the Z-plan. These blocks were only added by the third earl (yet another Patrick) after the Restoration, but the round flanking towers at their outer corners are evidence for a square barmkin surrounding the tower house. The eastern angle tower is sixteenth-century work but its twin on the west was largely rebuilt after a fire in 1800.

Visitors enter the tower house through a later extension at the rear. It leads into the retainers' hall, occupying the main block of the tower house at first-floor level. This long, barrel-vaulted chamber retains its early austerity, adorned only by the suits of armour on display. The window in the south wall was the original entrance to the tower house. Beyond a well chamber, the room in the jamb is equally bare. The spiral staircase in the first earl's stair turret descends in wide, easy steps to the ground floor, the original yett closing the entrance at the bottom. At this level the tower house is underlain by gloomy, vaulted undercrofts, unchanged since their first construction. The spiral stair ascends again to the magnificent contrast of the second floor. Here the main room is the great hall (now the drawing room), twice the height of the other floors. Its barrel vault is covered by elaborate plasterwork of 1621, while the contemporary fireplace overmantel depicts the royal arms. Another plaster ceiling adorns the adjacent chamber in the jamb, while the chapel (in an adjunct added by the third earl) is notable for its remarkable series of religious scenes, painted by the Dutch artist Jacob de Wet in the 1680s. The

other rooms on show in the later wings reflect the opulence of the Bowes-Lyon earls of Strathmore and Kinghorne.
Access: Open daily in summer (HHA).
Reference: Guidebook by R. Innes-Smith.
Relations: Scottish Baronial masterpieces such as Castle Fraser, Craigievar and Crathes. Contemporary plaster ceilings at Craigievar, Thirlestane and Muchalls.

GUTHRIE CASTLE, on an estate just west of the village, is primarily a Victorian mansion but is dominated by an L-plan tower house, attributed to Sir David Guthrie around 1468. The jamb is just a small staircase projection, while the corbelled-out parapet and attic have been rebuilt.
Access: A functions venue.

HATTON CASTLE overlooks the B954 just south-east of Newtyle village, in a garden beside the track up to Hatton Farm. This is a good example of a Z-plan tower house, consisting of a main block flanked by massive square towers at diagonally opposite corners. All three elements are four storeys high, including the attics with their renewed crow-stepped gables, but the roof line is relatively plain. Some of the windows are large but the walls are generously provided with shot holes low down. The entrance is in one of the towers, closely flanked by the main block and overhung by a blank heraldic panel. It leads to an early example of a grand staircase rising in straight flights to the hall on the first floor. The upper floors and the flanking towers provide ample accommodation. A rounded turret, occupying the re-entrant angle between the other tower and the main block, contains a spiral staircase leading all the way up. In the main block a corridor runs past two barrel-vaulted undercrofts to the vaulted kitchen, with its arched fireplace. The tower house is believed to have been erected around 1575 by Laurence, fourth Lord Oliphant. It was captured by the Marquis of Montrose in 1645. After a long period of abandonment and decay it was restored and re-harled from 1983.
Access: Well seen from the footpath.
Relations: Lord Oliphant's work at Kellie (Fife). Z-plan tower houses such as Claypotts, Colliston and Vayne.

INVERMARK CASTLE   At Gannochy a sideroad leaves the B966 and meanders for fifteen miles up Glen Esk to this remote stronghold beyond Lochlee church. A lofty oblong tower house overlooks the Water of Lee before it flows into the River North Esk. It is now an empty shell but structurally complete, if slowly decaying. The thick walls with rounded corners to deflect attacks by pick suggest a tower of some antiquity. Another indication of an early date is the first-floor entrance, now inaccessible but apparently once reached by a stone staircase with a void crossed by a drawbridge. The doorway is still barred by the original yett. It leads into a chamber with two modest fireplaces, indicating it was partitioned into two. A spiral staircase in one corner descends to a barrel-vaulted ground floor with wide-mouthed gunports. The same stair once ascended to the two upper storeys. These also appear to have been subdivided, so the tower lacked a conventional hall. It is generally accepted that the tower was built in the 1520s by David Lindsay, eighth Earl of Crawford, the archaic defensive features reflecting the frequent danger of Highland clansmen passing through the glen. The top of the tower seems to have been remodelled by the eleventh earl of the same name around 1605. It bears twin attic gables, high chimneys and a single corner bartizan.

Access: Exterior only.
Reference: *PSAS* (68).
Relations: Castles of the Lindsay earls at Edzell, Finavon and Lordscairnie.

INVERQUHARITY CASTLE, just east of the village, is a gaunt L-plan tower house with a lofty, barrel-vaulted hall and a corbelled-out parapet. Alexander Ogilvy, Lord Inverquharity, erected it on receipt of a licence to crenellate in 1444. The gabled jamb has been rebuilt.

Access: Private.

KELLY CASTLE, on an estate three miles south-west of Arbroath, is dominated by a T-plan tower house with bartizans. It occupies one corner of a walled barmkin with round flanking turrets at two corners. They were raised by the Auchterlony family early in the sixteenth century.

Access: Private (now a holiday let).

MAINS CASTLE, like Dudhope, sits in a Dundee park. This one is Caird Park, entered off Mains Loan about two miles north of the city centre. Mains is also a sixteenth-century courtyard castle but a more modest affair than Dudhope, lacking the flanking towers and gatehouse that characterise the latter. Over the gateway there used to be a plaque bearing the year 1562, along with the initials of Sir David Graham of Fintry and his wife Margaret Ogilvy. The castle was originally called Fintry but later restyled the Mains (i.e. the chief farm) of Fintry. A nephew of Cardinal Beaton, Sir David was later beheaded for his part in a Catholic plot.

The castle forms a simple square enclosure. In the middle of the west facade is the round-headed entrance arch, oversailed by machicolations. Windows though the curtain wall show that a range once existed on this side of the barmkin. The south side of the barmkin is closed off by a plain wall, while the east wing dates only from the late seventeenth century. The north range, overlooking the Gelly Burn, is the dominant one: a laird's house rather than a tower house proper, just two storeys and an attic in height with prominent crow-stepped gables. It was restored from ruin by the city council in the 1980s.

A tall jamb at one end gives the castle its idiosyncratic appearance. It rises six storeys to a corbelled-out caphouse, with a gable on each of its four faces. This caphouse is an addition dated 1630. A doorway in the side of the jamb leads to a renewed spiral staircase. It ascends to the hall and solar on the first floor. Below are storerooms which, unusually, are not vaulted.

Access: A functions venue but well seen from the park.
Relations: Dudhope. There is another Mains Castle in Lanarkshire.

MELGUND CASTLE stands amid fine gardens above the Melgund Burn. A mile south of Netherton, it is reached via a zigzag of sideroads off the B9134. It is tempting to yield to the tradition that attributes Melgund to David Beaton, the celebrated cardinal and Archbishop of St Andrews, who was murdered at St Andrews Castle in 1546. He supposedly built it as a hideaway for his mistress, Marion Ogilvy, and their children. However, the similarity in layout to Carnasserie in Argyll makes it more likely to belong to the 1560s, which would put it in the time of the cardinal's nephew, David Bethune of Balfour.

The complex consists of an L-plan tower house and an attached hall range to the east. From the lack of any join in the masonry and the similar architectural details, it is evident that they are of the same date, as at Carnasserie. Both portions are well supplied with shot holes. Unfortunately, the hall range is now quite ruinous and the ground-floor undercrofts have lost their barrel vaults. Unlike Carnasserie, the first floor was divided into a hall and solar, the former with a fine fireplace. At the solar end projects a staircase jamb, with a slender round turret attached. A wide corridor ran along the front of the hall range, but this has mostly perished.

By contrast, the tower house was restored from ruin for occupation in the 1990s. Although it contained private chambers, it is not isolated from the hall range and seems to demonstrate the symbolic importance of the tower house theme. It is entered from the jamb, but the doorway is in the side wall facing the hall range, not the tower. The ground floor houses two barrel-vaulted cellars. The wide spiral staircase provided access to both the hall and the three storeys of tower rooms above the undercrofts. A renewed parapet overhangs elaborate corbelling that rounds at the corners for bartizans. The recessed attic and the caphouse over the jamb are both modern reconstructions.

Access: The gardens are open occasionally.
Relations: Carnasserie.

MURROES HOUSE lies in secluded grounds next door to Murroes church, half a mile south-east of Kellas. This charming late sixteenth-century laird's house of the Fotheringham family is unusually well proved with gunports and has a semi-circular stair turret in the middle of one side.

Access: Private.

PITCUR CASTLE stands forlornly by the roadside three miles south-east of Coupar Angus, just off the A923. This ruin, nearly intact externally but gradually deteriorating, was the seat of the Halyburtons of Pitcur. The main block appears to have begun in the fifteenth century as a two-storey hall house, vaulted on both levels, though the vaults have since fallen in. Later, perhaps early in the sixteenth century, a third storey was added. At the same time a four-storey jamb was appended to create an L-plan tower house, though as the jamb is slightly offset against the main block it is sometimes described as T-plan. There is a vaulted kitchen in the ground floor of the jamb. Later still a rounded stair turret was inserted in the re-entrant angle. Oddly, the moulded entrance archway isn't in the re-entrant angle but in the front wall of the jamb.

Access: Exterior only.
Relations: The branch of the Halyburtons at Dirleton.

POWRIE CASTLE, on a farm three miles north of Dundee, was the seat of the Fotheringhams of Powrie. The truncated ruin of a sixteenth-century oblong tower house has a round corner tower. Opposite is an intact residential block, also with a circular corner tower, dated 1604.

Access: Private.

RED CASTLE is a romantic sight on a promontory above Lunan Bay. Taking the road running south from Lunan village, a steep path is soon encountered on the left. From the approach it appears to be a substantial ruin, but the illusion is shattered on closer inspection as all that still stands is part of a tower house and a featureless stretch of curtain wall. They are both built in the deep red sandstone that gives the castle its name. William the Lion first established a castle here, but the curtain is generally attributed to Ingram de Balliol, who died in 1244. The remaining western stretch, returning for a short distance on the north, suggests a simple oblong enclosure without flanking towers.

The oblong tower house was probably added towards the end of the fifteenth century. Hence its builder would either be Walter Stewart, first Lord Innermeath, or his son Thomas who fell at Flodden. Owing to erosion it now perches precariously over the steep drop down to the beach. The stark north wall and part of the west wall still rise to the row of corbels that supported the vanished parapet, rounding at the corners for bartizans. A small chunk of the east wall hangs menacingly overhead. The tower contained four unvaulted storeys plus an attic (now fragmentary) but the rest is reduced to its base. For two years from 1579 the castle was damaged in frequent attacks by the estranged and deranged husband of Lady Innermeith. It has slowly decayed ever since and its neglected condition in such a spot is a great pity.

Access: Freely accessible with caution (uphill walk).
Reference: *PSAS* (75).
Relations: Early curtains such as Castle Sween, Castle Roy and Kinclaven.

VAYNE CASTLE, on a farm two miles south-east of Fern, is a massive Z-plan tower house, now badly ruined and still decaying. There is one round and one square flanking tower, only the latter still standing high. It was built late in the sixteenth century by the Lindsays of Vayne.

Access: On farmland.

OTHER SITES The present *Brechin Castle* (HHA limited opening) is an eighteenth-century mansion in wooded grounds. Nothing is left of the original royal castle where John Balliol was forced to abdicate. It was captured by Edward I in 1303, following a siege in which the constable was felled by a catapult stone. Excavated fragments recall *Panmure Castle* (near Muirdrum), a small quadrangle with square corner towers destroyed during the Wars of Independence. Early strongholds at *Forfar*, *Montrose* and *Dundee* were also destroyed, though the latter retains the Wishart Arch – a simple gateway in Cowgate – from its town wall (1591). The tree-clad motte of *Hynd Castle* (near Hayhillock) bears fragments of a later tower house on top.

Kinnaird Castle (near Haughs of Kinnaird) incorporates some masonry from a fifteenth-century courtyard castle of the Carnegies, though the stately complex is now mostly Victorian and later. As for tower houses, E-plan *Careston Castle* has been much altered and extended into a mansion, the Old Mansion House at *Auchterhouse* incorporates a vaulted undercroft, while *Flemington Castle* (near Aberlemno) is an overgrown stump. A D-shaped barmkin tower with gunports survives from *Ruthven Castle*.

ARGYLL: ISLANDS

The romantic islands forming the southern half of the Inner Hebrides have a small group of castles chiefly memorable for their dramatic coastal settings. Originally part of the Norse Kingdom of the Isles but long attached to Argyll, they were the seats of warring clans who resisted royal control under the leadership of the MacDonald lords of the Isles. The fortified hall house at Aros and the simple walled enclosures of Duart and Achanduin are probably early efforts by the MacDougall lords of Lorne. Duart's tower house, added in the fourteenth century, was a forbidding residence for the chiefs of the powerful MacLean clan. Offshoots of that family built the fifteenth-century tower houses at Moy and Old Breachacha, the latter forming part of a compact barmkin complex. (There are ferries from Oban to Craignure on Mull, Achnacroish on Lismore and Arinagour on Coll.)

County reference: RCAHMS *Argyll* (vols 2 and 3). BoS *Argyll and Bute*.

ACHANDUIN CASTLE, sometimes transcribed as Achadun, rises above the west coast of Lismore. It commands a panoramic view up the Sound of Mull and is an intriguing sight from the Oban-Craignure ferry. A rough footpath from Maccoll, near the south-western tip of the island, winds along for about a mile to the castle, which crowns a ridge ending in a cliff face on one side. This shattered ruin formed a small quadrangle but only the north-east stretch of curtain wall still rises to any height, along with a portion of the north-west. A simple gateway pierces the middle of the surviving wall, though now reduced to a jagged hole. There are remains of a mural staircase up to the vanished parapet. A chunk of masonry indicates that one side of the compact courtyard was filled by the hall. This must have stood above an undercroft, hence the elevated entrance to a latrine passage in the curtain. Achanduin became the residence of the bishops of Argyll – the remains of their cathedral on Lismore are embodied in Clachan church. Its simplicity suggests an early castle of enclosure, first mentioned in 1304 though probably raised by the MacDougalls in the previous century. In 1508 Bishop Hamilton transferred his seat to Saddell Castle on Kintyre and Achanduin was left to decay.

Access: Freely accessible with caution.
Reference: *PSAS* (145).
Relations: Saddell. The episcopal castles of Carnasserie, Kilmartin and Saddell.

AROS CASTLE occupies a weather-beaten promontory on Mull, just to the north-east of Salen. Overlooking what was for centuries the island's chief harbour, it is one of a chain of strongholds built to guard the Sound of Mull at a time when Norse invaders were still a potential threat. The landward approach is cut off by a ditch. At the highest point of the enclosure, once protected by a length of wall, is the chunky ruin of a strong hall house. Only two sides still stand, along with a fragment of a third. The hall itself stood over an undercroft, now filled with debris from the fallen walls. The remains of pointed doorways and windows suggest that it was built towards the end of the thirteenth century, probably by the MacDougalls of Lorne who dominated Mull until their defeat by Robert the Bruce. It later passed to the MacLeans of Duart. In 1608 the king's viceroy Lord Ochiltree invited the lawless island chiefs onto his ship, moored in the bay below, for a parley. Once aboard they were arrested and imprisoned in Edinburgh.

Access: Freely accessible with caution.
Relations: MacDougall hall houses at Castle Coeffin and Ardtornish (across the Sound).

CASTLE COEFFIN   From the south end of Clachan on Lismore a footpath runs towards the island's west coast, becoming rough and twisty as it descends towards the shore of Loch Linnhe. After half a mile or so there appears to be a giant stegosaurus slumbering at the water's edge, such is the strange appearance of this narrow, rocky knoll with the upstanding masonry reduced to several jagged crags. They mark another defensible hall house, tentatively attributed to the MacDougalls of Lorne in the thirteenth century. It was an oblong structure with one canted corner, owing to the confines of the rock, the hall standing above an undercroft now filled by grass-covered rubble. There are some remains of a curtain wall around a lower ledge, guarding the approach. The site was still occupied in the fifteenth century, by which time it was a possession of the all-powerful Campbells.

Access: Exterior only (uphill return).
Relations: MacDougall hall houses at Aros and Ardtornish.

DUART CASTLE crowns the Black Point (Dubh Ard) at the north-eastern tip of Mull. Three miles from the jetty at Craignure, it is a beacon of arrival for passengers on the ferry from Oban. This magnificent setting commands the junction between the Sound of Mull and Loch Linnhe. On two sides the castle rises dramatically above cliffs. The plain curtain wall may well date from the thirteenth century. Its origin is obscure, but it has been suggested that it was raised by one of the MacDougalls of Lorne in conjunction with their mainland castle of Dunstaffnage.

By 1390 the castle had begun its long association with the MacLeans of Duart. Lachlan MacLean obtained much of Mull through marriage to the MacDonald heiress – a union achieved by kidnapping her father. Many of

Duart Castle, Argyll Islands

Lachlan's descendants, who feuded endlessly with other clans, bore the same name. One of them was murdered in Edinburgh in 1523, in a revenge attack following a failed attempt to drown his Campbell wife by tying her to a rock in the bay. Another attacked the MacDonalds and their allies in 1588, with the aid of Spanish troops from a foundered Armada galleon (see Mingary). The MacLeans were impoverished by their loyalty to the Royalist cause in the Civil War. They survived an invasion by the Earl of Argyll in 1674, but Sir John MacLean lost Mull for his part in the 1689 Jacobite uprising. Duart was garrisoned by Hanoverian troops until 1751, then decayed into a ruined shell. In 1911 it was purchased by Sir Fitzroy MacLean, a veteran of the Crimean War. He commissioned the architect John Burnet to restore his ancestors' home. Although modernised internally, the castle remains one of the most evocative Hebridean strongholds.

The thirteenth-century castle formed a small, square enclosure without towers. Only three sides were walled originally, the cliff being regarded as adequate defence on the north-east. A simple gateway (renewed by Burnet) pierces the middle of the south-west wall. Later buildings surround the other three sides of the little courtyard. The sixteenth-century south-east range backs onto the older curtain, while the north-east range closing the gap above the cliff was remodelled by Allan MacLean in 1673. Both ranges are now very much restored.

Running the full width of the castle on the north-west is the oblong tower house, which dominates the rest. This is grafted onto the older curtain but is entirely outside the original courtyard, occupying a ledge between the curtain and the cliff. Its form is severe enough to justify its traditional attribution to the first Lachlan MacLean in the late fourteenth century. Though still sparsely fenestrated, the tower house was considerably altered within by Burnet. A chunk was taken out of the courtyard side to create a bay window. The partitioned undercroft has lost its vault but retains a rock-cut well. At the north end a mural passage leads to a small annexe containing a grim prison cell. From the courtyard a staircase ascends to the first-floor hall, which is loftier than the other storeys. This and the rooms on the floor above, reached by a spiral stair, form a repository of clan memorabilia. The parapet and recessed attic were rebuilt by Burnet. He also added the Sea Room above the old prison annexe, its incongruous glass front providing a roofed vantage point on the frequent rainy days.

Access: Open daily in summer (HHA).
Reference: Guidebook (Jarrold Publishing).
Relations: Dunstaffnage and the other MacDougall castle at Dunollie. The MacLean castles at Moy and Old Breachacha. Other restorations at Eilean Donan and Kisimul.

MOY CASTLE   A forbidding tower house overlooks Loch Buie on the south coast of Mull, half a mile east of the coast road at Lochbuie. It has changed little since it was built, perhaps early in the fifteenth century by Hector MacLean, brother of Lachlan MacLean of Duart. The square-plan tower is pierced only by slits low down and small windows on the upper floors. A ground-floor doorway leads into the barrel-vaulted undercroft. From the entrance passage a straight mural staircase ascends to the hall, passing a narrow chamber in the thickness of the wall. The hall is also vaulted but the vault springs from the opposite pair of walls. A mural passage contains the opening to a pit prison beneath. From the hall a spiral staircase rises to another mural chamber, then to the roofless solar on the top floor and finally the embattled parapet.

Around 1600, little gabled caphouses were added at the two south-western corners. Otherwise, virtually the only alteration is the insertion of a fireplace in the solar. Originally there were no fireplaces in the tower, suggesting that the normal accommodation must have been located in the vanished barmkin. Hector's descendants, the MacLaines of Lochbuie, often feuded with the MacLeans of Duart. Sometimes there was discord within the family itself, as when Iain the Toothless killed his own son in a skirmish. In 1752 they abandoned the tower for Lochbuie House, which stands close by and preserves the tower's yett.

Access: Exterior only.
Relations: The MacLean castles at Duart and Old Breachacha.

OLD BREACHACHA CASTLE is an appealing little complex on the remote Isle of Coll. It stands at the head of Loch Breachacha, a mile south-west of Uig. Lachlan MacLean of Duart gave the island around 1430 to his son, John Garbh, who probably built the castle. Rivalry gradually developed between the MacLeans of Coll and Duart. The latter captured Breachacha in 1578 and 1593 during clan feuds, though on both occasions the MacLeans of Coll were soon reinstated. After these attacks they remodelled the castle, understandably still with some regard for defence. In 1750 Hector MacLean abandoned it for New Breachacha Castle, a striking Georgian mansion close by. A descendant, Major Nicholas MacLean-Bristol, restored the old castle to a habitable condition from 1965.

The castle consists of an oblong tower house in the north-west corner of a diminutive, walled barmkin, with a big oval tower at the south-east angle. Every surface has been re-harled a severe grey. While the tower house does not project beyond the curtain wall, the other tower is a bold flanker. Two narrow doorways pierce the curved curtain. Both are overlooked by box machicolations, added during the sixteenth-century remodelling when the curtain was heightened. A gabled house against one side of the curtain embodies the hall of the original castle. Presumably this always formed the main accommodation, because the tower house had no fireplaces originally.

The tower house rises with minimal fenestration to an embattled parapet. Unusually, none of its four storeys are vaulted. During the remodelling the straight mural stairs were supplanted by a spiral staircase well hollowed out in one corner. Around the same time a gabled attic was added behind the old parapet and the ground level within the barmkin was raised. As a result the original tower house entrance was buried, a new doorway being inserted at first-floor level. A stone-lined rampart behind the tower house was constructed for use as a gun battery in the seventeenth century but left unfinished.

Access: Well seen from the footpath to the beach.
Reference: *PSAS* (102).
Relations: The MacLean castles at Duart and Moy. Kisimul is similar in form.

OTHER SITES *Dunyvaig Castle*, overlooking Lagavulin Bay on Islay, is reduced to one truncated side of a tower or hall house clinging to the rock face. *Claig Castle*, the stump of a fifteenth-century tower house, occupies a cliff on Am Fraoch Eilean, a small island off Jura in the Sound of Islay. The dramatic Cairn na Burgh Mor, one of the Treshnish Isles, is naturally defended most of the way round by basalt cliffs. This formed the setting for *Cairnburgh Castle*, probably established by James IV as a bastion of royal power. The only remains are bits of curtain wall, the gable ends of a simple chapel and a later barrack block.

ARGYLL: MAINLAND

Apart from the spectacular scenery, the mainland of Argyll is to be commended for its high proportion of visitable castles. There is also an unusual amount of variety, since castles that pre-date the Wars of Independence were not destroyed as they often were elsewhere but became strongpoints in the frequent royal campaigns for mastery over the clans of the wild west. The story begins with Castle Sween, a simple enclosure erected before 1200 and, as such, one of the oldest stone castles in Scotland. Castles of the thirteenth century, or soon after, range from the plain curtain walls at Mingary, Innis Chonnell and (possibly) Duntrune, to the sophistication of Dunstaffnage with its flanking towers and Skipness with its arrow slit embrasures.

Following the Wars of Independence there is the usual succession of austere towers, changing little from Carrick in the fourteenth century to Castle Stalker, Dunollie, Kilchurn and Saddell over the next century or so. A number of clans are represented, though the county came to be dominated by the Campbell earls of Argyll and their many cadet branches. The last phase of Scottish castle building is relatively scarce in Argyll, though Barcaldine, Dunderave and Gylen are good L-plan tower houses and there is an interesting tower and hall range at Carnasserie. The Jacobite wars are reflected in the private barracks added to Kilchurn and Mingary. Most Argyll castles overlook the long coastline or the many lochs. They may seem remote now but the sea lanes to the Hebrides provided an easy form of transport. Their strategic positioning is immediately apparent in the way they line the Sound of Mull and Loch Linnhe.

County reference: RCAHMS *Argyll* (vols 1, 2, 3 and 7). BoS *Argyll and Bute*; BoS *Highland and Islands* (for the part transferred to Highland). *Dunstaffnage and the Castles of Argyll* by G. Stell.

ARDTORNISH CASTLE occupies a promontory jutting into the Sound of Mull on the Morvern peninsula. It lies on the Ardtornish estate and can only be reached by taking a track from Achranich that skirts the east shore of Loch Aline. Towards the end of this scenic four-mile walk the ruin at last comes into view. It is basically a hall house, its chief defensive strength coming from the commanding knoll on which it stands. Little more than the basalt walls of the undercroft survive, though the joist sockets for the wooden floor that carried the hall above can be seen in the side walls. One section of wall facing Mull rises higher but the window within it is part of an abortive attempt to restore the building from 1910.

This is probably one of the chain of early strongholds guarding the Sound of Mull, raised by the MacDougall lords of Lorne in the thirteenth century. After the dispossession of the MacDougalls in 1309, Ardtornish was granted to the MacDonald lords of the Isles and became one of their principal seats. A meeting in 1461 between the Lord of the Isles and the exiled Earl of Douglas led to the Treaty of Westminster-Ardtornish – a secret pact to divide Scotland between them under English overlordship. Its discovery by James III marked the beginning of the end for the MacDonald lords.

Access: Freely accessible with caution. Visible from ferries to the Western Isles.

Relations: MacDougall hall houses at Aros (across the Sound) and Castle Coeffin. Castle Sween and Strome also belonged to the lords of the Isles.

BARCALDINE CASTLE, two miles north of Benderloch via a sideroad off the A828, overlooks the shore of Loch Creran. This fine example of a late L-plan tower house was one of several strongholds raised by Sir Duncan Campbell of Glenorchy, otherwise known as Black Duncan. A heraldic panel over the entrance bears his initials, the year 1609 and the motto 'Follow me'. The Black Book of Taymouth relates that the structure cost a total of £10,000. Campbell gave it to his son Iain. Abandoned for nearby Barcaldine House in 1735, it became a roofless shell. In 1896 it was purchased by a descendant, another Sir Duncan Campbell, who restored the tower for occupation.

Though rising to four storeys, including the gabled attic, the main block is longer than it is high. By the end of the sixteenth century the traditional L-plan was becoming more domestic in character, but this tower house is still quite severe, with small windows except for a few later enlargements. As usual by that time there is no parapet. Round corner bartizans with renewed conical roofs are corbelled out at the top. The large jamb, almost as big as the main block, projects mainly to the south but also a little to the west. In the re-entrant angle, a rounded turret contains the broad spiral staircase. Here is the entrance, preserving the upper part of its yett. At ground level the main block contains a barrel-vaulted undercroft and kitchen, linked by a corridor, and a pit prison beneath. The hall above now has a Victorian air, while the upper floors have been partitioned.

Access: No longer open but well seen from the road (now a guesthouse).
Reference: Guidebook by R. Campbell.
Relations: Black Duncan's tower houses at Edinample and Finlarig.

CARNASSERIE CASTLE was built by the Protestant scholar John Carswell, rector of Kilmartin, a village that lies a mile to the south via the A816. He was made Bishop of the Isles by Mary Queen of Scots in 1567, though his appointment was no more than titular owing to the upheaval of the Reformation. There is a Gaelic dedication to the Earl of Argyll above the entrance. From the architectural details it would seem that Carswell employed the team of masons who had just completed Torwood Castle in 1566; it was complete by the time he died in 1572. Carnasserie has been an empty shell since 1685, when the Earl of Argyll blew it up during his rebellion against James VII.

Although the complex consists of a square tower house and a hall range to its west, it is clear that both elements are products of the same building campaign, the tower serving merely as a chamber block for the hall. At the other end of the hall is a projecting staircase jamb. It contains the entrance, flanked by the main block as in contemporary L-plan tower houses. Three undercrofts supported the hall, but their crowning vaults have perished as a result of the explosion. One of them was the kitchen, as shown by the arched fireplace. Beyond is the undercroft of the tower house, which retains its vault.

A straight mural stair ascends from here to the solar on the first floor of the tower. Above can be seen two further storeys of private quarters and an attic, now open to the sky. The attic gables are recessed within the parapet walk. Carnasserie shows the arrival of Renaissance ornament in such features as the doorways in the hall, the mutilated fireplace in the solar and the framed heraldic panels over the entrance. Nevertheless, it also demonstrates some regard for defence in its prominent position on a ledge and the wide-mouthed gunports at ground level. All the windows were originally small, those lower down being seventeenth-century enlargements by the Campbells of Auchinbreck.

Access: Open daily (HES – uphill walk).

Relations: Torwood. Melgund has a similar layout. The episcopal castles of Kilmartin, Saddell and Achanduin.

CARRICK CASTLE romantically occupies an outcrop of rock jutting into the western shore of Loch Goil, six miles south of Lochgoilhead. According to tradition there was a royal hunting lodge here. However, the impressive tower house was probably built before 1400 by the Campbells of Lochawe – the emerging dynasty who would become earls of Argyll. Their tower forms a mighty rectangle with one canted corner. Recessed within the plain parapet (with prominent gargoyles) is a gabled attic, added in the sixteenth century. By that time the tower was occupied by the Campbells of Ardkinglas, a cadet branch of the family who served as hereditary captains to the earls of Argyll. It was burnt by James VII's supporters during the Campbell rebellion in 1685 and remained a shell for three centuries. Restored from 1988 to serve as a residence, its austere exterior remains unspoilt.

At the rear (only viewable from the loch) are some vestiges of a tiny walled barmkin, with a gateway providing access from the loch. The two entrance doorways to the tower are placed on this side, the upper one a fine Gothic arch. Unusually, none of the floors are vaulted. Above the plain undercroft is a lofty hall, its pointed windows backed by arched recesses with stone seats. One of these recesses is flanked by straight mural staircases on either side. They ascend to the second floor, which was divided into private chambers. One of the stairs continues up to the parapet. The end walls of the tower contain mural latrines discharging into chutes.

Access: Exterior only.
Reference: PSAS (128).
Relations: Castles of the Campbell earls at Innis Chonnell, Skipness and Castle Campbell.

CASTLE STALKER is one of the most stunningly sited of all Scottish tower houses. It occupies a rocky islet in Appin Bay, off the mainland coast facing Portnacroish. This austere tower is attributed to Sir John Stewart of Lorne, who was murdered in 1463. Windows are few and small, while the embattled parapet does not project on corbels. Around 1620 the tower was acquired by the Campbells of Airds, supposedly as the result of a drunken bet with the Stewarts. During the Jacobite uprising of 1689 the Stewarts of Appin seized the rock, only to be driven out following a blockade lasting several months. The building decayed after serving as a Hanoverian garrison post but was restored for habitation from 1965 by Lieutenant-Colonel Stewart Allward.

The islet is approached off the A828, along a potholed road that starts nearly opposite Portnacroish Church. There are two entrances to the tower house, both overlooked by single machicolations at the wall-head. The lower doorway leads into the barrel-vaulted undercroft, one end of it walled off to form two small chambers. An external stone staircase now rises against the tower wall to the first-floor entrance but, in the original arrangement, a free-standing wooden stair ascended to a void crossed by a drawbridge. Above the entrance arch is a weathered heraldic panel. Filling this level of the tower is the spartan hall. A window embrasure contains the narrow opening to a pit prison in the thickness of the wall. The spiral staircase in one corner leads to all levels, but a dividing wall makes it impossible to bypass the hall. Above is the solar, similarly austere, though a carved figure on one of the fireplace columns provides a hint of decoration. The attic with crow-stepped gables, recessed within the parapet, is a Campbell addition. They also added the gabled caphouse at the head of the spiral stair. From here there are spectacular views across Loch Linnhe.

Access: Limited opening times in summer (pre-book) – a boat service is provided. There is a good view from the Castle Stalker Viewpoint.
Relations: Island castles such as Innis Chonnell, Eilean Donan and Kisimul.

Castle Stalker, Argyll Mainland

CASTLE SWEEN crowns a rock overlooking the east shore of Loch Sween, seven miles south of Achnamara. It takes its name from Suibhne or Sven, the shadowy Norse ancestor of the MacSween clan. Their ruined stronghold is one of the oldest stone castles in Scotland and its walls still rise virtually to full height. The circumstances of its construction are inevitably quite obscure. Shallow 'pilaster' buttresses – a Norman motif – appear at the angles and in the middle of each side. An eleventh-century origin has been claimed, though a date nearer to 1200 seems more realistic. The castle forms a small quadrilateral, not quite oblong in plan. It bears a superficial resemblance to some of the hall-keeps of Norman England but appears in fact to have been a small courtyard castle. There is no evidence that a roof ever covered the whole structure. A simple, round-headed arch midway along the south wall forms the main entrance. Against the curtain wall are the remains of a staircase that ascended to the parapet. One angle contains a tiny mural chamber.

A doorway in the west wall leads into the shattered remains of a square projection added in the thirteenth century. This ends in a circular tower flanking the north-west corner of the castle. Around 1262 Alexander III granted Sween to his loyal vassal Walter Bailloch, titular Earl of Menteith, and this tower may be his. The MacSweens, dispossessed because of their token adherence to the rulers of Norway, tried several times to recover their lordship. A Gaelic poem proclaims that one sea-borne attack was a short-lived success.

In 1376 the castle was granted to John of Islay, the MacDonald Lord of the Isles. The last addition to the castle is the two-storey oblong projecting from its north-east corner. It is known as MacMillan's Tower after Alexander MacMillan, keeper of the castle in the 1470s. Its ground floor (with arrow slits) contained the kitchen. In this period the main enclosure was filled by a hall on one side and a domestic block on the other, with just an unroofed passageway between them. James III dispossessed the troublesome MacDonalds in 1475, granting the castle to the Earl of Argyll. It decayed under the Campbells but remained strong enough to be attacked and burnt by the Royalists in 1647.

Access: Freely accessible (HES).
Reference: *Transactions of the Glasgow Archaeological Society* (55).
Relations: MacSween work at Skipness and Lochranza. Walter Bailloch probably raised the first Brodick Castle. Ardtornish and Strome were other seats of the lords of the Isles.

DUNDERAVE CASTLE A lofty tower house guards the north shore of Loch Fyne, five miles east of Inveraray in wooded grounds off the A83. This elaborate version of the stepped L-plan has a square tower in the re-entrant angle and a circular tower projecting at the rear corner. The tower house rises to five storeys, including the attic stage with crow-stepped gables supporting chimneys. As usual in the later tower houses, there is no parapet. Round corner bartizans are corbelled out at the top of the jamb. Windows are mostly quite small, so security was still a consideration in these wild parts. Carved heads (now badly weathered) provide a decorative touch on the doorway at the foot of the re-entrant tower. Above it a panel bears the initials of the builders, John MacNaughton and his wife Anna MacLean. It also has an incomprehensible inscription ending in the clan motto, 'I hoip in God'. Above is the year 1598, while higher still a blank heraldic panel is contained within an elaborate frame.

The entrance leads into a typical group of barrel-vaulted undercrofts linked by a corridor. One of them is a kitchen with the customary arched fireplace. In the entrance tower a wide spiral staircase ascends to the first floor. Here the main block is occupied by the hall with its wide fireplace. The upper floors attest the work of Sir Robert Lorimer, who restored the tower house from an empty shell for Sir Andrew Noble in 1911. Though largely respecting the original exterior, he augmented the number of gunports for aesthetic effect and added the low wings.

Access: No longer open.
Reference: *Dunderave Castle and the MacNachtans of Argyll* by M. Cock.
Relations: L-plan tower houses with an additional corner tower at Killochan, Invergarry and Dundas.

DUNOLLIE CASTLE occupies a precipitous rock overlooking the Firth of Lorne at the north end of Oban, off Ganavan Road. It is a prominent sight from ferries heading to Mull and the Western Isles – Sir Walter Scott remarked that 'a more delightful and romantic spot can scarce be conceived'. The kings of

Dalriada had a dun on this summit but the present ruin comprises a forbidding tower house at the north-east corner of a compact, roughly square barmkin. On the two sides adjoining the tower the plain curtain wall survives to a reasonable height, with a simple gateway positioned close to the tower, but the two seaward sides are fragmentary. This curtain possibly represents one of the thirteenth-century castle enclosures of the western seaboard. Dunollie was one of the strongholds of the MacDougalls of Lorne. The presence of another castle just a few miles from their chief stronghold at Dunstaffnage would be explained by its strategic view up the Sound of Mull.

Although the MacDougalls forfeited the lordship of Lorne in 1309, John MacDougall regained possession of Dunollie in 1452. The tower house was probably erected by him soon after. This massive, three-storey cube is consistent with that time. It is still virtually complete, except for the parapet, but all doorways and windows have been robbed of their worked stone. An inserted doorway leads into the barrel-vaulted undercroft. From here a straight mural staircase ascends to the hall, with a torn-out fireplace and a latrine. This level has the original entrance, presumably reached by a wooden stair. Dunollie was captured by the Covenantors under General David Leslie in 1647 and again by Hanoverian troops during the Jacobite rising of 1715. The MacDougalls abandoned it for nearby Dunollie House (now the clan museum) in 1746. After a long period as a crumbling ruin, the walls were consolidated in 2014–20 by the Dunollie Preservation Trust.

Access: Open daily in summer (uphill walk).
Reference: Guidebook by T. Donovan and C. Gillies.
Relations: Other MacDougall castles at Dunstaffnage, Gylen and Duart.

DUNSTAFFNAGE CASTLE is four miles north of Oban, taking the turning off the A85 to Dunbeg. It rises at the end of a promontory jutting into Ardmucknish Bay. This naturally defensive site may have been occupied by an older stronghold, as the prefix 'dun' implies. Rising compact on its rocky outcrop, this is one of the most complete of Scotland's thirteenth-century castles of enclosure and the most ambitious of those erected by the rulers of the western seaboard. It was the chief seat of the MacDougalls of Lorne, descendants of the shadowy Somerled, King of the Isles. The thick curtain wall may have been raised by Duncan MacDougall early in the century, with mural towers added later by his son Ewen. The castle demonstrates the arrival of feudalism in the West under Alexander III, during his struggle to wrest the Hebrides from the Norse. Hence the surprisingly up-to-date defences, along with the finesse of the contemporary ruined chapel in the woods nearby.

After initial resistance, Ewen found it pragmatic to submit to royal overlordship. During the Wars of Independence, however, John MacDougall decided that his best hope of regaining autonomy lay in supporting the English. In 1308 Robert the Bruce defeated him at the Pass of Brander; the castle

Dunstaffnage Castle, Argyll Mainland

fell and Robert then garrisoned it against the western clans. A branch of the ubiquitous Stewarts later received the lordship of Lorne. Alan MacDougall made good his ancestral claim by murdering John Stewart of Lorne and seizing the castle in 1463. It took a royal force to dislodge him. The lordship was then granted to Colin Campbell, first Earl of Argyll. In 1502 the second earl installed his cousin, Alexander Campbell, as captain of the castle, a title passing on to his descendants. Owing to its strategic position on the Firth of Lorne, Dunstaffnage was frequently used as a base for the Stewart kings' expeditions to the Isles. It resisted the Marquis of Montrose in 1644 but was burnt by the Earl of Argyll in 1685, during his rebellion following the accession of James VII. The castle was garrisoned by Hanoverian troops throughout the Jacobite wars. Flora MacDonald, who helped Bonnie Prince Charlie escape, was temporarily imprisoned here in 1746.

The castle is a substantial ruin. It forms an irregular quadrilateral with round corner towers, closely tailored to the knob of rock on which it stands. Excavations have shown that the towers were additions to an originally plain curtain. On all four sides the curtain rises from the low cliff, so the towers project only slightly from the line of the curtain. A stone flight of steps now leads up to the gatehouse, at the eastern angle of the enclosure. Originally the castle seems to have been entered through a gateway beside the flanking tower here. This tower has largely perished but part of its circumference is incorporated into the present gatehouse, which explains its irregular shape. The gatehouse is the only significant later addition to the castle and an unusual feature for its time. Alexander Campbell probably built the curved outer front but the rest of the four-storey structure – with the usual gabled attic – dates from the late sixteenth century. It provided a convenient residence for the captain – a late but modest example of the keep-gatehouse theme. Unlike the rest of the castle the gatehouse is still roofed over, having been restored and modernised after a fire in 1810. A narrow gate passage, flanked by the porter's lodge, ascends to the courtyard.

The courtyard is now empty except for the remains of a modest house of 1725 against the north-west curtain, incorporating the older kitchen with a large fireplace. Between the gatehouse and the North Tower stood the great hall. Its position is marked by two pairs of blocked windows piercing the thick curtain (only visible from outside). Elsewhere the curtain has a series of embrasures containing arrow slits, some of them later modified for use with handguns. A long stretch of wall walk is still accessible. The musket ports in the parapet are also seventeenth-century embellishments. The circular North Tower is a little larger than the others and may be regarded as a modest keep. Adjoining the vanished hall, it probably contained the MacDougalls' solar but a large chunk has fallen. Better preserved is the West Tower, another cylinder that contained three storeys surmounting a basement prison. The 'tower' at the south angle of the castle is no more than a shallow bulge in the thickness of the curtain.

Access: Open daily in summer and regularly in winter (HES).
Reference: Guidebook by D. Grove. *PSAS* (126 and 140).
Relations: The MacDougall castles of Dunollie and Duart. Mature castles of enclosure such as Kildrummy, Caerlaverock and Bothwell.

DUNTRUNE CASTLE, otherwise spelt Duntroon, crowns a rock jutting into Loch Crinan, five miles south-west of Kilmartin. Its 'dun' prefix suggests an earlier fortification on the site. The castle forms a roughly pentagonal enclosure, bounded by a plain curtain with the angles rounded off. It is therefore tempting to regard it as one of the chain of stone enclosures erected by the MacDougalls on the western seaboard in the thirteenth century. The absence of any tower house in the original structure supports this view but the surface masonry is thought to be no older than the fifteenth century. By that time the castle was occupied by yet another Campbell branch, the Campbells of Duntrune. Apart from a latrine chute no features survive to provide any evidence for dating – the mock battlements and the simple entrance gateway were part of a Georgian restoration.

The present house was grafted on around 1600. A section of curtain on the south-east was removed to make way for it, but on the south-west the house rises awkwardly above the older parapet. Three storeys high with crow-stepped gables, the building follows an L-plan and has vaulted ground-floor rooms. However, it is more akin to a laird's house than a tower house proper. Duntrune suffered assaults by the MacDonalds during the Civil War in 1644, and again by the Earl of Argyll in the rebellion of 1685. The ancillary buildings around the rest of the tiny courtyard date only from the eighteenth century. In 1796 the impoverished Campbells sold the castle to the Malcolms of Poltalloch. Colonel George Malcolm restored it for occupation from 1954, after more than a century of abandonment.

Access: The gardens are open daily. Tours of the interior can be arranged.
Relations: The early castles of enclosure at Innis Chonnell, Mingary and Castle Tioram.

GLENSANDA CASTLE, or Castle Mearnaig, rises strikingly on a knoll above the west bank of Loch Linnhe, facing Lismore. It is the gaunt shell of an oblong tower house, just two storeys high and nearly intact, probably built in the fifteenth century by the MacLeans of Kingairloch.

Access: On private land within Glensanda Quarry.

GYLEN CASTLE is perched dramatically above the sea at the southern tip of Kerrera, an island separated by a narrow strait from mainland Argyll. Visiting entails a three-mile walk from the jetty along a rough pathway. Alexander II died here while campaigning against the Isles in 1249. It is possible that the earth bank around the elevated promontory is a relic of his time. The promontory narrows to an isthmus blocked by the graceful tower house, rising sheer above cliffs on either side. This L-plan structure was built by Duncan MacDougall of Dunollie – a stone bearing the year 1582 was once visible at the wall-head. A doorway leads into a vaulted passage that runs through the tower to the apex of the promontory, which formed a small barmkin. At the rear is the jamb, containing the entrance and spiral staircase. This stair ascends to the hall and onwards to the solar, similar rooms that are sparingly windowed in spite of the tower's precipitous location. Above are the attic gables, with a round bartizan at one corner and an oriel window. A crude head carved below this window provides a decorative contrast to the double machicolation beneath, poised above the entrance to the tower. The jamb culminates in a caphouse, reached by a corbelled-out stair turret. Captured and burnt by the Covenanters under General David Leslie in 1647, the tower has been an empty shell ever since, but is maintained in good condition.

Access: Freely accessible. A boat service operates to Kerrera from Gallanach, south of Oban.
Relations: Dunollie was the main seat of the MacDougalls of Dunollie.

INNIS CHONNELL CASTLE   Innis Chonnell (pronounced 'Inch Connell'), is a tree-clad islet in Loch Awe. It lies close to the shore facing the B840, half a mile south of Ardchonnell. The islet carries an enigmatic ruin. Like most of the early castles in the west, its origins are shrouded in mystery. It may perhaps be ascribed to Cailean Mor, the ancestor of the Campbells of Lochawe, who died in battle in 1294. Surviving capture by Robert the Bruce in 1308, Innis Chonnell remained their chief seat until the first Earl of Argyll,

Colin Campbell, built his new castle at Inveraray in the 1450s. After that it served primarily as a prison under the care of its hereditary captains, the MacArthurs. The young MacDonald heir Donald Dubh escaped from here in 1505, only to endure thirty-seven years' confinement in Edinburgh Castle. The castle was finally abandoned in the eighteenth century. Its compact main enclosure remains virtually complete, except for the parapet, and the castle deserves much better treatment than its current state of overgrown neglect.

The islet is almost split into two halves by a cleft, the castle occupying the south-western portion. An outer courtyard, bounded by a thin retaining wall, fronts the inner enclosure, rising from a rock above the water. This forms a simple rectangle surrounded by a strong curtain wall. It seems to have been towerless originally except for a shallow projection at the east corner, which is solid lower down. The curtain was repaired in the fifteenth century, when an oblong tower was added at the south angle. At that time the entrance took on its peculiar form: the gateway pierces the north-east curtain high up and is reached from without by an earth ramp, while a stone staircase descends into the inner courtyard.

Against the high walls are the Campbells' residential buildings. They also belong to the fifteenth-century reconstruction, presumably before the move to Inveraray. The principal range occupies the south-west side. The main floor, above a row of barrel-vaulted undercrofts, used to be divided into the kitchen, hall and solar, reached by an external staircase. A four-storey chamber block occupies the east corner of the courtyard. Another building closed the gap on the south-east, so only one corner of the little courtyard was free of buildings. Here a staircase against the curtain ascended to the wall walk.

Access: Visible from the loch shore. Caution needed if you do get across.
Relations: Carrick, Skipness and Castle Campbell were other seats of the Campbell earls. Simple enclosures like Mingary and Castle Tioram.

KILCHURN CASTLE rises near the northern tip of Loch Awe. It is reached from the A85, two miles east of Lochawe village, though the castle is seen at its best from a viewpoint beside the A819. The low rock on which it stands once formed an islet in the loch, but the water level was lowered in the nineteenth century and the castle is now reached along a promontory. This photogenic ruin is dominated by an oblong tower house attributed to Sir Colin Campbell of Glenorchy, who died in 1475. He probably built it on his return from Rhodes, where he had served with the Knights of St John, but the tower house is typically Scottish in conception. It still rises largely to its full height of three storeys below the parapet, with round bartizans corbelled out at the corners. From the barrel-vaulted undercroft a mural stair curves up to the first-floor hall, which contains the original entrance. Two tiny chambers occupy the thick end wall of the hall, one of them overlying a pit prison. In the late sixteenth century another Colin Campbell added the characteristic attic gables.

Further alterations took place in 1691, when the Earl of Breadalbane added a round stair turret in conjunction with his new barracks. The view from the top encompasses the loch and the wooded hills around it. One of the bartizans later fell during a gale – it survives upside down in the courtyard where it landed.

Sir Colin's tower house occupies the eastern angle of a five-sided enclosure. Part of the original barmkin wall survives on the south-west. However, the rest was rebuilt by John Campbell, first Earl of Breadalbane, who is notorious for contriving the Glencoe massacre. After the first Jacobite revolt of 1689 he converted the castle into a garrison post for 200 private soldiers. Around the courtyard are the gaunt ruins of the oldest purpose-built barrack blocks in Scotland. Even the three round angle towers with gunports belong to this phase, though they are deliberately archaic in style. The castle was garrisoned by Hanoverian troops during the subsequent Jacobite uprisings and then abandoned.

Access: Open daily in summer (HES).

Relations: Barcaldine and Edinample are later tower houses of the Campbells of Glenorchy. There is a comparable barrack block at Mingary.

KILMARTIN CASTLE is a small tower house overlooking the village. Attributed to Neil Campbell, Bishop of Argyll from 1580, it has been well restored from ruin. Prominently gabled but quite plain at the wall-head, its Z-plan form with round flanking turrets is unique in Argyll.

Access: Private (now a guesthouse).

KINLOCHALINE CASTLE, a mile west of Achranich, overlooks the River Aline. This oblong tower house with corner bartizans was built by the MacLeans of Kinlochaline in the late fifteenth century and restored from ruin in the 1990s. The recessed attic is a rebuilding.

Access: Visible from the bridge.

MINGARY CASTLE, a mile east of the Kilchoan ferry terminal, is reached via a long drive running from the B8007. On the south coast of the Ardnamurchan peninsula, it commands the entrances to Loch Sunart and the Sound of Mull. The castle is still largely intact, though the battlements have been restored. A high curtain wall, tailored to the edge of the sheer promontory on which it stands, bounds a compact, roughly hexagonal enclosure. It is cut off from the mainland by a rock-cut ditch and the curtain is much thicker on that side. Apart from a shallow latrine projection there are no flanking towers, but the angles are rounded off to thwart attacks by pick. Mingary resembles Castle Tioram so closely that they may have been built by the same masons. The origins of both castles are quite obscure. They have generally been attributed to either the MacDougalls or the emerging MacDonald clan in the late thirteenth century, though it is possible that Mingary was only built after the MacIains acquired Ardnamurchan in the following century.

In 1588 the castle resisted an attack by Sir Lachlan MacLean of Duart, who was aided by Spanish troops from an Armada galleon that had foundered off Mull. Soon after this episode the MacIains rebuilt the parapet with battlements pierced by gun embrasures. On the north (landward) side the curtain was heightened, the original parapet being converted into a mural passage with more gunports. Putlog holes show that a wooden hoarding projected from the new wall-head. The strengthened castle changed hands twice during the Civil War. After a long period of abandonment, the castle was restored to a habitable condition in 2013–16.

A simple doorway pierces the curtain, reached by a later bridge across the ditch. The little courtyard is dominated by the north range, attributed to Alexander Campbell of Lochnell after 1696. Its austere form, with renewed gables and dormer windows, suggests that it was built as a private barrack block on the pattern of his kinsman's barracks at Kilchurn. It occupies the site of the thirteenth-century hall, the narrow lancet windows through the curtain having been blocked when the MacIains strengthened the castle. The much-restored eighteenth-century ranges on the east and west reduce the courtyard to little more than a passage, ending in a small sea gate leading onto the rock.

Access: Now a hotel (non-residents can pre-book a meal and a tour).
Reference: *PSAS* (144).
Relations: Kilchurn and Castle Tioram.

OLD CASTLE LACHLAN stands on a knoll overlooking the east bank of Loch Fyne, seven miles south-west of Strachur. Externally this chunky ruin appears to be a typical tower house of the earlier kind, sturdy and oblong. The walls still rise mostly to parapet level, though there are breaches at opposite corners, exposing something of the interior. It comes as a surprise to discover that this interior consists of two residential blocks on either side of a central passage that was open to the sky. This is the layout that Castle Sween ultimately adopted. Both blocks rise above the usual barrel-vaulted undercrofts, one of them the kitchen. Each is entered separately from the central passage. Above, the building to the left housed a lofty hall and that to the right two storeys of residential chambers, served by a latrine in the thickness of the outer wall. At the rear an arched recess contains a well. The outer walls were probably raised by the MacLachlan clan around 1400, but they built or remodelled the internal buildings about a century later. Later still are the remains of a simple barbican in front of the entrance. Despite their involvement in the Jacobite risings, the MacLachlans continued to occupy the building until they built the new Castle Lachlan nearby around 1790. Afterwards it fell into ruins.

Access: Freely accessible.
Relations: Castle Sween.

SADDELL CASTLE overlooks a stretch of beach on the east coast of the Kintyre peninsula. It stands at the end of a long drive running south from the B842, starting near the scanty ruins of Saddell Abbey. When this Cistercian abbey was dissolved in 1507 its lands were granted to David Hamilton, Bishop of Argyll. He built the oblong tower house on receipt of a licence to crenellate the following year, to replace Achanduin Castle on Lismore as the episcopal residence. This commanding tower rises four storeys to an embattled parapet mounted on two rows of corbels, with a gabled attic recessed within. Machicolated round bartizans clasp the four corners. A fifth bartizan projects midway along the west wall, poised above the ground-floor entrance, while next to it a caphouse marks the top of the spiral stair. Small windows show the defensive austerity still prevailing early in the sixteenth century. The doorway leads into the barrel-vaulted undercroft, while the floor above retains the arched fireplace of the kitchen. In 1558 the Earl of Sussex raided Kintyre and burnt the tower. The interior was remodelled by the Campbells of Glensaddell in the 1770s to provide servant quarters for nearby Saddell House. Outbuildings of the same period incorporate a stretch of the barmkin wall.

Access: Well seen from the footpath (now a holiday let).

Relations: Achanduin and the other episcopal castles at Carnasserie and Kilmartin.

SKIPNESS CASTLE overlooks Kilbrannan Sound on the Kintyre peninsula, three miles north-east of Claonaig. It incorporates parts of a castle attributed to Dougall MacSween in the mid-thirteenth century. However, most of the existing complex seems to have been erected by John de Menteith of Knapdale, who is infamous for capturing Sir William Wallace in 1305. The oblong layout was partly determined by the older buildings. The north end of the enclosure incorporates three sides of the MacSween hall house. Two sides have been incorporated into the curtain wall, while the third underlies the still later tower house. (Dougall built another hall house at Lochranza, which survives in a more complete state across the sound on Arran.) As well as the hall, one wall of a chapel is embedded in the thickness of the south curtain. When Sir John erected a new hall on the site, he built another chapel outside the castle, the ruin of which still stands.

The level site of the castle is unusual for Argyll. Its surrounding curtain is virtually complete, though only one section of parapet survives. On the south is the original entrance, a pointed gateway occupying a slight projection in the wall. It has a portcullis groove and was once overlooked by machicolations. A corresponding archway through the north curtain is a later insertion. Two sides of the curtain are pierced by rows of cross-slits within arched embrasures. They must have been reached from the upper floor of residential ranges that stood against the curtain. These courtyard buildings were demolished in the eighteenth century, including the new hall referred to above. The adjoining solar occupied a square tower projecting eastwards only at the south-east corner of the enclosure. A smaller square tower housing latrines projects from the west curtain.

As a reward for their support, Robert the Bruce granted Knapdale to the MacDonald lords of the Isles in 1325. After their forfeiture in 1493, Archibald Campbell, second Earl of Argyll, contrived a tower house at the north-east corner of the enclosure. Its north and east sides rise from the older curtain, while its west wall incorporates the gable end of the MacSween hall. This tower house survives intact and roofed above a vaulted undercroft. It can just about be called an L-plan because of a small corner jamb. A stone staircase ascends to the main entrance on the first floor, while there are two more storeys below the corbelled-out parapet with round bartizans (the intervening floors have perished). A later remodelling provided the gabled attic. The castle resisted a Royalist attack in 1645 but was subsequently abandoned for nearby Skipness House.

Access: Open daily in summer (HES).
Relations: Lochranza and the other MacSween stronghold at Castle Sween. Carrick, Innis Chonnell and Castle Campbell were other seats of the Campbell earls.

TARBERT CASTLE The royal burgh of Tarbert is the gateway to the Kintyre peninsula. Its shattered royal castle crowns a hill to the east, overlooking the natural harbour formed by East Loch Tarbert. It is reached up a flight of steps from the quayside. The ruinous tower house is the only upstanding feature and only two sides stand high. James IV added this modest tower to an older castle from 1494, following his campaign to drive out the MacDonalds. Enough survives to show that it was a four-storey oblong, with window recesses high up and early gunports near the base. Rubble from the two fallen walls has filled the lower part of the interior. Curiously, the tower was built astride the outer curtain wall of a rare two-courtyard castle.

The large outer courtyard, sloping down towards the sea, was added in 1325–26 by Robert the Bruce, better known as a destroyer of castles, but here strengthening his grip on the western clans. Very little of his surrounding wall survives apart from the stumps of two cylindrical towers on the north-east. They flanked the vanished entrance but are not close together enough to constitute a proper gatehouse. The smaller inner courtyard lies to the south-west. A substantial earth mound marks the buried foundations of this walled quadrangle, which may have been raised by Alexander III to consolidate his purchase of the Kingdom of the Isles in 1266. The decaying castle was captured during the Earl of Argyll's rebellion in 1685 and then fell into oblivion.

Access: Freely accessible (LA – uphill walk).
Reference: *The Royal Castle of Tarbert* (Tarbert Castle Trust).

Relations: James IV's work at Rothesay, Falkland, Edinburgh, Holyrood, Stirling and Linlithgow.

TOWARD CASTLE lies within the country estate of its 1820s successor mansion, Castle Toward, on the East Cowal peninsula. From Toward village a road runs west along the shore. After a mile or so a path leads off to the right through the woods, the remains coming into sight in a clearing a short distance beyond. Although badly ruined, it is of interest for the comparatively rare remains of its roughly oblong barmkin. Much of the surrounding wall still stands, with a finely moulded entrance arch of the late sixteenth century on the north. To the east it has been supplanted by the remains of a house built around 1630. At the south end is the fifteenth-century tower house, which was probably oblong in plan but only one wall stands to its full height. From here there is a commanding view of the Firth of Clyde. This was the seat of the Lamonts, some of whom were hanged by the Campbells following a siege in 1646 during the Civil War.

Access: Freely accessible. There is a ferry from Gourock to nearby Dunoon.
Relations: The fine barmkin gateways at Burleigh, Redhouse and Buckholm.

OTHER SITES   A royal castle overlooked *Dunoon* from the twelfth century. Roughly triangular with circular angle towers, it was blown up during the 1685 rebellion and is now reduced to a few fragments on a knoll in the grounds of the Castle House Museum. *Dunaverty Castle* is little more than the site of another early royal castle, on a rock near the southern tip of the Kintyre peninsula. Two early hall houses on Loch Awe are reduced to shattered ruins: *Fincharn Castle*, on a promontory jutting into the loch near its southern tip; and *Fraoch Eilean Castle*, on a tree-covered islet off its north shore (the upstanding portion is from a much later house). *Achadunan Motte* (near Lochgilphead) is the only castle mound in Argyll.

Inveraray Castle (HHA), the seat of the dukes of Argyll, overlooks Loch Fyne. The existing castellated mansion was built from 1746 by the third duke. However, it stands near the site of a large tower house erected in the 1450s by Colin Campbell, first Earl of Argyll, to replace Innis Chonnell as the clan's chief seat. *Ardmaddy Castle* (near Clachan; gardens open) and *Craignish Castle* (near Aird) are later mansions incorporating much altered tower houses. Badly ruined towers include *Achallader Castle* (near Bridge of Orchy), *Caisteal na Nighinn Ruaidhe* (on a wooded islet in Loch Avich) and *Castle Shuna* (on Shuna Island, near the modern Shuna Castle).

AYRSHIRE

This south-western coastal county has an interesting variety of castles. Norman colonisation is attested by impressive mottes at Dalmellington and Dinvin. The destruction wrought during the Wars of Independence was heavy and Loch Doon's simple curtain wall is the only substantial thirteenth-century masonry to survive, astonishingly moved from its original islet location. There are also early fragments at Ardrossan and Dundonald, which were both rebuilt as tower houses after the wars. The latter, raised by Robert II, remains impressive. Other early tower houses of note are massive Dean and L-plan Portencross, both erected by the Boyds. Dean was expanded into a courtyard castle in the fifteenth century, while the picturesque courtyard complex at Rowallan dates mainly from the following century. Other sites consisting of more than a single tower are the barmkin at Glengarnock, the succession of buildings on a promontory at Dunure, and Seagate Castle's fine entrance range. Crossraguel Abbey has some rare monastic fortifications, while Craigie's shattered hall house bears the remains of a ribbed vault.

Ayrshire has one of the largest groups of later tower houses, though some are quite modest efforts and the wall-heads are generally much tamer than their counterparts in the north east. Inevitably, many of these towers are now in private occupation or shattered ruins. The vast majority are simple oblongs (Barr, Fairlie, Hunterston and Mauchline), though Dalquharran is a more ambitious structure with a round tower flanking one corner. L-plan tower houses include Baltersan, Maybole and soaring Killochan. Kelburn is the only surviving Z-plan tower house in the south-west. A number of Ayrshire castles were built by the bellicose Kennedy earls of Cassillis (appropriately pronounced 'Castles') and their feuding cadet branches. They are scattered broadly around the county though more densely near the coast, with concentrations around Maybole, West Kilbride and Kilmarnock.

County reference: BoS *Ayrshire and Arran*.

AIKET CASTLE stands in its own grounds two miles south-west of Dunlop. This gabled, oblong tower house was probably built sometime after the Cunninghams of Aiket acquired the estate in 1479. There is a sixteenth-century extension of nearly the same height alongside.

Access: Private.

AILSA CASTLE Ailsa Craig rises out of the Firth of Clyde, ten miles from Girvan on the mainland. This huge volcanic mass has cliffs all around, except on the east where there is a less precipitous ascent. From the jetty it is possible to take a steep and narrow path that runs up the hillside to Ailsa Castle, but it is not for the faint hearted. This gaunt, oblong tower rises near the south end of the island, 300 feet above the sea. Although small it has all the necessary attributes of a tower house. The entrance is poised on the edge of the precipice. Beneath the vaulted undercroft, a narrow basement is contrived owing to the sloping ground. From the entrance a straight mural stair ascends to the vaulted kitchen with a big fireplace. A spiral stair then conducts the visitor to the upper floor – it can scarcely be called a hall – that is now open to the sky. The tower may have been raised before the Reformation by the Abbot of Crossraguel, though it was repaired by Thomas Hamilton in 1580. In 1597 Hew Barclay tried to seize the island with the intention of making it a Catholic refuge, but he plummeted to his death in the ensuing skirmish for control.

Access: Freely accessible, though great caution should be exercised (uphill walk). There are regular boat trips to Ailsa Craig from Girvan (weather permitting).

Relations: The similar crag setting of Bass Castle.

ARDROSSAN CASTLE sit on top of Castle Hill in a public park, overlooking the port and the Firth of Clyde. It consists of a small, square enclosure, the most conspicuous parts being the tower house and the kitchen, but everything is quite ruined. The original castle of the Barclay family was captured and destroyed in 1297 by William Wallace, who is said to have stuffed the bodies of the English garrison into a cellar. Part of this castle survived destruction during the Wars of Independence. The ground floor of the tower house features a blocked archway showing that it originated as a modest gate tower, probably in the late thirteenth century and thus one of the earliest examples of its type in Scotland.

Sir John Montgomerie of Ardrossan rebuilt the superstructure as an oblong tower house, supposedly with his share of the ransom money for Sir Henry Percy (Hotspur), captured at Otterburn in 1388. It stands high on two sides, but the rest has collapsed. The gateway was blocked to form a standard tower house, a new entrance being inserted through the north range alongside. An undercroft beneath this fragmentary ruin contains a mural stair descending to a subterranean well. Not much survives from the rest of the Montgomeries' courtyard except for the barrel-vaulted ground floor of part of the south range, which housed the kitchen. Wide-mouthed gunports have been inserted here and in the tower house. Roundhead troops captured the castle in 1648 and subsequently used it as a quarry for Cromwell's Citadel at Ayr.

Access: Exterior only (LA). There are plans to consolidate and make accessible.
Reference: *PSAS* (104).
Relations: The blocked gatehouses at St Andrews and Crichton.

BALTERSAN CASTLE is barely half a mile north-east of Crossraguel Abbey, in a field off the A77. This brooding ruin of an L-plan tower house stands mainly to full height, though the one surviving gable looks precarious. The tower once bore an inscription stating that it was begun in 1584 by John Kennedy of Pennyglen and his wife Margaret Cathcart. Four storeys high including the attic, it is entered through a doorway in the side of the jamb. This has a broad spiral staircase rising to second-floor level, from which it transferred to the remains of a square turret corbelled out in the re-entrant angle. The top of the jamb forms a caphouse projecting on continuous corbelling, while there is one surviving corner bartizan at the top of the main block. The architectural details are quite fine but the ground-floor vaults have fallen.
Access: Well seen from the road.
Reference: *PSAS* (130).
Relations: Nearby Crossraguel. John Kennedy also remodelled Greenan.

BARR CASTLE The town of Galston has developed around this massive, oblong tower house, which rises implausibly on Barr Street. It is sparingly fenestrated and lined with mural chambers. The ground floor and the lofty hall above are barrel vaulted, with two further storeys above. At the wall-head is a double row of alternating corbelling, rounding at the angles for vanished bartizans, but the parapet has given way to a low pyramid roof. The first-floor entrance is covered by a modern porch, while another doorway has been inserted at ground level. Sir William Wallace is said to have taken refuge in an earlier stronghold here, but the existing structure was built by one of the Lockharts of Barr in the fifteenth century – it is alternatively known as Lockhart's Tower. Another tradition asserts that John Lockhart gave refuge to two successive Protestant reformers, George Wishart and John Knox. The Lockharts abandoned the tower in 1670. It was put to various utilitarian uses before being restored as a Masonic Lodge.
Access: Exterior only.
Relations: There is another Barr Castle in Renfrewshire.

CARLETON CASTLE is prominently situated high above the coastal village of Lendalfoot, from which it is reached by a sideroad. Strongly positioned overlooking the Water of Lendal, this austere, oblong tower house stands virtually to full height except for one collapsed corner that denotes the position of the spiral stair. The gap has been partly filled by a thinner wall. The tower contained five storeys, the lower two vaulted though the vaults have mostly collapsed. There are denuded and precarious gable ends, recessed within the vanished parapet. The tower was built by the Cathcarts of Carleton, probably in the fifteenth century, but supplanted as the family residence after a century or so by nearby Killochan Castle. It continues to moulder on a farm. There is a motte (Little Carleton) in the field across the road.

Access: Well seen from the road.
Relations: Killochan.

CARNELL HOUSE occupies an estate two miles north-west of Crosshands. One side of William Burn's Victorian mansion incorporates an oblong tower house with an embattled parapet resting on continuous corbelling. It was built in the fifteenth century by the Wallaces of Carnell.

Access: A functions venue.

CASSILLIS HOUSE, original seat of the Kennedy earls of Cassillis, stands on an estate four miles north-east of Maybole. This lofty tower house is attributed to John Kennedy after 1373, with a later stair jamb converting it into an L-plan. A Victorian mansion has been added in front.

Access: Private.

CESSNOCK CASTLE, in secluded grounds south-east of Galston, is a seventeenth-century courtyard mansion with a severe oblong tower house at one end. Built by the Campbells of Cessnock in the fifteenth century, the thick walls of this tower may incorporate an older keep.

Access: Private.

CRAIGIE CASTLE is a couple of miles from Craigie village. It stands a mile south-east of Bogend off the B730, forlorn on a knoll overlooking Craigie Mains farm. The structure has deteriorated considerably since MacGibbon and Ross sketched it but, while very ruinous, it is interesting for its architectural detail. It seems to have begun as a thirteenth-century hall house of the Lindsays, now reduced to the two quite ruinous side walls. They bear the imprint of a ribbed vault, carried on arches that are now reduced to the delicate brackets from which they sprang. This vault, no doubt inspired by the one in nearby Dundonald Castle, was inserted into the older walls in the fifteenth century by the Wallace family, who were descendants of the national hero's elder brother. (Blind Harry consulted William Wallace of Craigie while writing his epic poem, *The Wallace*.) They also added another storey, walling up the battlements of the original building, but little is left of the superstructure. There are fragments of barmkin wall on either side. Craigie was abandoned in 1588 and has been decaying ever since.

Access: On farmland.
Relations: Dundonald.

CRAIGNEIL CASTLE is prominently sited, overlooking Colmonell from across the River Stinchar. Beyond the bridge, at a bend in the road, a gate marks the beginning of the ascent to this chunky tower house ruin. It occupies a ridge made more dramatic by past quarrying – it now stands on a cliff's edge. One corner has indeed collapsed down it and more looks ready to follow. The tower is oblong and rises to nearly its full height of four storeys, though the parapet has gone. The second floor was the hall, loftier than the others, with the remains of a barrel vault and a torn-out fireplace. There was a spiral staircase in one corner. The austere form of the tower suggests the fifteenth century or even the fourteenth, though its connection with Robert the Bruce's brother Neil is spurious. It is first mentioned in 1484 as a possession of Lord Kennedy, whose son became the first earl of Cassillis.

Access: Well seen from the footpath (uphill walk).

Relations: Castles of the Kennedy earls at Cassillis, Dunure, Maybole and Castle Kennedy.

CRAUFURDLAND CASTLE occupies an estate three miles north-east of Kilmarnock. Projecting inconspicuously to one side of this neo-Gothic mansion is a modest oblong tower house, built around 1500 by the Crawfurds of Craufurdland, with a corbelled-out parapet.

Access: A functions venue but open by appointment.

CROSSRAGUEL ABBEY is two miles south-west of Maybole, beside the A77. This monastery of the Cluniac order was founded by the Earl of Carrick in 1244. The ruined church and claustral buildings were largely rebuilt following destruction during the Wars of Independence. East of the cloister is a shattered row of storerooms that underlay the abbot's house, with the Abbot's Tower attached to one corner. Traditionally attributed to Abbot William Kennedy around 1530, though it may be older, this is a rare tower house within a Scottish monastery. Much of the oblong structure stands to its full height of four storeys, though one corner has collapsed and the parapet has vanished. A ruinous porch on the north side contained the main entrance, reached from the abbot's house. It led into the hall at first-floor level. Another doorway opens into the undercroft, with its broken vault.

Abbot Kennedy is also credited with building the abbey gatehouse, shortly before his death in 1547. This three-storey gate tower rises intact above the vaulted entrance passage to a corbelled-out parapet. The rounded stair turret to one side is crowned by a gabled caphouse. Dumbbell gunports in the adjoining lengths of precinct wall show their defensive nature. At the rear a round corner turret with more gunports doubled up as a dovecote and is capped by a beehive dome. This precinct wall can at best have only defended the monastic outer court. It was no doubt a response to the threat from England during the Rough Wooing of 1543–51, though it did not stop the abbey from being pillaged by reformers in 1561.

Access: Open regularly in summer (HES).
Reference: Guidebook by A. Cox.
Relations: Arbroath has another monastic tower house, while Pittenweem and St Andrews were other fortified monasteries.

DALMELLINGTON MOTTE is a good example of an earthwork castle mound, classically conical with a flat top, which no doubt supported a palisade and a wooden tower. Modern steps ascend to the summit. The surrounding ditch is still discernible but the oblong bailey has perished. The prominent site, overlooking the Water of Muck, lies just to the south-east of Dalmellington town centre and is reached from the High Street. This motte is tentatively attributed to Thomas de Colville, who received the barony from the mormaer of Carrick around 1200, but otherwise its history is quite obscure.
Access: Freely accessible (LA).
Relations: Mottes such as Dinvin and Druchtag.

DALQUHARRAN OLD CASTLE stands in the grounds of the present Dalquharran Castle, a Robert Adam mansion that is now also a decaying shell. Thomas Kennedy of Dunure abandoned the original structure for its successor in 1790. On a low knoll overlooking a bend in the Water of Girvan, the Old Castle ruin is reached from the village of Dailly by taking the metal footbridge across the river, then following a path north-east through the woods.

What remains is two sides of a courtyard mansion held by cadet branches of the Kennedy family. The north-east range was added in the 1670s by John Kennedy of Girvan Mains. Its courtyard front has collapsed, though the rear incorporates the old barmkin wall. The south-east side is formed by an elongated L-plan tower house, probably dating from the late fifteenth century – a Gilbert Kennedy of Dalquharran is mentioned in 1474. It is still virtually intact, though a neglected and decaying shell. Two gabled stair turrets project from the courtyard front: that to the right is the original jamb, while the other is an addition of 1679 as demonstrated by a heraldic panel. The austere main block preserves many corbels at the wall-head, though the embattled parapet that MacGibbon and Ross drew has vanished. At the east corner is a circular flanking tower, now badly cracked, while the base of a bartizan can be seen high up at the south corner. From the barrel-vaulted undercroft a straight mural staircase ascends to the first floor. It was divided into a hall and solar with separate fireplaces, though the partition between them has vanished. An ornate aumbry bears the Kennedy arms. The flanking tower no doubt housed a bedchamber. The upper floor repeated the arrangement but there is no trace now of any later attic.
Access: Exterior only.
Relations: Kennedy branches at Baltersan, Greenan, Kirkhill, Newark and Pinwherry.

DEAN CASTLE, beside the Fenwick Water, occupies an estate that has become a country park. There is an older, tree-clad motte close by. Originally known as Kilmarnock Castle, it stands on the northern outskirts of that town, off Glasgow Road. For centuries the castle was the seat of the Boyds of Kilmarnock, who received extensive lands as a result of Robert Boyd's fidelity to Robert the Bruce. His son Thomas probably built the oblong tower house before his death in 1365. It remains intact and little altered, preserving the severe aspect of early Scottish tower houses. Windows are few and small, the walls rising to a parapet unadorned by corbels or bartizans. Only the recessed attic and a corner caphouse, marking the top of the spiral stair, are later additions. Below the attic the tower house comprises three unequal storeys. A cross-wall divides the ground floor into a kitchen and storeroom, both covered by unusual segmental vaults. This level has its own entrance but the main doorway is on the first floor, now reached by a stone stairway. Here is the hall, much higher than the other storeys and crowned by a barrel vault. A mural chamber surmounts a pit prison, while a wall passage leads to a latrine. The spiral stair ascends to the upper floor. Twin fireplaces show that it was divided into two rooms, with an oratory occupying an alcove.

Robert Boyd, created Lord Boyd in 1454, added an oblong courtyard to the east of the tower house. Its plain curtain wall survives intact on the north and east, while the south side is occupied by a residential block. The early move to more palatial quarters explains the unspoilt condition of the tower house, which stands detached from the rest and was relegated to humbler purposes. Lord Boyd's new range contains the great hall, standing over vaulted undercrofts. One of them formed a new kitchen, with a large fireplace. The four-storey, oblong Laigh (low) Tower forms one end of the range, with a solar at hall level. Its machicolated parapet is supported by finely carved corbels. Together the hall and the new tower reflect the growing importance of this Lord Boyd. He became regent during James III's minority and his son married the king's sister, incurring the fury of the king. In 1469 Boyd had to flee into permanent exile in England, though the line continued.

The Boyds sold the castle following their involvement in Bonnie Prince Charlie's rising. Already gutted by fire in 1735, the hall block remained a shell until Lord Howard de Walden restored it for occupation it in the 1930s. He added the authentic-looking gatehouse on the north curtain (a copy of the one at Tolquhon Castle). Another fanciful touch is the pentise roof covering the parapet of the curtain. Lord Howard's collection of armour and fine Brussels tapestries is displayed inside the castle.

Access: Open daily in summer and regularly in winter (LA).
Reference: LA guidebook.
Relations: The Boyd tower houses at Law, Portencross and Bedlay. Early tower houses such as Dundonald, Drum, Lochleven and Threave.

DINVIN MOTTE is a prodigious earthwork. An oval motte is surrounded by a deep ditch and a strong rampart, beyond which is a second ditch within a slighter rampart. It is a reminder that concentric principles were sometimes employed in earth-and-timber castles. A gap in the ramparts marks the start of a causeway leading up the side of the motte. There is no trace of any accompanying bailey. Traces of a stone wall were once visible around the summit. Its history is quite obscure, though it is presumably the work of an Anglo-Norman settler in the twelfth century. The motte occupies an elevated position about a mile south-east of Pinminnoch; it entails walking up a field from a layby on the winding A714.

Access: Freely accessible with caution (uphill walk).
Relations: Mottes such as Dalmellington and Druchtag

DUNDONALD CASTLE crowns a commanding hill four miles north-east of Troon, above the B730. Excavations have shown that an older dun on the site was burnt down around the year 1000, perhaps in the struggles between the Britons of Strathclyde and the Scots. The site was reoccupied by Walter the Steward, one of the Normans invited to Scotland by David I. His position as High Steward of the royal household became hereditary, his descendants adopting the surname Stewart. Nothing survives of their earthwork castle and little of the first stone fortress that followed. Probably begun by Alexander Stewart before his death in 1283, it was a strong enclosure of the new type with round flanking towers. Not one but two twin-towered gatehouses were placed at opposite ends of the oval courtyard. The later tower house is built over the remains of the western gatehouse, as the shallow projection at its rear demonstrates. It represents the base of one of the half-round towers that flanked the gate passage. There is no record of its role during the Wars of Independence, but the castle seems to have been thoroughly demolished as part of Robert the Bruce's strategy of denying potentially dangerous strongholds to the English. Otherwise, one might have expected Robert Stewart to utilise more of such a substantial structure.

Robert Stewart, grandson of Robert the Bruce, was Guardian of Scotland during the long confinement in England of his uncle, David II, in 1346–57. He succeeded as Robert II, the first Stewart king, in 1371. The castle, now thus a royal stronghold, may already have been rebuilt by then. It shows the more utilitarian style prevailing after Scotland's liberation. In place of the towered curtain wall there was an oblong barmkin, its simple curtain now reduced to foundations except for one stretch. The massive tower house dominates the site, surviving virtually to full height though now a ruin. This rectangular block is longer than it is high and its oblong bulk is filled by two lofty halls. The present height of the lower hall is misleading, because a vanished wooden floor separated it from storerooms beneath. This barrel-vaulted chamber accommodated the retainers. More sumptuous was the great hall above, for Robert and his household. Its elaborate, ribbed vault has sadly fallen, leaving only the vaulting shafts on the side walls. Both halls were reasonably well lit for the time, though the window embrasures of the lower hall pierce the vault high up for greater security. The solar must have been consigned to the ruinous annexe appended as an afterthought at one end of the tower house. A grim pit prison, reached by a modern ladder, occupied its base. Another addition appears to be a narrow annexe that covered the original first-floor entrance – a rare throwback to the forebuildings of Norman keeps in England. In front are the foundations of a chapel.

Robert II often resided in semi-retirement at Dundonald. He died here in 1390 and it was neglected under his successors. After purchasing the decaying castle from the Crown in 1638, Sir William Cochrane used it as a quarry for building Old Auchans House, itself now a ruin a mile further west.

Access: Open daily (HES – uphill walk).
Reference: Guidebook by D. Forbes and K. Murray.
Relations: The Stewart castle at Rothesay. Robert II's work at Kindrochit, Dumbarton, Edinburgh and Stirling.

DUNURE CASTLE, on a rocky coastal promontory overlooking the village, is a forlorn but dramatic sight. It was the principal residence of the lords Kennedy, earls of Cassillis from 1509, until they moved down the coast to Culzean Castle in the seventeenth century. The killing of an envoy of the Lord of the Isles here in 1429 sparked a MacDonald uprising. Dunure is notorious for a grizzly incident in 1569, when the fourth earl Gilbert allegedly roasted the commendator of Crossraguel Abbey over an open fire until he agreed to sign over the abbey's lands. Thomas Kennedy of Bargany came to the rescue and stormed the castle, only to find himself in turn besieged by Earl Gilbert. A settlement was reached whereby the commendator handed over the lands but received a pension.

The castle was already in ruins by 1694 and very much remains so, though well consolidated. Owing to the confines of the site it forms a long residential block with a tower house higher up at the apex of the promontory. To appreciate the castle chronologically it is best to bypass the newer parts and head straight for the apex. You can get as far as the footings of a wall with a drawbridge chasm in front. This bounded the tiny enclosure established here in the thirteenth century. Straight ahead is the stump of a fourteenth-century oblong tower house. More remains of a roughly V-shaped extension, like the prow of a ship, added on the tip of the promontory in the following century. Returning the way you came, you first pass the fifteenth-century hall, then the sixteenth-century kitchen and bakehouse with their fireplaces. They are linked by a later corridor. These residential buildings are reasonably well preserved but decidedly modest. Presumably there was a barmkin on the level ground in front, where an excellent beehive dovecote still stands.

Access: Freely accessible (LA).
Relations: Cassillis, Craigneil, Maybole and Castle Kennedy were other seats of the Kennedy earls.

FAIRLIE CASTLE is just inland from the coastal village of Fairlie. From the south end of Castlepark Drive a footpath runs east past this oblong tower house, on a knoll overlooking the Firth of Clyde. It comprises four storeys, connected by a spiral staircase near one corner. Windows are small and are confined mostly to one wall. The ground floor is divided into two barrel-vaulted storerooms. At hall level a narrow kitchen with a deep fireplace was partitioned off at one end – an awkward trait that the tower shares with nearby Law, Skelmorlie and Little Cumbrae castles. It suggests that the four towers were all built around the same time and probably by the same team of masons. At the wall-head are three rows of alternating corbels, rounding at the corners for bartizans, again closely resembling the work at Little Cumbrae. The actual parapet has perished. According to tradition the tower was raised by Sir Robert Fairlie in 1521. It was restored from an empty shell for occupation in the early 2020s.

Access: Well seen from the footpath.
Relations: Law, Skelmorlie and Little Cumbrae.

GLENGARNOCK CASTLE, though badly ruined, is attractively situated in rugged terrain on a rocky promontory jutting into the River Garnock. Dipple Road heads north out of Kilbirnie and, after a mile or so, an unsignposted turning leads off to the left. Further on there is a track to the right, passing a farm and continuing until the castle appears amid the trees across a field to the left. The only level approach is cut off by a ditch. In front are the remains of a walled barmkin, a gap in the curtain wall denoting where the gateway stood. The compact interior was made smaller by various buildings, though the only substantial survivor is the vaulted kitchen. Ahead rises an oblong tower house on the edge of the ravine. It has collapsed towards the barmkin and only two walls stand entire, along with part of a third. The interior now appears to be a lofty hall, though the lower part was an undercroft and there may have been another dividing floor. It was covered by a pointed vault as the remaining fragment shows. The castle was raised by the Cunninghams of Glengarnock, probably in the fifteenth century. It was repaired in 1841 after a partial collapse, but nothing has been done since and the castle continues to crumble.

Access: Freely accessible with caution.
Relations: There was another Cunningham branch at Aiket.

GREENAN CASTLE is daringly poised on the edge of a cliff overlooking Doonfoot and the Firth of Clyde, three miles south-west of Ayr. It is been seen from the beach below but is approached by a path starting near the west end of Greenan Road. Remains of earthworks barring the approach may go back to the castle mentioned in 1199 or even an Iron Age hillfort. On closer inspection the oblong tower house is a fairly modest affair, comprising three storeys and an attic. Two sides stand to full height, including an attic gable with a crowning chimney and the remains of three corner bartizans, but the other two sides are more ruinous. There is the usual vaulted undercroft. The tower is tentatively attributed to Thomas Davidson, who was here in 1510. The original first-floor entrance was replaced by a ground-floor doorway (now walled up). Its lintel bears the year 1603, along with the initials of John Kennedy of Pennyglen and his wife Florence MacDowell. A fragment of barmkin wall survives alongside.

Access: Exterior only – great care should be taken owing to the sheer drop.
Relations: The cliff-top position of Old Keiss. John Kennedy also built Baltersan.

HUNTERSTON CASTLE can be found three miles north of West Kilbride. It is approached along Beech Avenue, off the A78. In sight of the Firth of Clyde, the complex occupies a wooded estate that was formerly marshland. This has been the seat of the Hunter family, who held the hereditary office of Royal Huntsman, since the twelfth century. A previous dwelling stood to the north-west, but the oldest part of the present complex is a modest oblong tower house. Built around 1500, it rises four storeys to an embattled parapet on a row of corbels. Recessed within is a later attic with crow-stepped gables. Running south from the tower is a lower extension of two storeys and an attic, added early in the seventeenth century. This has a gabled staircase jamb at the junction between the two, resulting overall in a T-plan structure. The first-floor entrance to the tower is now inside the wing. From the hall a spiral staircase ascends to the upper floors and parapet. The undercroft, which originally could only be reached through a hatch in the barrel vault, has a blocked archway from the days when the family saloon was parked there. Victorian extensions in the Scottish Baronial style have created a courtyard beyond. There is also a successor mansion – Hunterston House – close by.

Access: Open by appointment only but well seen from Old Road.

KELBURN CASTLE is set in a large estate – now a country park – two miles south of Largs, off the A78. Since the twelfth century the lands have continuously been held by the Boyles of Kelburn, who fought at the Battle of Largs nearby in 1263. The existing structure is primarily a mansion built by David Boyle, first Earl of Glasgow (d.1733), and extended in Victorian times. However, projecting from the rear and overlooking the steep bank of the Kel Burn is a Z-plan tower house – the only one in the south west that is not a fragmentary ruin.

The tower house comprises four storeys, including the gabled attic, but its axis is strangely askew to the later mansion. There are round towers at diagonally opposite corners and round bartizans at the other two corners, all enlivened by conical roofs. It is a complete example of its kind, but much altered within and concealed on two sides by the extensions, one of the flanking towers being entirely embedded in the later work. Sash windows have been inserted to match the rest of the mansion. The entrance, now within the later house, is in the customary position beside the flanking tower. Its lintel bears the year 1581 and the initials of John Boyle and his wife Marion Crawford. It is possible that John merely remodelled and added flanking towers to an older oblong tower house. The roof contains many original timbers. Kelburn is certainly the most colourful of British castles, its harled walls having been brightly painted by Brazilian street artists in 2007.

Access: Exterior daily. There are regular tours of the interior during high summer (HHA).

Relations: Z-plan tower houses such as Claypotts, Noltland, Drochil and Castle Menzies.

KILBIRNIE HOUSE, in a field south-west of Kilbirnie town, is the overgrown ruin of a massive oblong tower house, attributed to Malcolm Crawfurd of Kilbirnie around 1470. A seventeenth-century wing has been reduced to fragments since MacGibbon and Ross drew it.

Access: On farmland.

KILHENZIE CASTLE stands beside a farm two miles south-east of Maybole. This modest, oblong tower house has corner bartizans with conical roofs and dormer windows. It was probably built by John Baird of Kilhenzie in the late sixteenth century. A later wing is attached.

Access: Private.

KILLOCHAN CASTLE rises four miles north-east of Girvan, overlooking the Water of Girvan on a country estate off the B741. A long inscription over the entrance to this stepped L-plan tower house begins: 'This work was begun the I of Marche 1586 be Ihone Cathcart of Carltoun and Helene Wallace his spouse.' It continues with a quotation from the Book of Proverbs; there is a heraldic panel above. John Cathcart clearly desired an upgrade from his spartan tower house at Carleton, but he may have adapted an older tower if the thick walls are anything to go by. Killochan is one of the finest tower houses in the south west, commandingly tall with the stair turret a little higher still. An embattled, circular tower flanks the east corner, while the south-west gable end has corner bartizans with conical roofs. The curious, splayed window opening on this wall is considered further evidence of an older structure, though it would look odd at any period. The tower house in its current form has no parapet, but the third floor of the main block juts out on the south-east side above a row of continuous corbelling. The tower house now forms one wing of a much lower, eighteenth-century mansion.

A box machicolation oversails the entrance high up. The square turret in the re-entrant angle forms a porch leading into the ground floor of the main block. This comprises two undercrofts and a kitchen, all barrel-vaulted and linked by a corridor. The jamb contains a generous staircase rising in straight sections to the first-floor hall, which now forms the panelled dining room. The staircase then transfers to a spiral in the re-entrant turret, serving the two upper floors and the gabled attic. A second stair turret is corbelled out in the round flanking tower. The upper floors, with extra accommodation provided in the jamb and the round tower, have been transformed by later occupation. The Cathcarts remained here until they sold up in 1954.

Access: A functions venue.
Relations: Carleton. L-plan tower houses with an additional corner tower at Dunderave, Invergarry and Dundas.

KIRKHILL CASTLE, in the grounds of Kirkhill House at Colmonell, is the shell of an L-plan tower house with tall gables and corner bartizans. Even the original iron window grilles survive. Above one window is carved the year 1589 and the initials of Thomas Kennedy of Kirkhill.
Access: On private land.

KNOCKDOLIAN CASTLE is situated in the grounds of Knockdolian House, three miles west of Colmonell. Built early in the sixteenth century by the Grahams of Knockdolian, it is the intact shell of an oblong tower house with a plain parapet supported on continuous corbelling.
Access: On private land.

LAW CASTLE Law Brae ascends eastwards from West Kilbryde to this simple, oblong tower house overlooking the village. Now coated in gleaming white harling, it was restored for occupation from an empty shell, work being completed in 2005. The tower is said to have been raised after Thomas Boyd, Earl of Arran, married James III's sister Mary in 1467. However, just two years later he followed his father, Lord Boyd, into exile. Similarities to Fairlie, Skelmorlie and Little Cumbrae castles suggest the builder may actually have been another member of the Boyd family early in the sixteenth century. So do the wide-mouthed gunports low down, though they could be insertions. The tower rises four storeys to a renewed parapet resting on rows of continuous corbelling. Little bartizans clasp the corners, while a gabled attic with a tall chimney is recessed within. The ground-floor entrance leads into the first of two barrel-vaulted chambers. A spiral staircase in one corner ascends to the top. The first floor is mostly occupied by the hall, though one end was partitioned off to form a cramped kitchen with an arched fireplace, as at the other towers mentioned.

Access: Well seen from the road (now a holiday let).

Relations: Fairlie, Skelmorlie and Little Cumbrae. Dean and Portencross were other Boyd castles.

LOCH DOON CASTLE Two miles south-east of Dalmellington, a sideroad leaves the A713 and meanders along the bank of Loch Doon for seven miles until it reaches this castle. A rather ruinous curtain wall of fine ashlar masonry runs in straight sections around a polygonal courtyard – one so small that the whole ensemble resembles an English shell keep. One stretch is longer than the others, resulting in a roughly D-shaped enclosure. There are no flanking towers. Foundations show that residential buildings surrounded the courtyard – a fireplace is embedded in the curtain at first-floor level. The curtain is pierced by a fine Gothic entrance arch with a portcullis groove; there is also a narrow postern.

The ruin is of interest as one of the older stone castles of Scotland, for its Bruce connections and as the castle that moved. Castle Island, visible a quarter of a mile away in the middle of the loch, was the original location and determined the shape of the courtyard. However, plans to raise the water level prompted the Office of Works to painstakingly dismantle the castle stone by stone and re-erect it safely on dry land in 1935–36. The orientation of the re-assembled structure is almost the same as its original location. Only the foundations and doorway of a later Kennedy tower house were re-erected. Its two surviving walls had dominated the rest but were omitted to present the castle in its original form.

According to tradition the castle was built by Robert the Bruce. However, it is more likely to be the work of his father Robert, lord of Annandale, towards the end of the thirteenth century. It had a stormy history, first being mentioned in 1306 when it surrendered to the English. Bruce's brother-in-law Sir Christopher Seton, who had taken refuge here after the defeat at Methven, was hanged. The castle went on to change hands three more times in the next eight years but was left standing in contravention of Bruce's usual policy of destruction, probably because of its isolation. It was more successful in 1335, being one of only five castles to withstand the English during Edward Balliol's campaign to gain the Scottish throne. After passing to the earls of Cassillis, the castle succumbed to further attacks by the Black Douglases in 1446 and the Crawfords in 1511. Further disturbances induced James V to seize and dismantle the castle.

Access: Freely accessible (HES).

Relations: Other Bruce work at Tarbert, Lochmaben and fragmentary Turnberry. The Wallace Tower (Aberdeenshire) has also been moved.

MAUCHLINE CASTLE stands in the centre of the little burgh of Mauchline that grew up around it. The property was a grange of Melrose Abbey until the Reformation and Andrew Hunter (abbot 1444–65) built his residence in tower house form. Although in private grounds, the tower faces a public alley off Castle Street, immediately north of the parish church. The oblong structure, known as Abbot Hunter's Tower after its builder, is quite modest and rises three storeys to a simple row of corbelling. The parapet had to be removed to reduce the weight on the walls. Recessed within is a gabled attic, no doubt added in the sixteenth century. Above twin vaulted undercrofts is the hall, with the unusual luxury of a ribbed vault. A boss at the intersection of the ribs bears Hunter's arms. Other refined touches are the projecting latrine chute and a mutilated twin-light window with a carved head. The tower is still intact but derelict, supported in places by iron braces to counteract the pressure from the hall vault. It is attached to a later house, which has eradicated the other buildings of the grange.

Access: Exterior only.

Relations: Abbots' tower houses at Crossraguel and Pinkie.

MAYBOLE CASTLE dominates the High Street of the little burgh of Maybole. It was a seat of the notorious Kennedy earls of Cassillis. Their lofty L-plan tower house was probably built around the middle of the sixteenth century by Gilbert Kennedy, the third earl, who survived capture by the English at the battle of Solway Moss in 1542. The grey-harled tower is quite austere up to the crow-stepped gables, though round bartizans with conical roofs are corbelled out at two of the corners. The jamb, which contains the spiral stair all the way up, boasts an ornate oriel window in the caphouse, embellished with carved heads. This window, along with the little dormer windows at the wall-head, attest a remodelling by Gilbert's great-grandson John, the sixth earl, around 1620. Lower down the tower house is hemmed in by additions made when the twelfth Earl of Cassillis restored the building in 1812, after a period of decay. Hence the entrance to the tower, in the side of the jamb, is now approached from within. The ground floor retains its two vaulted compartments and the hall above is still one chamber, but the upper storey and attic have been subdivided. At attic level the bartizans provide little chambers. The earls have their burial vault in the ruined collegiate church nearby.

Access: Exterior only.

Relations: Cassillis, Craigneil, Dunure and Castle Kennedy were other seats of the Kennedy earls.

NEWARK CASTLE, one of four bearing that name in Scotland, occupies an estate a mile south-west of Alloway. One end of this mainly Victorian mansion is formed by an oblong, sixteenth-century tower house of the Kennedys of Bargany, with a plain parapet and bartizans.

Access: Private.

NEWMILNS TOWER   A handsome if modest oblong tower house stands on Castle Street in the heart of this little burgh. It rises three storeys to rows of continuous corbelling that round at the corners to support vanished bartizans; the cannon spouts are restorations. Recessed within the parapet is an attic with crow-stepped gables. The ground-floor entrance arch is surmounted by a blank heraldic panel. There are shot holes in the vaulted undercroft and each of the storeys above forms a single room, linked by a spiral staircase at one corner. The tower is attributed to Sir Hugh Campbell of Loudoun around 1530. It was converted into a prison for Covenantors, some of whom were rescued in 1685 by a local mob who stormed the tower. Having fallen into decay, the tower was restored and re-harled in the 1990s.

Access: Well seen from the road.

Relations: Campbell branches at Barcaldine, Castle Stalker, Duntrune and Kilchurn.

PENKILL CASTLE is a small, oblong tower house with two corner bartizans, a mile south-east of Old Dailly. It was built by the Boyds of Penkill, probably towards the end of the sixteenth century. It adjoins a house rebuilt in 1857 and dominated by an over-the-top staircase tower.

Access: Private.

PINWHERRY CASTLE stands on a tree-clad knoll in the garden of Pinwherry House, overlooking the Duisk River just south of Pinwherry. It is the prominent ruin of an L-plan tower house with precarious gables, attributed to John Kennedy of Banquarrie in the 1590s.

Access: Visible from the road.

PORTENCROSS CASTLE, in a village two miles west of West Kilbride, squats on a rock jutting into the Firth of Clyde, with views across to Little and Great Cumbrae. There is an older motte-and-bailey earthwork on Auld Hill, a little inland, but this tower house is believed to have been built in the late fourteenth century by the Boyds of Kilmarnock. Robert II and III were frequent visitors *en route* to Rothesay Castle, as attested by the number of charters sealed here. Abandoned to tenant occupation in the seventeenth century, the tower gradually decayed but was well restored by the Friends of Portencross Castle in 2009–10 – a glowing example of local initiative.

This is an early version of the L-plan but, unusually, the jamb projects from the gable end of the main block and is nearly as wide. There is both a ground-floor entrance to the main block, flanked by the jamb, and a first-floor entrance to the jamb, flanked by the main block (another doorway has since been cut through below the latter). From the vaulted undercroft a straight stair ascends to the hall. It is covered by a barrel vault which seems to be a later addition, judging from the change in masonry. The present lofty appearance of the hall is misleading, as the vault space was divided into two by a wooden floor, the upper level forming a dimly lit sleeping loft. The solar must have been squeezed into the second floor of the jamb, above two storeys of kitchens. A modern spiral staircase in the original stair well ascends to the remains of a corbelled-out parapet, with the ruinous gable ends of a later attic recessed within. At four storeys the jamb rises a little higher than the rest.

Access: Open regularly in summer.

Relations: Dean, Law and Bedlay were other castles of the Boyds.

ROWALLAN OLD CASTLE forms a picturesque little quadrangle in extensive grounds that have become a golf course, four miles north of Kilmarnock. It was long the seat of the Muirs of Rowallan. This low-lying site was once surrounding by marshland, long since drained. Gilchrist Muir received the lands as a reward for his role at the Battle of Largs in 1263. The shattered ruin of an oblong tower house, forming the north-east side of the present castle, is traditionally attributed to him. Another suggested builder is Sir Adam Muir, whose daughter Elizabeth married the future Robert II, but it is more likely to date from the fifteenth century.

Rowallan developed into a compact courtyard mansion in the sixteenth century, probably under Mungo Muir, who fell at the Battle of Pinkie in 1547. Its two main ranges are still intact and roofed. The tall south-east range is the show front. The entrance portal in the middle is flanked by slender, half-round turrets, their four stages delineated by string courses and capped by conical roofs. These turrets were added by Mungo's son John in 1562, as recorded on a panel high up. As the ground level within the castle is considerably higher than outside, the round-headed gateway is approached by a staircase. A vaulted gate passage, flanked by porter's lodges, leads into the little courtyard. To the right it is bounded by the stump of the older tower house, which was abandoned at an early stage. Enough survives to show that the ground floor had the customary vault. The tower is adjoined by an annexe of the 1640s, also now ruined, while a plain wall closes off the courtyard at the rear.

On the left is the south-west range, flanked by spiral staircase turrets. It stands over a row of barrel-vaulted compartments that may be contemporary with the tower house. One of them became the kitchen. Dumbbell gunports show some attention to defence here. The hall occupies the central part of the range, flanked by two storeys of private chambers. One of them is the solar, reached from the hall by an original panelled door. Further rooms occupy the two main floors of the south-east range, while a long gallery – following the Elizabethan trend – fills the attic.

In front of the castle there is a forecourt, with a gateway bearing the year 1611. The last Muir died in 1700 and the castle was let to tenant farmers. Occupation continued on a humble scale, too impoverished to modernise, which explains its remarkable preservation. Apart from some later panelling, the interiors have been little altered since. From 1902 the architect Sir Robert Lorimer built the new 'castle' nearby.

Access: Formerly in state care but now private (a functions venue).
Reference: *A Palace Fit for a Laird* by G. Ewart and D. Gallagher.
Relations: Late courtyard castles such as Tolquhon, Edzell and Cawdor. The twin-towered gatehouses of Fyvie, Tolquhon and Dudhope.

SEAGATE CASTLE stands in the centre of the royal burgh of Irvine. It is on or near the site of an older castle first mentioned in 1184. This was the probable scene of the Capitulation of Irvine, where Robert the Bruce and other Scottish nobles submitted to the English in 1297. Bosses in the gate passage vault depict the Montgomerie and Drummond arms, indicating that the present structure was built by Hugh Montgomerie, third Earl of Eglinton, and his wife Agnes Drummond. They were married in 1562. A visit by Mary Queen of Scots is recorded the following year, though how much existed at that point is an open question. The castle was abandoned in 1746, when the tenth earl removed the roof. It has been a ruin ever since.

The existing building is a long residential range fronting the street known as Seagate. A round-headed gate arch in the middle of the range is decorated with 'dogtooth' ornament more common in early Gothic work. It has been suggested that they were robbed from nearby Kilwinning Abbey. To the left the range stands to its full height of three storeys, including the attic gables. Large first-floor windows are surrounded by a cable moulding. These and the absence of any shot holes demonstrate the castle's defensive limitations. To the right of the gateway the range is reduced to just its lowest storey. The rib-vaulted gate passage and a fragment of return wall at the rear indicate that the range formed one side of a vanished barmkin. The rear elevation has a round stair turret projecting beside the plain inner gate arch. The ground floor consists of a row of barrel-vaulted undercrofts entered from the courtyard, along with a kitchen with a huge arched fireplace. Two well-appointed chambers occupy the surviving part of the first floor.

Access: Exterior only (LA).
Relations: Tower houses of the Montgomerie earls at Little Cumbrae and Lochranza.

SKELMORLIE CASTLE stands a mile south of Skelmorlie village via Skelmorlie Castle Road. It is positioned on a ridge overlooks the A78 and the Firth of Clyde. This is mainly a Victorian mansion but the wing to the left, as seen from the approach, is a gabled oblong tower house. It was built early in the sixteenth century by the Montgomeries of Skelmorlie, a descendant of whom is commemorated by a monumental tomb in the Skelmorlie Aisle at nearby Largs. The tower has been restored since and any old details are buried beneath the white harling. It consists of four storeys, include the attic with restored crow-stepped gables. Round bartizans are corbelled out high up at alternate corners. The first-floor hall had a narrow kitchen at one end – a trait shared by the nearby towers at Fairlie, Law and Little Cumbrae. Incorporated at the other end of the mansion is an embattled round tower from the barmkin defences.

Access: There is a good view from the road.
Relations: Fairlie, Law and Little Cumbrae.

SORN CASTLE, on an estate outside the village, began as a modest oblong tower house beside the River Ayr. Traditionally built in 1409 by the Hamiltons of Sorn, it was extended into a longer block in the following century. This now forms just one wing of a Victorian mansion.

Access: A functions venue.

THOMASTON CASTLE is a massive L-plan tower house with an unusually squat profile, situated beside the A719 two miles south-west of Pennyglen. Though now an empty shell, it rises three storeys to rows of continuous corbelling at the wall-head. A square stair turret in the re-entrant angle contains the entrance to the tower. Unusually, the jamb is pierced by a vaulted gate passage that led into the vanished barmkin. High above the outer archway is a blank heraldic panel. The ground floor contains a kitchen and the usual storerooms, all barrel vaulted. The upper floors have lost their partitions, and the interior is very overgrown. There is no trace of an attic. Despite the completeness of the tower house, the masonry is unstable and there is a deep crack in the jamb. Robert the Bruce's nephew, Thomas Bruce, is said to have built an earlier castle here (hence the name). However, the existing structure is attributed to the Corrys of Kelwood, who obtained the lands in 1507.

Access: Well seen from the road.

OTHER SITES   The vanished royal castle at *Ayr* was sacked by Robert the Bruce in 1298 but survived the Wars of Independence. The site, in a triangle between the coast and the River Ayr, is overlooked by the remains of Oliver Cromwell's Citadel. Robert also demolished *Turnberry Castle*, his probable birthplace. It occupied a headland jutting into the sea. A lighthouse marks the spot but only scraps of masonry cling to the rock. *Terringzean Castle* (near Cumnock) is reduced to part of a rare octagonal corner tower from a small quadrangle. *Kerelaw Castle* (near Stevenston) has shattered fragments of another small quadrangle but its most prominent feature – a wall with traceried windows – is a nineteenth-century folly. *Auchinleck Castle* is a fragmentary ruin on a rock near Ochiltree, while *Tarbolton* has a motte-and-bailey earthwork.

Culzean Castle (NTS – near Pennyglenn), Robert Adam's cliff top masterpiece, incorporates an older tower house of the earls of Cassillis, though it is unrecognisable. Some other tower houses survive in a much-altered or very ruinous condition:

Ardstinchar Castle (ruin, at Ballantrae)
Auchenharvie Castle (ruin, near Torranyard)
Blair Castle (near Dalry)
Caprington Castle (near Kilmarnock)
Cloncaird Castle (near Kirkmichael)
Dunduff Castle (near Fisherton)
Kilkerran Castle (ruin, near Dailly)
Kingencleugh Castle (ruin, near Mauchline)
Knock Old Castle (near Largs)
Loudoun Castle (ruin, near Galston)
Montfode Castle (ruin, near Ardrossan)
Stane Castle (near Irvine)
Sundrum Castle (near Coylton)

BANFFSHIRE

This former north coast county retains two plain, thirteenth-century curtain walls – of the Black Comyns at Balvenie and of a royal castle at Banff – which survived the Wars of Independence. The courtyard theme continues later with the daring promontory ruins of Findlater and the barmkin wall at Auchindoun. In the 1550s the Earl of Atholl gave Balvenie a new residential block of some distinction, while the Ogilvys built the remarkable sixteenth-century quadrangle with corner towers that forms the sadly neglected Boyne Castle. Tower houses range from the early austerity of Drumin and the grim massiveness of Auchindoun, to the simple elegance of Blairfindy and the petite charm of Fordyce. Ballindalloch Castle is a stately home incorporating a Z-plan tower house.
   County reference: BoS *Aberdeenshire: North and Moray*.

AUCHINDOUN CASTLE   Two miles south-east of Dufftown, off the A941, a track ascends in half a mile to this brooding ruin. It stands on a knoll above the River Fiddich in a gaunt moorland setting. The impressive banks and ditches that surround it are older and may belong to an Iron Age fort. This castle comprises a massive tower house, concentrically surrounded by a simple barmkin wall. Although the tower follows the L-plan, it is unusual for having no doorway in the re-entrant angle. On three sides it rises nearly to full height but the collapsed front wall reveals its structure. Over a barrel-vaulted undercroft rises a lofty hall, with a tall fireplace at one end and the springers of what must have been a finely ribbed vault. Otherwise, the tower has been robbed of all architectural features. Above are the remains of another spacious chamber, while further rooms occupied each of the three levels in the jamb. The fallen spiral staircase at one corner has left another gaping hole.
   The builder of the tower is a matter of some dispute. James III granted Auchindoun to his brother John Stewart, Earl of Mar and Garioch. John died in suspicious circumstances in 1479 and James is then said to have awarded the lands to his master mason Thomas (or Robert) Cochrane. According to tradition it was he who built the tower house, only to be hanged from the bridge at Lauder – along with other low-born favourites of the king – by jealous nobles in 1482. The story of his rise seems to have grown in the

telling, however. It is more plausible that John Stewart employed Cochrane to build the tower. The ribbed vault suggests an architect of some distinction.

The castle is first mentioned in 1509 as a possession of a branch of the Ogilvy family. They probably built the barmkin wall. This wall is complete all round except for its parapet, though propped up by later buttresses in places. It is pierced by a plain gate arch on the south and has the remains of a circular flanking tower at the north-west corner. Later windows pierce the south front, with the foundations of a domestic range behind. Adam Gordon of Auchindoun burnt Corgarff Castle and its occupants in 1571. The castle suffered several raids in ownership disputes. Bonnie Dundee used it as a base during his Jacobite campaign of 1689, but it fell into decay afterwards.

Access: Freely accessible (HES).

Relations: Cochrane is said to have built Kilravock. Ribbed vaulting at Dundonald and Old Tulliallan.

BALLINDALLOCH CASTLE occupies extensive grounds in the valley of the River Spey, entered off the A95 just north of Bridge of Avon. At its core is a Z-plan tower house, rising four storeys including the gabled attic, though later remodelling and extensions on either side now obscure the original layout. Round towers flank diagonally opposite corners, while the semi-circular Watch Tower projects from the middle of the west side. The top of this tower is corbelled out into a gabled caphouse that was the dominant feature of the original structure. It is now matched by another caphouse on the south-east corner tower, but that was only added during the remodelling of the 1850s. The north-west tower, with its conical roof, still rises no higher than the main block. It commands the original entrance doorway in the side of the Watch Tower, which is overlooked by a projecting machicolation high up on the caphouse. The current entrance through the south-east tower, crowned by a flamboyant arms panel, is a Victorian insertion.

The tower house was for long the residence of the Grants of Ballindalloch. A fireplace lintel in one of the bedrooms bears the year 1546, but this commemorates the marriage of Patrick Grant to Margaret Gordon and seems rather early for the Z-plan. Another lintel in the Watch Tower caphouse, referring to a later Patrick Grant and his wife Helen Ogilvy, is inscribed with the year 1602. It has been inferred that the caphouse is an addition of that time but the entire tower house could be of that period. The ground floor retains two vaulted compartments connected by a corridor, while a spiral stair ascends the Watch Tower to the caphouse. Otherwise, the interior reflects successive later transformations, the first-floor hall now forming the panelled dining room. The flamboyant General James Grant added an extension to the west of the tower house in the 1770s, while the big courtyard to the north is all Victorian. The grey harling lends a false sense of unity to the complex.

Access: Open regularly in summer (HHA).

Reference: Guidebook (Heritage House).
Relations: Z-plan tower houses such as Carnousie and Brodie.

BALVENIE CASTLE This striking ruin on a steep knoll overlooks Dufftown and Glen Fiddich. The walled quadrangle was probably erected by Alexander Comyn, second Earl of Buchan, who died in 1289. His branch of the family was known as the Black Comyns to distinguish them from the Red Comyn lords of Badenoch. In 1304 Edward I restored the castle (then called Mortlach) to Alexander's son, John. Four years later Robert the Bruce defeated the Comyns at Inverurie and devastated Buchan, John Comyn fleeing to exile in England. Balvenie escaped significant damage and re-emerged in the fifteenth century as the seat of the Douglas lords of Balvenie, an offshoot of the redoubtable Black Douglas family. After their downfall in 1455 the castle was granted to Sir John Stewart, half-brother of James II, who became first Earl of Atholl two years later. His descendant John, the fourth earl, built the splendid Atholl Lodging in the following century. He briefly became Lord Chancellor but died in 1578 – allegedly poisoned by Regent Morton. Jacobites occupied the castle during their 1689 revolt. It was garrisoned by

Balvenie Castle, Banffshire

Hanoverian troops during the later Jacobite risings but was abandoned for a nearby mansion (since demolished) in 1724.

As seen from the approach, the south-east range consists of two contrasting parts, both largely complete though now roofless. The austere block on the left, with large windows piercing the older curtain high up, probably dates from the Douglas occupation. To the right is the fourth earl's more elaborate Atholl Lodging, which bears a marked resemblance to the contemporary palace block at Huntly Castle. Heraldic shields near the wall-head include the arms of his first wife, indicating a date between 1547 and 1557. Wide-mouthed gunports show some regard for defence, while the two rows of large windows were barred by the usual iron grilles. Even the circular tower projecting boldly at the east corner dates only from this time, though it may occupy the site of an older flanking tower. A central gateway preserves its original double yett. It leads into the vaulted gate passage, with a porter's lodge to one side. Though forming an L-plan in one corner of the castle, the Atholl Lodging is emphatically a residential wing as opposed to a tower house proper. The round tower provided a secure location for the bedchambers of the earl and countess, reached from their separate suites on the first and second floors. Gables attest an attic above, while the customary barrel-vaulted storerooms occupy the ground floor. Two stair turrets face the courtyard, one rising to a gabled caphouse. On the other side of the gate passage is the Douglas block. This cavernous, vaulted space was originally divided by a wooden floor into two storeys, containing the great hall over a bakehouse.

The other three sides of the courtyard take us back to Alexander Comyn's castle. This simple enclosure was probably inspired by the royal castle at Banff. One two sides the wide ditch remains outside. Against the curtain are fragments of other domestic buildings from the Douglas period. Though lacking its parapet, the thick curtain survives largely to full height. Neither windows nor arrow slits break its solidity. There is just a square latrine turret, shallowly projecting from the north corner.

Access: Open daily in summer (HES).

Reference: Guidebook by C. Tabraham. *PSAS* (60).

Relations: Huntly Castle. Banff and other early curtains such as Castle Roy and Kinclaven.

BANFF CASTLE can be found off Castle Street, at the heart of this little royal burgh and harbour town. All that remains is the plain curtain wall, deprived of its parapet, that bounded the north and east sides of the courtyard. The wall is fronted by a deep ditch with an outer rampart, beyond which the land drops steeply towards the shoreline. This royal castle was probably established in the twelfth century and the earthworks could date from that time. The stone wall, which does not align neatly with the ditch, is usually attributed to Alexander II as part of his attempt to impose royal control over rebellious Moravia. As a simple quadrangle without flanking towers, this is quite plausible. It surrendered to Edward I without a fight in 1296 and was the last castle in the north to be retaken by the Scots in 1310. No doubt its usefulness as a garrison post in Comyn territory saved it from the usual destruction and a vanished tower house was later built within the courtyard. Nevertheless, the castle eventually decayed. The curtain survived as the garden wall of a house built for the Earl of Findlater by the architect John Adam in 1750.

Access: Now a community centre (LA).
Relations: Alexander II's curtain at Kinclaven.

BLAIRFINDY CASTLE, overlooking the River Livet, stands a short distance south-east of the Glenlivet Distillery, off the B936. This handsome tower house was built by John Gordon of Strathavon, whose arms – along with the year 1586 – are displayed in a worn panel above the entrance. The second Marquis of Huntly, a leading Royalist, was imprisoned here in 1647. He refused his kinsmen's offers to rescue him and went on to execution at Edinburgh. Burnt by Hanoverian troops after the Battle of Culloden in 1746, the ruin was stabilised and consolidated in 2019.

The L-plan tower is an empty shell but still rises to full height. It comprises four storeys including the attic gables, which rise with no intervening parapet. The jamb projects unevenly in two directions. In the re-entrant angle of the jamb is the entrance, overlooked at the wall-head by a row of machicolations – an archaic touch for its date. The ground floor was divided into a kitchen and a storeroom but their vaults have collapsed. A staircase in the jamb ascended to the first-floor hall. From here upwards the stair transferred to a shallow turret in the re-entrant angle, the upper part of the jamb containing chambers at three levels. A round bartizan is corbelled out high up at one corner.

Access: Freely accessible.
Reference: Guide by S. Forder.
Relations: It supplanted nearby Drumin.

BOYNE CASTLE can be found a mile and a half east of Portsoy. At a bend in the B9139, just after crossing a bridge over the Burn of Boyne, a footpath leads northwards across a field to this overgrown ruin hiding in the woods. It stands on a steep-sided promontory within a loop of the burn. A wide ditch cuts off the landward approach from the south, crossed by a causeway leading to the entrance. The ground plan suggests some Edwardian quadrangle in Wales, with its round corner towers and twin-towered gatehouse. It can only be supposed that the castle was a deliberate homage to that form but it is attributed to Sir George Ogilvy of Dunlugas, who inherited in 1575. James VI visited in 1589 but the castle was abandoned in the eighteenth century and has been crumbling ever since.

The castle is still very substantial in parts but is lamentably neglected and hopelessly overgrown. The large window openings – all torn into jagged holes – demonstrate that this is no Harlech, though the walls are well provided with shot holes. The most substantial part now is the west range, which comprised four storeys including the attic gables and the row of barrel-vaulted cellars at ground level. The first floor was presumably divided into the great hall and solar. Domestic buildings around the other sides of the courtyard have perished though a kitchen fireplace can be discerned against the east curtain. Three corner towers still rise high, one surmounted by a tall chimney, but the north-east tower is reduced to a stump. The shattered south curtain includes the remains of the gatehouse, actually two half-round towers flanking a simple gateway.

Access: Freely accessible with caution.

Relations: Late quadrangular castles with twin-towered gatehouses at Fyvie, Tolquhon and Dudhope.

CARNOUSIE CASTLE, in secluded grounds five miles west of Turriff, is a Z-plan tower house consisting of a long main block with round and square flanking towers. Well restored from dereliction, it was the seat of the Ogilvys of Carnousie and bears the year 1577 on a stair turret.

Access: Private.

CROMBIE CASTLE stands in its own grounds by the Crombie Burn, three miles north of Bridge of Marnoch. This is a small courtyard mansion of various dates. The oldest part still dominates: a severe L-plan tower house probably built by James Innes of Crombie in the 1540s.

Access: Private.

DRUMIN CASTLE stands on an eminence above the River Livet near its confluence with the Avon, in hilly terrain five miles south of Ballindalloch via the B9008. This is a severe oblong tower house, ruined but well maintained. Only two walls stand complete and one has perished entirely, exposing the barrel-vaulted undercroft. There are three storeys above, with small windows, fireplaces and corbels to support the vanished floor joists. Some lengths of parapet corbelling can be discerned. The entrance and staircase must have been in the fallen portion. The barony was granted by Robert II to his son, the infamous Wolf of Badenoch, but the tower is more likely to have been built early in the fifteenth century by Sir Andrew Stewart, one of his illegitimate sons. It was sold to the Gordons of Strathavon, who abandoned it in favour of nearby Blairfindy Castle. Drumin thus escaped the usual sixteenth-century makeover.

Access: Freely accessible (uphill walk).

Relations: Blairfindy.

EDEN CASTLE Four miles south-east of Banff on the A947, a sideroad (signposted Scatterty) heads west, leading in another mile and a half to this gaunt, ruined tower house. The front is virtually complete and shows a three-storey main block with traces of an attic above. There are several shot holes. At one corner is a square flanking tower with a doorway covered by the main block. A staircase in the tower ascended in straight flights to the first-floor hall. From there a turret stair, corbelled out in the re-entrant angle, led to the upper floors. The ground floor was divided into two vaulted undercrofts but little more than half of the main block is still standing. The rest has been torn down, along with the round flanking tower that stood at the corner diagonally opposite, thus forming a Z-plan. The tower house was built by the Meldrums of Eden, probably in the late sixteenth century. Extensive later additions have all vanished.

Access: Exterior only.
Relations: Z-plan tower houses such as Ballindalloch and Carnousie.

FINDLATER CASTLE occupies a dramatic promontory jutting into the North Sea. The car park is a mile west of Sandend. From there it is a half-mile walk to the cliffs, which provide a spectacular viewpoint for the castle on an isthmus lower down. The castle is first attested in 1246 and fell briefly to the Norsemen during King Haakon's invasion of 1263. However, the present very ruinous remains date from around 1445, when Sir Walter Ogilvy of Findlater obtained a licence to crenellate. In 1562, during the Earl of Huntly's revolt, his son Sir John Gordon (the real instigator of the rebellion) refused to admit Mary Queen of Scots. Her troops besieged the castle and Sir John was hanged after the Battle of Corrichie. Another Sir Walter Ogilvy abandoned the castle around 1600 for nearby Cullen House. It has been crumbling ever since.

The fearless may gingerly take the steep path down the isthmus, first reaching a long forework or barbican that is now just a massive stone base. Beyond is a featureless chunk of walling that may represent one side of a gate tower. On the promontory the main survivor is a truncated tower house, rising audaciously from a ledge on the steep western side of the rock. It seems destined one day to collapse into the cove below. One end of the structure even projects forward as a jamb. Both of the surviving storeys are below courtyard level but it is conjectured that there were at least two more floors above. Partly cut out from the rock face, they are barrel vaulted with gaping apertures marking the windows. Footings of a curtain wall extend to the northern tip of the promontory. There is a beehive dovecote close by on the mainland.

Access: There is a good view from the cliff top. Access to the promontory is possible but hazardous owing to steep drops.
Relations: Dramatic coastal ruins such as Castle Sinclair Girnigoe, Tantallon and Fast Castle (Berwickshire).

FINDOCHTY CASTLE overlooks a farm to the south-west of the village. This truncated ruin of an L-plan tower house, with a shallow staircase jamb, was probably built by Thomas Ord of Findochty late in the sixteenth century. Fragments of barmkin wall can also be seen.
Access: On farmland.

FORDYCE CASTLE stands among the houses of a neat village, three miles south-west of Portsoy. Fordyce was already a small burgh when the tower house was built so this is a rare surviving example of a fortified house in a communal setting. The handsome little L-plan tower was erected in 1592 by Thomas Menzies of Durn, a former provost of Aberdeen. Just three storeys high including the gabled attic, the original entrance is in the side of the jamb, though a later doorway has been cut through the main block as well. In the re-entrant angle between them, a stair turret projects on diminishing rows of ornate corbelling with cable moulding and other motifs. The stair turret is pierced by two rows of ornamental shot holes. A round bartizan, with a conical roof and more shot holes, is also corbelled out at one corner of the main block at attic level. On the other side of the jamb is a lower wing added around 1700. The remains of the medieval parish church are close by, with an armoured effigy.
Access: Exterior only (now a holiday let).
Relations: Drumlanrig's Tower and Queen Mary's House are other 'urban' tower houses.

INCHDREWER CASTLE, in a field four miles south-west of Banff, is a picturesque but derelict L-plan tower house with a stair turret on the side. Erected by the Currour family, probably in the 1540s, it forms one end of a very ruinous barmkin with a round corner tower.
Access: On farmland.

KININVIE HOUSE, on an estate a mile north of Dufftown, is a Victorian mansion incorporating an L-plan tower house at one end. The rare, semi-circular jamb is surmounted by a square caphouse. It was built sometime in the sixteenth century by the Leslies of Balquhain.
Access: Private.

KINNAIRDY CASTLE stands in its own grounds two miles north of Bridge of Marnoch. This truncated tower house followed the L-plan but the re-entrant angle has been filled in. Built by the Innes family around 1420, it is adjoined by a much lower sixteenth-century range.
Access: Private.

MILTON TOWER, otherwise known as Castle Oliphant, overlooks the River Isla on Station Road, near Keith railway station. At first glance it appears to be the shell of a small oblong tower house with a gabled top. However, the south gable end shows it to have been part of a longer range that has otherwise disappeared, along with the accompanying barmkin. Various openings embedded in this wall indicate four storeys, including an attic, while the fireplace (with restored lintel) no doubt heated the dais end of the hall. You can peer through the yett into the barrel-vaulted ground floor. The building is attributed to George Ogilvy of Milton around 1480, though the gables may be among the alterations recorded in 1601.

Access: Exterior only.

Relations: There were other Ogilvys at Auchindoun, Boyne, Carnousie and Findlater.

OTHER SITES   The shattered remains of a hall house on a promontory near Maggieknockater represent *Gauldwell Castle*, first raised by the Flemish settler Hugh de Freskin (see Duffus). *Inaltrie Castle* (near Lintmill) is marked by a chunk of curtain wall, believed to date from the thirteenth century. Among tower houses, stately *Cullen House* has grown out of a much-altered L-plan tower, the *Castle of Park* (near Cornhill) is a mutilated Z-plan, while *Kilnmaichlie House* (near Drumin) incorporates a jamb. *Pitlurg Castle* is reduced to a circular barmkin tower.

BERWICKSHIRE

Berwickshire is Border territory but the visitor expecting a counterpart to Northumberland may be disappointed. This sparsely populated Southern Upland county was a no man's land, often devastated during the centuries of Anglo-Scottish hostility. The Home (pronounced 'Hume') family was the most prominent, often holding the office of Warden of the Eastern March, but their simple courtyard castles have all but disappeared. Fast Castle at least retains its dramatic coastal setting. There are plain tower houses, akin to the pele towers on the other side of the Border. Bemersyde and Greenknowe are good examples, but most are private residences or badly ruined. The most interesting castles in the county are the two late, elongated tower houses of Nisbet and Thirlestane. Eyemouth has the impressive earthworks of a short-lived artillery fort. The Elizabethan fortifications at Berwick-on-Tweed are noteworthy but the much-besieged town has mostly been in English hands since its bloody capture by Edward I in 1296.

County reference: RCAHMS *Berwickshire*. BoS *Borders*.

BEMERSYDE HOUSE stands a mile and a half north of Dryburgh, on a country estate reached via a drive off the B6356. The handsome oblong tower house overlooks the River Tweed. It was built by the Haigs of Bemersyde, probably early in the sixteenth century. There are four main floors connected by a spiral stair in one corner, which continues to the plain parapet with angle bartizans. The first floor is barrel-vaulted and the hall above it has a small mural chamber. A two-storey attic, recessed within the parapet on its longer sides, was added later in the sixteenth century. Everything is much altered inside and the tower is now sandwiched between lower Georgian wings. The tower was burnt by the English in 1545. The thirteenth-century poet and seer Thomas the Rhymer is said to have predicted there would always be Haigs at Bemersyde, the best known so far being the First World War field marshal Douglas Haig.

Access: A functions venue. The gardens are open by appointment (HHA).

COWDENKNOWES HOUSE, on an estate a mile south of Earlston, was the seat of the Homes of Cowdenknowes. A square tower of 1554, originally forming one corner of a walled quadrangle, has been adapted to form the entrance to the present, mainly Victorian mansion.
Access: Private.

CRANSHAWS CASTLE, in its own grounds a mile west of Cranshaws village, is a picturesque, oblong tower house. Built by the Swintons of Cranshaws late in the sixteenth century, it has rounded corners and an embattled parapet rising from a simple row of corbels.
Access: Private (now a holiday let).

EVELAW TOWER is the decaying shell of a forbidding L-plan structure, standing amid farm buildings three miles north-east of Westruther. Both the ground and top floors are vaulted. It was probably built after William Douglas purchased the land from Dryburgh Abbey in 1576.
Access: On private land.

EYEMOUTH FORT occupies a rocky promontory jutting into the North Sea, just behind Eyemouth Holiday Park. It is a rare example of a purely military post erected during the age of the castle and demonstrates what was possible, if desired, against the growing power of artillery. The principles involved the use of earth ramparts to cushion the shock of cannonballs and angular bastions equipped with artillery to provide cross-fire. Although the stone facing has vanished, the ramparts and bastions still survive as prominent, grassy mounds. There are actually two successive forts here. The first was one of the group raised by the English in 1547 during the Rough Wooing. This consists of an earth rampart cutting off the promontory with a single bastion (the King's Mount) projecting from the middle. The fort was designed by the military engineer Sir Richard Lee and the bastion is a crude attempt to emulate the arrow-head bastions that had recently been pioneered in Italy. The fort was destroyed under the terms of the Treaty of Boulogne three years later. In 1557 a French expeditionary force landed and added an outer rampart on the lower ground in front. The bastions at either end are of the fully developed arrow-head type. They were soon emulated by Lee in the new town ramparts at nearby Berwick, which were commenced in response. The second fort also had a short life, being dismantled two years later as a result of the Treaty of Cateau-Cambresis.
Access: Freely accessible with caution (LA).
Relations: There were other English artillery fortifications at Thirlestane and Roxburgh.

FAST CASTLE Seven miles east of Cockburnspath, a side road off the A1107 (signposted to Dowlaw) ends at a farm. From here a coastal footpath descends in three-quarters of a mile to a dramatic rock rising sheer from the sea. The natural cleft separating the headland from the mainland is crossed by a rickety bridge. Its spectacular situation, 'overhanging the raging ocean', as Sir Walter Scott put it, amply compensates for the meagre remains. This was one of the Border castles held by the lords Home, though frequently in English hands. It is first recorded when it was recaptured from the English in 1410. The castle was largely rebuilt from 1521, after being destroyed by the Duke of Albany. An English plan, drawn shortly before they lost it to a surprise attack in 1548, helps identify the layout. The small summit was surrounded by a wall and divided into two courtyards crammed with buildings. Only fragments and foundations remain, except for a tall finger of masonry representing one corner of the hall block and a seaward gun battery forming a revetment against the rock. Destroyed again by the English in 1570, it has been crumbling ever since.

Access: Freely accessible with caution (uphill return).
Reference: *PSAS* (55).
Relations: The rebuilt castle of the lords Home at Hume.

GREENKNOWE TOWER, overlooking the A6105 on a knoll to the west of Gordon, is an unspoilt example of an L-plan tower house. Subsequent alterations have been minimal, though it was only abandoned as a residence in the nineteenth century. Now an empty shell, the tower lacks little more than its roof and floors. A few slits for handguns pierce the ground level, one of them commanding the entrance in the jamb. This doorway preserves its yett. A carved lintel above it bears the year 1581 and the initials of the builders, James Seton of Touch and his wife Janet Edmonstone, though they may have just remodelled and embellished an older structure. The ground floor of the tower, covered by a barrel vault, formed the kitchen. It retains a large fireplace and an aumbry at one end. A spiral staircase in the jamb ascends to the first-floor hall. From here the stair transfers to a rounded turret, corbelled out in the re-entrant angle. It rises to two upper floors in the main body of the tower and a series of small chambers in the jamb. Large windows light all three upper floors. Though once closed by iron grilles, they show the defensive limitations typical of the period. Round corner bartizans and crow-stepped gables enliven the roof line but, as usual by this time, there is no parapet. An adjoining hall range has vanished.

Access: Open daily (HES).
Relations: Touch House was another residence of the Setons of Touch.

HUTTON CASTLE overlooks the Whiteadder Water on an estate west of the village. This extensive mansion of various periods incorporates a modest, oblong tower house and a much-altered residential block, both erected by the Homes of Wedderburn in the sixteenth century.

Access: Private.

NISBET HOUSE lies in its own grounds off the A6112, two miles south of Duns. At first glance it looks like a tower house with an attached range, but the tower dates only from 1774 and is a rare Georgian homage to the genre. The attached range is actually an elongated variant of the tower house theme, nearly as high as the later tower, containing five storeys including the gabled attic. Cylindrical turrets clasp the southern corners of the building, a bartizan is corbelled out high up at the north-east corner, while two square turrets project from the north side. These contain wide spiral staircases lower down but the last flight to the attic is transferred to matching turrets that are corbelled out in the re-entrant angles. The entrance lies between them, leading into a ground-floor corridor linking three undercrofts and a kitchen, all barrel vaulted as usual. The hall and solar on the floor above have been transformed to reflect later tastes and so have the upper storeys. Thicker walling in the eastern half of the building suggest an older tower may be incorporated.

The remarkable feature here is the number of wide-mouthed gunports and heart-shaped shot holes peppering the harled walls at all levels, showing some lingering regard for security. The building is attributed to Sir Alexander Nisbet during the reign of Charles I. Such a structure would be old-fashioned by that time, and it could actually be older – Alexander inherited the property around 1609, which would be a more plausible time. Alexander showed great loyalty to the Royalist cause during the Civil War. This ruined him and he had to sell Nisbet to John Kerr. It is the latter's arms that appear in a panel over the entrance, though a panel containing the Nisbet arms has been reset above it.

Access: Private.
Relations: Thirlestane has a similar layout.

THIRLESTANE CASTLE, a Scottish Baronial mansion in extensive grounds overlooking the Leader Water, stands just to the north-east of Lauder. It is reached down a long drive off the A68. The complex occupies the site of Lauder Fort, one of the artillery defences raised by the English during their invasion of 1547 but soon abandoned. Sir John Maitland, Lord Chancellor to James VI from 1587, built the unusually elongated tower house that forms the core of the present complex before his death in 1595. However, the majestic south-west front of the mansion dates mostly from later times. The tall centre marks one side of Chancellor Maitland's building, but this end was heightened by his grandson John, Duke of Lauderdale, who ruled Scotland as one of Charles II's 'cabal' of five chief ministers. Lauderdale's architect, Sir William Bruce, added the lower square towers that flank the older block, while the side wings with matching towers date only from an expansion by the ninth Earl of Lauderdale in the 1840s.

The original tower house projects to the north-east behind this show front. Four storeys high including the gabled attic, it has round towers with gabled caphouses projecting at all four corners – an unusual conceit in Scotland. Bruce put balustrades on the twin towers on the south-west, but the north-eastern pair remain unspoiled. Stair turrets project in the re-entrant angles of all four towers. Three semi-circular turrets punctuate the long sides of the building, the middle pair containing spiral staircases. These turrets are connected by squat arches just below the wall-head. Bruce inserted the sash windows and the parapet balustrades.

Each level was divided into four main chambers, but the interior has been transformed by later generations into a stately home. Even the ground floor was converted into living rooms by the ninth earl, its barrel vaults being removed in the process. Among the portraits in the Panelled Room is one of Chancellor Maitland. From 1672 the Duke of Lauderdale remodelled the first floor as a series of majestic state rooms with one of the finest groups of plaster ceilings in Scotland. Nevertheless, Chancellor Maitland's original decoration must also have been of a high quality, as shown by a plaster ceiling of the Nine Worthies on the abandoned floor above.

Access: Open regularly in summer (HHA).

Reference: Guidebook by J. Jauncey.

Relations: Lennoxlove was another Maitland residence. Plaster ceilings at Craigievar, Glamis and Muchalls.

WEDDERLIE HOUSE is on a farm two miles north-east of Westruther. It dates mainly from 1680 but one end is formed by a small L-plan tower, the upper part of which rises above a row of corbels resembling machicolations. It was built by the Edgar family in the late sixteenth century.

Access: A functions venue.

OTHER SITES   Fragments of masonry on a low motte near Marygold recall *Bonkyll Castle*, destroyed during the Rough Wooing. *Hume Castle* (open), on a commanding knoll between Kelso and Greenlaw, was an early walled quadrangle of the lords Home. It saw much action during the conflicts of the sixteenth century but was slighted in the Civil War. The existing curtain wall with big mock battlements was built as a folly in 1794, though a chunk of old masonry survives within the courtyard. Incorporated in the Regency mansion of *Duns Castle* is an L-plan tower house, doubtfully attributed to Robert the Bruce's staunch supporter Thomas Randolph, Earl of Moray. It was heavily restored when the rest of the mansion was built. *Blanerne Castle* (near Edrom), *Carfrae Bastle* (near Carfraemill), *Cockburnspath Tower*, *Corsbie Tower* (near Legerwood), *Leitholm Peel*, *Old Thirlestane Castle* (near Thirlestane village), *Whitslaid Tower* (near Nether Blainslie) and the *Rhymer's Tower* at Earlston are all badly shattered tower houses.

BUTE COUNTY

Previously part of the Norse Kingdom of the Isles, these scenic islands in the Firth of Clyde formed the old county of Bute. Rothesay Castle on Bute itself was a power base of the Stewarts, hereditary High Stewards before they inherited the throne. It is notable for its circular, thirteenth-century curtain wall and its James IV gatehouse. On Arran, Brodick has been transformed from another early castle into a stately home, while Lochranza Castle was a hall house later converted into a conventional L-plan tower house. Another tower stands sentinel on Little Cumbrae. They are all on or very close to the coast. (There are ferries from Wemyss Bay to Rothesay, Ardrossan to Brodick and Claonaig to Lochranza.)

County reference: BoS *Argyll and Bute*; BoS *Ayrshire and Arran*.

BRODICK CASTLE romantically overlooks Brodick Bay, two miles north of Brodick harbour on the Isle of Arran. On the site of an older fortification, it was probably established as a castle after the Battle of Largs (1263) by Walter Bailloch, a younger son of the Lord High Steward, who married the Menteith heiress Mary. His descendants were the Stewart earls of Menteith and something of their original castle survives in a mutilated form. Robert the Bruce captured the castle from the English in 1307. The castle's stormy history also includes attacks by the English in 1406, the MacDonalds in 1455, the Campbells in 1528, the Earl of Lennox in 1544 and the Campbells once again in 1646, during the Civil War. James III granted the castle to the Hamiltons. James Hamilton, created first Earl of Arran in 1503, probably raised the tower house that forms the north-east end of the present complex. This tower was later doubled in size, perhaps by his son of the same name who was regent in 1542–54. A beleaguered Roundhead garrison strengthened the site in the 1650s. Later decay was halted from 1844 onwards when William, eleventh Duke of Hamilton, restored and greatly enlarged the castle as a residence.

The present castle consists chiefly of one long residential range. Its south-east front overlooks splendid gardens descending steeply towards the bay. The left half, including the ambitious entrance tower that now dominates the rest, is entirely Victorian and the join with the older work midway along is clearly visible. Of the remainder, the left half represents the later sixteenth-century extension, the right half the original oblong tower house. Both parts present a unified front of three storeys and a gabled attic, with regular rows of enlarged windows. However, there is continuous corbelling at the top of the original tower that is missing on the extension (though copied in the Victorian part). The north-eastern end of the complex forms a discordant cluster. A projection from the main block, with a half-round turret, connects with the gabled East Tower, positioned at right angles to the rest. These structures also date mainly from the sixteenth century in their present form, but their lower parts incorporate older work as detailed below. A stone gun battery beyond dates from the Roundhead occupation.

Internally the main suite of state rooms was transformed by the Duke of Hamilton and there is no sense of transition from the new part to the old, though the older parts are apparent in the greater thickness of their walls. The hall on the first floor of the original tower house is now the grand dining room. Beyond this, at ground-floor level a vaulted passage in the connecting block leads to the East Tower, with a spiral staircase in the half-round turret seen outside. This represents the gate passage of the Stewarts' original courtyard castle of the late thirteenth century. No doubt the flanking turret was originally duplicated on the other side of the passage. The East Tower may have originated as a barbican in front of this gate, while the tall plinth at the base of the later tower house may be a relic of an older hall block.

Access: Open daily in summer (NTS).
Reference: NTS guidebook.
Relations: Walter Bailloch's work at Castle Sween. Castles of the Hamilton earls at Cadzow, Craignethan and Kinneil.

KAMES CASTLE, in secluded grounds a mile west of Port Bannatyne on Bute, is a lofty oblong tower house with renewed battlements, built around 1500 by the Bannatynes of Kames but transformed internally. A courtyard of Victorian guest cottages has supplanted the barmkin.

Access: Private.

LITTLE CUMBRAE CASTLE   This island off the Ayrshire coast was a hunting ground of the early Stewart kings. The oblong tower house, which rises on an islet separated from the main island by a tidal channel, was probably built by Hugh Montgomerie, first Earl of Eglinton, after he was appointed keeper of the island in 1515. His brief was to 'resist ye personis yat waistis' the island, which might refer to poachers or pirates. By 1599 it was let to Robert Boyd of Badenheath, whose attempt to construct a harbour incurred the wrath of the fifth earl. He sent thirty men to ransack the tower and the inventory of the items taken offers an interesting glimpse of how such a residence was furnished. Roundhead troops are said to have burnt the tower in 1653 and it has lain empty ever since, making its excellent condition all the more remarkable.

The tower is a shell but virtually intact. It rises austerely to a double corbelled-out parapet, rounding to bartizans at three of the corners. A modern stair rises to the original first-floor doorway (a late example of such positioning). This leads into a handsome little hall with a lofty barrel vault and three quite generously sized window openings. A narrow kitchen with an arched fireplace was walled off at one end – an awkward feature also found in the neighbouring mainland castles of Fairlie, Law and Skelmorlie. From the entrance a spiral staircase in one corner of the tower leads down to two storerooms with wide-mouthed gunports. The same stair ascends to the second floor, now open to the sky but formerly partitioned into two residential rooms, both with fireplaces and latrines. It then continues to the parapet, providing an exhilarating view. Part of an attic gable remains.

Access: Freely accessible at low tide. There are periodic boat trips from Largs Yacht Haven (pre-book).

Relations: Fairlie, Law and Skelmorlie. Castles of the Montgomerie earls at Seagate and Lochranza.

LOCHRANZA CASTLE, near the northern tip of Arran on a spit jutting into Loch Ranza, is the shell of an L-plan tower house. At least it looks that way, but the main body of the tower originated as a strong hall house, probably in the mid-thirteenth century. The hall was at first-floor level over an undercroft. It retains slit windows and a straight mural staircase connecting with a blocked doorway high up, facing the loch. This was originally reached by a wooden stair. The hall is attributed to Dougall MacSween, who is credited with another hall house that partly survives in Skipness Castle, across Kilbrannan Sound in Kintyre. In 1262 Alexander III deprived the MacSweens of their possessions in favour of the loyal Walter Stewart, titular Earl of Menteith, who fought at the Battle of Largs the following year. Robert the Bruce, emerging from his mysterious hiding place, traditionally landed at Lochranza in 1306 to launch his bid for the Scottish throne. After Robert Stewart became king in 1371 the place was used as a royal hunting lodge, before being granted in 1452 to Alexander, Lord Montgomerie.

Towards the end of the sixteenth century the building was remodelled to its current form by one of the Montgomerie earls of Eglinton, five of whom successively bore the name Hugh. As seen from the approach, the left part of the hall block was partitioned off to form three storeys of residential chambers above a pair of undercrofts that were originally vaulted. These levels are connected by a spiral staircase. A prominent gable rises above the older wall-head, surmounted by a chimney and flanked by a round bartizan. In addition, a tall jamb was added at the right end of the hall block, rising five storeys to a corbelled-out parapet. Even now defence was clearly a consideration, windows remaining small and few in number, while the new ground-floor entrance (its yett still in place) is covered by a box machicolation at the wall-head. Abandoned since the eighteenth century, the walls are complete except for the collapsed rear corner of the chamber block.

Access: Open daily in summer (HES).

Relations: Skipness and the other MacSween stronghold at Castle Sween. Castles of the Montgomerie earls at Seagate and Little Cumbrae.

ROTHESAY CASTLE   This is one of the oldest stone castles of enclosure in Scotland, now thoroughly hemmed in by the little harbour town (a royal burgh) that surrounds it. Rare for its wet moat and even more so for its circular layout, it was a seat of the Stewart family long before they gained the throne. William the Lion granted the Isle of Bute to Alan fitz Walter, second High Steward of the royal household. The curtain wall was probably built by his son, Walter Stewart. It certainly existed by 1230, when Gillespec MacDougall arrived with a Norse fleet to reclaim the Kingdom of the Isles. Rothesay fell despite a determined resistance. *King Haakon's Saga* relates that 'the Norwegians hewed the wall with axes, because it was soft'. However, they abandoned Bute when a Scottish relieving fleet appeared. In 1263 King Haakon IV of Norway made another attempt to reclaim his ancestors' territory. This time the castle was occupied without resistance. Alexander, the fourth High Steward, led the Scots at the Battle of Largs, an inconclusive struggle that nevertheless persuaded Haakon to withdraw. The dispute was settled three years later when Scotland formally purchased the Isles. It was probably after this second occupation that Alexander added four flanking towers and a small gate tower to the circumference of the curtain.

Rothesay became a royal castle after Robert Stewart succeeded to the throne as Robert II in 1371. He used it as a retreat from the burdens of monarchy. His infirm son Robert III, self-styled 'worst of kings and most miserable of men', died here in 1406. James IV made the castle a base for his attempts to control the Hebrides and his additions are still defensive in character. His new gatehouse appears to have been left unfinished following his death at Flodden in 1513 and was only completed in the last years of James V. The castle resisted an attack by the Master of Ruthven (the heir of Lord Ruthven) in 1527 but fell to the Earl of Lennox, who supported the English invasion of 1544. Slighted during the Roundhead occupation, the castle was further damaged in 1685 during the Earl of Argyll's revolt against James VII. Decay ensued until the 1870s when that great castle restorer, the third Marquess of Bute, consolidated the ruins and re-flooded the moat.

Chronologically it is better to ignore the massive gatehouse projecting on the north and proceed around the edge of the moat. This surrounds the well-preserved curtain, one section still retaining its battlements. There is no sign of the breach made by the Norsemen in 1230. James IV heightened the curtain – some of the older battlements lower down can still be discerned to the right of the gatehouse. Unfortunately, three of the four round flanking towers have been reduced to their bases. The one that does survive on the north-west is a fine example of a thirteenth-century tower, rising from a plinth and well provided with arrow slits. It is called the Pigeon Tower owing to later use as a dovecote. Excavations within the round courtyard have uncovered some of the buildings that filled it but only the shell of St Michael's Chapel survives. This unusually grand castle chapel stood over an undercroft. Its builder is unrecorded but James IV seems more likely than his son. The Gothic windows with stumps of tracery show no sign of the Renaissance detail we might expect of James V.

Returning to the gatehouse, we can trace the evolution of this massive oblong block that projects into the moat. A small gate tower (the first of its kind in Scotland) was added in front of the original entrance arch by Alexander Stewart. Under James IV this became the inner end of a much longer, vaulted gate passage. An opening in the floor looks down into a sinister pit prison, while a postern opens onto the strip of land between the curtain and the moat. The small gateway at the far end of the passage, framed in a drawbridge recess, leads to a wooden bridge across the moat on the site of the original. Above the gate passage is a large hall, served by a gabled latrine turret. Its present completeness is due to the Marquess of Bute, who rebuilt the collapsed east wall and put on a new roof. Passages through the heightened curtain led to the two adjacent mural towers, while royal quarters occupied the ruinous top storey. James IV in fact had revived the old concept of the keep-gatehouse.

Access: Open daily in summer and regularly in winter (HES).

Reference: Guidebook by N. Scott. *Transactions of the Glasgow Archaeological Society* (9).

Relations: The Stewart castle at Dundonald. Work of James IV and V at Tarbert, Dumbarton, Dunbar, Tantallon, Falkland, Edinburgh, Holyrood, Stirling, Blackness and Linlithgow. Keep-gatehouses at Caerlaverock, Tantallon, Crichton and Doune.

OTHER SITES *Kildonan Castle*, a shattered fifteenth-century tower house on the south Arran coast, has decayed badly since it was sketched by MacGibbon and Ross. The handsome tower of *Wester Kames* (close to Kames Castle) on Bute was largely rebuilt in 1905.

CAITHNESS

Until 1196 the northernmost tip of mainland Scotland was ruled by Norse jarls, one of whom may have built the Castle of Old Wick – a ruined tower on a rocky promontory. Later the tempestuous Sinclair earls of Caithness enjoyed a considerable degree of autonomy. Along with a few cadet branches they are responsible for most of the county's castles. Tower houses progress from austere, fourteenth-century Braal to the contrasting Z-plans of Old Keiss and the Castle of Mey. Castle Sinclair Girnigoe is a ruined courtyard stronghold of the earls, while Bucholie's majestic setting compensates for the meagre remains. The multi-turreted tower house forming Dunbeath Castle was built as late as the 1620s. These castles cling mostly to the rugged coastline, often on the edge of a cliff, with a particular concentration on the east around Sinclair's Bay.

County reference: RCAHMS *Caithness*. BoS *Highland and Islands*.

ACKERGILL TOWER, overlooking Sinclair's Bay on an estate two miles east of Reiss, is a lofty oblong structure. Probably built early in the sixteenth century by William Keith, the second Earl Marischal, the parapet was renewed and the interior transformed by David Bryce in 1851.

Access: Formerly a hotel but now private.

BRAAL CASTLE   From Bridge Street in Halkirk an unsignposted road runs nearly a mile north-east to this house beside the River Thurso. The present Braal Castle is a mansion of the 1850s, now divided into flats, but in the woods just behind is the neglected ruin of a ramshackle tower house, almost square in plan with one canted corner. The inaccessible first-floor entrance has a straight mural staircase leading to the upper floor; there was no stair to the undercroft below, which must have been reached via a ladder. Prominent corbels projecting from the walls show that the floors were wooden throughout. The tower stands nearly to full height but has lost its parapet. Like the Castle of Old Wick, the thick walls and rather crude construction have prompted speculation about it being a keep from the Norse period. There is no actual evidence for this, and the tower seem more likely to date from the fourteenth century. A possible builder is Malise, the last mormaer of Caithness. It evidently existed by 1375, when the 'castle of Brathwell' was granted to

David Stewart, Robert II's son and Earl of Caithness. Along with the earldom it passed to the Sinclairs in 1455. Its inland position is almost unique among the castles of Caithness.

Access: Exterior only.
Relations: The Castle of Old Wick.

BRIMS CASTLE   About a mile and a half east of Forss, an unsignposted road runs north from the A836 to this unassuming structure in a splendid position overlooking the Pentland Firth. It could almost be dismissed as an abandoned Highland farmhouse but the main block is actually a small L-plan tower house of three storeys plus an attic. Chimneys surmount the crow-stepped gables. The ground floor, originally reached only via a trapdoor in the vault, has wide-mouthed gunports. The jamb, which is an early addition, contains a spiral stair. Unusually for its date, the original entrance was at first-floor level, in the jamb but not in the re-entrant angle. The lower wing is partly contemporary but greatly altered. Much of the barmkin wall survives in a ruined condition, with a small gateway. This modest structure was built late in the sixteenth century by Henry Sinclair of Broubster for protection against his kinsman, the Earl of Caithness. Standing by the entrance to a farm, it was occupied as recently as the 1970s but is now roofless.

Access: Well seen from the road.
Relations: Other Sinclair branches at Dounreay and Dunbeath.

BUCHOLIE CASTLE   About a mile south of Freswick on the A99, opposite a solitary bungalow, a gated track following the edge of a field descends towards the coast. The castle doesn't come into view until it is quite close. Bucholie or Bucholly Castle is to be recommended for its spectacular position on a promontory with sheer drops into the North Sea, but the remains are scant and destined to become scantier. The narrow neck of land connecting the castle to the mainland is interrupted by a rock-cut ditch. With the loss of the bridge the castle is hazardous to enter but you can see the little gate tower that forms the principal remnant, its outer wall pierced by a tall archway with two windows above. A long, walled passage, which could be pelted from above, leads onto the promontory. This carries the footings of two rows of barmkin buildings with no more than a lane between them – the steep cliffs rendered artificial defence superfluous. Although a Norse origin has been claimed, the present castle was built by the Mowats of Freswick, probably in the fifteenth century.

Access: There is a good view from the approach, but great caution is required.
Relations: Dramatic coastal settings such as the Castle of Old Wick, Castle Sinclair Girnigoe, Dunbeath and Old Keiss.

CASTLE OF MEY overlooks Pentland Firth on the north coast of Caithness, six miles west of John o' Groats off the A836. Orkney beckons in the distance. George Sinclair, fourth Earl of Caithness, obtained the lands of Mey in 1549. A plaque formerly above the entrance bore the year 1566, probably commemorating the completion of the building. The son to whom George gave it was murdered by his elder brother in 1573. The Sinclair earls remained in possession until their line died out in 1889. In 1952 the castle was purchased by the newly widowed Queen Elizabeth the Queen Mother, who had it restored it from a derelict state as her Highland retreat. She also revived its original name after centuries of being known as Barrogill Castle. It is now something of a shrine to her memory.

Externally this is a complete example of a Z-plan tower house, with square towers flanking the diagonally opposite corners of the main block. Its dominant feature is the south-east tower, which at five storeys is one stage higher than the rest. The corners of the towers and the main block have round bartizans corbelled out near the top, though their original conical roofs have been replaced by mock battlements. Wide-mouthed gunports guard the approach low down but all the windows are Georgian enlargements. Later additions obscure the original symmetry. In his remodelling from 1819 the architect William Burn added a dining room to the west of the main block and a large porch on the south front. The original doorway, flanked by the main block, is at the base of the north-west tower, which contains a wide staircase ascending to the former hall. The interior is a twentieth-century recreation of Burn's Regency elegance. Lower side wings to the north attest the presence of a barmkin but only the gateway in the end wall is original. Fine gardens complement the charming setting.

Access: Open daily in summer.
Reference: Guidebook by N. McCann.
Relations: Strongholds of the Sinclair earls at Castle Sinclair Girnigoe, Freswick, Old Keiss, Rosslyn and Ravenscraig (Fife).

CASTLE OF OLD WICK   Reached by a coastal path a mile or so south-east of Wick, this dramatic ruin crowns a narrow promontory with steep cliffs battered by the North Sea. Sheer drops isolate it on either side, while a rock-cut ditch preceded by a rampart cuts off the landward approach. Just behind the ditch rises a square-plan tower, occupying nearly the full width of the promontory. Built of the local basalt, it stands to near full height on two sides and part of a third. The rest has collapsed, taking all evidence of the entrance with it. There was no vaulting – the floor beams of its four storeys rested simply on internal offsets in the walls. A couple of slit windows show an uncompromising attitude to defence, though remains of simple fireplaces demonstrate some regard for domestic comfort.

It is possible that the 'Old Man of Wick' is one of Scotland's few early keeps. The similar Cubbie Roo's Castle in Orkney is known to have been built in 1145. Although history is silent here, Old Wick is traditionally attributed to Harald Maddadson, Jarl of Orkney, in the 1160s. Like the other early stone castles it would thus have been built by a Norseman, though William the Lion drove Harold out of his mainland possessions in 1196. Nevertheless, there is no hard evidence to confirm such an early date and it may in fact have been raised by the Sutherlands in the fourteenth century or the Oliphants in the fifteenth. What remains is little altered despite much later occupation. A siege is recorded in 1569, when the Oliphants were starved out by the Master of Caithness (the son of the earl). Two rows of buildings along the promontory behind the keep reflected this later history but are now just outlines in the turf.

Access: Freely accessible with caution (HES).
Relations: Cubbie Roo's. Castle Sween would be nearly as old.

CASTLE SINCLAIR GIRNIGOE is dramatically poised on a promontory jutting into Sinclair's Bay, four miles north of Wick off the road to Noss Head. Though badly ruined, it is in an exhilarating location. This is a castle of two parts. A long and narrow inner enclosure occupies the bulk of the promontory but is separated from the mainland by a roughly square outer

Castle Sinclair Girnigoe, Caithness

courtyard delimited by cliffs. It is likely that William Sinclair, created first Earl of Caithness in 1455, erected the inner courtyard, while George, the fifth earl, built or rebuilt the outer courtyard. In 1606 he changed the name from Girnigoe Castle to Castle Sinclair. However, the latter name became synonymous with the outer courtyard alone, perpetuating the myth that it was a separate stronghold rivalling rather than complementing the main enclosure. This impression is accentuated by the deep chasm between the two and the fact that both portions have their own tower house. The current designation unites them once again.

A ditch separates the outer courtyard from the mainland. The void is crossed by a modern bridge. The long, barrel-vaulted gate passage is flanked by George Sinclair's oblong tower house, positioned to command the entrance. This is reduced to little more than one gable end, precariously crowned by a chimney. Very ruinous ranges of lodgings overlook the cliff on the other two sides.

The natural chasm between the two courtyards was crossed by a drawbridge, with William Sinclair's older tower house rising immediately behind. Filling the narrowest part of the promontory, it contains the entrance to the inner courtyard – a narrow passage with a right-angled turn to confuse the unwary. This tower is the best-preserved portion of the castle, rising virtually to its full height of three storeys, plus basement rooms below and later attic gables above. It could be said to form an asymmetrical E-plan. A staircase jamb at the east corner is countered by a much bigger jamb on the north, containing the vaulted kitchen at ground level. Turf-covered footings of ranges extend on both sides of the promontory towards its north-eastern tip, leaving just a narrow lane in between. The sheer north-western face did not require artificial defence, but the gentler south-east front was guarded by a stretch of curtain wall with gun slits, now largely reduced to footings.

Sir John Campbell of Glenorchy purchased the earldom from the impoverished Sinclairs after the Civil War. George Sinclair of nearby Keiss, who claimed the title himself, seized and dismantled the castle in 1679 but his followers were massacred when the Campbells showed up in force soon afterwards. It has been a wind-battered ruin ever since, though the Clan Sinclair Trust has been consolidating the remains since 2003.

Access: The outer courtyard is freely accessible in summer but great care should be taken.

Relations: The Castle of Mey, Freswick, Old Keiss, Rosslyn and Ravenscraig (Fife) were other strongholds of the Sinclair earls.

DOUNREAY CASTLE is the decaying ruin of a simple L-plan tower house, stranded on the shore behind the defunct Dounreay nuclear power station. Built late in the sixteenth century by the Sinclairs of Dunbeath, it endured a siege by the Earl of Caithness' brother in 1614.

Access: On private land.

DUNBEATH CASTLE stands a mile and a half south of Dunbeath village, just off the A9. A long drive passes fine gardens before reaching this iconic stronghold, perched dramatically on a cliff above the North Sea. The paved forecourt takes the place of a ditch that cut off the promontory. The old portion faces the approach: an elongated oblong tower house of four storeys, including the gabled attic. It is well provided with shot holes. The antiquity of the structure is concealed beneath white harling and the regular fenestration is a Victorian enhancement. Tall bartizans with conical roofs clasp three corners high up, while the facade is punctuated by two half-round stair turrets that project from the first floor upwards. They are crowned by square caphouses. The renewed ground-floor doorway between them leads into a row of barrel-vaulted undercrofts, the one to the left a kitchen with the usual big fireplace. A straight staircase ascends in the thickness of the wall to the first floor, which was divided into a hall and solar, but this and the upper floors have been transformed by centuries of continuous occupation.

Although it may incorporate older work from a castle first mentioned in 1428, the existing tower house is said to have been built by the merchant John Sinclair of Geanies after he purchased the lands in 1624. That would make it a very late one, which is plausible in the far north. Royalist forces captured the castle in 1650, during the Marquis of Montrose's abortive attempt to put Charles II on the throne, but following his defeat at Carbisdale it was soon retaken. In 1853 the building was restored by the architect David Bryce and large additions were subsequently put up at the rear, extending to the cliff's edge. The Sinclairs finally sold up in 1945.

Access: A functions venue. The adjacent gardens are open by appointment.
Relations: Other Sinclair branches Brims and Dounreay.

FRESWICK CASTLE is a gaunt sentinel overlooking Freswick Bay and just a mile north of Bucholie Castle. This tall tower house was probably raised by the fourth Earl of Caithness in the 1580s. It originally followed the L-plan but the main block was later extended to form a 'T'.

Access: Private (now a holiday let).

OLD KEISS CASTLE A path from Keiss harbour runs north-east along the dramatic coastline, passing the scanty remains of two ancient brochs. A little further on is this ruined tower house, daringly perched on the edge of a sheer cliff overlooking Sinclair's Bay and looking likely to fall into it sooner or later. It was erected around 1600 by George Sinclair, fifth Earl of Caithness. The building was abandoned in 1755 for the present Keiss Castle a little further inland.

The calculated irregularity and decorative corbelling are hallmarks of the Scottish Baronial style, so the inevitable decay of the tower house is unfortunate. Owing to the confines of the site it forms a curious variant of the

Old Keiss Castle, Caithness

Z-plan. Two round flanking towers are placed at diagonally opposite corners but they do not comprehensively flank the main block. The tower at the east angle projects mainly to the south-east, while that on the west projects only south-westwards towards the sea. For most of its height the latter contained the spiral staircase, though the top is squared off to form a caphouse, the stair transferring to a turret alongside. A round bartizan is corbelled out at the south angle of the tower house, directly above the sea. Presumably the vanished entrance occupied the collapsed north corner. This fallen portion serves to expose the interior structure. Three storeys of chambers plus the remains of attic gables surmount the barrel-vaulted undercroft.

Access: Exterior only. Great caution should be exercised owing to the steep drops.

Relations: Castle Sinclair Girnigoe was also remodelled by the fifth earl. The Castle of Mey, Freswick, Rosslyn and Ravenscraig (Fife) were other strongholds of the Sinclair earls.

OTHER SITES   *Forse Castle*, on a spectacular coastal promontory near Latheron, is a fragment of a shattered tower that continues to crumble. Like Old Wick, a Norse origin has been doubtfully suggested. There was a Norse castle at *Thurso* but the existing ruin was a Victorian mansion. *Berriedale Castle* is reduced to courtyard fragments on another dramatic promontory cut off by a ditch. There were several other extraordinarily sited coastal towers that are now little more than sites, such as *Gunn's Castle* (near Bruan).

CLACKMANNANSHIRE AND KINROSS-SHIRE

These two contiguous counties north of the Forth punch above their weight when it comes to the castles within their small confines. Clackmannanshire has two early and impressive tower houses at Alloa and Clackmannan, the latter with a massive added jamb. Sauchie, smaller and later, is another good example. The tower house at Castle Campbell is just part of a courtyard complex of the earls of Argyll, while Menstrie preserves two sides of another courtyard castle. Kinross-shire's chief stronghold is the island castle of Lochleven, with an early royal tower house where Mary Queen of Scots was imprisoned. Burleigh is interesting for retaining part of its barmkin wall in addition to the tower house.

County reference: RCAHMS *Fife, Kinross and Clackmannan*. BoS *Perth and Kinross*; BoS *Stirling and Central Scotland* (for Clackmannanshire).

ALDIE CASTLE crowns a knoll on an estate a mile east of Powmill. This picturesque little complex is still dominated by an oblong tower house with corner bartizans, built by the Mercers of Aldie early in the sixteenth century. The annexes in front date from the following century.

Access: Private.

ALLOA TOWER rises in a precarious swathe of green in the centre of the little burgh. It is only the view from the parapet that reminds us of its urban setting. Over eighty feet high, this is one of the tallest and strongest of Scottish tower houses but its appearance has been softened by later alterations. Sir Robert Erskine obtained Alloa in 1368. He may have built the lower part of the oblong tower – changes in the masonry halfway up suggest a pause in building, at which point the tower was really just a hall house. It has been suggested that his grandson, another Robert, heightened the tower following his elevation as Lord Erskine in 1438.

In 1565 Mary Queen of Scots rewarded the Erskines with the earldom of Mar. Their prosperity was shattered by John, the sixth earl, who planned the 1715 Jacobite rising from Kildrummy Castle. Before fleeing into exile he expanded the tower house into a grand mansion. This was later demolished, leaving the tower alone once more, but the expansion explains the sash windows on the north-west facade. False windows were even inserted at each end, in denial of the immense thickness of the walls. The Classical doorway is an insertion of the same period, replacing a first-floor entrance at the rear. At the top the tower retains its stepped battlements, with round bartizans corbelled out at the corners and in the middle of the main front.

Internally the sixth earl transformed the character of the tower house. The main chambers were all reduced in size by the insertion of a large, circular staircase filling one end of the tower. At hall level on the first floor, a passage beside this grand stair leads to the original well, rising in a shaft from the base of the tower. The truncated hall forms a spacious chamber with mural passages between the deep window embrasures. A spiral stair in one corner ascends to the so-called Charter Room, the only vaulted stage in the tower, then up to the solar. Only at this level does the interior show its original dimensions, being above the plaster dome of the grand staircase. There is a fifth storey above, but the intervening floor has vanished. Hence the solar now appears to be a lofty chamber, covered by the original oak roof. It is perhaps fortunate that the sixth earl had to flee, because his unrealised plans included the removal of these rare old timbers in favour of a roof garden with a fish pond!

Access: Open regularly in summer (NTS).

Reference: *Alloa Tower and the Erskines of Mar* (Clackmannanshire Field Studies Society).

Relations: Kildrummy. Braemar and Mar's Wark (Stirling) are later seats of the Erskine earls.

ARNOT TOWER, a mile west of Auchmuirbridge, is a ruined oblong tower house of ashlar masonry with an adjoining stretch of barmkin wall. Probably built after 1507, when Walter Arnot was made a baron, the tower stands in the gardens of a successor mansion that shares its name.

Access: On private land.

BURLEIGH CASTLE is an unusual and striking sight beside the A917, half a mile east of Milnathort. In addition to the ubiquitous tower house, we find an unusually bold flanking tower and a short stretch of curtain wall linking them. They formed the west side of an oblong barmkin. The linking wall has an arched gateway flanked by wide-mouthed gunports, with an empty heraldic panel above. The modest oblong tower house is now a shell, rising four storeys to a corbel table that rounds at three corners to support vanished bartizans. Above that are the ruined gable ends of an attic, recessed within the parapet. A ground-floor doorway leads to the vaulted undercroft, a spiral staircase in one corner ascending to the upper floors. The other tower, which is still roofed, forms a three-quarter circle in its lower two storeys to flank the west and (vanished) south sides of the barmkin. There are more gunports near the base and shot holes below the rather large windows. The upper storey is corbelled out to form an oblong caphouse. In contrast, the tower house does not project beyond the wall at all.

Carved on the gable of the flanking tower are the year 1582 and the initials of Sir James Balfour and his wife Margaret. This tower and the barmkin wall are no doubt theirs but the tower house was built by a previous Balfour of Burleigh, perhaps early in the sixteenth century. Sir James' son Michael was a favourite of James VI, who visited several times. The last Balfour laird, already in exile after shooting dead a love rival, was dispossessed for his role in the 1715 Jacobite rising.

Access: Open regularly in summer (HES).

Relations: Good barmkins at Old Breachacha, Auchindoun and Muchalls.

CASTLE CAMPBELL, originally known as Castle Gloom, occupies a promontory with steep drops on either side to the Burn of Sorrow and the Burn of Care. Such names are an injustice to this picturesque tower house and courtyard ensemble, spectacularly positioned high up in the Ochil Hills, a mile north of Dollar. An older tower of the Stewarts of Lorne, raised over a truncated motte, was destroyed in 1466 by Walter Stewart in a family dispute. The present tower house, perhaps incorporating something of the older one, was built by Colin Campbell, first Earl of Argyll, who married the Stewart heiress. Made Lord Chancellor in 1483, he obtained royal approval to change the name to Castle Campbell. His son Archibald probably added the south range before his death at Flodden in 1513. The other buildings date from the time of the seventh earl, another Archibald, who inherited in 1584. Hence the castle expanded in the course of a century from a tower house to a courtyard mansion, but the fully developed complex had a short existence. In 1654 it was burnt by Royalist rebels. No attempt was made to repair the damage, the ninth earl moving to Argyll's Lodging in Stirling. Apart from the re-roofed tower house and east range, the castle is now a ruin.

Rising four storeys to a corbelled-out parapet with shallow corner bartizans, the tower house dominates the castle from the north-east corner of the courtyard. It retains the uncompromisingly defensive style of earlier Scottish tower houses. The north facade, overlooking the approach, is particularly severe, with just one narrow window on the top floor. By contrast, the late sixteenth-century curtain wall bounding the north and west sides of the courtyard is hardly a serious obstacle, though the diminutive gatehouse close to the tower house is flanked by wide-mouthed gunports. Vanished lodgings against this wall would have made the courtyard even smaller than it is now.

The second earl's ambitious range fills the south side of the courtyard, supplanting his father's tower house as the main residence except in times of danger. Most of the upper floor formed the great hall. Its outer wall is pierced by a row of windows overlooking the promontory, showing little concern for defence. Beneath the hall, a row of barrel-vaulted undercrofts is fronted by a ruinous corridor with stair turrets at either end. A vaulted passage leads to the apex of the promontory, once occupied by terraced gardens.

Closing the narrow gap between the tower house and the hall block is the east range, its little Renaissance loggia of just two arches facing the courtyard. This was built by the seventh earl. He also added a jamb to the tower house, thus converting the oblong structure into a T-plan. The jamb contains a broad spiral staircase, supplanting an older stair in one corner of the tower. It ascends to the first-floor entrance, from which a side passage leads to a prison cell. Straight ahead is the vaulted hall, retaining a large fireplace. A mural stair descends to the undercroft, also vaulted, with its own doorway from the courtyard. Returning to the main spiral stair, we ascend to the two upper storeys of the tower house, no doubt forming the first earl's solar and bedchamber. The seventh earl added the ribbed vault over the bedchamber (note the two green man carvings at the apex), showing that the tower still contained important accommodation. He also added the gabled attic, though this has been rebuilt.

Access: Open daily in summer and regularly in winter (HES – uphill walk).
Reference: Guidebook by C. Tabraham.
Relations: Castles of the Campbell earls at Carrick, Innis Chonnell and Skipness. Lauriston, Drummond and Queen Mary's House are other T-plan tower houses.

CLACKMANNAN TOWER stands in a field to the west of the old burgh, commanding a view from the Ochil Hills to the Firth of Forth. It began as an oblong tower house, erected according to tradition by Robert the Bruce himself as a hunting lodge. Another Robert Bruce, illegitimate son of David II, obtained Clackmannan in 1359 and is more likely to be the builder. Towards the end of the fifteenth century the Bruces heightened the tower and added a jamb on the south side. Unusually, this jamb is almost as big as the main body of the tower and rises an extra storey. Both portions are built in fine ashlar, but windows are few and small. The jamb is distinguished by a machicolated crown, whereas the reconstructed parapet of the main block is carried on a double row of corbels. Catherine Bruce took it upon herself to knight Robert Burns with Robert the Bruce's supposed sword when he visited in 1787. She was the last Bruce of Clackmannan and after her death the tower was abandoned.

When the tower house was extended into an L-plan, a ground-floor entrance was created in the side of the flanking jamb for greater security (the re-entrant angle has subsequently been filled in with a low staircase annexe). Around 1600 this arrangement was superseded by a Renaissance portal in the opposite (east) wall, reached from a forecourt of which some footings survive. The ground floor of the main block is the customary vaulted undercroft, once divided into two levels by a wooden floor. A mural stair rises to the hall, another barrel-vaulted compartment that was nevertheless of some dignity, as the monumental fireplace shows. At this level the doorway forming the original entrance to the fourteenth-century tower was retained as the entrance to the jamb. Owing to the loss of their wooden floors the storeys above the hall now appear to form one tall chamber, covered by a modern roof. In fact, there are four levels here. The first two mark the limit of the original tower house. Another storey was added in the fifteenth century, with a mural passage along one side. At the top are attic gables, added later still. The unvaulted jamb, which has lost all its floors, housed a kitchen at hall level and further accommodation in the storeys above. It suffered from subsidence caused by mining below. In 1955 a collapse left a deep gash in the middle of the east front, but this has been rebuilt using the original materials.

Access: Exterior only (HES). There are occasional open days.
Reference: *The Tower of Clackmannan* by T. C. Gordon.
Relations: Early tower houses such as Alloa, Lochleven, Drum and Threave.

CLEISH CASTLE, a mile west of the village, is an L-plan tower house of ashlar masonry. Probably begun by Robert Colville of Cleish in the mid sixteenth century, but later heightened, it is prominently gabled but plain at the wall-head. The blocked barmkin gateway stands nearby.

Access: Visible from the road.

DOWHILL CASTLE is in the grounds of Dowhill House, two miles east of Cleish. This ruin was a seat of the Lindsays of Dowhill. It began around 1500 as a small oblong tower house, later extended into a longer range with a round corner turret. A barmkin tower also survives.

Access: On private land.

LOCHLEVEN CASTLE is an evocative island ruin, comprising an early tower house and a walled courtyard. Tree-clad Castle Island in Loch Leven was little larger than the castle itself until the water level was lowered in the nineteenth century. A castle existed here by 1301, when Sir John Comyn drove off an English besieging force. Robert the Bruce, departing from his usual policy of destroying castles during the Wars of Independence, chose it as a residence. By 1335 Lochleven was one of only five castles still loyal to the exiled David II. In that year Alan Vipont successfully defended it against the English, who were fighting to put Edward Balliol on the throne. It is possible that the five-storey tower house still dominating the castle already existed by that time, but it is more likely to have risen later in the century, perhaps after David II returned from English captivity in 1357. It is thus an early royal tower house (compare David's Tower at Edinburgh), but in 1390 the castle was granted to a branch of the powerful Douglas family.

Lochleven Castle, Kinross-shire

The oblong tower house is massive, plain and impossible to date with any precision. It is virtually intact though now roofless. A corbelled-out parapet is the only embellishment, with round bartizans projecting at three of the corners. The original entrance is placed at second-floor level for maximum security and would have been reached as now by a removable wooden staircase. It leads into an austere space that would have formed the hall, which is thus unusually high up in the tower. You can look up into the solar above, with a window recess that served as a simple oratory, and the top floor (probably occupied by retainers). A corner spiral stair leads up to these chambers and down to the vaulted kitchen below. At the bottom is an undercroft, also vaulted. This was once only accessible from a hatch in the barrel vault, the ground-floor doorway being a much later insertion.

The tower house abuts the north wall of a low curtain wall surrounding a roughly square courtyard. In its current form it was probably built soon after the tower, though it seems to incorporate earlier work on two sides. A simple archway beside the tower house is the sole entrance now, though there is a blocked postern in the wall opposite. This entrance was only defended by a gate, implying that the vanished outer courtyard had more substantial defences of its own. The north and east sides of the curtain are straight. The other two follow a more irregular course, determined by the footings of the earlier curtain that probably existed at the time of the 1335 siege. Among the foundations of courtyard buildings is the great hall, its gable end rising above the curtain. Originally there were no flanking towers. The circular, four-storey Glassin Tower, projecting boldly at the south-east corner, was added by Sir Robert Douglas of Lochleven after he inherited the castle in 1540. Its lower floor contains wide-mouthed gunports commanding two sides of the curtain.

Lochleven is haunted by tragic memories of Mary Queen of Scots. Having stayed as a guest here in 1563, debating with John Knox, she returned a prisoner in 1567 after her ignominious surrender at Carberry Hill. Here she miscarried twins and was coerced into signing her abdication. After ten months' confinement (first in the Glassin Tower and later in the tower house) she escaped with the help of her jailor's brother, only to suffer swift defeat at the Battle of Langside and long imprisonment in England. The former Regent Morton spent his final years here before his execution in 1581. Afterwards the castle gradually fell into decay.

Access: Open daily in summer (HES). A boat service operates from Kinross.
Reference: Guidebook by C. Tabraham. *PSAS* (116).
Relations: David II's work at Edinburgh Castle. The early tower houses at Alloa, Drum, Dean and Threave.

MENSTRIE CASTLE is an improbable survivor in a workaday village beneath the Ochil Hills, four miles north-east of Stirling. The west range and part of the south range remain of a quadrangular mansion, probably built by Sir William Alexander soon after he obtained Menstrie in 1598. Despite its stocky appearance, the castle has only limited pretensions as a defensive structure. For once, a tower house never formed part of the complex and there is even a surprising lack of shot holes, except for a couple of ornamental ones in the round bartizan corbelled out at the south-west angle. Both ranges are handsomely lit on the two upper floors, though the windows would have been protected by iron grilles. In the middle of the west range an ornate, round-headed entrance archway is set in an ashlar panel. It leads into the barrel-vaulted gate passage. The rest of the quadrangle has vanished and the current courtyard is completed by modern housing.

Sir William held high office under James VI and was later created first Earl of Stirling. An abortive attempt to found a Scottish colony in Nova Scotia resulted in his impoverishment. In 1645 the mansion was burnt by the Marquis of Argyll during his Civil War duel with the Marquis of Montrose. Having narrowly escaped demolition, the surviving ranges were converted into flats in 1961.

Access: Exterior only (LA).
Relations: Late courtyard castles such as Fyvie, Tolquhon and Dudhope.

SAUCHIE TOWER is a worthy companion to the larger tower houses at Alloa and Clackmannan nearby. It stands a short distance to the north-west of Fishcross, overlooking the River Devon off Collyland Road. The tower was probably built by Sir James Schaw, Comptroller of the Royal Household. He joined the 1488 revolt against his patron, James III, and was rewarded by James IV with the captaincy of Stirling Castle. The tower forms the usual massive oblong of the period, finely built of ashlar with relatively small window openings even high up. A dainty caphouse crowns the spiral stair, while the corbelled-out parapet rounds at the corners into tiny bartizans. The gabled attic, a later addition, was largely rebuilt in 2002 when the tower house was restored from dereliction by the Friends of Sauchie Tower.

A round-headed doorway at ground level leads into a passage through the thickness of the wall. There is a guard chamber on one side and a spiral staircase on the other. A wooden floor, attested by the surviving corbels, divided the vaulted undercroft into two levels. Mural chambers, including a narrow kitchen, are accommodated at each level in the entrance wall, which is thicker than the others. The stair ascends to the hall, a handsome chamber with a wash basin in an arched recess. Its large fireplace has a flat lintel supported on columns. In the solar above, a vaulted recess occupies the thick wall on the entrance side. These main chambers are well provided with mural latrines, but the next floor is an ill-lit space for guards or servants.

Access: Exterior only (LA). There are occasional open days.

Relations: Nearby Alloa and Clackmannan. There is also an Old Sauchie House in Stirlingshire.

TULLIBOLE CASTLE lies in secluded grounds a mile east of Crook of Devon. It consists of an oblong tower house and a slightly lower extension with a projecting jamb, added by the advocate John Halliday in 1608. An inscription over the doorway invokes peace and prosperity.

Access: A functions venue with occasional open days.

OTHER SITES   For once there is nothing in this category.

DUMFRIESSHIRE

Motte-and-bailey earthworks recall the Norman presence in the south west. The first major castle is the triangular, moated stronghold of the Maxwells at Caerlaverock, which eventually attained its intended form despite two slightings during the Wars of Independence. Auchencass and (probably) Morton are other castles of that period that escaped destruction by Robert the Bruce. However, they are much less well preserved, apart from Morton's hall. Lochmaben Castle is a curious English outpost of the fourteenth century, also fragmentary apart from the wing walls crossing the moat, while the Crichtons created a small and now ruinous quadrangle at Sanquhar in the fifteenth.

Otherwise, this is the usual tale of tower houses, beginning with the gaunt, fourteenth-century structure at Torthorwald, and reaching a peak in the following century with mighty Comlongon Castle, noted for its mural chambers and machicolated crown. In terms of numbers, the sixteenth century predominates as usual. Bonshaw and Repentance towers are still very austere, but the mood lightens with the corbelled-out parapets and corner bartizans of Gilnockie and Hoddom. It culminates in the riot of turrets and caphouses for which Amisfield Tower is noted. A number of other towers survive as restored private homes or shattered ruins in fields. This is to be expected in a county that was in the front line of the Border conflicts, with defence coordinated by the Warden of the Western March (a hereditary post of the lords Maxwell). When it was not a corridor for invading armies, the county was frequently devastated by reiving and feuding, though Border families like the Armstrongs of Gilnockie gave as good as they got.

County reference: RCAHMS *Dumfriesshire*. BoS *Dumfries and Galloway*.

AMISFIELD TOWER, long the seat of the Charteris of Amisfield family, is one of the most attractive of the later tower houses, rising impressively to a Scottish Baronial skyline. Round corner bartizans, with shot holes pointing downwards, are corbelled out near the wall-head of this square-plan tower. They are capped by semi-conical roofs that recede into the crow-stepped gables of the main block. As usual in the later towers, there is no parapet. A round corner turret marks the position of the spiral stair. Higher up this turret squares out into a three-storey caphouse, crowned by its own gable. Behind it another caphouse, higher still, crosses the east gable of the tower house.

Nevertheless the exterior is austere for most of its height and the tower is actually believed to date from early in the sixteenth century, with the upper embellishments added nearly a century later. Wide-mouthed gunports threaten at ground level. The fenestration is reasonably generous, but all windows were barred by iron grilles. A dormer window contains a machicolation, poised high above the entrance on the south front. Two panels on this front bear the arms and initials of Sir John Charteris and his wife, Agnes Maxwell of Hoddom. On one of them the year 1600 is inscribed – probably commemorating the completion of the alterations.

The entrance passage is flanked on one side by a tiny guardroom, and on the other by the straight staircase leading to the first floor. Above the barrel-vaulted undercroft is the retainers' hall. A spiral staircase then ascends to the second floor, retaining a fireplace with carved side columns and a faded frieze. This is the tallest room in the tower, serving as a more private hall for the laird. The third floor was divided into two bedrooms with tiny closets in the bartizans. Owing to the loss of the intervening floors this level is now open to the attic. The crowning roof retains much original timber. Each level of the tower house is disturbed by a jutting staircase projection – the consequence of a wide spiral stair in a tower without a jamb. The little chambers in the two caphouses are reached by a narrower spiral stair between them.

A successor mansion stands close by. Its oldest part was built in 1631 by John's son of the same name, once more settled conditions had arrived. The tower house was retained for service accommodation and stands amid fine gardens a mile north-west of Amisfield Town.

Access: There are occasional open days.
Reference: Guidebook by A. M. Maxwell-Irving.
Relations: The Scottish Baronial crowns at Craigievar, Glamis and Crathes.

AUCHENCASS   Two miles north of Beattock, off the B7076, a lodge marks the entrance to the present Auchen Castle, a mansion of 1849. Continuing past it, a road, then a track, wind up to its predecessor, in a field behind Lawesknowe Farm. Though sadly crumbling, this square enclosure is still substantial in parts. Its massive curtain wall rises from a wider stone base, suggesting that the intended thickness was reduced in the course of building. There are remains of a staircase that led to the wall walk. The stumps of solid, round towers survive at two corners and at least one more existed. No windows pierce the curtain, though timber domestic buildings presumably stood against it. The gateway occupied the fallen stretch on the north. Beyond the surrounding ditch is a broad outer rampart. These featureless ruins probably represent an early castle of enclosure. Roger de Kirkpatrick was here in 1306, so it may be one of those castles built by supporters of Edward I. Thomas Randolph, the redoubtable Earl of Moray who probably built Morton Castle, is another possible contender. Evidently Auchencass evaded Robert the Bruce's

policy of castle demolition. The slender south-east corner turret was probably added under the Douglas earls of Morton, but the absence of any later adaptations suggests an early abandonment.
Access: Freely accessible with caution.
Reference: *PSAS* (65).
Relations: Morton.

BARJARG TOWER occupies an estate four miles north-west of Auldgirth. At one corner of this mainly nineteenth-century mansion is an altered L-plan tower house with prominent round corner bartizans. It was probably built after Thomas Grierson acquired the lands in 1587.
Access: The gardens are open occasionally.

BONSHAW TOWER, just to the south-east of Kirtlebridge, stands on a bluff overlooks the Kirtle Water. Just six miles from Gretna, the tower is the very epitome of a Border stronghold. This massive oblong is small-windowed and little altered since it was built. Of four storeys including the attic, the tower rises to a corbelled-out parapet without battlements. Above the entrance (within a later porch) is a Latin inscription meaning 'honour and glory to God alone'. It leads into the vaulted undercroft, with shot holes and a little prison in one corner. A spiral stair in one corner ascends to the hall, with a large fireplace and a Gothic aumbry, then past a little stone sink to the upper floors. The existing tower was probably built by Edward Irving of Bonshaw soon after the English blew up a previous house here in 1570 (there had been other English attacks). From 1585 Lord Maxwell besieged it four times without success during a protracted feud with the Irvings, who later got together with the Johnstones and killed him in a skirmish nearby. The tower now stands intact alongside a successor mansion built in 1770.
Access: A functions venue.

CAERLAVEROCK CASTLE AND OLD CASTLE   An impressive ruin overlooks the Solway Firth, eight miles south of Dumfries off the B725. Long the chief seat of the powerful Maxwell family, Caerlaverock enters recorded history in 1300. In that year Edward I captured the castle. The siege is commemorated in an epic poem, *The Roll of Karlaverock*, and though lasting only two days it was a hotly contested affair with the furious exchange of arrows, bolts and catapult stones (there is a replica trebuchet outside the castle). Edward allowed the Maxwells to remain here, in return for their support, but in 1312 Sir Eustace Maxwell changed sides. Having resisted an English attempt to recapture the castle, he made the great sacrifice of destroying it in accordance with Robert the Bruce's strategy. After David II's capture at Neville's Cross in 1346, the Maxwells were forced to submit again to the English. This led to another slighting by the Scots in 1355.

Caerlaverock Castle, Dumfriesshire

The lords Maxwell became hereditary wardens of the war-torn Western March and their castle stood in the front line of Border warfare. Caerlaverock was occupied by the English in 1544, during the Rough Wooing, and captured again by the Earl of Sussex in 1570. Robert Maxwell, first Earl of Nithsdale, rebuilt the domestic accommodation in the 1630s. Peace seemed to have descended on the Borders at last, but the splendid new buildings had a very short life owing to the earl's loyalty to Charles I. In 1640 the castle surrendered to the Covenanters after a three-month bombardment. Despite the generous terms negotiated, the Covenanters slighted the castle for the last time.

The present Caerlaverock Castle was not the first here. Hidden in woods a short distance to the south is the oblong site of the Old Castle, bounded by a now-dry moat and an outer rampart. Excavations have exposed its mid-thirteenth-century foundations: the surrounding wall has square turrets projecting diagonally at three of the corners, while domestic buildings filled the little courtyard. The site was prone to flooding from the Solway and Sir Herbert de Maxwell transferred to the new location in the 1270s. The regular layout with flanking towers shows an awareness of developments in England but the plan is most unusual. It is almost an equilateral triangle, with a twin-towered gatehouse at the northern angle and circular towers at the other two.

The walls and towers rise directly from a wide, wet moat – a rarity in Scotland. Beyond is a concentric outer moat, now dry.

Despite the uniform layout, the walls of Caerlaverock Castle reveal a complicated building history. Herbert de Maxwell's ashlar masonry is evident only in the gatehouse and the footings of the north-west curtain wall. Evidently the destruction of 1312 was thorough, though it is possible that the castle was still incomplete at that time. Most of the existing masonry is fourteenth century but from two building campaigns, probably interrupted by the second slighting of 1355. It is surprising that the castle was rebuilt to the original specification after the age of the tower house had dawned. Two sides of the castle remain virtually intact. Apart from the gatehouse, the chief feature is Murdoch's Tower – supposedly the prison of Murdoch Stewart, Duke of Albany (d.1425). This slender, four-storey cylinder at the western apex of the triangle is crowned by the corbels of a machicolated parapet. However, the matching tower at the east angle was demolished to its base by the Covenanters, along with most of the south curtain.

Unusually for a Scottish castle, the gatehouse is the dominant feature. With its twin round towers flanking the entrance it is a rare example of a keep-gatehouse, more familiar in Wales. Only the gate passage and the western flanking tower are Herbert's. The eastern tower was built or rebuilt in the fourteenth century, while the entire structure was remodelled by Robert, Lord Maxwell (d.1488). He built the shallow forework between the flanking towers, containing a recess for the drawbridge. He also added a machicolated crown, again represented now only by the corbels. Above them, the caphouse with round bartizans dates from the late sixteenth century, along with the wide-mouthed gunports piercing the flanking towers. A plaque over the entrance depicts the stag emblem of the Earl of Nithsdale. The entrance arch, retaining its portcullis groove, leads into a narrow gate passage flanked by guard chambers. The three upper floors may have contained the constable's residence, starting with a hall (later subdivided) over the gateway. Another of Lord Maxwell's additions is the soaring arch covering the inner end of the gate passage. It contains a nasty surprise at the summit in the form of a murder hole.

The courtyard within is all the smaller owing to the high buildings that surround it, the oldest range standing against the north-west curtain. This austere block, later serving as retainers' lodgings, was erected in the fifteenth century by Lord Maxwell. Opposite is the majestic shell of the Nithsdale Apartments, with its rows of windows topped by ornate pediments. This masterpiece of the Scottish Renaissance was built in 1634 by the Earl of Nithsdale. He also remodelled the great hall and solar on the south side of the courtyard, now fragmentary owing to the 1640 slighting.

Access: Both sites are open daily (HES).

Reference: Guidebook by D. Grove and P. Yeoman. *PSAS* (57). *The Siege of Caerlaverock* by C. Scott-Giles.
Relations: Mature castles of enclosure such as Kildrummy, Rothesay, Old Inverlochy and Bothwell. Keep-gatehouses at Rothesay, Tantallon, Crichton and Doune. Towers of the lords Maxwell at Buittle and Mearns.

CLOSEBURN CASTLE, in its own grounds a mile south-east of Closeburn village, once stood on a promontory jutting into a now-drained loch. Attributed to Sir Thomas Kirkpatrick around 1390, this austere, oblong tower house with phoney battlements is vaulted at three levels.
Access: Private (now a holiday let).

COMLONGON CASTLE is one of the finest fifteenth-century tower houses in Scotland. Complete and unspoiled, it is notable for the mural chambers that supplement the main rooms on each floor. The tower was built by the Murrays of Cockpool. It could be contemporary with Borthwick (the 1430s) and probably predates the licence to crenellate granted to John Murray soon after 1500 (the exact year in unclear). The tower house forms a massive oblong, magnificently severe between the plinth and the embattled, machicolated

Comlongon Castle, Dumfriesshire

parapet. On each floor small windows are symmetrically distributed. A particularly strong yett still guards the ground-floor entrance. This leads into a passage through the great thickness of the wall, with a doorway to the spiral staircase in one corner. At the end of the passage is the barrel-vaulted undercroft, once divided into two storeys by a wooden floor as demonstrated by an offset in the walls. These levels are only lit by slits and no weakening mural chambers pierce the walls here. There is a well in the floor.

The spiral staircase is supplemented by a service stair in the opposite corner of the tower. Both ascend to the hall, a lofty chamber covered by a beamed ceiling. A grand fireplace occupies the west (dais) end, with carved capitals and a frieze over the lintel. Nearby is an aumbry framed by an ornate Gothic arch. Two window recesses with stone seats pierce the south wall but there is only one on the north, because part of this wall is occupied by a mural chamber. Another chamber contains the hatch to a pit prison beneath. Other small chambers, one a latrine, fill the two corners not occupied by stairs. The kitchen is curiously squeezed into an alcove at the east end, divided from the hall by a later stone screen.

The main spiral staircase continues to the two upper storeys, now one big space owing to the loss of their dividing floor. They repeat the basic layout of the hall, with windows and mural chambers in virtually the same positions. When the solar was later partitioned into two rooms, the large fireplace was divided down the middle. One chamber in the north wall served as an oratory. Twin fireplaces suggest that the top floor was always divided into two bedrooms. The spiral stair rises to the parapet. Only this level shows significant later alteration. Around 1600 gabled caphouses were added at two corners, while the entire western parapet was roofed over to form a watching gallery.

A Victorian mansion stands beside the tower house. The earls of Mansfield, descendants of the Murrays, kept the tower in good repair while not attempting to modernise it. They stand nine miles south-east of Dumfries, in extensive grounds just west of Clarencefield. (See plan on page 359.)

Access: The mansion was a hotel but is currently closed.
Reference: *PSAS* (126).
Relations: Borthwick. The tower house oratories at Affleck, Dean and Lochleven.

ELSHIESHIELDS TOWER, in its own grounds three miles north of Lochmaben, is a modest L-plan structure with big corner bartizans and a taller jamb. The tower was probably built by Wilkin Johnstone of Elshieshields, after a previous house here was burnt in a raid in 1602.

Access: Private (now a retreat). Group tours can be arranged.

FOURMERKLAND TOWER stands in a copse by a farm, three miles north of Terregles. This picturesque little oblong tower house has round bartizans at alternate corners high up. A plaque over the entrance bears the year 1590 and the initials of Robert Maxwell of Fourmerkland.

Access: On private land.

FRENCHLAND TOWER, a decaying ruin in a field a mile east of Moffat, was originally oblong but later given a jamb to convert it to the L-plan. Its gables are complete but much of the main block has collapsed. The tower was built by the French family in the sixteenth century.

Access: On farmland.

GILNOCKIE TOWER overlooks the River Esk, four miles south of Langholm off the A7. Sometimes known erroneously as Hollows Tower, it is still owned by the once-notorious Armstrongs. They had a long-running feud with their English neighbours, the Grahams. In 1527 both Gilnockie and the Grahams' similar tower at Kirkandrews, across the Cumbrian border, were burnt in tit-for-tat raids. At that time the celebrated reiver, Johnny Armstrong of Gilnockie, dominated the locality. In 1530 James V invited him to a hunt but, once there, had him hanged along with fifty of his entourage. This treachery is bewailed in the ballad *Johnie Armstrang*, though it did not deter the surviving Armstrongs from pursuing their accustomed livelihood.

Gilnockie is an evocative Border tower house, restored and re-floored in 1979 by Major Roy Armstrong-Wilson. The windows are tiny throughout. At the wall-head is an elaborate corbel table, rounding at the corners to support vanished bartizans. One of the crow-stepped gables carries a chimney and the other a beacon platform. A joint in the masonry suggests that the third floor and the recessed attic are later sixteenth-century additions. Otherwise the oblong structure may well have been built by Johnny Armstrong. A simple doorway leads into the barrel-vaulted ground floor. Above is the hall, its large fireplace heating the dais end. The upper storeys are disfigured by modern partitioning. As in some other south-western tower houses, the spiral staircase intrudes into the body of the tower at one corner.

Access: Open daily.

HODDOM CASTLE stands close to the River Annan, six miles north-west of Annan via the B723. It occupies an estate that has suffered the indignity of becoming a caravan park. Around 1565 an English spy reported that John Maxwell, Lord Herries, was building a castle here and the buildings are consistent with that date. Three years later it surrendered to Regent Moray, following Mary Queen of Scots' defeat at the Battle of Langside. Recovered by supporters of the exiled queen, Hoddom was damaged in 1570 during a raid by the Earl of Sussex.

The south-west wall of a square barmkin survives, sporting a round flanking tower with gunports at each end and a rebuilt gateway in the middle. Within the barmkin rises the massive L-plan tower house. It comprises four storeys below the parapet, all divided by a later cross-wall. An attic is recessed within the corbelled-out parapet, which rounds into bartizans at the corners. Wide-mouthed gunports pierce not only the vaulted ground floor but also the third storey, which seems to have housed the garrison. A more traditional defensive touch is the machicolation high above the original entrance, located as usual in the side of the jamb. In the 1630s the first Earl of Annandale enlarged the windows and added two more storeys on top of the jamb. A wide staircase, with a pit prison beneath, rises in the jamb up to second-floor level. The interior of the tower has suffered many later alterations and is now thoroughly derelict. It became the core of a later mansion, but that has been demolished except for the Victorian stable block.

Access: Exterior only.
Reference: *PSAS* (117).
Relations: Lord Herries also built nearby Repentance Tower.

ISLE TOWER, in secluded grounds two miles north of Holywood, is a modest oblong structure with bartizans at alternate corners and a later house attached. Carved over the entrance are the year 1587 and the initials of John Ferguson. (The county has another Isle Tower near Bankend.)

Access: Private.

LOCHHOUSE TOWER, in its own grounds just north of Beattock, is a well-restored oblong with rounded corners and a corbelled-out parapet. This tower belonged to the Johnstones of Corehead and existed by 1567. The top storey and gabled attic are clearly later additions.

Access: Private (now a holiday let).

LOCHMABEN CASTLE Beside Kirk Loch Brae at the south end of Lochmaben town is an oval motte called the Old Castle. Raised by the Bruces of Annandale in the twelfth century, it may have been the birthplace of Robert the Bruce, though Turnberry Castle has a stronger claim. Edward I chose a new location for one of his invasion forts in 1298. It occupies a promontory on the south shore of Castle Loch, over a mile further south. Then known as the Peel of Lochmaben, it was a simple earthwork created by digging a moat to cut off the promontory. This simple fortification – such a contrast to Edward's castles in Wales – resisted Robert the Bruce in 1299 but changed hands several times during the Wars of Independence. Despite the failure of Edward Balliol's invasion in 1332, it remained a precarious English outpost in Scotland. Within the moated enclosure are the remains of a small oblong courtyard, with a hall block at the rear and a simple barbican in front, but these buildings are now reduced to featureless stumps of walling. They were probably raised in the 1340s by William de Bohun, Earl of Northampton.

The more substantial additions are often attributed to Edward III in the 1370s, after the extinction of the Bohun line. However, the English royal accounts record only minor repairs, so they may represent a later phase of building by the Bohuns. The courtyard was extended southwards as far as the moat. A thick chunk of curtain wall still stands high. Massive wing walls project at either end of this screen wall, both with archways spanning the moat. Hence the theory that the stone-lined moat (now often dry) served as a canal across the promontory, the wing walls protecting an artificial harbour for boats.

Archibald Douglas, 'the Grim', finally wrested Lochmaben Castle from English control in 1384. After the fall of the Black Douglases in 1455, Lochmaben was seized by the Crown. Although regarded as one of the strongest places on the Border, it was captured by the Earl of Hertford in 1544 during the Rough Wooing. James VI ordered repairs as late as 1624 but the castle was already drifting into ruin.

Access: Freely accessible (HES).
Reference: *PSAS* (106).
Relations: Bruce family work at Tarbert, Loch Doon and vanished Turnberry. Roxburgh Castle was another English outpost.

MORTON CASTLE now consists of little more than the substantial ruin of a large hall block. It cuts off a triangular promontory jutting into Morton Loch, two miles north-east of Carronbridge and reached by a warren of minor roads. A scrap of wall projecting from the hall is evidence for a curtain wall running to the apex of the promontory, so it would appear that the castle had a triangular courtyard with the great hall at its base. At either end of the landward front are the remains of flanking towers. Only a segment is left of the circular south-east tower, but the D-shaped south-west tower is more complete. Part of an arch springing from the jagged end suggests that it was actually one of a pair flanking a gate passage, though these towers oddly projected to either side rather than in front of the outer gateway. Enough survives to show that the gate passage was protected by a drawbridge, a portcullis and two pairs of doors – an unusually strong concentration of entrance defences. A row of tall windows lit the hall, above the tiny openings of an unvaulted undercroft. Facing the former courtyard is the first-floor doorway to the hall, once reached by a wooden stair.

The castle is traditionally attributed to James Douglas of Dalkeith, who became first Earl of Morton in 1456. However, the triangular layout with gatehouse and angle towers is reminiscent of Caerlaverock. It may have been erected by Robert the Bruce's nephew, Thomas Randolph, Earl of Moray – here flouting the king's de-fortification strategy. If so, the existing hall windows and doorway reflect a remodelling around the time of the traditional dating.

The castle was important enough to be one of those slighted under the terms of David II's release from English captivity in 1357. It is likely that the rest of the castle was destroyed at that time, the hall being allowed to remain as a residence. Further damage may be due to James VI, who ordered an attack on the castle when he was defied by the Catholic Lord Maxwell in 1588.

Access: Freely accessible (HES).
Reference: *PSAS* (12 and 92).
Relations: Caerlaverock. Thomas Randolph may also have built Auchencass.

REPENTANCE TOWER   Just south of Hoddom, a footpath from the B725 ascends to a squat tower on the summit of Trailtow Hill, commanding a panoramic view across the Solway Firth. John Maxwell, Lord Herries, built this square tower in conjunction with Hoddom Castle in the valley below, as reported by an English spy in 1565. This was a watch tower rather than a tower house proper, forming a small garrison post to provide advanced warning of raids. Three storeys culminate in a barrel vault. The pyramid roof within the parapet is an eighteenth-century embellishment, though the beacon platform no doubt reflects the original arrangement. Later stone steps ascend to the first-floor doorway. On the lintel the word 'Repentance' is still legible. Various explanations have been put forth for this, since Maxwell had his fair share of guilt. The tower resisted the English attack in 1570, when Hoddom Castle was sacked.

Access: Exterior only.
Relations: Hoddom. The watch towers at Ardclach and Castle Varrich.

SANQUHAR CASTLE stands in a field on the south-eastern edge of the old burgh, just off the A76. Now an overgrown and neglected ruin, it was built by the Crichtons of Sanquhar. The oldest part is a four-storey tower house at the south corner, probably dating from the late fourteenth century. During the fifteenth century they expanded the castle into a compact quadrangle with ranges on all sides. Although the first Duke of Queensberry erected Drumlanrig Castle as its magnificent successor, he took an instant dislike to it and continued to live at Sanquhar. Only after his death in 1695 was the castle finally abandoned. Efforts by John Crichton-Stuart, third Marquess of Bute, to restore the castle as a residence were thwarted by his untimely death in 1900.

The castle occupies a bluff overlooking the River Nith, while a broad ditch and rampart cover the landward approaches. An outer enclosure had a surrounding wall that is now reduced to foundations. Ahead is the inner courtyard, fronted by the remains of an oblong gatehouse that forms most of the north-west range. The entrance is flanked by the stump of a single half-round flanking tower containing a well (compare Doune). It leads into a gate passage with an undercroft on one side, its vault reconstructed by the Marquess of Bute. A hall occupied the floor above but is now very ruinous.

Remains of the south-west range include a kitchen with a large fireplace, but the other two sides of the enclosure are now fragmentary. Although the square-plan tower house appears largely complete, the Marquess of Bute was active here too, rebuilding one fallen corner and inserting new windows.
Access: Exterior only.
Relations: Doune. The Marquess of Bute's restorations at Rothesay, Falkland and the Old Place of Mochrum.

SPEDLINS TOWER is a large oblong in its own grounds, three miles north-east of Templand. It was built by the Jardines of Applegarth in the fifteenth century but remodelled with twin gables around 1605. The ornate hall fireplace is identical to one at Newark (Renfrewshire).
Access: Private.

STAPLETON TOWER is an intact shell in the grounds of a demolished mansion, four miles north-east of Annan. Built by the Irvines of Stapleton early in the sixteenth century, this oblong tower house has an elaborate corbel table supporting the parapet and corner bartizans.
Access: On private land.

TORTHORWALD CASTLE crowns a hillock overlooking the village, four miles north-east of Dumfries. This ruinous oblong block is attributed to Humphrey de Kirkpatrick, who acquired the barony in 1321. If so, it is one of the oldest tower houses in Scotland, but the structure was remodelled and extended in finer masonry by the Carlyles of Torthorwald towards the end of the fifteenth century. Much of the tower – including the extension – has collapsed, leaving only two walls and part of a third standing high. The walls were thickened to support two levels of barrel vaulting but these vaults have largely fallen. Only the south end of the upper vault survives – enough to show that it covered a lofty hall. The original first-floor entrance became a window during the remodelling and a new doorway was inserted below. A finger of masonry at one corner denotes an upper floor above the hall. The ditch and rampart around the hilltop probably date from Norman times. Despite a sacking in 1544 during the Rough Wooing, the tower remained occupied until the eighteenth century. It is now in a parlous state.
Access: Well seen from Linns Road.
Relations: Early tower houses at Drum, Hallforest and Duffus.

OTHER SITES The *Mote of Annan* is a substantial motte-and-bailey earthwork of the Bruces at Annan, half washed away early in its history by the River Annan flooding. Several others mottes recall the Flemings and Normans who settled here in the twelfth century, such as *Auldton* (near Moffat), *Barntalloch* (near Burnfoot), *Dinning* (near Closeburn), *Lower Ingleston* (near

Kirkland), *Rockhall* (near Collin) and *Wamphray* (near Newton Wamphray). Robert the Bruce seized the early royal castle at *Dumfries* in 1306, after infamously murdering John Comyn of Badenoch in the vanished Greyfriars' church nearby. He destroyed the castle after capturing it again in 1313. The site is by the River Nith in Castledykes Park.

Drumlanrig Castle (HHA), the Duke of Queensberry's mansion near Carronbridge, was built in 1679–90 and must be considered an early sham despite its castellated grandeur with four massive corner towers. It occupies the site of an older Black Douglas stronghold. Close by are the meagre remains of *Tibbers Castle*, a towered enclosure built from 1298 but soon destroyed. The county has its fair share of shattered or much-altered tower houses:

Blacket Tower (ruin, near Eaglesfield)
Breconside Tower (near Moffat)
Dalswinton Old House (ruin)
Isle Tower (ruin, near Bankend)
Lag Tower (ruin, near Dunscore)
Langholm Castle (ruin)
Lochwood Tower (ruin, near Beattock)
Mouswald Tower (ruin)
Robgill Tower
Woodhouse Tower (ruin, near Kirtlebridge)

DUNBARTONSHIRE

This small county is squeezed between the Firth of Clyde and the bonny banks of Loch Lomond. Dumbarton Castle, on its great rock above the Clyde, was an important royal stronghold but only a few scattered portions have survived its transformation into a Hanoverian fortress. Elsewhere there is a just a handful of tower houses, along with shattered ruins on islets in Loch Lomond.

County reference: BoS *Stirling and Central Scotland. The Castles of Glasgow and the Clyde* by G W Mason.

DUMBARTON CASTLE, on a basalt rock overlooking the royal burgh and the Firth of Clyde, is one of the most spectacularly sited of all Scottish castles, reminiscent of Edinburgh and Stirling. It emerged as Dun Breatann, the chief stronghold of the British kingdom of Strathclyde. In the year 870 the rock was sacked by Vikings from Dublin after a four-month siege. Occupation continued but it only seems to have become a castle in the accepted sense when Alexander II founded the royal burgh below in 1222. Henceforth it was an important royal stronghold, guarding the route to the Highlands and the base for many expeditions to the Hebrides. The beleaguered child monarchs David II and Mary Queen of Scots were both sent here before sailing to safety in France, in 1333 and 1548, respectively.

Although it emerged unscathed from the Wars of Independence, Dumbarton saw much action in the troubled era of the Stewart monarchs. James IV battered it into submission following his disputed accession in 1489, while Regent Arran captured it from English sympathisers in 1545. The most audacious attack took place in 1571, when the castle was holding out for the exiled Mary Queen of Scots. Captain Thomas Crawford, with 100 men, scaled the rock under cover of night. They reached the lower summit undetected, then turned its guns on the rest of the castle, which quickly surrendered. As a result of its strategic importance the existing complex, like Edinburgh, is largely a fortress of the Jacobite period. The defences were gradually rebuilt from 1675 but were never put to the test. Declared obsolete in 1865, the castle was reoccupied by the military during both world wars.

Man-made defences were always of secondary importance on this precipice and only a few scattered pieces remain of the medieval castle. The site consists of two unequal summits separated by a deep cleft, forming a natural motte-and-bailey stronghold on a gigantic scale. It is now entered at the foot of the cleft through King George's Battery, built by General Wade in 1735. The wall winding westwards over the crags from here is entirely of the Hanoverian period. King George's Battery is overlooked by the handsome Governor's House, on the site of the outer gatehouse. Beyond a small forecourt bounded by cliffs is the Guard House, an oblong inner gatehouse of the sixteenth century, with shot holes below the roofline. From here the narrow cleft provides the only way up. Steps ascend to another obstacle, known as the Portcullis Arch. This tall, pointed gateway also serves as a bridge between the two summits. Although it dates only from Robert II's reign, it is the oldest masonry on the site.

The cleft broadens into a saddle between the two summits. A length of late medieval curtain wall closes off the comparatively gentle ascent at the north end of the Castle Rock. This curtain contained a gateway flanked by the Wallace Tower, an oblong tower house probably added by James IV. In the 1790s the curtain was thickened to support a gun battery. As a result, the gateway was blocked and the Wallace Tower was reduced to the sorry stump that remains.

A Georgian powder magazine now occupies the lower summit. This open space formed the main courtyard of the original castle and the existing gun batteries probably follow the line of an older curtain. A steep ascent to the higher summit, 240 feet above the Clyde, is rewarded by panoramic views. It was crowned by the White Tower but the existing foundations belong to a much later windmill.

Access: Open daily in summer and regularly in winter (HES).
Reference: Guidebook by C Tabraham. *Dumbarton Castle* by I. MacPhail.
Relations: The royal castles of Edinburgh, Stirling and Blackness have also been adapted into later fortresses.

DUNGLASS CASTLE, beside the River Clyde west of Bowling, consists of an irregular courtyard raised by the Colquhouns of Dunglass. Ruined stretches of curtain wall built around 1380 survive, along with a derelict, late sixteenth-century laird's house and an obelisk of 1839.

Access: On private land within a disused oil depot.

INVERUGLAS CASTLE, facing Inveruglas village on a wooded islet in Loch Lomond, is the squat ruin of the MacFarlanes' sixteenth-century tower house, damaged in the Civil War. Originally oblong, it was converted to the Z-plan by the addition of twin round flanking turrets.

Access: The island is visible from the shore at Inveruglas.

KILMARONOCK CASTLE, otherwise known as Mains Castle, is two miles south-west of Drymen. This oblong tower house, built by the Dennistouns in the fifteenth century, now stands as an ivy-clad ruin in the garden of Kilmaronock House. There is a deep breach in one corner.

Access: On private land.

OTHER SITES Castles occupy three other islands in Loch Lomond: there are the shattered remains of a walled courtyard on Inchmurrin (*Lennox Castle*) and very ruinous tower houses on *Inchgalbraith* and *Vow*. As for other tower houses, *Kilmahew Castle* (near Cardross) has undergone a neo-Gothic transformation, *Bannachra Castle* (near Cross Keys) is badly ruined, while *Rossdhu Castle* (near Luss) is reduced to one complete side.

EAST LOTHIAN

Despite its position astride one of the chief invasion routes, much early masonry escaped the total destruction usually wrought during the Wars of Independence. Although slighted by the Scots, one section of John de Vaux's multi-towered castle at Dirleton has survived and must have looked very advanced when it was built in the mid-thirteenth century. There are also the remains of a more modest enclosure at Hailes and the mysterious Goblin Hall at Yester. After the wars, Dirleton was rebuilt on the old lines but without the flanking towers that had been demolished. Nevertheless, the Earl of Douglas revived the theme of the towered curtain wall at Tantallon, on a coastal promontory where only one side needed serious defences. Later on it proved able to withstand the artillery of both James IV and V.

From the sixteenth century the county preserves an unusual number of courtyard strongholds: the Bass Rock castle on its narrow ledge and the well-preserved barmkin walls of Garleton, Redhouse and Saltcoats. They culminate in Sir John Seton's remarkable, though sadly incomplete, towered quadrangle at Barnes. The gun battery added to the fragmentary royal castle of Dunbar shows its strategic importance in the ongoing Border conflicts, as do the upgrades to Tantallon. Fine tower houses at Lennoxlove, Preston and Redhouse follow the L-plan, while Fa'side offers the curious case of two conjoined tower houses.

County reference: RCAHMS *East Lothian*. BoS *Lothian*.

BARNES CASTLE   Sir John Seton of Barnes, brother of the Earl of Dunfermline, was a diplomat who rose to become Treasurer of the Royal Household. He began 'ane great building at the Barnes' but work was abandoned, far from complete, on his premature death in 1597. Only the ground floor levels of this unusual palace-fortress had been completed – the complex is known locally as 'The Vaults'. Prominently positioned in the Garleton Hills, the castle is about two miles north-east of Haddington and not far from Seton's other castle at Garleton. A turning for Barney Mains is signposted on the A199. Near the end of this sideroad, a public footpath skirts the edge of a field to the neglected ruin.

The visitor first passes the long north-west wall with its four square flanking towers, then turns to follow the north-east wall with a row of ragged window openings exposing a line of barrel-vaulted undercrofts within. The other two sides of the courtyard are bounded by the remains of a plain curtain wall with two further towers, including one at the south angle. In fact, this is an unusually large quadrangle with towers at all corners, except the east, and three intermediate towers, including the two on the north-west. They are well provided with wide-mouthed gunports, though no attempt was made to make the walls artillery-proof. It seems odd that defence should be most concentrated on the side where there is a steep drop towards the Cogtail Burn, but it has been pointed out that attackers could mount this bank unobserved, whereas the other three sides offer a clear field of view. The entrance was on the south-west, where there is now a gap in the curtain.

On the north-east side of the courtyard a mansion of some sophistication was intended. The row of vaulted undercrofts, linked by a corridor, has already been noted from outside. The middle compartment is not vaulted and was intended for a grand staircase. In front of them are two matching blocks (one of them the kitchen), forming an E-plan towards the courtyard with stair turrets in the re-entrant angles. Remains of another range line the north-west side.

Access: Freely accessible with caution.

Relations: Garleton. Seton's brother's work at Fyvie and Pinkie. There is also a Barns Tower in Peeblesshire.

BASS CASTLE　The Bass Rock is an astonishing sight in the Firth of Forth, rising out of the sea about a mile from Tantallon Castle as the gannet flies (they defend the place tenaciously). This huge volcanic plug is sheer on all sides except at the south end, where there is a more gradual ascent from the jetty. This approach is guarded by the Bass Castle – basically a long screen wall forming a revetment against the cliff, its courtyard a narrow ledge of level ground behind. The eastern part of the curtain wall has three shallow towers project from its face, two half-round and one square-fronted. A spur wall containing a mural staircase projects from the square tower. It descends steeply to a battery with large gunports overlooking the jetty. A crane hoisted provisions and even people up from here. The steep approach, fully exposed to the parapet above, entails passing through a doorway in the spur wall and then another in a re-entrant portion of the screen wall.

A castle is first recorded here in 1405, when the future James I took a ship *en route* to his capture and long imprisonment in England. However, the existing remains are dated to the sixteenth century. Although it was long held by the Lauders of the Bass, the castle was used as a state prison from time to time. It twice resisted the English in 1548–49 and endured a long blockade before surrendering to Roundhead troops in 1652. In 1691 four Jacobite prisoners seized control and held out for three years. The lighthouse now dominating the site was built in 1902.

Access: Well seen from the harbour. There are regular boat trips around the rock from North Berwick in summer.
Relations: Ailsa Castle on its much bigger crag.

DIRLETON CASTLE sits on a crag overlooking a pleasant village two miles west of North Berwick. It began as the seat of the Vaux family – Normans who settled here at the invitation of David I. John de Vaux raised the original castle around the middle of the thirteenth century. He was seneschal to Alexander II's queen, Marie de Coucy, and the dynamic layout with round flanking towers may reflect her father's mighty castle at Coucy in Picardy as well as recent developments in England. It may have been the first of its type in Scotland. In 1298, following the Battle of Falkirk, the castle fell to Bishop Bek of Durham after a protracted siege. It was recovered by the Scots in 1311, then slighted to make it untenable by the English. Thankfully the destruction here was not as severe as usual.

Dirleton rose again under the Halyburtons of Dirleton, who inherited the lordship soon after. Evidently the east side of the castle had suffered the most damage and John Halyburton erected a massive hall block in its place towards the end of the fourteenth century. In 1515 the castle passed to the

Dirleton Castle, East Lothian

Ruthvens of Huntingtower, whose political ambitions led to their downfall. William Ruthven, first Earl of Gowrie, abducted the young James VI in the Raid of Ruthven and was later executed. His sons perished in 1600 during a supposed attempt to assassinate the king at Perth. Dirleton became an outpost of Royalist resistance after Cromwell's invasion in 1650 but its gates were blasted down by General Lambert. It soon fell into its present ruined state.

John de Vaux established the layout of the castle – a quadrilateral enclosure, naturally protected on the north and west by the crag. On the east his curtain wall has been absorbed by the Halyburtons' hall block but the foundations of two round angle towers are exposed. Only the southern end of the Vaux castle can still be appreciated. Owing to the confines of the rock there is an awkward cluster of three towers here. The largest, rising from a plinth, is D-shaped. Although no bigger than the destroyed towers of the east curtain, it is regarded as a keep owing to its salient position. A smaller half-round tower flanks the west side of the castle, while a square turret occupies the angle between them.

The simple gatehouse stands beside the keep, on the short south-eastern stretch of curtain. It is part of John Halyburton's work. A modern bridge crosses the rock-cut ditch to the gateway, recessed in a tall archway with remains of machicolated bartizans above. Within the gate passage can be seen the pit into which the inner part of the drawbridge fell when the outer half was raised. Beyond is the compact courtyard. John de Vaux's curtain survives as a low retaining wall on the north and west, but, owing to the cliff, there are no flanking towers here. A flight of steps descends the rock to the Ruthvens' re-planted garden and a beehive dovecote with 1,100 nesting-holes.

Several doorways lead into the cavernous, barrel-vaulted undercroft of the Halyburtons' hall block. Note the imprint of the wooden frame used in the construction of the vault. The east wall of the undercroft incorporates John de Vaux's curtain. It preserves the original entrance gateway, now blocked by the greater thickness of the later masonry. Above it, the great hall once formed a lofty chamber but is now largely reduced to its lower courses. At the service end is a delicately carved recess where the food was laid out. In the fifteenth century the Halyburtons extended the hall block northwards to accommodate a solar beyond the dais end of the hall. Beneath it is a narrow, vaulted chapel, with a priest's chamber in the thickness of the wall. An inhospitable prison cell lurks beneath the chapel. Still further down is a grim pit prison, formed in the ditch of the original castle.

From the south end of the hall a passage connects with the lofty kitchen, part of John Halyburton's hall block. It preserves two large fireplaces and a hole in the crowning vault to allow the smoke to escape. The passage continues to a portcullis chamber over the gatehouse. Beyond is the gabled Ruthven Lodging, built by the Earl of Gowrie before his execution in 1584. This handsome residential block isolates the three Vaux towers at the southern apex of the castle. The so-called 'keep' is only two storeys high. Both levels are polygonal internally and covered by pointed vaults. Above the ground floor with arrow slits is the Lord's Chamber, with a hooded fireplace. A passage leads from here to a small room in the adjoining turret.

Access: Open daily in summer and regularly in winter (HES).
Reference: Guidebook by C. Tabraham.
Relations: Towered enclosures such as Dunstaffnage, Caerlaverock and Bothwell. Work of the Ruthvens at Huntingtower and Scone.

DUNBAR CASTLE occupies a small but precipitous headland overlooking the harbour of this old royal burgh. It consists of two portions, the outer nearly an islet, linked Tintagel-style to the mainland by a narrow causeway being undermined by the sea. The castle was established by the Cospatrick earls of Dunbar before 1216 on the site of an older dun. In 1296 it surrendered to Edward I following his victory over John Balliol at the first Battle of Dunbar, fought just outside the town. Edward II took refuge here after Bannockburn before sailing back to England. Then in 1338 came one of the most memorable of medieval sieges. Although the story was embellished in Blind Harry's poem, *The Wallace*, it is clear that the garrison held out for at least six weeks against an English army led by the Earl of Salisbury. As well as the missiles hurled from the battlements, the earl had to endure the obscene taunts of the redoubtable 'Black Agnes' Randolph, Countess of Dunbar. A Scottish fleet broke the blockade and raised the siege.

With the loss of Berwick to the English in 1296, Dunbar had become the chief port on this stretch of coast. Parliament ordered the destruction of the castle in 1488 to prevent its use by the English, but just six years later James IV began rebuilding as a royal castle. Only fragments survive on the islet portion, pieces of curtain wall clinging precariously to the cliff face. A tall finger of masonry may be the last vestige of a tower house. Facing land are some remains of a cross-wall with early gunports of the inverted keyhole type, along with one side of a gate tower. More is left on the smaller but higher crag forming the landward part of the isthmus. Here is a polygonal gun battery raised by John Stewart, second Duke of Albany and regent during James V's minority. It was begun in 1515 after the disaster at Flodden. Notwithstanding the experiment in the fifteenth century at Ravenscraig, this gun battery represents a new stage in the development of artillery defence. The wide-mouthed gunports in the outer walls are probably the first of this type in Scotland. A second tier of cannon was mounted on the vanished parapet, supported by the immensely thick walls.

Despite these new defences the castle was sacked by the Earl of Shrewsbury in 1548. Following her contrived abduction in 1567, the Earl of Bothwell brought Mary Queen of Scots to the castle and browbeat her into marrying him. After their swift downfall, parliament again ordered the slighting of the castle and it has decayed ever since. The burgh was one of the few in Scotland to have a stone town wall, but nothing remains of it.

Access: Well seen from the harbour (LA).

Relations: Ravenscraig (Fife). Work of James IV and V at Falkland, Edinburgh, Holyrood, Stirling and Linlithgow.

FA'SIDE CASTLE   Birsley Road runs south-west from Tranent for two miles to this white-harled tower house at a sharp bend in the road. It is otherwise known as Falside, though the family that occupied it until 1631 is usually called Fawside. In 1547 the original tower was caught up in the Battle of Pinkie, being burnt by the English and its garrison slaughtered when Lady Fawside dared to put up resistance. It was rehabilitated enough for Mary Queen of Scots to stay here the night before her defeat at Carberry Hill in 1567. Having narrowly escaped demolition as a dangerous ruin, the building was restored to a habitable condition in the 1970s. The property boundary incorporates some of the old barmkin wall.

This is the unusual case of an oblong fifteenth-century tower to which an L-plan extension has been added, so that it looks on plan like two tower houses back-to-back. The older part is four storeys high with much thicker walls than the addition. It has a ground-floor entrance and a spiral stair in one corner. The second-floor hall features a huge fireplace and a modern beamed ceiling, painted in traditional style. Only the top floor is barrel vaulted. This tower has been restored with battlements but without an attic in an attempt to evoke its original appearance, though the corner caphouse is a plausible embellishment. The main block of the extension also has four storeys, including the attic, but the floor levels are different and only the ground-floor kitchen is vaulted. The jamb is divided into six storeys and there is a slender stair turret in the re-entrant angle. The roofline of the extension is gabled and typical of the late sixteenth century. Both corner bartizans have been rebuilt above the level of the corbelling.

Access: Well seen from the road (now a guesthouse).

FENTON TOWER, in its own grounds overlooking Kingston, is a long and lofty L-plan structure with a stair turret projecting in the re-entrant angle and another at the rear. Probably built soon after John Carmichael obtained the lands in 1587, the tower has been well restored.

Access: Visible from the road (now a holiday let).

GARLETON CASTLE lies in the shadow of the Garleton Hills, a mile and a half west of Athelstaneford off the B1343. A castle on this site may have been the birthplace of the Renaissance poet and playwright Sir David Lyndsay around 1490. However, the existing complex dates from the second half of the sixteenth century. It is attributed to Sir John Seton of Barnes, Treasurer of the Household under James VI, probably before he began building nearby Barnes Castle.

Like Barnes, Garleton is a courtyard castle. Though less ambitious in scale it was evidently completed, unlike its neighbour. The barmkin, now a domestic garden, is roughly oblong and the surrounding curtain wall survives in a ruinous state except on the west side. Astride the curtain at what would have been the western corners are two oblong lodges (towers would be too strong a word). That on the north-west is much restored as a residence but the south-west lodge survives intact in its original form. Three storeys high, including the attic with its crow-stepped gables, it is divided by a cross-wall and has a kitchen at ground level. There is a projecting stair turret in the outer face. However, the main residence was an L-plan tower house or laird's house at the north-east corner of the barmkin. Only the two precarious walls doubling up as the curtain now survive, but the vestiges of three barrel-vaulted cellars protrude at ground level. Projecting from the middle of the east curtain is a round flanking tower with a tall chimney. This tower and the two lodges are guarded by wide-mouthed gunports.

Access: Exterior only.

Relations: Barnes. The barmkins at Redhouse, Old Breachacha, Auchindoun and Muchalls.

HAILES CASTLE incorporates one of the early stone castles of Scotland, probably raised by the Gourlay family before 1250. Though changing hands several times, the castle appears to have survived the Wars of Independence unscathed – perhaps a reflection of its unimportance. In the fourteenth century the castle was extended, probably by Sir Patrick Hepburn of Hailes who distinguished himself at the Battle of Otterburn (1388). Sir Henry Percy, better known as Hotspur, unsuccessfully attacked the castle in 1400. Hailes fared less well in 1443 during a feud with Archibald Dunbar, who slaughtered the garrison. It fell to Lord Grey of Wilton during the English invasion of 1547. James Hepburn, fourth Earl of Bothwell, was probably born here. His forfeiture in 1567, after his scandalous marriage to Mary Queen of Scots, ended the Hepburn association with Hailes, though the castle was garrisoned during Cromwell's invasion. It is now very much a ruin.

The castle forms an elongated enclosure on the south bank of the River Tyne, two miles south-west of East Linton. Its western part is the fourteenth-century extension, bounded by a thick curtain wall pierced by a simple gateway. The curtain bends to an oblong tower house that succeeded the original keep but is now just as ruinous. It stands at the western extremity of the castle, five storeys high with a pit prison at one end, but only two sides remain. Beside the tower house a postern leads onto the riverbank. A group of buildings backs onto the north curtain, overlooking the river. First comes the large fifteenth-century chapel, standing above a barrel-vaulted undercroft that served as the bakehouse. Though structurally intact, the chapel has been mutilated by later use as a granary. Only the piscina and a blocked Gothic window reveal its original function.

Beyond the chapel is the junction with the thirteenth-century castle. It begins with a three-storey oblong tower, smaller than the later tower house nearby. This was a modest copy of the oblong keeps of Norman England and as such lagged behind the round-towered castle of Dirleton. Only two sides remain to full height, but the pit prison at its base is probably the first of its kind in Scotland. Attached to the keep are the footings of an early hall, beyond which the stump of a narrow projecting tower contains a rock-cut well. The early curtain continues to fragments of a later great hall bounding the east side of the courtyard. No doubt the curtain returned on the south to join up with the fourteenth-century extension, but this stretch has perished.

Access: Freely accessible (HES).
Reference: Guide by J. S. Richardson.
Relations: Early keeps at Aberdour, Cubbie Roo's and (possibly) the Castle of Old Wick. Castle chapels at Kildrummy, Rothesay and Edinburgh.

INNERWICK CASTLE lies midway between the village and the east coast. The seat of the Hamiltons of Innerwick, its position close to the Great North Road condemned it to a short and stormy history. The castle is first mentioned in 1403 when it was captured by Sir Henry Percy (Hotspur), who would soon meet his end at the Battle of Shrewsbury. Recaptured and destroyed by the Duke of Albany in 1406, it was subsequently rebuilt, only to be stormed and destroyed again by the Duke of Somerset in 1547 during the Rough Wooing. The ruins were used briefly as a base to harry invading Roundheads in 1650. They have been decaying ever since and are now thoroughly unstable.

From Crowhill, three quarters of a mile west of the A1, there is an easily missed public footpath running south through the wooded Thornton Glen Wildlife Reserve. It becomes a rather hair-raising ledge, with steep falls to the Thornton Burn below, but the castle is soon encountered on a small promontory jutting into the burn. A rock-cut ditch cuts off the only easy approach from the west, which is the side that confronts the visitor. The confusion of the remains is exacerbated by dense foliage. The castle followed a wedge shape dictated by the confines of the rock. It was surrounded by a curtain wall of which portions survive, including what appears to be the remains of a gate tower at the north-west corner. The whole of the compact interior seems to have become filled with buildings crammed around an oblong tower house, of which only the two barrel-vaulted undercrofts survive. The masonry suggests at least two periods of construction, no doubt undertaken between the destructions of 1406 and 1547.

Access: Well seen from the footpath (uphill walk).
Relations: Hamilton branches at Preston and Redhouse.

LENNOXLOVE HOUSE is an attractive complex in extensive grounds. It is reached via a long drive starting a mile south of Haddington, off the B6368. A massive tower house at one corner dominates the rest. This fine L-plan structure was originally known as Lethington. In 1702 the Duchess of Lennox bequeathed it to Lord Blantyre on condition that he call it 'Lennox love to Blantyre' – a surreal name for an aristocratic mansion.

According to tradition the tower house dates from 1345. It was more likely raised sometime in the following century by the Maitland family, who would later build Thirlestane Castle. Its middle storey is the hall, twice as high as the other floors and covered by a barrel vault. Three holes in the vault seem to be smoke outlets for a central hearth, suggesting that the tower was originally a hall house and the solar above is a later addition. It cannot be much later, though the monumental fireplace now in the hall dates only from 1912. Beneath the hall, the vaulted undercroft now serves as a chapel. A passage has been cut through to a pit prison in the jamb, reached originally only by an opening in the vault. Another feature here is the well, rising via a shaft to the kitchen, which occupies the jamb at hall level. Externally the tower house is little altered, despite a sacking by the Duke of Somerset in 1549. At that time it was occupied by the blind poet, Sir Richard Maitland.

Sir Richard's grandson John, first Earl of Lauderdale, remodelled the tower house. As well as enlarging some windows, he added the gabled attic above the corbelled-out parapet with its tiny round corner bartizans. There is also a caphouse at one corner. A Latin inscription of 1626 above his new entrance commemorates these works. The sturdy yett suggests that the tower house might still be regarded as a refuge. Nevertheless the earl went on to build the residential range to the east of the tower, which fills in the re-entrant angle and bears the year 1644. A tall jamb projects at the opposite end of the range, showing a continuity of old defensive forms if not of purpose. Extensions after the Restoration by the Duke of Lauderdale (who also remodelled Thirlestane) created a small courtyard on the site of the old barmkin, of which only the gateway remains. The mansion is now filled with the treasures of the dukes of Hamilton, who purchased it in 1946.

Access: Open regularly in summer (HHA).
Reference: Guidebook by R. K. Marshall.
Relations: Thirlestane.

LUFFNESS CASTLE occupies wooded grounds a mile north-east of Aberlady. This Victorian mansion incorporates a gabled L-plan tower house with prominent chimneys. Built by Sir Patrick Hepburn of Luffness around 1584, the main block was soon extended to form a T-plan.

Access: Private (now a holiday let).

NUNRAW TOWER, east of Garvald and close to the modern abbey, is a late sixteenth-century Z-plan tower house with square flanking towers. Built by the Hepburns of Beanston and later extended, one room has a contemporary painted ceiling depicting exotic animals and heraldry.

Access: Private.

PRESTON TOWER rises in a historic village just inland from Prestonpans. This gaunt tower house, now roofless but otherwise complete, was built by the Hamiltons of Preston around 1400. It seems to be an early example of the L-plan – the entrance is not yet placed for security in the re-entrant angle. The jamb forms an annexe for small chambers, including a pit prison at the base. Instead there are two entrances in the opposite wall, in line with twin corbels that supported a box machicolation high up. One doorway opens into the vaulted ground floor, while the other must have been reached by a wooden stair. It led into the lofty hall on the first floor, which is also vaulted. The only communication between the hall and the undercroft is a hole in the vault. From the hall a spiral stair ascended to the solar and on to the parapet.

Instead of the usual attic gables there are two further storeys recessed within the corbelled-out parapet. They were added by Sir John Hamilton in 1626, their pedimented windows contrasting with the plain openings below. The tower had been burnt by the Earl of Hertford in 1544 and was again by Cromwell's troops in 1650. After a third, accidental fire thirteen years later, it was abandoned. Hamilton House and Northfield House are attractive lairds' houses close by.

Access: Exterior only (NTS). There are plans to consolidate and open the interior.

Relations: Hamilton branches at Innerwick and Redhouse.

REDHOUSE CASTLE crowns a low rock overlooking the B1377 beside Redhouse Nurseries, a mile and a half north-west of Longniddry. This compact courtyard castle exudes neglect and its building history is complex. Above the Renaissance doorway to the tower house are the initials of John Laing of Redhouse and his wife Rebecca Dennistoun, along with a Latin quote meaning 'without the Lord, all is in vain'. In 1608 they made over the property to their son-in-law, Sir Andrew Hamilton. Opinions vary, but the consensus is that Laing built the barmkin sometime before 1600, while Hamilton converted an older laird's house into a tower house.

The square barmkin is surrounded by a wall of no great height. A moulded gate arch in the middle of the south wall is overlooked by machicolation corbels. The cellars of an ancillary range line the east wall of the barmkin. However, it has lost its upper floors apart from the dovecote at the south end, which thus looks like a modest tower. The striking tower house at the north-west corner of the courtyard is a ruin but stands mostly to full height. It seems to have originated as a long residential block, of which only the western half remains. This portion was built up into a tower house, with a narrow extension joining it to the north barmkin wall; the corridors thus created at each level are the only vaulted compartments within the tower. Additionally, a jamb was added to create an L-plan, but an unusual one insofar as the jamb acts as a flanking tower at the north-west corner of the barmkin. Oddly, the architectural details of the tower house are somewhat finer to the outside world than they are towards the barmkin, apart from the doorway already mentioned, which is surmounted by an ornate heraldic panel. The tower is four storeys high. A kitchen occupied the ground level of the wrecked interior.

Access: The courtyard is freely accessible.

Relations: Hamilton branches at Innerwick and Preston. The barmkins at Garleton, Old Breachacha, Auchindoun and Muchalls.

SALTCOATS CASTLE, half a mile south of Gullane, is reached by a footpath running south from Saltcoats Road. It is named after the flat salt marshes that originally surrounded it. A heraldic panel (reset in a ruined cottage in front) from the castle bears the year 1390, apparently amended from 1590 by someone who wished to increase the castle's antiquity. It also shows the arms of Patrick Livington of Saltcoats and his wife Margaret Fettis. According to legend, Patrick had been given the lands for single-handedly slaying a particularly wild boar that was running amok in the neighbourhood.

His square barmkin survives as a ruinous enclosure wall on all sides but the west. The residential buildings that surrounded the barmkin are reduced to fragments and there is no indication of a tower house. At the north-east corner is the barrel-vaulted kitchen. The south side was filled by a four-storey hall range but the wall facing the courtyard has fallen. The west end of this range is the highlight: it somewhat resembles the gatehouse at Dirleton but was merely a showy facade. Two flanking turrets, semi-circular at ground level, are corbelled out to square for the remaining four storeys. At the top they are linked by a round-headed arch that seems to be an early seventeenth-century embellishment. Several of the gargoyles that formed a row above this arch cling on precariously, but the castle is overgrown and steadily decaying. There is a ruined dovecote nearby.

Access: Freely accessible with caution.

Relations: Dirleton.

STONEYPATH TOWER stands by a farm, half a mile north-east of Garvald. This austere, L-plan tower house was built sometime in the fifteenth century by the Lyells of Stoneypath. It was restored from quite a ruinous condition and the corbelled-out parapet is entirely renewed.

Access: Private.

TANTALLON CASTLE majestically crowns a coastal promontory, three miles east of North Berwick. Commanding a view of the Bass Rock and the Firth of Forth, it is one of the most dramatically sited of all Scottish castles. First mentioned in 1374, when it was probably newly built, the castle is a testimony to the ambition of William, first Earl of Douglas. Its massive curtain wall and flanking towers hark back to the castles of enclosure erected before the Wars of Independence, though owing to the terrain only one side required much defending. William died in 1384 and Tantallon passed to his illegitimate son George, first Earl of Angus and ancestor of the Red Douglas line. They emerged as rivals to their Black Douglas kinsmen, supporting James II when he crushed the latter in 1455. Inevitably, the Red Douglases became over-mighty barons in turn. Archibald, the fifth earl, hanged James III's unpopular favourites at Lauder, thus earning the nickname Bell the Cat. He then conspired against James IV. As a result, James brought his artillery to besiege Tantallon in 1491. Unable to take it by storm, the king was reluctantly reconciled with his rebellious vassal.

Archibald's grandson and namesake, the sixth earl, married James IV's widow Margaret Tudor. His guardianship of her son, James V, bordered on imprisonment. The seventeen-year-old king escaped his clutches in 1528 and immediately laid siege to Tantallon. Once again royal cannon were brought up to its walls but the besiegers' pledge to 'ding doun Tantalloun' was thwarted by lack of ammunition. After twenty days the siege was abandoned. It was a remarkable demonstration of a strong castle's ability to withstand the fury of a king, but Archibald was forced to flee to England. James then took possession and strengthened the castle. A third bombardment took place in 1651, when the castle was garrisoned by the Royalists. This time General Monck's artillery was not deficient and the Roundheads stormed the castle through one of the breached towers. The rest gradually fell into its present ruined state.

A sixteenth-century earthwork ravelin fronts the castle. Behind are the bank and ditch of an outer courtyard, with the collapsed remains of a stone outer gateway. Crossing the south end of the ditch, a spur wall with gunports ends in a squat round tower. These were probably added by Archibald Douglas before the 1528 siege. Only an oblong dovecote occupies the outer courtyard now.

Just behind the rock-cut inner ditch rises the great screen wall that divides the two courtyards. Built by William Douglas, it is one of the most formidable medieval fortifications in Scotland. The high curtain had a flanking tower at each end and an impressive gatehouse in the middle. Unfortunately, the end towers were both devastated in 1651. A huge chunk was taken out of the D-shaped tower on the right of the facade, while the cylindrical Douglas Tower to the left was largely destroyed to its base. The mighty gate tower survives to full height but its outer front is obscured by a forework with rounded corners added by James V. Wide-mouthed gunports are positioned to rake the approaches. A small doorway, suitable only for pedestrians, leads into a narrow passage where the gunners operated. Beyond is the original gate passage – once defended by a drawbridge, a portcullis and three pairs of gates. Above it, now open to the sky, are four storeys of chambers. They probably formed the constable's residence, so the building was a rare example of the keep-gatehouse theme.

The gatehouse leads into a roughly oblong inner courtyard delimited by the cliffs. James V did not need to thicken the screen wall to make it artillery-proof. He merely blocked up a few mural chambers and rebuilt the embattled parapet. This parapet is reached by two straight staircases in the thickness of the wall, their vaults formed by a series of transverse arches. In the courtyard is the well, hewn out of the rock to a depth of nearly 100 feet.

Despite the cliff, the curtain continues along the north side of the courtyard. Against it are the ruins of a gabled great hall over a row of barrel-vaulted undercrofts. It joins up with the Douglas Tower at the north-west corner of the enclosure. This contained the lord's private suite, a rare instance in the later medieval period of a round tower house, recalling the cylindrical keeps of the previous century. Six storeys rose above the basement prison, but the tower is now just a fragment of its former self. The jagged end of the D-shaped tower at the other end of the screen wall shows at least an intention to continue the curtain along the south side of the courtyard as well, though the cliffs are ample defence in themselves. A cleft on the east side of the promontory contains a gateway providing access from the sea.

Access: Open daily (HES).
Reference: Guidebook by C. Tabraham and N. Scott.
Relations: The Black Douglas castles at Old Tulliallan, Threave, Bothwell, Hermitage and Newark (Selkirkshire). James V's work at Dunbar, Falkland, Edinburgh, Holyrood, Stirling, Blackness and Linlithgow.

WHITTINGEHAME TOWER occupies an estate two miles west of Stenton. This modest L-plan structure has an embattled parapet with tiny corner bartizans, supported on corbels. The tower was built by the Douglases of Whittingehame, probably in the late sixteenth century.

Access: Private.

YESTER CASTLE occupies a steep-sided promontory on the wooded Yester estate, two miles east of Gifford. Reaching it is something of an expedition. From the B6355 you can take the invariably muddy Yester Way alongside the Gifford Water, turning left after about a mile to follow Hopes Water for another mile. However, the path becomes a narrow ledge with a steep drop to the rushing water below, so it is not for the faint-hearted. Eventually it descends to cross the burn and then ascends the other bank. The castle is concealed in the woods and not apparent until you are almost there. The neglected ruins represent an irregular, roughly oblong enclosure on a promontory between Hopes Water and a tributary burn. It was probably erected after the Hays of Neidpath Castle obtained the site in 1357. Only the deep ditch remains on the landward approach, but the curtain wall cutting off the north-eastern apex of the promontory stands high, with a small postern. There is also a tall fragment from a hall range on the south-east, overlooking the burn, with a section of vaulted cellar. This castle resisted an English attack before the Battle of Pinkie in 1547 but succumbed to them the following year.

Beyond the postern is the castle's one remarkable and perfectly preserved feature – a subterranean hall at the north end of the promontory, outside the confines of the courtyard. This is an older structure, attributed to Sir Hugo de Gifford who died in 1267. Known as the Goblin Hall, its low position in relation to the rest of the castle does not commend it as the undercroft of a vanished keep, while the theory that it was a hideout for a beleaguered garrison seems at odds with the fine masonry. The mystery adds spice to the myth that Hugo conjured it up as a place to practice his sorcery. A wooden floor originally divided the space into two levels, each with its own arched entrance in the south wall, so the current loftiness is misleading. The ashlar walls are crowned by a pointed vault with closely spaced ribs. Remains of a first-floor fireplace in the far wall show that it was meant to be occupied, despite the lack of natural lighting. On one side, a vaulted passage leads to a postern overlooking a stream. On the other, a stair descends steeply through the bedrock to a filled-in well. The rest of this early castle was presumably destroyed following its recovery from the English in 1311.

Access: Freely accessible with caution (uphill walk).

Relations: Neidpath. The early hall at Kirkwall.

OTHER SITES *Elphinstone Tower*, on a farm near Tranent, was probably the greatest loss to castellated architecture anywhere in Britain in the twentieth century. This massive oblong tower house was built by Sir Gilbert Johnstone around 1440. Like its near contemporary, Borthwick Castle, the five-storey tower had a lofty hall with a pointed vault and was honeycombed with mural chambers, passages and stairs. Unfortunately, it stood over a coal seam and the subsiding structure was demolished in 1955. Only the lower courses were left standing, with the ground-floor entrance complete on one side.

Fragments of a small enclosure attest *Markle Castle* (near East Linton). Tower houses are embedded in *Ballencrieff Castle*, *Biel House* (near Stenton) and *Woodhall House* (near Pencaitland). *Tranent* has the shell of a very plain tower off Church Street. Another tower, twice burnt by the English in the 1540s, has been extended into the tithe barn that overlooks the fifteenth-century parish church at *Whitekirk*. A ruined jamb on a rock ledge survives from the tower house of *Waughton Castle* (near East Fortune).

The so-called *French Camp* at Dunglass is the denuded earthwork of one of the artillery forts erected by the English during their invasion of 1547. They also fortified the royal burgh of *Haddington*, resisting all attempts by the French and Scots to dislodge them until withdrawing two years later. The earth ramparts with early arrow-head bastions were then levelled.

FIFE

Some castles take advantage of the dramatic coastline surrounding this peninsula between the Firths of Forth and Tay. Fife is one of the best counties for castles, though several rewarding sites are not normally accessible. Part of a rare oblong keep at Aberdour is the only early stonework. From the fourteenth century there is the hall house of Old Tulliallan, with its remarkable ribbed vaulting, and the ruinous curtain walls around Ballinbreich and St Andrews. Numbers increase in the following century, with the courtyard castles of Balgonie and Wemyss and several other tower houses, such as Rosyth. However, the most fascinating survival from this period is James II's artillery screen wall at Ravenscraig, with its two massive flanking towers.

In terms of volume, the sixteenth century predominates as usual. There are numerous tower houses, but a considerable proportion are in private occupation or cast adrift on farmland. Lordscairnie and Monimail are typical examples but the best are L-plan Scotstarvit, built in fine ashlar masonry, and (almost) Z-plan Earlshall with its painted ceiling. A curious variant is the soaring oblong that formed the fortified bell tower of Dysart Old Church. Aberdour and Ballinbreich were given fine residential buildings, while Kellie and Rossend are curious T-plan complexes, the former with three towers at the extremities. The royal palace at Falkland, a sadly incomplete Renaissance gem, is entered through James V's semi-fortified gatehouse. St Andrews Castle was rebuilt after sustaining damage in the great siege of 1546, which has bequeathed the unique legacy of the besiegers' rock-cut mine and the defenders' counter-mine. In the town we find a defensive wall around the old cathedral precinct and the only substantial town gate in Scotland.

County reference: RCAHMS *Fife, Kinross and Clackmannan*. BoS *Fife. Castles of Fife* by R Fawcett.

ABERDOUR CASTLE overlooks the Firth of Forth in a village astride the A921, three miles west of Burntisland. Alan de Mortimer, a Norman settler, received lands here from David I. Although there is no mention of a castle until 1361, there remains the stump of a sizeable tower that must have been built early in the thirteenth century at the latest, making it a rare Scottish example of a Norman-style keep. Its curious plan is a parallelogram rather than oblong. Shallow 'pilaster' corner buttresses recall Norman keeps in England, while two round-headed windows survive at ground-floor level. The adjacent parish church is partly Romanesque too. In the fifteenth century the building was remodelled as an L-plan tower house, the ground floor being divided into two barrel-vaulted cellars. By that time Aberdour was held by the earls of Morton, a branch of the Douglas family. Unfortunately the heightened walls proved too heavy for the older base and the keep gradually collapsed. Only one chunk survives to full height along with the added jamb, which contains the spiral stair. Part of the superstructure collapsed in 1919, but astonishingly remains in one piece on the ground.

Attached to the keep via the staircase jamb is a gabled residential block added by James Douglas, fourth Earl of Morton, probably in the 1570s when he was regent. He did not have long to enjoy it, being executed in 1581, ostensibly for his part in the murder of Lord Darnley. Regent Morton's handsome dwelling contains a pair of residential chambers on its two upper storeys, above a vaulted ground-floor kitchen and storeroom. Though structurally complete, it has been a shell since it was accidentally burnt by Hanoverian troops during the 1715 Jacobite rising. An east wing with a long gallery on the upper floor, added by the eighth earl in 1632, survived this fate and retains its roof and floors. There is a gabled corner tower with a contemporary painted ceiling on the first floor. The Morton buildings are purely domestic in character, forming one side of a thinly walled barmkin of which some foundations remain. A recreated terraced garden and a particularly fine beehive dovecote lie beyond. After the fire, the Mortons moved to nearby Aberdour House.

Access: Open daily in summer and regularly in winter (HES).
Reference: Guidebook by K. Owen.
Relations: Early keeps at Hailes, Cubbie Roo's and (possibly) the Castle of Old Wick. Regent Morton's work at Edinburgh and Drochil.

BALCOMIE CASTLE stands on a farm two miles north-east of Crail. The surviving portion is a tall L-plan tower house, built by the Learmonths of Balcomie. It was actually one of a pair flanking the south front of a late sixteenth-century courtyard castle, now otherwise fragmentary.

Access: Visible from the road (now a holiday let).

BALGONIE CASTLE, an impressive tower house and courtyard complex, stands on a bluff overlooking the River Leven, just west of Milton of Balgonie via a minor road. The oldest part is the oblong tower house of ashlar masonry, rising more than seventy feet high. It is traditionally attributed to Sir Thomas Sibbald around 1360, though the fifteenth century is more likely. Its austere form allows little window space, especially lower down. There were two entrances, at ground and first-floor levels, both now reached from a later staircase block. The ground floor is an undercroft with a pointed vault, not communicating with the rest. Above is a lofty hall, crowned by a barrel vault. Window embrasures with stone seats pierce the thick walls. A spiral stair in one corner ascends via two upper floors to the corbelled-out parapet, with tiny round corner bartizans and a little caphouse marking the head of the stair. Recessed within the parapet is a sixteenth-century attic.

Balgonie passed from the Sibbalds to the Lundies by marriage. In 1496 Sir Andrew Lundie of Balgonie became Lord High Treasurer and entertained James IV here. Like other aspiring nobles of the period, Sir Andrew sought a more spacious residence beyond the confines of the tower house. James made a small donation towards the cost of the long residential range east of the tower. This contained a new great hall with a solar beyond, standing over three barrel-vaulted compartments. One of them was the kitchen, which is now used as a chapel. Nevertheless, the tower house was preserved as an isolated unit for times of danger. The old hall in the tower appears to have been reached from the new hall by a drawbridge, crossing the narrow chasm that originally lay between them. Tower house and hall range together form the north side of an oblong barmkin, given its surrounding curtain around the same time. There is a gateway in the south wall but the principal entrance is the little gatehouse (with an incongruous wooden shack on top) at the south-west corner. Porters' lodges flank the gate passage, one of them forming a half-round turret with keyhole gunports.

The castle's most famous owner was Alexander Leslie. After long service in the Swedish army during the Thirty Years War, he returned home to lead the invasions that forced Charles I to recall the English parliament. Charles made him first Earl of Leven in the settlement of 1641, but Leslie played a leading role in the Civil War that followed (he should not be confused with General David Leslie). He was saved from execution under Cromwell at the request of the Queen of Sweden. Leslie remodelled the great hall, reducing its two fireplaces and adding an attic above. He also built new lodgings on the east side of the courtyard and the staircase block filling the narrow void between the tower house and the hall block. After that the castle decayed and, apart from the tower house, its buildings are now roofless shells. In 1971 David Maxwell began a long process of conservation.

Access: No longer open but well seen from a footpath.

Relations: Fifteenth-century tower houses like Affleck, Castle Campbell, Cardoness and Newark (Selkirkshire). Good barmkins such as Old Breachacha, Auchindoun and Muchalls.

BALLINBREICH CASTLE overlooks the Firth of Tay, on the edge of a field three miles north-east of Newburgh. Otherwise known as Balmbreich, this substantial but heavily overgrown ruin is arranged around a roughly oblong courtyard. In 1312 Robert the Bruce granted the lands to the Leslies, who were ennobled as earls of Rothes in 1457. The thick curtain wall, quite plain and originally towerless, probably dates from the late fourteenth century. On the north it has been supplanted by a thin boundary wall. Domestic buildings stood against the curtain from the beginning but only the hall block at the south-west corner is original. Its west end has fallen. Sometime in the fifteenth century the great hall on the first floor was given a pointed barrel vault. The collapse of this vault has exposed three sedilia from a chapel that originally overlay the hall.

Apart from the hall block the internal buildings of the castle are largely the work of Andrew Leslie, fifth Earl of Rothes. His initials and the year 1572 were once visible over the entrance – a modest doorway through the east curtain. Andrew heightened the hall block to contrive a tower house and provided the corbelled-out wall-head. He also added the ruinous eastward extension that completes the south side of the courtyard – an exceptionally tall chimney rises above the gable. A semi-circular tower projecting from the middle of the south front is also his, though the shot holes are negated by the large windows he inserted through the older curtain on either side. Three-storey lodgings in fine ashlar masonry occupied the long west side of the courtyard, with gabled turrets for spiral staircases projecting at either end. The southern part of this range is reduced to its footings, except for the kitchen fireplace backing onto the curtain, but the northern part is complete to the gables. Little survives of the north range. Although the Leslies were still here when elevated to ducal status in 1680, they soon abandoned the castle.

Access: On farmland.

BALMUTO TOWER occupies an estate a mile south of Auchtertool. This little mansion of various dates is wrapped around an oblong tower house of the Boswells of Balmuto, erected sometime in the fifteenth century. A rebuilt attic is recessed within the embattled parapet.

Access: Private.

COLLAIRNIE CASTLE, two miles south-east of Dunbog, stands amid farm buildings off the A913. The main block of this tower house is reduced to a stump but the jamb is complete, though sadly derelict. It rises five storeys to the gabled attic. A rounded stair turret in the re-entrant angle is crowned by a square caphouse. The entrance lintel bears the year 1581 and the initials of David Barclay of Collairnie and his wife, Margaret Wemyss. The jamb may be an addition, converting an older oblong tower to the L-plan. Two beamed ceilings within have lost most of the painted coats of arms for which they were noted.

Access: Well seen from the road.
Relations: Branches of the Barclay family at Towie Barclay and Ardrossan.

CREICH CASTLE is the battered ruin of a stepped L-plan tower house beside Creich Farm, half a mile north-east of Brunton via a minor road. The walls stand virtually to full height – a stretch of elaborate corbelling survives at the summit of the tower in the re-entrant angle. Evidently this continued all the way around. The main block was of three storeys and the jamb of four, linked by a fallen spiral staircase in the re-entrant tower. The usual vaults cover the ground floor. Close by are the remains of a barmkin tower. A charter of 1553 mentions the tower house, which may have been built by Robert Beaton of Creich not long before. It stands on a low mound in what was once marshland.

Access: Exterior only.

CRUIVIE CASTLE occupies a knoll overlooking a farm, half a mile north-west of Lucklawhill. This squat ruin is an L-plan tower house, its featureless walls now rising little more than two storeys high. The tower was built by the Sandilands of Cruivie, probably in the fifteenth century.

Access: On farmland.

DENMYLNE CASTLE can be found just off the A913, a mile south-east of Newburgh. It is the handsome shell of a rare T-plan tower house, in the forecourt of Denmylne House. The main block rises three storeys to a corbelled-out wall-head, with attic gables above. Each floor of the overgrown interior is divided by a cross-wall into two rooms, the ground floor being vaulted as usual. The jamb, containing the entrance in a side wall, projects off-centre. Rising taller than the rest to its own crowning gable, it contains a broad spiral staircase. A smaller projecting turret at the rear of the tower contained latrines serving each floor. The large windows are compensated for by wide-mouthed gunports low down. Patrick Balfour of Denmylne was ordered to build a hall here in 1541 and this tower may be the result. In the following century it was occupied by the historian Sir James Balfour, Lord Lyon King of Arms.

Access: Well seen from the road.
Relations: T-plan tower houses such as Castle Campbell, Lauriston and Drummond.

DYSART OLD CHURCH   The picturesque royal burgh of Dysart is now on the eastern edge of Kirkcaldy. Overlooking the harbour are the ruins of the old parish church, dedicated to St Serf. Abandoned for a new building in 1802, it has perished apart from the west front, the porch and a few arches from the nave arcades. However, the bell tower – positioned at the south-west corner – is intact and one of the most impressive in Scotland. Apart from its exceptional height (more than eighty feet) it is almost indistinguishable from contemporary tower houses. Architectural details suggest the church was built around 1500 and the tower, at least in its lower part, is of one build with it.

The plain parapet of St Serf's Tower is supported on a row of corbels, with a corner caphouse crowning the spiral stair. Nevertheless the tower was not a 'vicar's pele' like a few in northern England. In all its seven storeys only the gabled attic had a fireplace (probably for a watchman), while the tall sixth storey is pierced by a narrow lancet window on each side to transmit the peal of bells. The lower storeys are lit only by narrow slits. Hatches in the barrel vaults that cover the bottom two floors probably allowed bells to be hoisted and lowered. The first-floor entrance, from the ruined nave, is now reached up a flight of stone steps. Clearly this was a place of refuge when required, since the port's position on the Firth of Forth was a vulnerable one. It survived as a landmark for seafarers after the rest was abandoned.

Access: Exterior only (LA).

Relations: Ecclesiastical fortifications at Arbroath, Crossraguel and St Andrews.

EARLSHALL CASTLE, a mile east of Leuchars along Earlshall Road, is still intact owing to a sensitive restoration by the young architect Robert Lorimer from 1891. A panel on the great ceiling of the long gallery declares that the castle was built (more probably begun) by Sir William Bruce of Earlshall in 1546. A survivor of Flodden, he died in 1584 at the age of ninety-eight. His longevity is recorded on a tablet in the fine Romanesque church of Leuchars nearby. Earlshall is almost a Z-plan tower house and, if that panel is accurate, one of the earliest of this type. A round tower flanks the north-east corner of the main block, but its counterpart at the diagonally opposite angle is a square jamb projecting southwards only. The picturesque skyline reflects a remodelling by Sir William's great grandson of the same name, who died in 1636.

A rounded stair turret projects in the angle between the south-west jamb and the main block. This is crowned by a square caphouse with a plain parapet, but the wall-head is otherwise typical of the later castles. Pitched roofs are framed by crow-stepped gables, while the skyline is enlivened by chimneys and dormer windows. The doorway in the stair turret leads to a barrel-vaulted undercroft. A spiral staircase ascends to the hall, with its Lorimer panelling and screen. In the jamb at this level is a painted ceiling of 1636. More astonishing is the great ceiling of the long gallery that fills the floor above. It bears the initials of the second William Bruce and the year 1620. The many painted panels (somewhat restored by Lorimer) depict figures of the virtues, exotic beasts and heraldic shields. More painted beams can be seen in the bedchamber occupying the round tower at this level. Both flanking towers are four storeys high.

Much of the sixteenth-century barmkin remains, amid fine gardens. A short stretch of wall, with corbelling at the top, runs south from the jamb. It contains the small entrance gateway, surmounted by a panel containing Sir William's arms. The wall ends in a square corner tower with vaulted chambers and a gunport. A seventeenth-century kitchen block bounds the barmkin on the south, but the east side of the enclosure has vanished.

Access: No longer open, though the gardens are open occasionally.

Reference: Guidebook (Pilgrim Press).
Relations: Ferniehirst follows another near Z-plan layout. Painted ceilings at Delgatie, Crathes and Huntingtower.

FALKLAND PALACE   Although it ranks alongside the other quadrangles of the Stewart monarchs, this royal palace is not safely behind castle walls as at Stirling and Edinburgh, nor a fortified enclosure in its own right like Linlithgow. However, it began as the outer courtyard of an older castle of which a fragment survives, and the grand entrance has some of the characteristics of a keep-gatehouse.

The solid base of a circular keep can be seen in the gardens. This thirteenth-century seat of the earls of Fife was sacked by the English in 1337. Here Robert III's son, the Duke of Rothesay, died in suspicious circumstances in 1402, while in the custody of his uncle, the Duke of Albany. James I seized Falkland after his return from English captivity in 1424 and his successors used it as a hunting lodge. The palace courtyard rose under James IV but was left incomplete following his death at Flodden. James V remodelled the facades in Renaissance style in 1536–41. He died here in 1542, still only thirty but weary of life after the rout of his army at Solway Moss. Charles II was the last royal visitor, during his premature attempt to gain the throne in 1651. In the ensuing centuries of absent rulers, Falkland was left to decay. John Crichton-Stuart, third Marquess of Bute, restored the palace after he acquired the office of keeper in 1887.

The great hall on the north side of the quadrangle is reduced to foundations, while there was only a plain wall on the west. Elegant buttresses and portrait medallions on the surviving two ranges are reminiscent of Loire chateaux, James V employing a number of French masons in the construction. Only undercrofts and the courtyard facade survive of the east range, carelessly burnt down when Roundhead troops were billeted here in 1654. The square tower at the rear was largely rebuilt by the Marquess of Bute. Most of the principal floor in the intact south range is occupied by the majestic Chapel Royal, its painted ceiling installed for Charles I's visit in 1633.

Facing East Port, one of the old streets in this picturesque royal burgh, is the handsome gatehouse at the west end of the south range. This was the last part of James V's building campaign and John Brownhill is known to have been the master mason. In relying on a gatehouse as the only strongpoint, the palace compares with some of the semi-fortified mansions of late medieval England. Large windows higher up are barred by iron grilles, like those in the south range. Twin round towers with wide-mouthed gunports flank the gateway, the elevation recalling the James IV Tower at Holyrood Palace. An attic storey rises within the corbelled-out parapet, while the recessed upper stages of the flanking towers are capped by conical roofs. Vaulted guard chambers flank the gate passage, with a pit prison beneath one. The three upper floors formed a self-contained residence for the keeper of the palace, linked by a spiral stair in one of the towers. Their Victorian interiors evoke the Marquess of Bute's restoration, though he imported some authentic pieces of furniture.

Access: Open daily in summer (NTS).
Reference: NT guidebook.
Relations: The royal palaces at Edinburgh, Holyrood, Stirling and Linlithgow. The Marquess of Bute's restorations at Rothesay, Sanquhar and the Old Place of Mochrum.

FERNIE CASTLE stands in its own grounds just off the A92, four miles west of Cupar. From the approach Fernie appears to follow the Z-plan, but the entire eastern half of this long range dates only from the eighteenth century. The original portion is the taller block at the west end – an L-plan tower house with a slightly taller jamb. A round turret, projecting from one corner at the rear, is corbelled out to a square caphouse at the summit. The main block is four storeys high and the gabled roof line is completely unadorned. The entrance, in the side of the jamb, leads to a generous spiral stair. The windows are later enlargements and the interior has been completely modernised, apart from the barrel-vaulted ground floor now housing a bar. There is a big Victorian extension to the west, while a neo-Gothic forework has been added to the jamb. The Fernies sold up to the Arnots of Newton in 1580, so it isn't clear which family was the builder.

Access: Now a hotel.

FORDELL CASTLE stands on an estate two miles north of Dalgety Bay. This charming little tower house with bartizans and dormer windows has twin square flanking turrets that almost form a Z-plan. A lintel bears the year 1580 and the initials of James Henderson of Fordell.

Access: Private.

KELLIE CASTLE is a Scottish Baronial array of crow-stepped gables, turrets and chimneys, rising amid fine gardens three miles north-west of Pittenweem, off the B9171. It was the seat of the Oliphants, who obtained the lands in 1360. The unusual layout consists of a main residential block with three projecting towers. One tower rises at the east end, while the other two flank the western end of the block, resulting in a T-plan layout overall. However, two of the towers are older than the rest. The north-west tower, a simple oblong with vaults on two of its original four floors, was built as a free-standing tower house around 1500. Laurence, fourth Lord Oliphant, added the eastern tower, which bears the initials of his wife Margaret Hay and the year 1573. This five-storey L-plan structure, with a spiral staircase in the jamb, would appear to be a second tower house, added on the other side of a vanished barmkin. As a castle with dual tower houses Kellie is not unique.

The fifth lord, another Laurence, inherited Kellie in 1593 and set about uniting the two towers. His mansion appears to have been completed by 1606 – the year carved on one of the dormer window of the main block. Chiefly domestic in character, the addition of the south-west tower may suggest some lingering defensive intent, though a desire for symmetry was probably more compelling. Its five storeys culminate in a gabled attic with corner bartizans. A matching attic was added to the north-west tower, but on a different axis. The south-west tower contains the entrance, flanked by the main block in the customary way. It leads to a grand staircase rising in straight flights to the first floor. This was divided into a hall and solar (now the drawing room and dining room, respectively). Spiral staircases lead upwards in all three towers, including a corbelled-out re-entrant turret on the south-west tower. The upper floor was originally partitioned into separate family suites. Among the barrel-vaulted undercrofts is the original kitchen with a large fireplace.

In 1613 Oliphant's expenditure forced him to sell up to Sir Thomas Erskine, who became first Earl of Kellie. There is an intricate plaster ceiling of 1617 on the first floor of the east tower. The Royalist third earl, Alexander Erskine, returned from exile after the Restoration to remodel the building. He enlarged the windows of the main floor. Several of his fireplaces and plaster ceilings survive but Georgian embellishments have transformed the interior into elegant state rooms. In 1878 Professor James Lorimer, father of the architect Robert, began a sensitive restoration.

Access: Open regularly in summer (NTS).
Reference: Guidebook by H. Lorimer.
Relations: The twin tower houses at Huntingtower and the Old Place of Mochrum. The fourth lord probably built Hatton as well. There is also a Kelly Castle in Angus.

LOCHORE CASTLE This shattered ruin, otherwise known as Inchgall Castle, stands near the entrance to Lochore Meadows Country Park, a mile and a half south of Ballingry off the B920. Until the water level of Loch Ore was lowered in the eighteenth century, the castle occupied an islet (possibly a crannog) near the shore of the loch. The oblong tower house occupies a low mound that may be a motte. The tower is reduced to two storeys and only the corners of the building stand high, with curious breaches in between. Despite the lack of features the thick walls suggest a relatively early date, perhaps in the late fourteenth century when it was held by the Valognes or Valence family. The tower is placed in the middle of a roughly oval barmkin, added by the Wardlaws of Torrie in the following century. Several battered sections of the surrounding wall remain, though none of the half-round turrets that projected from it. In 1547 the invading English considered Lochore to be one of the four strongest castles in Fife.

Access: Freely accessible with caution (LA).

LORDSCAIRNIE CASTLE, in a field three miles north-west of Cupar, is reached via a sideroad (signposted Moonzie) off the A913. This decaying ruin of a late fifteenth-century tower house stands almost to full height. It was probably built by Alexander Lindsay of Auchtermoonzie, who later became the seventh Earl of Crawford. The austere tower follows the L-plan, though here the jamb is just a small projection containing the entrance and spiral stair. It was divided into four storeys but the ground-floor vaulting has fallen. Low down the worked corner blocks have been prised away by stone robbers, while the window openings are reduced to ragged holes. A round barmkin turret with wide-mouthed gunports also survives.

Access: Well seen from the road.

Relations: Castles of the Lindsay earls at Edzell, Finavon and Invermark.

MACDUFF'S CASTLE occupies the edge of a cliff overlooking the Forth behind East Wemyss cemetery, off the A955. It has no connection with Macduff, the thane of Fife who appears in *Macbeth*. An earlier castle here was burnt by the English in 1306. The castle was rebuilt as a compact quadrangle, probably by a branch of the Livingstones shortly before 1400. After centuries of abandonment it is reduced to overgrown fragments, except for the melancholy ruin of the later west range.

Unfortunately, the gate tower at the north end of this range – the main survivor from the original complex – was demolished owing to its precarious condition as recently as 1967. However, the oblong, three-storey tower house at the south end still stands to the wall-head. It is attributed to Sir John Colville of Ochiltree, who acquired the castle in 1530. Curiously windowless, all lighting must have been concentrated in the one wall that has collapsed. A circular stair turret projects at one corner. Colville also built a hall alongside, now reduced to a row of ruinous barrel vaults. One of them formed a new entrance passage, supplanting the entrance through the demolished gatehouse. Around the same time the landward sides of the castle were surrounded by a concentric outer curtain wall – a rare feature in Scotland. Much of the western wall remains in a ruinous state, with wide-mouthed gunports and a circular corner turret.

Access: Freely accessible (LA).

Relations: The concentric outer wall at Lochindorb.

MONIMAIL TOWER is a small, harled oblong, its four floors linked by a spiral staircase in one corner. The moulded parapet has little angle bartizans, except for the corner occupied by a pyramidal caphouse with carved roundels. This parapet bears the year 1578 and the initials of Sir James Balfour of Pittendreich. The tower house now stands alone, apart from an ungainly lean-to building on one side. However, it once occupied one corner of a vanished residential range, itself just one side of a walled courtyard. The whole complex was in fact a palace of the archbishops of St Andrews, until falling into secular hands at the Reformation. Cardinal Beaton enlarged the palace before his murder at St Andrews in 1546, so it is possible that Balfour merely remodelled an existing tower. It survived unspoiled as accommodation for estate workers after Melville House was built nearby in 1697. Restored from dereliction by the Monimail Tower Project in the 1990s, the tower stands behind the Old Cemetery near the village centre, half a mile west of Letham.

Access: Open daily.
Relations: The archbishops' castle at St Andrews.

MOUNTQUHANIE CASTLE stands in the grounds of Mountquhanie House, west of Rathillet. It is the ivy-grown ruin of an oblong tower house with a corbelled-out parapet, probably built around 1592 by Sir Andrew Balfour of Mountquhanie. There is also a round barmkin turret.

Access: On private land.

MYRES CASTLE, on an estate a mile south of Auchtermuchty, is a sixteenth-century tower house of the Scrymgeours of Myres. This odd variant of the Z-plan consists of two conjoined blocks, both with a round corner turret. One of them is now embedded within a later extension.

Access: A functions venue.

NEWARK CASTLE is the most dramatic but battered of the four 'new works' bearing this name in Scotland. It tops a sheer promontory jutting into the Firth of Forth, half a mile south-west of the fourteenth-century church at St Monans. The castle is reached by following the Fife Coastal Path along the cliff's edge. There has been a castle here since the thirteenth century but the present ruin is later, consisting of one long range. The seaward part may be fifteenth-century work of the Kinloch family, but it is now reduced to a row of three barrel-vaulted undercrofts. Beyond them is an early sixteenth-century extension, built by the Sandilands of Cruivie, rising three storeys to a precarious gable end. A vaulted kitchen with a deep fireplace occupies the ground floor. Projecting from the outer corner are the remains of a round tower. It still rose to its full height of five storeys when sketched by MacGibbon and Ross around 1890, but only one segment stands high now. The windows in the tower were probably enlarged by the Covenanter General David Leslie, who became Lord Newark. From here a stretch of curtain wall ran to the cliff's edge. The remains of a wall opposite closed off the tip of the promontory; the fourth side of the small barmkin is now only bounded by the receding cliff. A Victorian proposal to restore the castle for occupation came to nothing and it continues to crumble. Overlooking the precipice close by is an excellent beehive dovecote.

Access: Exterior only.
Relations: The three other Newarks in Ayrshire, Renfrewshire and Selkirkshire. Cruivie was another tower of the Sandilands.

OLD TULLIALLAN CASTLE The present Tulliallan Castle (now the police college) is a nineteenth-century mansion at the north end of Kincardine-on-Forth, off the A977. Opposite, on the west side of the road, a pathway runs through the woods towards the old castle. This is a shell, but is virtually intact following a thorough consolidation in the 1990s. It formed a defensible hall house, standing within a D-shaped enclosure surrounded by a ditch. In 1304, Edward I ordered the sheriff of Clackmannan to strengthen Tulliallan and the earthwork may date from that period. The refined hall house in ashlar masonry seems to be an unlikely product of that phase and may have been erected by the Douglas family after the Wars of Independence. They went on to become the powerful earls of Douglas.

The walls rise to a corbel table that supported the vanished parapet. Polygonal stair turrets clasp the western corners of the hall block, while two contrasting projections flank the long north front. A narrow latrine wing on the left and a square tower to the right are probably fifteenth-century additions by the Edminston family. There are entrances at both ends of the south front. The main one is framed by a little drawbridge recess, the slot to receive its chain visible above. A portcullis groove can be seen within the arch. The other entrance was closed merely by a door. Both lead into the remarkable ground floor, its ribbed vaulting carried on a row of columns. Originally divided into two compartments, an additional cross-wall obscures one of the columns. The fine quality of the eastern undercroft, which contains a fireplace, shows that it was a residential chamber rather than a store. A passage leads to a latrine and prison in the added north-east tower.

The two spiral staircases ascend to the roofless great hall above. It was remodelled by the Blackadder family in the late sixteenth century. They enlarged the windows, walled off the west end to form a solar and heightened the north-east tower to provide further accommodation.

Access: On private land.

Relations: Black Douglas castles at Tantallon, Threave, Bothwell, Hermitage and Newark (Selkirkshire). The comparable hall house at Rait and remains of ribbed vaulting at Dundonald and Auchindoun.

PITCRUVIE CASTLE is the decaying ruin of an austere tower house, erected soon after the lands were acquired by the Lindsays of Pitcruvie in 1498. It followed the L-plan but the shallow stair jamb has collapsed. The tower stands by farm buildings a mile north-west of Upper Largo.

Access: On farmland.

PITCULLO CASTLE rises in its own grounds a mile north of Dairsie. This late sixteenth-century L-plan tower house, with restored dormer windows, was the seat of the Balfours of Pitcullo. A stair turret, corbelled out in the re-entrant angle, has a balustraded caphouse on top.

Access: Private.

PITEADIE CASTLE is a ruinous L-plan tower house, with a shallow staircase jamb surmounted by a gabled caphouse. Probably built by the Vallances of Piteadie in the late fifteenth century, it stands in the grounds of Piteadie House, three miles south-west of Kirkcaldy.

Access: On private land.

PITFIRRANE CASTLE stands in extensive grounds that are now a golf course, a mile south-west of Crossford. It began as a three-storey, oblong tower house, erected sometime after the Halkett family acquired the lands in 1399. Later, an attic adorned with gables, chimneys and round corner bartizans replaced the former parapet. A slightly taller jamb was also added, converting the tower into an L-plan. These additions are dated 1583 by a heraldic plaque above the original entrance. It also bears the arms of George Halkett of Pitfirrane and his wife, Jean Hepburn. The old yett still hangs nearby. In its lower part the jamb contains a broad spiral stair, leading up to the first-floor hall and the private chambers on the floor above. A corbelled-out stair turret continues to the attic. The yellow-harled tower looks authentic externally but the interior was transformed in Victorian times by the Halketts, who remained here until 1951. Wooden Renaissance panels bearing carved heads adorn the window recesses of the hall.

Access: Now part of Dunfermline Golf Club.
Reference: *Pitfirrane House and its Policies* by I. G. Dewar.

PITREAVIE CASTLE faces Castle Drive in a suburb two miles north of Rosyth. It was probably built soon after the queen's chamberlain, Henry Wardlaw of Balmule, purchased the lands in 1608 – his initials are inscribed over the entrance. Towards the street the building presents a sophisticated E-plan with a jamb at either end. In the re-entrant angles twin stair turrets, with shot holes below, are corbelled out at first-floor level. The handsome facade of ashlar masonry rises to four storeys, including the gabled attics. As its date suggests, this tower house has some of the characteristics of contemporary lairds' houses but the original entrance – a pedimented doorway occupying the traditional position in the side of the western jamb – is guarded by a fine yett. A matching doorway in the other jamb – now converted into a window – led only into an undercroft. In front of this facade was a walled barmkin, eradicated by the road.

The porch, the large window in the left jamb and the extension beyond are part of a drastic restoration by the architect Charles Kinnear in 1885. He transformed the interior, removing the ground-floor vaults and modifying the rear elevation. In 1651, survivors from the Battle of Inverkeithing are said to have sought refuge here but were pelted with stones. Since ceasing to serve as a NATO headquarters in 1996, the building has been converted into flats.

Access: Well seen from the road.
Relations: E-plan tower houses such as Craigston, Castle Stuart and Castle Kennedy.

PITTARTHIE CASTLE, in a field half a mile north of Lochty, is the handsome shell of a tower house of the stepped L-plan variety. A deep fissure disfigures one gable end. Probably erected in the 1580s by James Monypenny of Pitmilly, the large jamb projects in two directions.

Access: On farmland.

PITTENWEEM PRIORY can be found off Priory Court, uphill from the picturesque village harbour. It was a monastery of Augustinian canons, transferred here from the Isle of May in 1318. Two ranges from the claustral buildings survived the Reformation and are embodied in the existing house. Because of its exposed position overlooking the Firth of Forth, the priory was surrounded by a strong precinct wall with a parapet. This has disappeared but the gatehouse survives as an empty shell in front of the house. Probably dating from the fifteenth century, it is a simple oblong with a central gate arch and just one storey above. At the wall-head is a bold line of corbels that supported a vanished machicolated parapet.

Access: Exterior only. There are occasional open days.
Reference: *Pittenweem Priory* by R. A. Lodge.
Relations: Fortified monasteries at St Andrews, Arbroath and Crossraguel.

RAVENSCRAIG CASTLE occupies a rocky promontory jutting into the Firth of Forth. The coastal setting is offset by unsympathetic tower blocks on the northern outskirts of Kirkcaldy, off the A921. James II began the castle in 1460. Ostensibly a dower house for his queen, Mary of Gueldres, the castle must also have been intended to defend the coastline at a time when the Wars of the Roses sparked renewed tensions with England. The French master mason, Henri Merlzioun, designed a castle that is recognised as the first in Britain to show some serious regard for defence against the growing power of artillery. Ironically, the gun-loving king was killed by one of his own cannon while besieging Roxburgh Castle later that same year. Construction continued during James III's minority but the castle was left unfinished when Queen Mary died in 1463.

The defences are concentrated entirely on the landward side and suffer the disadvantage of being overlooked by higher ground, as well as being constructed on a slope. Behind the rock-cut ditch is a massive block with a D-shaped tower at either end. Its unusually thick walls were designed to withstand the bombardment of early cannon, while gunports of the inverted keyhole type show that the castle was intended to have guns of its own. In the middle of the facade is a gateway, reached by a modern bridge across the chasm. In fact the entire complex could almost be described as a keep-gatehouse on a grand scale. The entrance leads into a long gate passage, with a guard room in the thickness of the wall. On either side are vaulted chambers where gun powder was stored. The dominant West Tower, rising from the edge of the cliff, formed a self-contained tower house. Above the barrel-vaulted undercroft were three storeys of residential chambers, squared off internally for domestic convenience. Owing to the sloping terrain the three-storey East Tower rises from a much lower level. Its top storey is only level with the ground floor of the West Tower. There is a well in the vaulted undercroft of this tower.

Ravenscraig did not remain a royal castle for long. In 1470 James III granted it to William Sinclair, first Earl of Caithness. Changes in masons' marks suggest that the castle was left even more unfinished in 1463 than previously supposed. The West Tower and much of the central block may actually be William's work but, if so, he adhered faithfully to the original design. His descendants completed the castle on a reduced scale in the sixteenth century. A large hall was probably intended to occupy the floor of the central block above the gate passage. Instead the Sinclair earls converted this space into an open artillery platform, with wide-mouthed gunports facing landward. They also gave the two towers their now ruinous attic gables. The narrow promontory behind is a paltry courtyard for such a mighty screen. Too sheer to require additional defence, it contains the foundations of a small ancillary range and a low breastwork for guns to command the Forth. These also date from the Sinclair occupation. General Monck bombarded the castle into submission in 1651 and it has been a ruin ever since.

Access: The interior is no longer open but the courtyard is accessible daily (HES).

Relations: Work of James II and III at Stirling and Linlithgow. The Castle of Mey, Castle Sinclair Girnigoe, Old Keiss and Rosslyn were also held by the Sinclair earls. There is another Ravenscraig in Aberdeenshire.

ROSSEND CASTLE rises on a hill overlooking Burntisland harbour and the Firth of Forth. Reached off Melville Gardens, it consists of an L-plan tower house with a long wing projecting to its west. They are both of equal height and four storeys tall, including the attics, but the white harling conceals a complex history. The jamb contains the entrance doorway, though owing to the adjacent range it is not flanked by the main block. A plaque above bears the year 1554 and the arms of George Dury, commendator of Dunfermline Abbey. So the tower house in its current form is mid-sixteenth century, though it is said to embody a much older keep.

The west range contains a spacious hall and upper chambers over a row of three vaulted undercrofts, linked by a corridor. Part of a painted ceiling from the hall is now on display at the National Museum of Scotland in Edinburgh. It bears the initials of Sir Robert Melville of Murdocairney, who inherited Rossend in 1581. Hence the wing would seem to be early addition, though slit windows on the ground floor may be relics of an older chapel when the site was a grange of Dunfermline Abbey. Gunports facing the harbour at ground level show some attention to defence. Furthermore, the south end of the tower house, with its corbelled-out top floor, may have supported a gun platform. During a visit by Mary Queen of Scots, the lovelorn French poet Chastelard was discovered hiding under her bed and was summarily beheaded. After narrowly escaping demolition on account of its derelict state, the building was restored to a habitable condition from 1975.

Access: Well seen from the road.
Relations: Kellie follows a similar T-plan layout.

ROSYTH CASTLE is surrounded by the reclaimed land forming Rosyth Dockyard. From the Fife end of the Queensferry Crossing it is approached along Milne Road. Originally the castle occupied an islet in the Firth of Forth, reached only by a causeway at low tide. Sir David Stewart received the barony in 1428. One of his descendants, the Stewarts of Rosyth, erected the tower house before the end of the century. Complete to the wall-head, though now roofless, this tower may be described as an L-plan, though the staircase jamb is only a shallow projection. A doorway flanked by the jamb leads into the barrel-vaulted undercroft, retaining corbels to support a dividing floor. Owing to the collapse of the spiral stair, the vaulted hall and the chamber above are no longer accessible. Larger windows were inserted at this level by James Stewart in 1639 – one of the transoms bears that year and his initials. Recessed within the parapet are the remains of his attic gables.

The tower house stands at the north-east corner of an oblong barmkin. Toothings at the tower corners show that a curtain wall formed part of the original design, but only two sides stand above the foundations. The north wall is pierced by keyhole gunports and contains the entrance to the castle – a narrow porch immediately beside the tower house. A plaque above bears the royal arms, the initials MR and the year 1561, commemorating the homecoming of Mary Queen of Scots. The courtyard buildings added by Robert Stewart in the mid-sixteenth century are reduced to excavated foundations. In 1572 the castle resisted an attack by troops from Blackness Castle across the Forth, then holding out for the exiled queen. However, the Roundheads made short work of it in 1651. The castle was abandoned when the last Stewart of Rosyth died soon after.

Access: No longer in state care but well seen from Livesay Road.
Relations: Former island castles such as Kilchurn, Castle Kennedy and the Black Castle of Moulin.

ST ANDREWS CASTLE, PRECINCT WALL AND TOWN DEFENCES
On a headland projecting from the rocky shoreline of this cathedral town are the battered ruins of a castle built by the powerful bishops (later archbishops) of St Andrews. First established around 1200 by Bishop Roger de Beaumont, the castle changed hands several times during the Wars of Independence. The

St Andrews Castle, Fife

English strengthened it in 1336 but their brief occupation came to an end the following year. Sir Andrew Murray captured the castle after a three-week siege, then demolished it to prevent its future use by the enemy. Bishop Walter Traill (d.1401) re-established the castle as his episcopal residence. In 1513 four contenders fought for the vacant see. One of them seized the castle, only to be driven out by the prior of St Andrews, who was another candidate.

Dramatic events took place here in 1546. Cardinal David Beaton, then archbishop, made a martyr of the Protestant preacher George Wishart by burning him at the stake outside the castle gate. A few months later some of Wishart's disciples, led by William Kirkcaldy of Grange, entered disguised as masons. They stabbed the cardinal to death and hanged his mutilated body from the parapet. Queen Mary of Guise's forces were kept at bay for nearly a year, despite attempts to undermine the walls. Eventually a French fleet appeared, cutting off the garrison's English supplies and bombarding the seaward defences. The defenders, who included John Knox, were sentenced to become galley slaves. Although the castle was again dismantled, it was soon restored by Archbishop John Hamilton. After all Church lands were seized by the Crown in 1587, the castle became a quarry for the town.

Facing the town is the south front, now the best-preserved part of the castle. This side is dominated by the Fore Tower, a four-storey oblong rising from the ditch on a broad plinth. It began as Bishop Trail's gate tower. Just above the plinth can be seen the sides of the blocked gateway, while higher up is the recess for a drawbridge beam. Archbishop Hamilton capped the tower with a crow-stepped attic gable and a double corbelled-out parapet, rounding to support vanished bartizans at the corners. He also walled up the entrance, thus converting the gatehouse into a tower house. Hamilton transferred the castle entrance to a new range alongside. His badge – a five-pointed star – appears four times in the frieze above the Renaissance portal. It leads into a vaulted gate passage.

Once inside, it is clear that the rest of the castle is very much a ruin. Bishop Traill's curtain wall encloses a roughly oblong courtyard, now devoid of the many buildings it once contained. Eroding cliffs bound the castle headland on the north and east – most of the east curtain has collapsed into the water. Two very ruinous square towers clasp the northern corners, overlooking the sea. Many Protestants languished in the sinister bottle dungeon beneath the Sea Tower. At the south-west corner of the enclosure is a fragment of a large round tower added by Archbishop James Beaton, the cardinal's uncle, for defence by artillery. It was demolished after the siege of 1546 and a matching tower at the south-east angle has long been claimed by the sea. The full complexity of the Fore Tower becomes apparent from its collapsed courtyard front. This end incorporates an earlier gate tower, probably raised to the English in 1336.

Undoubtedly the castle's most important features lie underground. They are the mines dug through the rock in 1546, unique as the only siege tunnels still visible in Britain. Mary of Guise's troops drove a mine towards the Fore Tower with the intention of blowing up the foundations. However, they were intercepted by the Protestants, who broke into it with a counter-mine of their own. Steps below the Fore Tower descend to the cramped counter-mine, one aborted branch leading off in the wrong direction. The main tunnel descends until it breaks into the head of the besiegers' mine, beyond the castle ditch. One can then ascend the rock-cut steps of the besiegers' more generously proportioned tunnel.

Nearby is the old cathedral of St Andrew, once the largest church in Scotland with a priory of Augustinian canons attached to it. It was abandoned at the Reformation and is now reduced to some imposing ruins. The former cathedral precinct is surrounded by a fortified wall of its own. Extending for nearly a mile, it was longer than some town walls and most of it survives. Its lower part dates from the fourteenth century, at which time it was a conventional precinct wall without defensive pretensions. Early in the sixteenth century the wall was heightened and given a corbelled-out parapet by Prior John Hepburn. Panels bearing his arms can be seen on the slender towers with keyhole gunports that project at intervals. Eleven of the towers are semi-circular and two are square.

Another three have disappeared. The fortification of the precinct may reflect the pride of the pre-Reformation Church as much as the canons' insecurity. It must have been too long for a religious community to patrol effectively.

The precinct wall begins at the monumental east end of the cathedral. It follows the shoreline, where the two square towers are placed, then runs alongside the harbour. A gateway here, the Mill Port, is flanked by dumbbell gunports. We then turn inland to follow the wall along Abbey Walk, passing the double-arched gateway known as the Teinds Yett. After a short breach the wall runs north up Abbey Street. The last section leading back to the cathedral has vanished except for the main gatehouse, known as the Pends. Being part of the fourteenth-century precinct wall this structure is not overtly defensive, though the arches at either end of the long gate passage would have been closed by stout gates. The wall ended at the west front of the cathedral church, which thus formed a vulnerable part of the circuit, as at Arbroath.

St Andrews is a historic burgh with the oldest university in Scotland (1412). Like most Scottish towns there is no record of a town wall but the main routes in were barred by four stone gates. The only one to survive is the West Port, spanning South Street. A contract for its rebuilding was drawn up with the master mason Thomas Robertson in 1589. The only substantial town gate to survive in Scotland (though there is a simple gate arch at Dundee), it was considerably restored in 1843. The entrance here is also a simple gateway, supporting a parapet carried on a double row of corbels, but it is flanked by twin polygonal turrets with shot holes.

Access: The castle is open daily, while the precinct wall and the West Port are freely accessible (all HES).

Reference: Castle and cathedral guidebook by C. Tabraham and K. Owen.

Relations: Fortified episcopal residences at Carnasserie, Spynie and Kirkwall. The defensive monasteries of Pittenweem, Arbroath and Crossraguel.

SCOTSTARVIT TOWER, three miles south of Cupar off the A936, is an excellent example of an L-plan tower house. Its ashlar masonry is unusually fine and the tower rises complete to a corbelled-out parapet. The jamb is just a shallow projection containing the spiral staircase all the way up. It flanks the ground-floor entrance, leading into a barrel-vaulted undercroft that was once divided into two levels by a wooden floor. The staircase ascends to the hall, distinguished by its big fireplace and three windows – more than any other room in the tower. A restored wooden ceiling divides it from the solar above, which is covered by a second barrel vault. No doubt the spartan floor above housed the servants. Although the tower of Tarvit is first mentioned in 1579, the lack of any reference to it in an earlier document of 1550 should not be regarded as conclusive. Stylistically it belongs to the early sixteenth century and would therefore have been built by one of the Inglises of Tarvit.

The small windows indicate some genuine defensive intent, unlike the more comfortable towers prevailing later in the century.

In 1611 the advocate Sir John Scot purchased the tower, changing the name to Scotstarvit. He added the attic with its crow-stepped gables, giving six storeys in all, and the pointed stone caphouse over the spiral stair. The mansion called Hill of Tarvit, half a mile to the north-east, contains an ornate fireplace bearing his initials and the year 1627. It was taken from the attic where he wrote his satire on political corruption, *Scot of Scotstarvet's Staggering State of the Scots Statesmen*.

Access: Exterior at any time (HES). The key is available at Hill of Tarvit (NTS).

Reference: Guide by R. MacIvor.

SEAFIELD TOWER, though very ruined, is a landmark on the Fife Coastal Path, three miles south of Kirkcaldy. Situated on a rock that has been tailored to be more sheer, this modest tower house followed the L-plan though the stair jamb has disappeared. One and a half sides of the main body have also fallen away, allowing a view into the wrecked interior. It reveals the imprint of the hall fireplace and the curve of the undercroft vault against the side walls. The tower was divided into four storeys, no doubt with a vanished attic above. There is a chunk of concentric barmkin wall. Probably built early in the sixteenth century, the tower was the seat of the Moultrays of Seafield. It continues to decay – a portion of the superstructure collapsed in 2013.

Access: Freely accessible with caution.

STRATHENDRY CASTLE occupies its own grounds two miles west of Leslie. This mansion is dominated by a rare T-plan tower house with a half-round jamb. There are stretches of parapet along the gable ends only. It was raised in the sixteenth century by the Forresters of Strathendry.

Access: Private.

WEMYSS CASTLE (pronounced 'Weems') occupies extensive grounds overlooking the coast, just north of West Wemyss. It has been the seat of the Wemyss family since the thirteenth century. Here in 1565 Mary Queen of Scots first received her future husband, the troublesome Lord Darnley. The present mansion consists primarily of a long range with flanking wings, poised on the edge of the cliff. Begun in the 1640s by the first Earl of Wemyss, it is notable for its plaster ceilings. However, the northern flanking wing is actually an older tower house, built around 1421 by Sir John Wemyss. Only the two lower storeys of this structure are original, with a vaulted undercroft and a spiral staircase in one corner. The top floor has been rebuilt to match the rest of the mansion's facade.

Later in the fifteenth century the tower house became the south-west corner of an irregular, four-sided enclosure – now very much a service adjunct to the later mansion beyond. On the sheer north and east, overlooking the sea, the curtain wall with its corbelled-out parapet is still recognisable. Projecting at the northern angle is a bold cylindrical tower with a bottle dungeon at the base. There is another at the south-east corner (now at the junction with the later extension). A heraldic panel above the gate passage (now within the later house) bears the initials of David, first Baron of Wemyss – one of many who fell at Flodden in 1513. His son, another David, erected residential buildings around the tiny courtyard. These have been transformed in later centuries, apart from the vaulted ground floor of east range which underlay the great hall.

Access: Visible from the Fife Coastal Path. The gardens are open by appointment.

Relations: The Wemyss family also built Elcho.

OTHER SITES In Pittencrieff Park, close to Dunfermline Abbey, are the foundations of *Malcolm Canmore's Tower*, an early keep of the Scottish kings (though not as early as Canmore). *Crail*'s royal castle overlooked the harbour but was destroyed during the Wars of Independence. *Leuchars*, noted for its Romanesque church, has a low motte in a field to the north of the town. *Maiden Castle* is another motte at Kennoway.

A number of tower houses survive in a much-altered or very ruinous condition:

Ardross Castle (ruin, near Elie)
Balwearie Castle (ruin, near Kirkcaldy)
Bandon Tower (ruin, near Glenrothes)
Bordie Tower (ruin, near Kincardine)
Corston Tower (ruin, near Strathmiglo)
Couston Castle (near Aberdour)
Dairsie Castle
Kilconquhar Castle
Largo Tower (near Upper Largo)
Lundin Tower (near Lower Largo)
Pitcairlie House (near Auchtermuchty)
Struthers Castle (ruin, near Craigrothie)

INVERNESS-SHIRE

This is a large county of dramatic scenery, bisected by the huge fault line of the Great Glen. Its castles are scattered widely and were far enough away from the Wars of Independence to have preserved much early masonry. Castle Roy and Castle Tioram are simple walled enclosures of the thirteenth century. Old Inverlochy follows a more mature layout with corner towers, while a twin-towered gatehouse is the focal point of Urquhart Castle's two courtyards overlooking Loch Ness. The latter two were both built by John Comyn, lord of Badenoch, towards the end of the century. The Red Comyns went on to be driven out by Robert the Bruce. For the next 300 years there is surprisingly little: some domestic buildings at Tioram and the reconstruction of Urquhart on the original lines. Then appeared two late tower houses of unusual plan, Castle Stuart and Dalcross, both erected in the 1620s and attesting the unsettled conditions that still prevailed in the north. Invergarry may be later still, though it is more likely to be a remodelling of an older tower.

County reference: BoS *Highland and Islands*.

CASTLE ROY overlooks the B970, heading north out of Nethy Bridge. This walled enclosure forms a simple rectangle sitting on top of a low, natural mound. The curtain wall is plain but well preserved, much of it lacking little more than the parapet. Only the south corner has fallen. The angles are towerless except for a thinly walled square turret at the north corner, flanked by a postern. The main entrance is a simple archway through the north-east curtain, restored from a ragged hole. No residential buildings survive within. It is conjectured that there were timber ranges against at least some of the walls, since a recess near one corner probably marks a latrine passage. They would have reduced the small courtyard to a tiny space.

The curtain was probably built early in the thirteenth century and thus represents an early castle of enclosure, like Castle Tioram and others on the western seaboard. In the absence of any historical evidence it has been tentatively attributed to the Red Comyn lords of Badenoch, who were then emerging as one of the realm's most powerful families. Lack of later accretions suggests that the castle was abandoned when Robert the Bruce drove out the Comyns in 1308, but thankfully not destroyed as many castles were during

the Wars of Independence. Its long neglect makes its condition all the more remarkable. The ruins have now been consolidated by the Castle Roy Trust.
Access: Freely accessible.
Relations: The Red Comyn castles of Old Inverlochy, Urquhart and Lochindorb.

CASTLE STUART overlooks the Moray Firth in secluded grounds beside the B9039, eight miles north-east of Inverness. This sophisticated version of the tower house theme was built by James Stewart, third Earl of Moray, to replace Darnaway Castle as his chief seat. The year 1625 carved on two of the dormer windows may commemorate the completion of the structure. Just a year previously the castle had been seized by the MacKintoshes, who claimed possession and had to be bought off. Such dangers may explain the defensive character at so late a date. After more than a century of abandonment the building was restored for habitation by the thirteenth earl in 1869. An older fortification is attested by Auld Petty Motte, closer to the shore.

The tower house consists of an oblong main block with tall, square towers flanking the south and east corners – an E-plan designed to impress rather than the more defensively efficient Z-plan. There is a deliberate flouting of symmetry typical of the Scottish Baronial style. One tower is gabled while the other rises to an archaic parapet, though both have round corner bartizans. The other two angles of the main block are adorned simply by gabled turrets, projecting diagonally high up. Wide-mouthed gunports are concentrated on the entrance front and its flanking towers. The central doorway is a much later insertion but the original entrance survives in the side of the south tower, flanked by the main block as usual. It leads to a grand staircase, rising in straight flights to the first floor. From here twin spiral stairs occupy turrets corbelled out between the towers and the main block. Both the first and second floors are divided into a hall and chamber, probably forming separate suites for the earl and his countess. A long gallery filled the attic, while the flanking towers provided bedchambers and withdrawing rooms. All these interiors are quite modernised. The ground floor remains more authentic, consisting of a kitchen and a row of barrel-vaulted storerooms linked by a corridor.

Access: No longer open but visible from Auld Petty lane (now a holiday let).
Relations: Darnaway. The E-plan tower houses at Craigston, Borthwick and Castle Kennedy.

CASTLE TIORAM (pronounced Cheerum), despite continuing neglect, is a striking sight on a tidal islet in Loch Moidart, six miles north of Salen. The castle deserves better treatment, because it is one of the best of the early stone enclosures of the western seaboard. Its closest parallel is Mingary, at the other end of the Ardnamurchan peninsula in western Argyll. Both castles may have been erected towards the end of the thirteenth century but there is no documentary evidence as to their builders – the wide-ranging MacDougalls or the emerging MacDonald clan are equally possible. It is even plausible that Tioram was raised by the MacIains early in the fourteenth century. While lacking the mural towers and other defensive improvements characteristic of this period, they are nevertheless impressive walled enclosures, tailored to the rocks on which they stand. The angles are rounded off to make assault with a pick more difficult. At Tioram the solid curtain wall survives intact and encloses an irregular, five-sided courtyard. Chunky battlements and drainage spouts enliven the wall-head, though these are no doubt later embellishments. There are also putlog holes for a continuous wooden hoarding. A simple doorway, overlooked at parapet level by a box machicolation, admits at the north end, while two blocked posterns can be discerned elsewhere.

On the north-west side of the sloping courtyard a straight staircase leads to the parapet, while on the south-east a hall block was erected against the curtain in the fourteenth century. This may be associated with Amy MacRuari, who took up residence after she was divorced by the Lord of the Isles in 1350. Now a shell but otherwise intact, the entrance is also crowned by machicolations. It leads into the great hall on the first floor, with a fireplace and a spiral stair in one corner. Below is the usual vaulted undercroft, while the solar above was originally the top floor. A south-west range, consisting of twin chambers above more undercrofts, was built by the MacRuaris in the following century to supplement the accommodation.

In 1493 the castle passed to the MacDonalds of Clanranald. Towards 1600 they added a top storey and attic gables above the original hall block, making it more like a conventional tower house. Even so it does not rise much higher than the lofty curtain. They also heightened half of the south-west range to form another tower, with round corner bartizans and a spiral staircase jamb. The castle was captured by the fourth Earl of Huntly in 1554 and again by the Roundheads in 1651. Its Jacobite owner burnt it to a shell in 1715 to prevent its use by Hanoverian troops.

Access: Exterior only when the tide is out.

Reference: *Transactions of the Glasgow Archaeological Society* (13). *Castle Tioram: A Statement of Cultural Significance* by A. R. P. Lorimer and Associates.

Relations: Mingary and other simple enclosures such as Castle Roy and Innis Chonnell.

DALCROSS CASTLE occupies a country estate overlooking the Moray Firth, two miles south-west of Croy. This lofty, gabled L-plan tower house was built from 1621 by Simon Fraser, sixth Lord Lovat. Like Castle Stuart it is rather late for a new tower house of some defensive pretensions, though the layout is in keeping with trends in lairds' houses of the time. Beyond the main block is a lower extension of 1703. The Duke of Cumberland lodged here before the rout at nearby Culloden in 1746. The tower house decayed into a roofless shell but was restored to a habitable condition from 1896 by the architect William Carruthers.

The 'jamb' of the tower house is virtually a separate building and is only connected to the main block by one corner. At five storeys (including the attic) it has one storey more than the main block, though it rises only slightly higher. They are linked by a square stair turret in the re-entrant angle, which is a little higher again. This terminates in a caphouse with a round corner bartizan, while there are bartizans at three other corners of the tower house as well. There is, of course, no parapet. Wide-mouthed gunports pierce the walls near ground level and a number of shot holes can be seen in the walls higher up. The entrance in the stair turret is surmounted by a panel bearing the MacKintosh arms (they purchased the lands in 1702). It leads to a wide spiral staircase that serves the differing levels of both wings. On the ground floor is a row of barrel-vaulted storerooms linked by a corridor, one of them the kitchen with an arched fireplace. The monumental fireplace in the first-floor hall above is one of the few original features to survive in the upper storeys, which have been transformed in accordance with later tastes.

Access: Private (now a holiday let).
Relations: Castle Stuart. Castle Levan has a similar layout.

ERCHLESS CASTLE occupies an estate a mile north-east of Struy. This Victorian mansion is dominated by a tall L-plan tower house with corner bartizans and a re-entrant stair turret. The tower was built by the Chisholms around 1600 but has been thoroughly modernised internally.

Access: The grounds are open by appointment (now a holiday let).

INVERGARRY CASTLE overlooks Loch Oich, the smallest of the lochs filling the Great Glen. This strategically placed tower house of the MacDonells of Glengarry seems to have been built after they were driven out of Strome Castle in 1602, though it was described as 'new' when it was burnt by General Monck in 1654. Even for the early seventeenth century the walls are surprisingly thick, but there is no evidence for an older tower here. The layout is L-plan, with a round tower projecting at the east corner to the rear. Unusually, no vaults appear to have covered the main block, which comprised a kitchen at ground level, a hall above and private quarters on the three upper floors, all linked by a spiral stair (now fallen) in the corner tower. After Monck's incursion the tower house was rehabilitated, which might explain the loss of older features. Among other improvements a grand staircase block was added, filling in the re-entrant angle.

The MacDonells were staunch Jacobites and Invergarry was regarded as a place of great strength. Having surrendered to Hanoverian troops after a siege in 1716, they entertained Bonnie Prince Charlie here on his retreat in 1746. To forestall any further Jacobite activity, the Duke of Cumberland blew up the tower after the Battle of Culloden. As a result the main body of the tower house still stands mostly to full height but the jamb and the added stair block have been levelled, though the imprint of the staircase is embedded in the tower wall. It stands beside the long drive to Glengarry Castle, its Victorian successor mansion, a mile east of Invergarry village via the A82.

Access: Exterior only.

Relations: The MacDonell castle at Strome. L-plan tower houses with an additional corner tower at Dunderave, Killochan and Dundas.

LOCH AN EILEIN CASTLE Loch an Eilein, in Rothiemurchus Forest and fringed by the Cairngorms, is five miles south of Aviemore. It is reached via a sideroad off the B970. On an islet close to the west bank of the loch are the overgrown ruins of a small castle, the western facade being much the best-preserved part. It comprises a stretch of wall divided into three distinct sections. That to the right is the gable end of a little hall house of the bishops of Moray, probably built in the thirteenth century. To the left is one side of a modest oblong tower house attributed to Alexander Stewart, the Wolf of Badenoch, who is notorious for sacking Elgin Cathedral in 1390. The middle part is a chunk of curtain wall built by the Grants of Rothiemurchus to link the two. They also erected a domestic range to the rear, creating a small courtyard between that and the older structures. The tower has a vaulted ground floor. The castle was besieged by Jacobites in 1690 and sheltered survivors from the Battle of Culloden in 1746. Since then the level of the loch has been raised so the islet, which harbours a colony of ospreys, is smaller than it used to be.

Access: There is a good view from the loch shore.

Reference: *Antiquaries Journal* (17).

Relations: The bishops' palace at Spynie. Muckrach was another seat of the Grants of Rothiemurchus.

MUCKRACH CASTLE This tower house, restored from ruin, stands a mile west of Dulnain Bridge. Built by Patrick Grant of Rothiemurchus around 1598, the main block has a circular tower at one corner, corbelled out into a caphouse higher up. A barmkin turret also survives.

Access: Private (now a holiday let).

OLD INVERLOCHY CASTLE guards the entrance to the Great Glen, standing beside the River Lochy just before it flows into Loch Linnhe. Overshadowed by Ben Nevis, it is two miles north-east of Fort William and close to the A82. It seems to have been built by John Comyn, lord of Badenoch, one of the claimants to the Scottish throne following the death of the infant Queen Margaret in 1290. His line was known as the Red Comyns to distinguish them from the Black Comyn earls of Buchan. John's familiarity with

Edwardian-style principles is apparent in a group of castles protecting his extensive domains. The quadrangular plan with circular angle towers has been compared to Harlech Castle. Since there is no gatehouse – only simple portals midway along the north-west and south-east curtain walls – perhaps a closer parallel is the inner ward at Conwy. Those Welsh castles rose in the 1280s and Inverlochy is surely no earlier. Although the castle is now a ruin, it survives largely intact except for the parapet (the battlements on the west side are a clumsy restoration). A surrounding moat was fed by the river but has long been filled in.

The boldly projecting corner towers contained three storeys. Comyn's Tower at the west corner is larger than the others and may be regarded as one of Scotland's few surviving round keeps. One tower has suffered a deep breach. All four are entered at the corners of the courtyard. From each entrance passage a staircase curves upwards in the thickness of the tower wall to the upper floors. Arrow slits with fish-tail bases pierce the towers lower down. One particularly Edwardian motif is the way that the wall walk of the curtain bypasses the keep. The south-east (landward) gate is better preserved than the gate facing the water on the north-west, but both retain portcullis grooves.

John Comyn died here in 1300. His son of the same name, one of the Guardians of Scotland appointed after the Battle of Falkirk, was stabbed to death by Robert the Bruce at Dumfries in 1306. Bruce captured the castle the following year, during the campaign that drove the remaining Comyns into exile. Unlike many castles involved in the Wars of Independence it was not destroyed, no doubt because it could be garrisoned to keep the Highlanders in check. Nevertheless, its history is obscure until 1506, when the third Earl of Huntly obtained a licence to strengthen the castle. Despite the licence, his only contribution seems to have been a vanished residential block against the north-west curtain. Reoccupation seems to have been short-lived, so the castle was spared more extensive alterations. A Victorian mansion two miles away has usurped its name. Two battles of Inverlochy were fought close by. In 1431 the MacDonalds defeated James I's supporters, while in 1645 the Marquis of Montrose enjoyed a short-lived triumph over the Marquis of Argyll.

Access: Freely accessible (HES).
Reference: *PSAS* (128).
Relations: Urquhart and Lochindorb were also raised by John Comyn, along with destroyed Ruthven. Kildrummy, Dunstaffnage, Caerlaverock and Bothwell are other mature castles of enclosure.

URQUHART CASTLE Jutting into the mysterious waters of Loch Ness, two miles south-east of Drumnadrochit, is one of the most romantically sited of all Scottish castles. It was first established around 1230 by Sir Alan Durward, Alexander II's son-in-law and justiciar, in an attempt to bring royal control to the north. However, the extensive castle visible today was probably the

Urquhart Castle, Inverness-shire

creation of John Comyn, lord of Badenoch, who was granted the lordship in 1275. The English garrison installed without resistance in 1296 withstood a night attack by Andrew Moray the following year, but seems to have been dislodged not long after. The castle again fell to the English following a long siege in 1303 but was recovered by Robert the Bruce four years later (a replica trebuchet can be seen close by). Unlike the more southerly castles fought over during the Wars of Independence, Urquhart was not dismantled. By 1333 it was one of only five castles to remain loyal to the young David II during Edward Balliol's English-backed campaign to win the throne.

In the ensuing centuries the castle formed a bastion against the mainland ambitions of the MacDonald lords of the Isles, who often raided the Great Glen. Although belonging to the Crown, the castle was usually entrusted to loyal lords. Thus in 1509 James IV granted the castle to John Grant, the 'Red Bard' of Freuchie, on condition that he 'repair or build at the castle a tower, with an outwork or rampart of stone and lime, for protecting the lands and the people from the inroads of thieves and malefactors'. Grant gradually rebuilt the decayed castle, though he was temporarily driven out by the MacDonalds in 1514 and there were further devastating raids. In 1644 it was looted by the Covenanters. The castle met its end after the first Jacobite uprising. Having resisted 600 Jacobites here in 1689, the royal garrison blew up the gatehouse on their departure two years later.

Urquhart is an unusually extensive castle for Scotland, but it is now very much a battered ruin. Two main periods are represented, John Comyn's castle of enclosure having largely been reconstructed on the original lines by John Grant. Although overlooked by much higher ground, the long promontory above the loch is a strong site, naturally divided into two courtyards by a central inlet. Both courtyards are surrounded by stone curtain walls, now very ruinous but still thirteenth century in parts. To the west the landward approach is cut off by a deep ditch, crossed by a stone causeway with a gap for the drawbridge. A gatehouse bars the entrance, comprising a gate passage between U-shaped flanking towers, though the existing gate arches and barrel vaults belong to the Grant reconstruction. Fallen chunks of masonry here recall the explosion of 1691.

The gatehouse stands at the narrow neck between the two courtyards, an arrangement vaguely reminiscent of Caernarfon Castle. Opposite, where the enclosure is narrowest, a water gate leads to a landing place on the loch shore. To the south is the upper courtyard, its curtain largely reduced to foundations except for part of a mural tower facing the loch. It is overlooked by a rocky knoll forming a natural motte. A roughly oblong walled enclosure on its summit represents Alan Durward's original castle, itself on the site of a Pictish fort.

A smaller knoll in the lower courtyard carries the foundations of the chapel. The main domestic buildings here follow the bends in the curtain, overlooking the loch. They were probably erected when Alexander Stewart, the notorious Wolf of Badenoch, had custody. Only their lower parts survive, comprising a great hall undercroft flanked by the kitchen and a solar block. At the northern apex of the castle is the tower house, isolated from the courtyard by its own ditch. This oblong tower is the only part of the castle to survive in a reasonably complete state, except for the south wall, which collapsed in a gale in 1715. John Grant rebuilt the tower house after 1509, though the vaulted basement survives from a fourteenth-century predecessor. The ground-floor entrance leads into the hall. A spiral staircase winds past two similar floors on its way to the summit, offering panoramic views of the loch and – if you are very lucky – a glimpse of its monstrous inhabitant. The corbelled-out parapet has the remains of two corner caphouses. Another stair descends from the hall to the basement, below courtyard level, and further down to a postern overlooking the loch.

Access: Open daily (HES). A lift descends to the castle from the car park.
Reference: Guidebook by K. Grant, R. Pickering and N. Scott.
Relations: Durward's castles at Coull and Lumphanan. Comyn also built Old Inverlochy and Lochindorb. Castle Grant was the main seat of the Grants of Freuchie.

OTHER SITES   On a natural mound near Kingussie stands the gaunt shell of the *Ruthven* Barracks (HES), a Hanoverian garrison post of 1719. It occupies the site of another stronghold of John Comyn of Badenoch, blown up by the Jacobites. *Moniack Castle* (near Balchraggan) incorporates the jamb of an L-plan tower house, while the grounds of *Inshes House* (near Inverness) preserve a square flanking tower from the barmkin.

Inverness Castle, on a hill overlooking the River Ness at the heart of the old royal burgh, was the most important stronghold in the north. The original castle, perhaps first raised under David I, was destroyed by Robert the Bruce. It was rebuilt by the Earl of Mar in 1412–15 as a large tower house and walled courtyard. After the Jacobite rising of 1715, the castle was transformed into a Hanoverian garrison post. This was blown up by order of Bonnie Prince Charlie before the Battle of Culloden, fought close by. The remains were swept away in 1833 to make way for the present neo-Gothic courthouse and county jail, which together form an impressive castellated sham (LA). A well between the two buildings is the sole relic of the medieval castle.

KINCARDINESHIRE

Sandwiched between Aberdeenshire and Angus, this former east coast county boasts two exceptional castles: Dunnottar, the seat of the earls Marischal on its mighty coastal rock, has an early tower house, a sixteenth-century courtyard mansion and complex entrance defences utilising the natural terrain. Crathes is one of the finest of the later tower houses and preserves some excellent painted ceilings. Most of the county's tower houses follow the L-plan but the remainder are tucked away on private estates. The best are the Castle of Fiddes and Muchalls, the latter with its little barmkin and plaster ceilings. Both Crathes and Muchalls were built by the Burnetts of Leys.

County reference: BoS *Aberdeenshire: South and Aberdeen.*

ALLARDICE CASTLE, on an estate two miles north-west of Inverbervie, comprises two altered wings at right angles from a small courtyard complex. It was probably built by Sir John Allardyce before 1600. One of the wings is pierced by a gate passage with a fine entrance portal.

Access: Private.

BALBEGNO CASTLE, in its own grounds a mile south-west of Fettercairn, is an L-plan tower house with a later extension alongside. It bears the year 1569 and the initials of John Wood of Balbegno. The rare rib-vaulted hall suggests the same masons as Delgatie and Towie Barclay.

Access: Private (now a holiday let).

BENHOLM CASTLE occupies its own grounds a mile north of Benholm village. It consists of a Georgian mansion and an oblong tower house with a corbelled-out parapet and a prominent caphouse, built before 1500 by the Lundies of Benholm. Two sides collapsed in a gale in 1993.

Access: Private.

CASTLE OF FIDDES   This tower house is concealed in grounds off the road to Barras, which runs south from the A90 near Temple of Fiddes. It is an unusual and ingenious variant of the L-plan, picturesque despite the dull, grey harling. A window lintel bears the year 1592, which is a good approximation of the tower's date. It would put its construction in the time of Robert

Arbuthnott of Fiddes, who died around 1606. After a long period of dereliction, the building was twice restored for occupation in the twentieth century.

Rounded turrets flank the gabled south front of the main block. One of them is corbelled out high up into a square caphouse, diagonal to the rest. The other, with a double row of corbelling near the top, is awkwardly truncated in line with the curved gable end. The jamb to the east is nearly as large as the main block. On the north side, from the first floor upwards, a shallow round projection denotes a spiral staircase. The other corners have slender bartizans with conical roofs, rising up from second-floor level. These have shot holes angled downwards, while there are other shot holes near ground level. The original ground-floor doorway, flanked by the jamb, is overlooked high up by a little balcony containing three machicolations.

An entrance lobby contains separate doorways to the vaulted undercroft in the main block and the vaulted kitchen (with the usual arched fireplace) in the jamb. From the same lobby a spiral stair ascends in one of the flanking turrets to the first-floor hall in the main block. From here the stair transfers to the other flanking turret and on to an upper hall. A much smaller spiral staircase in the thickness of the wall leads to the attic rooms. There are chambers at each level in the jamb, connected by the spiral stair at the rear.

Access: Private.

CLUNY CRICHTON CASTLE, on a farm a mile east of Milltown of Campfield, is a ruined tower house of the stepped L-plan. Only the stair turret rises to full height. A panel over the entrance states that it was built by George Crichton in 1666, making it an exceptionally late one.

Access: On farmland.

CRATHES CASTLE In the exuberance of its upper parts, Crathes rivals Craigievar as the perfect later Scottish tower house. Only its stockier profile may push it into second place aesthetically. Over the original entrance doorway are the arms of the Burnetts of Leys and the years 1553 and 1596 – presumably marking the beginning and end of construction. However, a keystone on the hall vault bears the year 1554, suggesting a rapid building of the main structure by one Alexander Burnett, and a later campaign of roof-level embellishment by another in the new Scottish Baronial style. This second Alexander was the great-grandson of the original builder (father and grandfather both died soon after inheriting).

As usual at this late stage there is no parapet, but the wall-head is alive with dormer windows, cannon spouts and crow-stepped gables. The southern corners sport little round bartizans with conical roofs, while the others bear oblong caphouses projecting on corbels. Two more caphouses crown the jamb. These embellishments are attributed to one of the Bell family of master masons who adorned a number of north-eastern tower houses, including Craigievar.

The wide south gable with its corbelled-out stair turret midway along hints that the tower house is divided by a cross-wall, increasing the accommodation and explaining its generous width. Lower down this L-plan tower is quite austere and sparingly fenestrated, showing some lingering regard for defence, though a large Victorian window now lights the hall. Rounded corners accentuate the smooth effect of the harled walls – another parallel with Craigievar.

The original entrance is in the east wall, flanked by the jamb. However, the tower house is now entered through a low adjoining wing, added in the eighteenth century by a Burnett whose twenty-one children proved too numerous even for this tower to accommodate. Three vaulted compartments occupy the ground level of the tower, one of them a kitchen in the jamb. Closing the original entrance is a good example of a yett made from interleaving iron bars. A service stair ascends from the wine cellar but the main spiral staircase occupies the south-east corner of the main block, unusual for an L-plan tower in being away from the jamb. It leads to the High Hall, which is twice the height of the other storeys. The plain barrel-vault of this lofty chamber was once painted, as attested in the alcoves. Above the Italian Renaissance fireplace (a later insertion) is the ivory Horn of Leys, supposedly given to the Burnets by Robert the Bruce.

Although Crathes lacks the ornate plaster ceilings of Craigievar it is notable for its painted wooden ceilings, probably commissioned by the younger Alexander Burnett. The best are in the rooms on the third floor. In the long spaces between the beams of the Nine Nobles' Room are trios of pagan, Jewish and Christian heroes. The Muses' Room provides another treatment of mythological figures, while the ceiling of the Green Lady's Room is full of grotesque imagery. Admittedly unsophisticated when compared with Renaissance painting in Europe, they are nevertheless a colourful and rare survival, if somewhat restored. A four-poster bed in another chamber is believed to have been the younger Alexander Burnett's. Filling the attic, the long gallery is covered by a seventeenth-century oak panelled ceiling.

Crathes surrendered without a fight to the Marquis of Montrose in 1644 – the nearest it ever came to a siege. Relieved of Victorian extensions after a fire in 1966, the tower stands amid splendid formal gardens off the A93, three miles east of Banchory. (See plan on page 360.)

Access: Open daily in summer and regularly in winter (NTS).
Reference: Guidebook by O. Thomson.
Relations: The Burnetts also built Muchalls Castle. Craigievar, Midmar and Glamis are other masterpieces of the Scottish Baronial style. Painted ceilings at Delgatie, Earlshall and Huntingtower.

DUNNOTTAR CASTLE occupies a spectacular boss of rock projecting into the North Sea, two miles south of Stonehaven. This natural fortification no doubt supported an earlier dun, but it became sacred ground owing to

Dunnottar Castle, Kincardineshire

the tradition that the missionary St Ninian founded a chapel here. The rock emerged as an English stronghold during the Wars of Independence. According to Blind Harry, William Wallace scaled it in 1297, while Sir Andrew Murray definitely captured the rock in 1336. The presence of St Ninian's chapel on the summit caused Sir William Keith to be excommunicated when he later fortified the site. In 1395 he appealed to the Avignon Pope on the grounds that he needed a castle 'to protect himself from tribulations and from the malice of the tyrants of the kingdom'. This gives a plausible date for the tower house that dominates the castle. Sir William was Great Marischal (marshal) and the castle formed the power base of his descendants, the earls Marischal.

Another William Keith, the fourth earl, constructed the formidable entrance defences in the 1570s. He also began the courtyard mansion on the summit, completed by his son George, who inherited in 1581. In 1645 the Marquis of Montrose burnt the surrounding lands but did not attempt to take the castle. Dunnottar was finally put to the test in 1651, enduring eight months of siege under its governor, George Ogilvy. Nevertheless the surrender came swiftly once the Roundheads managed to bring siege guns to the site. The royal regalia in its care were spirited away before the fall, being hidden in Kinneff Old Church until the Restoration. Following the tenth Earl Marischal's involvement in the Jacobite rising of 1715, the castle was dismantled. It is now largely a ruin.

To reach the castle it is necessary to descend a steep flight of steps to the shoreline. A cleft in the rock forms a natural ramp to the summit, barred by a succession of defences built by the fourth earl. A stretch of wall closes the gap, flanked on one side by a tall, square tower built against the cliff face. Known as Benholm's Lodging, this has a double tier of wide-mouthed gunports sweeping the approach. Once through the narrow entrance gateway, a staircase ascends past vaulted guard rooms on either side. Benholm's Lodging is reached beyond the guard room to the right. It rises to a crowning vault, all the more impressive owing to the loss of the intervening wooden floors. A gloomy pit prison occupied the base of this tower. At the top of the staircase the visitor is confronted by a screen wall with more gunports, concealing another guard room cut out of the rock. The cleft, ascending steeply, is covered by two successive barrel vaults before finally emerging on the summit of the rock.

Turning right at the summit, the visitor passes the ruinous Waterton's Lodging of 1574, its stair turret crowned by a caphouse. Behind, a long range of stables rises from the cliff's edge. However, our attention is drawn to the tower house beyond, virtually intact though now an empty shell. It is one of the earliest L-plan tower houses to survive. Such towers would usually be entered in the angle between the jamb and the main block, but here the jamb overlooks the cliff. Consequently, the original entrance was placed in the east wall at first-floor level. It led into the hall, a well-lit chamber served by a kitchen in the jamb. Above is the solar, reached by a spiral stair, while vaulted undercrofts occupied the ground floor. The tower retains its parapet corbels, rounding at the corners to support vanished bartizans. In the late sixteenth century the tower house was remodelled to give the familiar gabled profile, but this attic stage is now quite ruinous except for the caphouse at the head of the spiral stair. At the same time a larger kitchen was installed in the ground floor undercroft, where the present entrance to the tower was inserted.

Across the plateau to the east is the courtyard mansion, overlooking the cliff. It forms an irregular quadrangle, purely domestic in character on this secure summit and partly open to the south. Two portions have been re-roofed: the drawing room in the north range and the Silver House projecting from the west. Spacious chambers over barrel-vaulted undercrofts provided separate dwellings for the earl and his countess, while a long gallery runs the length of the west range. A wing projecting eastwards contains a ponderous undercroft known as the Whigs' Vault, where 167 Covenanters were crammed after the Argyll revolt of 1685. In the courtyard is a large cistern. The simple chapel on the south side of the quadrangle was restored by the fifth earl (a rare undertaking by a Protestant lord) but embodies an earlier structure consecrated in 1276. William Wallace is said to have burnt this chapel – with the English garrison trapped inside – when he captured the rock.

Cliffs form an impregnable defence most of the way around the rock, so an enclosing curtain wall was not necessary. Only on the north is the descent anything less than sheer. Here the gap was closed by a stretch of wall built some way down the slope. Only fragments survive.

Access: Open daily (HHA – uphill walk).

Reference: Guidebook by A. Cunningham. *Dunnottar Castle* by W. D. Simpson.

Relations: Hallforest, Inverugie and Ackergill are other castles of the Keith earls. Early L-plan tower houses such as Craigmillar and Neidpath.

DURRIS HOUSE, on an estate two miles east of Durris, incorporates an early seventeenth-century tower house of the Frasers of Durris, with a tall jamb. Originally L-plan, the re-entrant angle has since been filled in. There is a motte (Castle Hill) to the north-west, by the River Dee.

Access: Private (now a holiday let).

INGLISMALDIE CASTLE is set in its own grounds two miles south-west of Luthermuir. This late sixteenth-century L-plan tower house of the Livingstones of Inglismaldie, with prominent bartizans, is somewhat restored and now sandwiched between the wings of a Victorian mansion.

Access: Private.

MUCHALLS CASTLE lies in wooded grounds half a mile north of Bridge of Muchalls, off the A92. The inscription in a plaque over the entrance gate says it all: 'This work begun on the east & north be Ar. Burnet of Leyis 1619: ended be Sr Thomas Burnet of Leyis his sonne 1627.' Alexander Burnett of Leys, who embellished the upper parts of Crathes Castle, acquired Muchalls in 1600. He died in 1619, so the bulk of this mansion must be due to Sir Thomas.

On the north and east sides are two harled ranges at right angles to each other, though as at MacLellan's Castle (which Muchalls seems to emulate) both ranges are rather long to be regarded as a conventional L-plan tower house. They are three storeys high, including the attic stage, and terminate in crow-stepped gables. The north front is mutilated by Victorian extensions. Several prominent chimneys crowning the roof ridges attest the ample fireplaces within. A jamb with a corbelled-out top projects at the south end of the east range, while several round bartizans clasp the corners high up. The other two sides of the stone-flagged barmkin are enclosed by a wall, ruined on the south but intact on the west. Its modest height does not offer much security, as might be expected at this late date, but it has a parapet walk with four projecting bartizans. In the middle is the arched gateway, flanked on either side by triple shot holes.

The main entrance is in the re-entrant angle between the east range and the jamb. It leads to a corridor linking three undercrofts and a kitchen in the east range. The north range contains two more undercrofts directly connected with each other (one has since been subdivided). All these rooms are groin vaulted and the southernmost is said to be the relic of an older tower house. The stair in the jamb winds up to the hall, a magnificent chamber with a plaster ceiling of hanging pendants and painted roundels featuring the heads of biblical and mythological heroes. The fireplace overmantel bears the royal arms, with lion and unicorn supporters and the year 1624. On either side pairs of caryatids appear to be doing the Egyptian walk. Within the fireplace is a listening hole (a laird's lug) from the chamber above. Beyond an ante-room at the north-east corner, the withdrawing room and laird's study in the north range also have fine plaster ceilings. The top floor is plainer and more altered, with little closets inside the bartizans.

Access: Private.

Relations: Crathes and MacLellan's. The plaster ceilings at Craigievar, Glamis and Thirlestane.

THORNTON CASTLE, in extensive grounds two miles west of Laurencekirk, was the seat of the Strachans of Thornton. It has an L-plan tower house built around 1531 and a tall, circular barmkin tower, linked by range built in 1662 over a row of older, barrel-vaulted undercrofts.

Access: Private (now a holiday let).

TILQUHILLIE CASTLE, in its own grounds three miles south-east of Banchory, is a well-restored Z-plan tower house with rounded corners and two square flanking towers, one of which is nearly as large as the main block. It is attributed to John Douglas of Tilquhillie around 1576.

Access: Private.

OTHER SITES   *Kincardine Castle* (not to be confused with the Victorian mansion of that name in Aberdeenshire) originally dominated a vanished royal burgh near Fettercairn. Built by Alexander II as a compact oblong enclosure with a gateway flanked by square towers, it is now attested only by fragments in the undergrowth. *Lauriston Castle* (near St Cyrus) preserves a length of barmkin wall with a flanking turret, on the site of an older stronghold strengthened by Edward III. *Glenbervie House* began as a fifteenth-century hall block with two round corner towers but has largely been rebuilt. *Hallgreen Castle* (at Inverbervie) incorporates a much-altered L-plan tower house. *Kaim of Mathers* (near St Cyrus) is a small and very ruinous watch tower, precariously perched on a sheer promontory overlooking the sea.

KIRKCUDBRIGHTSHIRE

Kirkcudbrightshire forms the eastern half of Galloway, which reluctantly succumbed to royal rule. Norman settlers encouraged here by David I account for the number of motte-and-bailey earthworks, among which the Mote of Urr is pre-eminent. Another motte at Buittle supports fragments of a castle of the Balliols, who briefly attained the Scottish Crown. The huge, fourteenth-century tower house on Threave Island, with its later surrounding wall showing early provision for artillery defence, is an appropriate monument to the ambitions of the Black Douglas dynasty before their downfall. Cardoness offers a tower house of some distinction from the following century, while Orchardton is uniquely circular. Carsluith, Drumcoltran and Buittle are more typical later towers. Kirkcudbright is dominated by MacLellan's Castle, a fine semi-defensive town mansion of the 1570s, matched by the more mutilated courtyard castle of Kenmure. Access is relatively good owing to several castles fortuitously being in state care.

County reference: RCAHMS *Galloway* (vol. 2). BoS *Dumfries and Galloway*.

BARHOLM CASTLE is an L-plan tower house of the McCullochs of Barholm, probably dating from the early sixteenth century. The ornate doorway may have been robbed from a monastery. The tower has been restored for occupation – one side had to be rebuilt with the old stones.

Access: There are occasional open days.

BUITTLE CASTLE, two miles west of Dalbeattie, is reached along a drive off the A745. Old Buittle Tower rises amid farm buildings that probably follow the outline of the barmkin. This tower house comprises three storeys and a rebuilt attic, with the usual vaulted undercroft. It may have been built by Robert, Lord Maxwell, who obtained the lands in 1535. John Gordon of Lochinvar added the jamb in the 1590s, creating an L-plan with a stair turret corbelled out in the re-entrant angle. This tower has a very plain aspect because a Victorian refurbishment robbed it of its corner bartizans – a deliberate deprivation of status when it was let to tenant farmers.

In fact, the tower occupies the bailey of an older castle and utilises its stones. Buittle (or Botel) began with the low, oval motte overlooking the Urr

Water, to the south-east of the later tower house. This was probably raised early in the thirteenth century by Alan, lord of Galloway. His daughter Devorgilla married the English baron John de Balliol of Barnard Castle. They founded Balliol College, Oxford, and probably rebuilt the castle in stone. It may well have been the birthplace of their son, another John, who gained the Scottish Crown as a result of Edward I's adjudication in 1292 but lost it when he attempted to defy his English master. This was a castle of enclosure, following the outline of the motte but with a straight north-west curtain facing the bailey. It is reduced to masonry fragments and the base of twin round towers that flanked the entrance. The castle was captured and thoroughly dismantled by Robert the Bruce in 1312. Edward Balliol used the site as his base while unsuccessfully attempting to regain his father's throne in the 1330s. Its defences do not seem to have risen again.

Access: The tower is open for pre-booked tours but the ruins are fenced off.
Relations: Barnard Castle (England). Caerlaverock and Mearns were other strongholds of the lords Maxwell, while Kenmure and Rusco belonged to the Gordons of Lochinvar.

CARDONESS CASTLE   This commanding tower house stands a mile south-west of Gatehouse of Fleet, overlooking the A75. Though still virtually complete it is now an empty shell. The Water of Fleet once came up to the ridge on which the tower stands. Gilbert McCulloch of Myreton was here by 1466 and either he or his son James built the oblong tower. In front are the foundations of ancillary buildings but – unusually – they were never enclosed by a barmkin wall, as an English spy reported around 1565.

The external severity of the tower house is typical of the fifteenth century, despite some reasonably large windows lighting the upper storeys. A few early gunports of the inverted keyhole type (no doubt inspired by Threave) pierce the ground floor. To the left of the entrance passage a porter's lodge occupies a mural chamber, while to the right is the spiral staircase. Twin doorways lead into the barrel-vaulted undercroft, reflecting the original division into two rooms. It was also once divided into two levels by a wooden floor, as shown by the corbels that supported the joists. The spiral stair ascends to two mural chambers. One contains an opening to the pit prison below, while the other has a murder hole poised above the entrance passage. Further up is the hall, twice as high as the other storeys. It has several mural chambers, one of them containing a latrine. The hall fireplace has lost its lintel but preserves the shafted columns that supported it. An aumbry alongside is framed by a delicately carved arch. A more complete fireplace of similar quality can be seen in the solar above. This floor is divided by a later cross-wall, supported by an arch over the hall. Above that a squatter storey may have contained bedchambers.

Tall attic gables crown the tower, giving six storeys in all. The attic is no doubt a sixteenth-century addition. It is recessed within the remains of the parapet, but the Elizabethan spy confirms that the tower had no battlements. He estimated that 200 men would be needed to mount a surprise attack. The McCullochs of Cardoness indulged in feuds with their neighbours. In 1690 Godfrey McCulloch was executed for shooting a neighbour and the building was left to decay.

Access: Open daily in summer (HES).
Reference: Guidebook by A. Cox and D. Grove (includes Carsluith).
Relations: Fifteenth-century tower houses such as Affleck, Castle Campbell, Balgonie and Newark (Selkirkshire).

CARSLUITH CASTLE overlooks Wigtown Bay. It is just off the A75 coast road, ten miles south-east of Newton Stewart. This attractive L-plan tower house has lost its roof and floors but is otherwise complete. It may incorporate an older tower raised by the Cairns family of Orchardton. Richard Broun rebuilt or remodelled the tower around 1568 – that year was once inscribed in the panel above the entrance, along with his arms. This doorway occupies the side of the jamb, protected by one of several wide-mouthed gunports in the main block. The jamb is devoted to a wide spiral stair and is crowned by a gabled caphouse. Two vaulted storerooms occupy the ground floor of the main block. Above them is the hall, followed by a floor once divided into the laird's solar and bedchamber, as twin fireplaces on opposite walls demonstrate. A blocked doorway at this level led onto a wooden balcony, long perished, while attic gables and a tall chimney rise above. Lengths of corbelled-out parapet line the two gable ends only, between little round corner bartizans. Richard Broun's son was fined for his part in the murder of a McCulloch from nearby Barholm Castle, which looked quite similar before its restoration. The Brouns of Carsluith abandoned the tower in 1748 and emigrated to India.

Access: Open daily (HES).
Reference: Guidebook by A. Cox and D. Grove (includes Cardoness).
Relations: Barholm. The Cairns seat at Orchardton.

DRUMCOLTRAN TOWER is an austere little L-plan tower house, standing intact amid farm buildings. It is believed to have been built by Sir John Maxwell of Terregles, around the time of his marriage to Agnes Herries in 1550. The tower is a conservative structure for its time, with modest-sized windows and a plain parapet supported on corbels. A gunport covers the doorway, placed in the projecting jamb. Above an empty panel for the Maxwell arms, a Latin inscription exhorts the visitor to speak little, be truthful, avoid wine and remember death. Within the barrel-vaulted undercroft, later divided into two rooms, is a large kitchen fireplace. A spiral staircase ascends in the jamb to a gabled caphouse, rising a little higher than the rest. As usual the first floor of the tower contained the hall, mutilated by eighteenth-century alterations. Two chambers occupied the floor above, the further one being reached by a passage from the spiral stair. Above them is the usual attic. Although the tower is still roofed over, the intervening floors have gone. It overlooks the road, a mile north of Kirkgunzeon.

Access: Open daily (HES).
Relations: Other Maxwell branches at Hills, Kirkconnell and Orchardton.

EARLSTOUN CASTLE lies on an estate two miles north of St John's Town of Dalry. This austere L-plan tower house has enlarged windows and a stair turret corbelled out in the re-entrant angle. It was raised late in the sixteenth century, probably by the Sinclairs of Earlstoun.

Access: On private land.

HILLS TOWER, on a farm a mile south-east of Lochfoot, was built by Edward Maxwell sometime after 1527. This oblong structure has an embattled parapet resting on a row of corbels and a later range alongside. A stretch of barmkin wall with a diminutive gatehouse also survives.

Access: Private.

KENMURE CASTLE occupies a wooded estate a mile south of New Galloway. Just beyond a row of houses, an unsignposted footpath leads east from the A762. There was an older stronghold on this prominent knoll near the head of Loch Ken. It may have been the birthplace of King John Balliol, though Buittle has a stronger claim. It was destroyed in 1568, after Mary Queen of Scots lodged here *en route* to English exile after the Battle of Langside. The existing structure was probably begun soon after by the Gordons of Lochinvar. It consists of two ranges from a late sixteenth-century courtyard complex. The layout is thus similar to MacLellan's Castle but Kenmure has suffered many alterations, followed by neglect. Damaged by Cromwell in 1650, the castle was modernised by the Gordons in Victorian times, then abandoned in the 1950s. Stripped of its roofs and floors, it has been going to rack and ruin ever since.

The grey-harled walls show little sign of antiquity externally, with rows of enlarged windows. In fact the south range was heavily restored in the nineteenth century, along with the stair turret in the re-entrant angle. However, the west range preserves a row of barrel-vaulted cellars linked by a corridor at ground level. This corridor continues to the kitchen, which is surmounted by the former great hall. Above the cellars are two storeys of residential chambers. Numerous shot holes are the only tokens of defence, though a wall with an arched gateway once closed off the barmkin on the north and east.

Access: Exterior only.
Relations: MacLellan's Castle. Buittle and Rusco were other towers of the Gordons of Lochinvar.

KIRKCONNELL HOUSE lies in its own grounds two miles north-east of New Abbey. This mansion of various dates incorporates at one end a sixteenth-century L-plan tower house, with a spiral stair in the jamb and a corbelled-out parapet. It belonged to the Maxwells of Kirkconnell.

Access: Private (now a holiday let).

MACLELLAN'S CASTLE dominates the little royal burgh of Kirkcudbright (pronounced 'Kirkoobree'). The earthworks of an earlier stronghold lie just outside the town but this imposing mansion, beside the River Dee, is named after Sir Thomas MacLellan of Bombie, provost of the town. In 1569 he obtained permission to build a house on the site of the recently dissolved Franciscan friary and construction began soon afterwards using its stones. It was probably completed in 1582 – the year inscribed on a large heraldic panel above the main entrance.

Although following a stepped L-plan, this is not so much a tower house as a more extensive mansion consisting of two ranges at right angles to each other. Nevertheless, the main entrance is conventionally located in the re-entrant angle between the two ranges, while the usual barrel vaults cover all the ground-floor rooms. A corridor connects three undercrofts in the south wing. Another corridor leads from the kitchen in the east wing, with its arched fireplace, to a square tower projecting at the south-east corner of the complex. This tower contains a second doorway from outside, again flanked by the main block for greater security. From the main entrance a straight staircase ascends to the principal floor. The great hall occupies most of the south wing at this level, with a solar beyond. Behind the hall fireplace is a mural chamber containing a spy-hole. Three spiral staircases ascended to the two upper floors, providing suites of accommodation for the MacLellans and their guests. The wall-head is an attractive array of crow-stepped gables, tall chimneys and round corner bartizans. The emphasis is on display and comfort, with only limited pretensions as a defensive structure. Large windows at all three upper levels were at least barred by iron grilles, as shown by the sockets in the masonry, while a few wide-mouthed gunports command the approach at ground level. Presumably there was a wall on the other two sides, bounding a little square barmkin, but nothing remains of it.

Sir Thomas died in 1597 and is commemorated by a fine tomb in Greyfriars' Church across the road. His descendants exhausted their wealth on the Covenanter side during the Civil War. The castle was abandoned and stripped of its roofs and floors in 1752. Since then it has been an empty shell but remains structurally complete.

Access: Open regularly in summer (HES).
Reference: Guidebook by D. Grove.
Relations: Kirkcudbright Castle is nearby. Kenmure and Muchalls follow a similar layout.

MOTE OF URR   This formidable earthwork rises two and a half miles north of Dalbeattie, in a field just off the B794 (level with the Urr Lodge Hostel). However, since that approach involves crossing a ford that is often too deep to attempt, a more round-about route via the A745 may be required. Overlooking the Urr Water, it is Scotland's largest motte-and-bailey castle and one of the most impressive in Britain. The roughly oval bailey (one corner is squared off) is surrounded by a double rampart with a deep ditch in between. It may be an adaptation of an Iron Age fort. Two causeways mark the entrances. The southern half of the enclosure is filled by the conical motte, huge if relatively low in relation to its girth. The motte has its own surrounding ditch, even where it is close to the bailey defences. This arrangement is unusual since motte and bailey are normally separate entities, linked only by their ditches.

Excavations on the motte top found evidence of destruction and subsequent heightening, after which there was a wooden keep surrounded by a stockade with turrets. No doubt the bailey ramparts had stockades too. The destruction is plausibly associated with the Galloway rising of 1174, when the Norman settlers were temporarily driven out. A castle here is first mentioned as being held by Walter de Berkeley, William the Lion's Great Chamberlain. He could have erected it shortly before the rising. An alternative theory is that it was raised earlier still by Fergus, lord of Galloway. Occupation continued here well into the following century, but no stonework ever replaced the wooden defences.

Access: Permission should be sought at the adjacent house.
Relations: Motte-and-bailey castles such as the Bass of Inverurie, the Doune of Invernochty and Duffus.

ORCHARDTON TOWER   Although some thirteenth-century castles adopted the prevailing fashion for round keeps, this is virtually unique among the later tower houses for its circular plan. Tantallon had the only other example but that was part of a walled complex, whereas Orchardton is almost freestanding. It probably followed Irish precursors. Cylindrical towers were often employed as flankers but they were never popular from a domestic point of view. This tower is said to have been built by John Cairns around 1456. Though quite austere, that year would be consistent with the few architectural details. The tower house stands at one end of a diminutive barmkin enclosure, formed by some rough buildings that are now reduced to ruinous undercrofts.

By contrast the tower is virtually intact, though now roofless. It rises to a plain, corbelled-out parapet, with a tiny caphouse at the head of the spiral stair. A doorway at ground level leads into the undercroft, which has no connection with the rest of the tower. Its straight sides support the usual barrel vault but the upper storeys of the tower are circular inside as well as out. The original entrance at hall level survives as an archway overlooking the barmkin. In the seventeenth century the Maxwells of Orchardton converted one of the hall's two windows into a new doorway, reached by a rough stone staircase. Beside the hall fireplace is a wash basin in a trefoil-headed recess – the only scrap of ornament in the tower. Above can be seen the solar and bedchamber, both with plain windows and fireplaces. The tower stands five miles south of Dalbeattie, on a sideroad off the A711. It should not be confused with nearby Orchardton Castle, a castellated Victorian mansion.

Access: Open daily in summer and regularly in winter (HES).
Reference: Guide by C. Tabraham.
Relations: Tantallon. The Cairns' tower at Carsluith.

PLUNTON CASTLE   Three miles south of Gatehouse of Fleet, a road signposted to Carrick diverges south from the B827. At Lennox Plunton, opposite some farm buildings, a gate marks the beginning of a footpath running south through woods to this tower house, about a quarter of a mile from the road. A tolerably complete though sadly neglected ruin, it is a homely specimen of the L-plan, built by the Lennoxes of Plunton late in the sixteenth century. The jamb is a modest projection that contained the fallen spiral stair. Above the barrel-vaulted ground floor are the hall, a storey once divided into two bedrooms and the attic, marked by eroded gables. There are shallow bartizans at the two rear corners.

Access: Freely accessible with caution.

RUSCO TOWER stands in wooded grounds four miles north of Gatehouse of Fleet. This oblong structure has an elaborately corbelled-out parapet and a corner caphouse. Attributed to Robert Gordon of Lochinvar around 1500, it has been well restored from dereliction.

Access: Private.

THREAVE CASTLE is a monument to the mighty Douglas family. Two miles south-west of Castle Douglas along the A75, a sideroad leads north towards this imposing ruin on Threave Island, in a loop of the River Dee. The massive tower house was erected by Archibald Douglas, known as 'the Grim'. In 1369 David II put Archibald in charge of rebellious Galloway. He became third Earl of Douglas in 1388, following his nephew's death at the Battle of Otterburn.

Archibald the Grim built what was then the biggest tower house in Scotland. It remains one of the largest, rising over eighty feet high. Just below parapet level, a triple row of putlog holes supported a wooden hoarding on three sides of the tower. A modern stair rises to the first-floor entrance, a tall archway reduced in size during the Napoleonic Wars when the tower accommodated French prisoners. It leads into the upper part of a cavernous, barrel-vaulted undercroft, once divided into two storeys by a wooden floor. This level housed the kitchen. One end of the storey below was walled off to form an unusually

Threave Castle, Kirkcudbrightshire

large pit prison – a reminder of Archibald's rough justice. A spiral staircase in one corner ascends to the great hall, occupying the full length of the tower house and permitted two large windows on the relatively secure side above the river. The floor above was divided into two private chambers, as twin fireplaces show. Above that was a fifth storey, its nine arched openings level with the putlog holes of the hoarding. This squat stage may have accommodated the garrison, at least in times of siege. As the tower house is now a shell, we can only look up into these rooms from the hall. Nevertheless, the tower remains complete except for its battlements.

Archibald, who also rebuilt Bothwell Castle, died peacefully here in 1400. His son of the same name was killed fighting the English at the Battle of Verneuil in Normandy in 1424, while the young sixth earl was murdered at the infamous Black Dinner in Edinburgh Castle in 1440. This was not the doing of James II, who was then barely ten years old. However, as he matured he had cause to regard the Black Douglases – so-called to distinguish them from the Red Douglas earls of Angus – as over-mighty rivals. In this climate of uncertainty William Douglas, the eighth earl, appears to have built the curtain wall forming a concentric defence around the tower house. It is fronted by a moat once fed by the river. Unfortunately, the curtain is mainly reduced to footings but the surviving one and a half sides are pierced by numerous arrow slits. Circular towers projected at three corners but only the east angle tower survives above the base. Its three gunports (of dumbbell and inverted keyhole type) were intended for small cannon of some kind. They are probably the earliest attempt at artillery defence in Scotland, though the gunports in a similar tower at Craigmillar might be older. A simple gateway through the curtain is aligned with the tower house entrance. Perhaps the two were linked by a drawbridge.

William Douglas in turn perished at Stirling Castle in 1452. Summoned for a reconciliation with James II, he was stabbed to death by the king and his followers, then hurled out of a window. In 1455 his brother James was defeated at Arkinholm and driven into exile in England, but Threave held out for more than two months in his name. The new curtain acquitted itself well against the king's dreaded cannon (not Mons Meg, which hadn't arrived yet) and the garrison negotiated generous surrender terms. Henceforth the castle was held by the Crown, though the lords Maxwell of Caerlaverock became its hereditary keepers. During the invasion of 1544 the English occupied the castle but were driven out after a short siege. Owing to the Earl of Nithsdale's loyalty to Charles I the castle was bombarded by the Covenanters in 1640. Again it eventually surrendered on terms but was then slighted.

Access: Open daily in summer (HES). There is a boat service to the castle from the jetty.

Reference: Guidebook by C. Tabraham. *Medieval Archaeology* (25).

Relations: Craigmillar. The Black Douglas strongholds of Tantallon, Old Tulliallan, Bothwell, Hermitage and Newark (Selkirkshire). Early tower houses such as Dean, Dundonald, Alloa and Lochleven. Early artillery fortifications at Dunbar and Ravenscraig (Fife).

OTHER SITES An unusual number of mottes attest the Norman and Flemish settlers of the twelfth century:

Balmaclellan Mote
Barmagachan Mote (near Borgue)
Boreland Mote (near Anwoth)
Dalry Mote at (St John's Town of Dalry)
Ingleston Mote (near Gelston)
Kirkclaugh Mote (near Anwoth)
Lincluden Mote (HES)
Minnigaff Mote
Roberton Mote (near Borgue)
Southwick Mote (near Caulkerbush)

The first castle at *Kirkcudbright* was destroyed by Robert the Bruce. Excavations have revealed a twin-towered gatehouse and round angle towers but only the ditched site can be seen now. Known as Castledykes, it lies by the River Dee to the west of the little burgh, off Castledykes Road. The *Abbot's Tower* overlooking New Abbey was rebuilt from ruins to serve as a residence in the 1990s. *Auchenskeoch Castle* (near Caulkerbush), *Balmangan Tower*, *Corra Castle* (Near Kirkgunzeon), *Cumstoun Castle* (near Tongland), *Edingham Castle* and *Garlies Castle* (near Minnigaff) are all badly ruined tower houses.

LANARKSHIRE

Much of this county is rolling southern upland but it includes the industry-scarred Clyde Valley – a few of its castles are now within the city of Glasgow. Mottes such as Carnwath and Coulter attest the period of Norman settlement. William de Moravia's Bothwell Castle, with its mighty round keep, is one of the finest strongholds pre-dating the Wars of Independence. Sadly, it suffered much in those wars and was later completed on a reduced scale by the earls of Douglas. The courtyard theme continued with the small enclosures and residential buildings at Provan and Corra. In the sixteenth century Sir James Hamilton of Finnart designed Craignethan Castle to withstand the artillery of the day. It is still very substantial, despite the loss of its massive screen wall, but his other castle at Cadzow has been reduced to a fragmentary state. Tower houses start in the fifteenth century with the ruinous examples at Crookston and Covington. Moving into the following century, the most striking are those at Craignethan and Dalzell. A good proportion of Lanarkshire castles occupy strong positions overlooking the Clyde or its tributaries.

County reference: BoS *Lanarkshire and Renfrewshire*; BoS *Glasgow. The Castles of Glasgow and the Clyde* by G. W. Mason.

ABINGTON MOTTE   This well-preserved motte-and-bailey earthwork, at Nether Abington, is sandwiched between the A702 and the River Clyde, just north of junction 13 of the A74(M) motorway. The low motte is surrounded by a deep ditch, while the D-shaped bailey is enclosed by a rampart except where the ground drops steeply to the river. A gap in the rampart denotes the entrance, while a nineteenth-century memorial stone crowns the motte. It may have been raised around the middle of the twelfth century by John of Crawford, a Norman or Flemish settler, or later by a descendant.

Access: Freely accessible.
Relations: The mottes at Carnwath, Coulter and Dalmellington.

BARNCLUITH TOWER stands in the garden of its Georgian successor, Barncluith House. It overlooks the Avon Water on the eastern edge of Hamilton. This simple oblong tower with crow-stepped gables is believed to have been built around 1583 by John Hamilton of Barncluith.

Access: Visible from the road.

BEDLAY CASTLE, in its own grounds south of Moodiesburn, began as a rather low L-plan tower house with a jamb projecting on two sides. Built late in the sixteenth century by Robert, Lord Boyd of Kilmarnock (see Dean Castle), it has been extended into a longer range.

Access: Private.

BOTHWELL CASTLE, perched on a rock above the River Clyde a mile west of Bothwell village, is reached via Castle Avenue. This is an extensive ruin incorporating one of Scotland's most ambitious thirteenth-century castles. William de Moravia, or Moray, began building sometime after he inherited in 1278. However, it would appear that little more than the circular keep had been completed when Edward I invaded in 1296. The castle became a bone of contention during the Wars of Independence that followed. In 1299 the Scots wrested it back from the English after a siege lasting fourteen months. Edward I recaptured it two years later with the aid of miners and a tall siege tower called 'the Belfry'. After the rout at Bannockburn in 1314 the constable surrendered to the triumphant Scots – a number of English knights and nobles who had taken refuge here after the battle were taken prisoner. The castle was then slighted in accordance with Robert the Bruce's strategy. A last English occupation ended in 1337 when Sir Andrew Murray, Guardian of Scotland, employed another siege tower against his own castle. Tradition ascribes the partial destruction of the keep to him rather than King Robert.

Nevertheless, the castle rose again under the powerful Douglas dynasty. Archibald 'the Grim', later third Earl of Douglas, acquired Bothwell by marriage in 1362. He began a slow reconstruction that continued under his son of the same name, who became the fourth earl. They were surprisingly faithful to the original layout, though they drastically reduced the size of the courtyard. By the time of the younger Archibald's death in 1424, leading a Scottish contingent to disaster at the battle of Verneuil in Normandy, the present castle was largely complete. However, the rivalry between the Stewart kings and the Black Douglases soon came to a head. James II murdered one Earl of Douglas at Stirling in 1452, and drove the last into exile three years later. In 1492 the Red Douglas earls of Angus obtained possession in exchange for Hermitage Castle. By 1700 they had built a new mansion (now demolished) close by, the old castle being left to decay as a landscape ornament.

Bothwell was originally conceived as an irregular, pentagonal enclosure with round flanking towers, resembling contemporary Kildrummy Castle but on a grander scale. Only the great keep and the short stretches of curtain wall on either side of it were actually built, but the whole site was laid out in preparation. Hence the foundations of a large gatehouse and one angle tower are exposed in front of the present castle. Had it ever been built, the gatehouse would have sported twin round towers flanking a long gate passage, as at Kildrummy. Beyond is the plain length of curtain erected by Archibald the Grim. He reduced Bothwell to an oblong courtyard occupying only the southern half of the intended enclosure. His south and east curtains stand on the thirteenth-century foundations. At the north-east corner he built a square-plan tower house to replace the slighted keep, which it rivalled in height (compare his tower at Threave). Sadly, this tower has been largely destroyed to its massive base. Like the older keep, the entrance was originally barred by a little drawbridge. The recess for its raising beam can be seen above the doorway, but it was later rendered redundant when the great hall was added in front.

The circular south-east tower is entirely the work of the fourth Earl of Douglas, its four storeys capped by a machicolated crown. Against the east curtain he built a great hall over three barrel-vaulted undercrofts. A large window lights the dais end, while the row of clerestory windows facing the courtyard was added after the Red Douglases took possession. A chapel stood beyond it, as denoted by the vaulting shafts and piscina in the curtain. Windows piercing the south curtain attest further residential buildings on this relatively secure side above the Clyde. The wall changes direction at the circular Prison Tower, a slender structure marking the transition to the older masonry at the west end of the courtyard.

Douglas Simpson described William de Moravia's keep as 'the grandest piece of secular architecture that the Middle Ages have bequeathed to us'. It is the most ambitious of the Scottish round keeps and, as seen from the courtyard, vies with the best in England and Wales. Despite the loss of the parapet, it rises ninety feet from the bottom of the broad moat that isolates it from the courtyard. A sluice gate in the south wing wall shows that the moat was water-filled. Two pointed windows pierce the ashlar facade of the keep. A modern bridge crosses the moat to the entrance archway, opening onto a passage that bends through the great thickness of the keep wall. Above is a mural chamber with cross-slits, from which the drawbridge and portcullis were raised.

Inside we see the stark effects of the Wars of Independence, because the outer half of the keep has been destroyed to its base. Archibald the Grim made no attempt to restore it to its former splendour. He merely built a crude blocking wall across the diameter, reducing the round keep to roughly a semi-circle. We enter at the level of the lord's hall, a once-octagonal room with blank arcading against its walls. A central pillar to support the roof is embedded in the blocking wall, while a well can be seen in the gloomy undercroft below. The floor above the hall lacks windows in the surviving portion and has been interpreted as a chamber for the garrison. Above is the solar, from which there was an escape route. A doorway opens onto the parapet of the southern wing wall, leading to the Prison Tower and down to its adjacent postern.

Access: Open regularly (HES).
Reference: Guidebook by C. Tabraham. *PSAS* (59 and 127).

Relations: Kildrummy and other mature castles of enclosure such as Caerlaverock and Dirleton. Tantallon, Old Tulliallan, Threave, Hermitage and Newark (Selkirkshire) were other Black Douglas strongholds.

BRAIDWOOD CASTLE This tall oblong tower house with straight mural staircases, a mile north-east of Crossford, has been well restored from ruin. Previously called the Tower of Hallbar, it may have been built by Harry Stewart of Gogar after he obtained the lands in 1581.
Access: Private (now a holiday let).

CADZOW CASTLE rises dramatically above a bend of the Avon Water in Chatelherault Country Park, three miles south-east of Hamilton off the A72. Chatelherault was a hunting lodge of the Dukes of Hamilton (its name recalls their ancestor's French title) and the castle was preserved as a romantic ruin in the extensive grounds. It is attributed to Sir James Hamilton of Finnart, James V's Master of Works, before his execution in 1540. The inner courtyard was a massive structure designed for artillery defence, like his castle at Craignethan. Defaulting to Sir James' half-brother, the Earl of Arran, the castle was repaired and strengthened after falling to the Earl of Lennox in 1570. It was captured again and slighted by the former Regent Morton on the downfall of the Hamiltons in 1579.

Cadzow consisted of two courtyards perched above the river. The inner was a compact, nearly oblong enclosure, now reduced to a heap of grass-covered rubble. Only the lower courses of the surrounding walls still stand, confined by a web of scaffolding in a long-term attempt to stabilise this precarious site. The base of a round tower projects at the south-west corner and there was another on the south-east. Beyond a ditch is the outer courtyard, again roughly oblong with much of its surrounding curtain wall still standing. The north wall with its double row of slit windows probably denotes the great hall, though this side – overlooking the gorge and the hunting lodge – was tampered with for visual effect during the ducal period.
Access: Exterior only (HES).
Reference: *Chateau Gaillard* (15).
Relations: Craignethan and Sir James' work at Blackness. Other castles of the Hamilton earls at Brodick and Kinneil.

CARNWATH MOTTE This big, artificial mound of classic conical form is a conspicuous feature on Carnwath golf course, just off the A70 at the west end of the village. It overlooks the Carnwath Burn. There are traces of a surrounding ditch but no sign of any accompanying bailey. William de Somerville accompanied the future David I to Scotland in 1107 and was later made lord of Carnwath. He or one of his descendants no doubt raised the motte. Nothing is known of the defences – presumably a wooden 'keep' and a stockade – but clearly no stonework ever crowned the summit. The Somervilles later abandoned it for nearby Couthally Castle, which has all but disappeared.

Access: Well seen from the road.
Relations: Mottes such as Abington, Coulter and Dalmellington.

CORRA CASTLE, otherwise known as Corehouse Castle, lies on the wooded Corehouse estate, two miles south of Kirkfieldbank. Corehouse Drive leads from this road to the West Lodge, from which a track runs eastwards through the woods. Where it begins to bend north to the nineteenth-century mansion, continue straight on towards the sound of rushing water. The estate is situated on a spectacular stretch of the River Clyde and the castle is perched on a sheer promontory with steep drops to the Corra Linn Falls below. When you reach the river the castle is just ahead, but this front is hidden beneath the vegetation. The wall on the only landward side, fronted by a ditch, is more apparent but even that is quite overgrown. It contains a keyhole gunport and a simple gate arch.

Within, the castle forms a compact enclosure tapering to the tip of the promontory. On the west are the remains of a residential block with a row of four barrel-vaulted undercrofts, three of them entered directly from the barmkin. Little remains of the superstructure except at the north end, where it rises to three storeys. It is unclear if the rest of the range was as high. Little stands above ground on the other side of the barmkin though there is an underground chamber. Probably dating from the sixteenth century, the castle was held by the Bannatynes of Corehouse, one of whom was implicated in the murder of Lord Darnley. It now shelters rare breeds of bat.

Access: Exterior only.

COULTER MOTTE HILL   Two miles south-west of Biggar, just before the A72 crosses the River Clyde, Cormiston Road leads north to this simple motte overlooking the river. Although of no great size, it is a well-preserved, conical example unencumbered by foliage. An Alexander de Cutir is recorded here in the thirteenth century, and it may have been raised by him or an earlier member of his line. The timber defences have long since perished, while the site of the bailey is now just a lawn in front.

Access: Freely accessible (HES).
Relations: Mottes such as Abington, Carnwath and Dalmellington.

COVINGTON TOWER stands forlorn in a field off Covington Road, a mile and a half north of Thankerton. It occupies the site of a Flemish settler's earthwork castle, but the present structure is the chunky ruin of an oblong tower house built by the Lindsays of Covington. It is said to date from the 1440s and that would be about right. The tower was four storeys high with a vaulted ground floor, but only one portion still rises to near its full height and the interior is now thoroughly overgrown. With its thick walls and mostly small windows, however, it is an evocative specimen of the earlier type of tower house. Gaping holes on the second floor denote larger windows that lit the hall, while a narrow cleft at one corner marks the position of the spiral stair. Close by is a sixteenth-century beehive dovecote.

Access: Well seen from the road.
Relations: Branches of the Lindsays at Crossbasket, Mains and Dowhill.

CRAIGNETHAN CASTLE was one of the last castles with some serious defensive intent to be erected in Scotland. It was designed to withstand the growing power of artillery, which explains its unusually squat profile. The castle was built by Sir James Hamilton of Finnart, an illegitimate son of the first Earl of Arran. Building was under way by 1532. As Master of Works to James V, Sir James supervised construction at the royal palaces until his suspicious master had him executed on a trumped-up charge of treason in 1540. It is likely that the inner courtyard, including the tower house and its protective screen wall, were standing by that time. The outer courtyard was added, or at least completed, by Sir James' legitimate half-brother. This James Hamilton was the second Earl of Arran, Duke of Chatelherault (a French title) and regent during the long minority of Mary Queen of Scots.

Their castle occupies a promontory with steep falls to the River Nethan and the Craignethan Burn. It stands about a mile west of Crossford as the crow flies, but three miles by tortuous roads. Guarding the only level approach is the outer courtyard, a large rectangle once filled by ancillary buildings. The surrounding curtain wall is crowned by a corbelled-out parapet and pierced by wide-mouthed gunports. Twin square towers flank the outer corners, while a gateway juts out in the middle of the entrance front. Nevertheless, the outer curtain is primarily for show, too low and too thin to be regarded as a serious obstacle against the cannon of the day.

Ahead lies the inner enclosure, more substantial than the outer but now quite ruinous, except for the tower house. It is separated from the rest by a broad, flat-bottomed ditch. At the south end of the ditch is a caponier, an Italian innovation unique for its time in Britain. This stone-roofed fighting gallery enabled defenders to rake the ditch with handguns, but would have proved unbearable in the suffocating smoke of gun fire. By contrast, a simple cross-wall with gunports closes the northern end. The stone revetment forming the inner edge of the ditch is all that remains of a powerful screen wall. It originally rose high enough to shield the tower house from bombardment from the higher ground to the west.

A modern bridge crosses the ditch directly into the inner courtyard but the original bridge lay further north. It led to a narrow strip of ground between the inner curtain and the steep drop to the river. Attackers would thus have to

Craignethan Castle, Lanarkshire

make their way under fire to a gate tower (now just a stump) midway along the north curtain. The inner courtyard is another rectangle, concentric to the large tower house within. Its west end is formed by the screen wall, with a spiral staircase descending to the caponier. Oblong towers guarded the eastern corners of the enclosure. Although the north-eastern tower has been reduced to foundations, the kitchen tower is complete. Its barrel-vaulted main floor housed an austere chapel.

The inner courtyard is dominated by the tower house, an oblong block that survives almost complete. Its plain exterior is relieved by the double row of corbelling that supported the parapet and round corner bartizans. A simple rectangle in outline, the tower house is a residential complex akin to the hall-keeps of Norman England. The ground-floor entrance leads into a narrow vestibule. Beyond is the great hall, rising the full height of the tower house and covered by a barrel vault. North of the hall are the kitchen (with a huge fireplace) and two floors of private chambers. A double-gabled attic above was divided into several bedrooms but this level has largely perished. From the vestibule a staircase descends to a complex of vaulted undercrofts, which are partly underground owing to the sloping site.

Craignethan did not have a long active life and was never tested in earnest. The second earl supported Mary Queen of Scots after her abdication. She was entertained here following her escape from Lochleven Castle in 1568. After the Earl of Morton drove the first Marquis of Hamilton into exile in 1579, the castle was slighted and the screen wall demolished. Andrew Hay built the laird's house occupying one corner of the outer courtyard in 1659.

Access: Open daily in summer (HES).
Reference: Guidebook by I. MacIvor and C. Tabraham. *PSAS* (125).
Relations: Sir James' work at Cadzow, Blackness and (probably) Strathaven. Other castles of the Hamilton earls at Brodick and Kinneil. Early artillery defences at Dunbar and Ravenscraig (Fife).

CROOKSTON CASTLE is five miles south-west of Glasgow city centre, in the suburb of Pollock. It stands overlooking the Levern Water, in public grounds off Brockburn Road. The site takes its name from Robert de Croc, a Norman who had settled here by 1180. The ditch of his roughly oval enclosure is still complete but, surprisingly, there is no trace of any rampart. In the middle rises an ambitious tower house, probably erected around 1400 by Sir John Stewart of Darnley. He became constable of the Scottish army in France, twice captured by the English before his death at the Battle of the Herrings in 1429. His building shows French influence in its *bastille* plan, rare in Scotland, the oblong main block originally having square flanking towers at all four corners. In 1489 his grandson John, first Earl of Lennox, rebelled against the new king, James IV. James brought Mons Meg and other cannon to besiege Crookston. It may have been then that the tower house was battered into its present ruined state. Nevertheless, it was still serviceable enough to be captured by Regent Arran in 1544, during the next Lennox rebellion.

The main body of the tower house stands high except for the collapsed west end, which evidently bore the brunt of the bombardment. Its ground-floor entrance, once barred by a portcullis, leads to a vaulted undercroft with transverse ribs. There is a well chamber in the great thickness of the wall. A straight stair, reached from the entrance passage, ascends to the spacious hall, twice the height of the other storeys and once covered by a pointed vault. Above are the remains of the solar, with a large fireplace. Of the four angle towers only that on the north-east stands to the wall-head, providing sweeping views over the suburban landscape. It rises to the corbelling that supported a vanished parapet and corner bartizans. The lowest level is a pit prison, with four storeys of chambers above. The other corner towers would have provided ample accommodation. However, the south-east tower is reduced to its vaulted ground floor, while the western pair have perished entirely.

Access: Open daily in summer and regularly in winter (HES).
Reference: Guide by C. Tabraham. *Transactions of the Glasgow Archaeological Society* (12).
Relations: *Bastille*-plan tower houses at Thirlestane, Holyrood and Hermitage.

CROSSBASKET CASTLE, in its own grounds roughly halfway between East Kilbride and Hamilton, is reached via a drive off the B7012. It overlooks a bluff above the river known as the Rotten Calder. Most of the complex is a showy mansion built by the Clark family in Victorian times but, to the left of the main facade, it incorporates a complete if modest oblong tower house, overawed by the rest. The tower rises three storeys to a plain parapet resting on a row of corbels. A restored attic with dormer windows is recessed within the parapet, while a tiny caphouse marks the head of the spiral stair at one corner. The interior preserves its barrel-vaulted undercroft but is otherwise transformed, while most of the windows are later enlargements. It was probably built early in the sixteenth century as a dower house by the Lindsays of Dunrod.

Access: Now a hotel.
Reference: *The History of Crossbasket Castle* by P. Veverka.
Relations: Mains Castle was the chief seat of the Lindsays of Dunrod.

DALZELL HOUSE (pronounced 'Deeyell') presents a splendid front: an austere tower house with wings projecting forward on either side, the gap between them being closed by an embattled stretch of barmkin wall. However, the wall with twin gateways is much restored, while the north range was built entirely by the future Baron Hamilton of Dalzell in the 1850s in mirror image to the one opposite. That leaves the south range, linking up via a kitchen with the original tower house on the east. The south range was probably built after Sir Robert Dalzell was ennobled in 1628. It is purely domestic in character, as might be expected by that time, though the undercrofts are vaulted in the traditional manner and a slender round turret with a conical roof projects at the south-west corner. This range was considerably restored after a fire in 1869.

The Dalzell family was here from the thirteenth century and their tower house dates from around 1500. This massive oblong rises to a parapet projecting from a double row of corbels, with small bartizans at three corners and a round caphouse on the fourth. Recessed within the parapet is a restored attic with crow-stepped gables. The original entrance passage, now reached from the seventeenth-century wing, retains its portcullis groove. It leads into a barrel-vaulted undercroft. A straight mural staircase ascends from the entrance passage to the floor above, also vaulted. It appears to be a lofty hall but was originally divided into two storeys by a wooden floor. From here a spiral stair leads to another floor above the vault and on to the parapet. At the rear the tower is perched above a steep drop to the Dalzell Burn. After narrowly escaping demolition, the mansion was converted into flats in the 1980s. It lies on the Dalzell estate, now a country park on the southern outskirts of Motherwell, and is reached along Dalzell Drive.

Access: Well seen from the road.

GILBERTFIELD CASTLE is a lofty, ruined tower house with prominent gables, rising in a field two miles south-east of Cambuslang. It follows the L-plan but half of the main block has fallen. The tower was built by the Hamiltons of Gilbertfield and used to bear the year 1607.

Access: On farmland.

HAGGS CASTLE has been swallowed up by Glasgow. It is an unexpected sight on Haggs Lane in the suburb of Pollokshields. Above the entrance a restored inscription, in a frenzy of cable moulding, bears the year 1585 and the legend: 'Sr John Maxwell of Pollok Knyght and Dame Margaret Conyngham his wyf bigget this hows.' Two letters survive to John's Cunningham father-in-law, pleading for financial help. In 1753 Baronet Maxwell abandoned this tower house for stately Pollok House nearby. It was freely restored for habitation by Sir John Maxwell in the 1850s.

This L-plan tower house is three storeys high, plus an attic with characteristic crow-stepped gables and restored dormer windows. The jamb has largely been rebuilt after falling into ruin. The original entrance, in the side of the jamb, connects with a corridor leading past two storerooms to a kitchen with a deep fireplace. These chambers are all barrel vaulted. A broad spiral staircase in the jamb ascends to the hall and solar on the floor above, the former with a fine fireplace. From here the stair to the upper floors transfers to a corbelled-out turret, though not in the usual position in the re-entrant angle. A second turret stair from the solar has been replaced by a bay window. The building is noted for its architectural detail but was well equipped with square gunports before the later alterations.

Access: No longer a museum but well seen from the road.

Relations: Maxwell branches at Fourmerkland, Stanely and Newark (Renfrewshire).

MAINS CASTLE is an oblong tower house on a low motte overlooking the James Hamilton Heritage Park, north of East Kilbride. It has a restored parapet, a corner stair turret and a recessed attic. The tower was built by the Lindsays of Dunrod in the late fifteenth century.

Access: A functions venue but visible from the park.

PROVAN HALL can be found in Auchinlea Park on the Easterhouse housing estate, six miles east of Glasgow city centre. Located a short distance north of junction 10 of the M8 motorway, it is a quaint and modest little quadrangle. Twin ranges occupying the north and south sides are linked by stretches of plain wall on the east and west. Although it incorporates earlier work, the south range was thoroughly remodelled in the eighteenth century. The north range is believed to date back to the 1460s, when it was the seat of a prebendary of Glasgow Cathedral. Its present form, however, with crow-stepped gables and dormer windows, suggests a thorough remodelling after the Reformation by Sir William Baillie. There are three barrel-vaulted undercrofts (including the kitchen) at ground level, while the floor above is divided into an unpretentious hall and solar. At the north-east corner a round flanking turret with a conical roof has one vertical gunport, supporting a fifteenth-century date. The moulded gate arch through the east wall is surmounted by a dainty pediment bearing the initials of Sir Robert Hamilton and the year 1647.

Access: Open regularly (NTS).

STRATHAVEN CASTLE, otherwise called Avondale Castle, sits on a knoll above the Powmillon Burn in the middle of the little burgh. An earlier stronghold of the Black Douglases was destroyed after their downfall in 1455. The site was then given to Andrew Stewart, Lord Avondale, who probably built the existing structure. It looks complete and severe towards the town but is otherwise fragmentary. The structure is long and low, more like a hall house than a tower house, though it did have a projecting jamb (reduced to foundations) facing the vanished barmkin. Only two walls and part of a third survive, while the ground-floor vaults have perished. A slender, round corner turret of four storeys dominates the rest, with regular string courses, wide-mouthed gunports, heraldic panels and an oddly low doorway at the base. It was added in the sixteenth century, probably by Sir James Hamilton of Finnart. The building was abandoned in 1716 and soon fell into ruins. The interior was given a veneer of concrete in 1912 in a lamentable attempt at stabilisation.

Access: Freely accessible (LA).
Relations: Finnart's work at Cadzow, Craignethan and Blackness.

TORRANCE HOUSE can be found in Calderglen Country Park, just south-east of East Kilbride off the A726. It overlooks the Calder Water. This mansion is dominated by a lofty, gabled L-plan tower house of five storeys, including the attic with its crow-stepped gables. The summit is further adorned with chimneys and dormer windows. There is an embattled stair tower in the re-entrant angle. A Victorian entrance porch fills up the rest of the re-entrant, covering the original doorway in the side of the stair tower. The tower house is said to have been built around 1605 by Roger Hamilton of Torrance, though the stair tower appears to have been an afterthought. Internally it has been converted into flats. In the eighteenth century the main block was extended and there have been further additions since to form a courtyard.

Access: Now part of Torrance House Golf Club.
Relations: Hamilton branches at Barncluith, Cadzow, Craignethan and Gilbertfield.

WAYGATESHAW HOUSE, in its own grounds a mile north of Crossford, incorporates a truncated oblong tower house. There is a moulded barmkin gateway flanked by gunports alongside. They were built by the Lockharts of Waygateshaw sometime in the sixteenth century.

Access: Private.

OTHER SITES   Beside *Glasgow*'s splendid cathedral stood the castle of its bishops and archbishops, dominated by a tower house. The site is now occupied by St Mungo's Museum. The Stewarts' thirteenth-century towered enclosure at *Rutherglen* was recaptured from the English by Edward Bruce in 1313. It avoided the usual fate of slighting but the site, around Castle Street, has long been built over. *Douglas Castle*, one of the chief strongholds of the Black Douglases, was destroyed after their rebellion in 1455. The existing round tower ruin is a relic of a Georgian successor mansion. William Wallace sparked his rebellion in 1297 by killing sheriff Heselrig at *Lanark*, though this event seems to have taken place outside the vanished royal castle that stood on the hilltop.

There are motte-and-bailey earthworks at Biggar (*Gillespie Moat*), *Roberton* and *Crawford*, the latter bearing the jagged ruins of a seventeenth-century house. *Eastend House* (near Thankerton), *Garrion Tower* (near Dalserf), *Shieldhill Castle* (now a hotel near Quothquan) and The Peel at *Busby* all incorporate much-altered tower houses, while *Lamington Tower* is an abject ruin. The fine fifteenth-century tower of *Cathcart Castle* was demolished as recently as 1980 owing to its dangerous condition. Only the base remains in Linn Park. Two round turrets and the remains of a stair jamb survive from the courtyard castle of *Boghall*, in a field just outside Biggar.

MIDLOTHIAN

Edinburgh Castle, on its great rock at the top of the Royal Mile, is the very soul of Scotland. Some interesting portions of the royal castle-palace have survived its transformation into a Hanoverian fortress standing sentinel against the Jacobite threat. Nevertheless, as a *castle* it isn't as pre-eminent in the county as one might expect, since there is a concentration of unusually grand baronial strongholds guarding the southern approaches to the city. It is strange in a land of so many tower houses that one in particular rises literally above all others, but that distinction can be claimed by Borthwick. This prodigy was built by Sir William Borthwick in the 1430s and is unusual for its pair of jambs facing the same direction. Craigmillar and Crichton are unusually complex courtyard strongholds of the fifteenth century, stemming from older tower houses. Dalhousie would be another good example but for later mutilations. On a more modest scale, Rosslyn and Hawthornden are courtyard castles notable for their audacious promontory locations.

Holyrood Palace grew out of an unusual tower house begun by James IV, with round turrets at three of the four corners. Merchiston is a fine L-plan tower house of the fifteenth century, while Carberry and Lauriston are good examples of later towers. As usual there are others that are badly ruined or privately occupied, though Midlothian offers a good level of accessibility on the whole. A number of these castles are now within the city of Edinburgh.

County reference: RCAHMS *Midlothian and West Lothian*; RCAHMS *City of Edinburgh*. BoS *Lothian*; BoS *Edinburgh*.

BAVELAW CASTLE, in its own grounds two miles south of Malleny Mills, is really an L-plan laird's house but it is well equipped with gunports. In its present form it is attributed to Laurence Scott of Harperrig, who acquired the estate in 1628, but it probably incorporates older work.

Access: Private.

BORTHWICK CASTLE possesses the tallest and strongest of all Scottish tower houses. Rising nearly 100 feet and still intact, it was built by Sir William Borthwick on an older castle site. In 1424 he stood as a hostage for James I's release from his long captivity in England. He was rewarded in 1430 with a licence to crenellate and was later ennobled as first Lord Borthwick.

Borthwick Castle, Midlothian

The magnificent tower house is the result. It was surrounded by a strong curtain wall enclosing the roughly triangular promontory on which the castle stands. William's armoured effigy, with his wife beside him, can be seen in the adjacent parish church.

In 1567 Mary Queen of Scots and the Earl of Bothwell sought refuge here after their scandalous marriage precipitated a general revolt. Bothwell withdrew to avoid a siege and Mary escaped in male costume, only to surrender at Carberry Hill. The castle proved a thorn in the side of Oliver Cromwell during his invasion of 1650. He wrote to the fifth Lord Borthwick: 'You have harboured such parties in your house as have basely unhumanely murdered our men. If you necessitate me to bend my cannon against you, you must expect what I doubt you will not be pleased with.' Perhaps confounded by this double negative, the garrison surrendered after a token bombardment.

Although the tower house escaped destruction, the curtain was probably slighted. Except for the western stretch facing the approach, which maintains a level parapet despite the steep slope, most of the existing wall is Victorian on the old foundations. So is the gateway, guarding the only level approach. It is immediately flanked by a squat round tower at the south-west corner of the courtyard. The wide-mouthed gunports in this tower and the western curtain were inserted in the sixteenth century. Except on the east, where it extends to the tip of the promontory, the curtain formed a concentric defence around the tower house. It is necessary to follow the narrow space between them to reach the entrance.

The tower house was sensitively restored from dereliction by the twentieth Lord Borthwick from 1892, and again by Helen Bailey from 1973. From the west its unusual layout is apparent. A deep recess in the middle separates two jambs projecting from the main body of the tower house – the first example of the so-called E-plan. The whole ashlar facade is magnificently severe – even high up the windows are small in relation to the amount of wall surface. A machicolated parapet projects from the summit but never appears to have been embattled. Near the top the east side bears the scars of Cromwell's bombardment. The main body of the tower comprises three vaulted stages of similar height but two of them are divided by wooden floors, making five storeys in all. Only the middle stage is not subdivided, forming an ambitious hall within. Masons' marks are consistent from ground to top, confirming that the entire structure is the product of one great building campaign.

Surprisingly, the entrance is not located between the jambs but on the north side at first-floor level. It is now reached via a staircase and a stone bridge but, when the curtain stood intact, the void was crossed by a drawbridge from the wall walk. The entrance passage demonstrates the great thickness of the walls. On the left is the guardroom, a mural chamber with a spiral stair descending to the lower storeys. To the right a mural passage leads to the kitchen in the north jamb, with a deep fireplace. Straight ahead is the lofty great hall, crowned by a pointed vault. Pairs of window embrasures pierce the south and east walls. There is another on the west, in the recess between the two jambs. At the dais end the fireplace has a carved canopy, modelled on French examples. To the right, beside the doorway to the parlour in the south jamb, is an ornate aumbry. It is matched by a wash basin – as delicate as a church piscina – at the screen end of the hall. Beside it a spiral staircase leads upwards.

The floor above the hall was originally partitioned into two private chambers, a solar containing a hooded fireplace and another room with an oratory in one of the window embrasures. It is likely that the vaulted chamber at the top of the tower house, now used as a chapel, housed Lord Borthwick's servants. Ample private accommodation was provided in the two jambs, which contain eight storeys and are served by their own spiral stairs. Apart from the kitchen and parlour at hall level, the other floors contained bedrooms for members of the family or important retainers, so Borthwick provided much more accommodation than other tower houses of the period.

Another doorway from the courtyard leads to a stair descending to the undercrofts. Though modernised, the three vaulted compartments of the main block are still divided into two levels by wooden floors. At ground level the

northern jamb contained a pit prison and the southern a well. The castle stands three miles south-east of Gorebridge, on a sideroad off the A7.
Access: Well seen from the gate. The castle is primarily a functions venue but there are periodic open days.
Reference: Borthwick Castle: Its Place in History by H. Bailey.
Relations: Later E-plan tower houses at Craigston, Castle Stuart and Castle Kennedy. Comlongon and Spynie are comparable tower houses in scale.

BRUNSTANE CASTLE, otherwise called Brunston, stands on a farm three miles south-west of Penicuik. This crumbling oblong enclosure has a shattered hall range and a square corner tower, but no tower house. It bears the year 1568 and the initials of John Crichton of Brunstane.
Access: On farmland.

CAIRNS CASTLE, by a farm three miles south-west of Ainville, now overlooks Harperrig Reservoir. This austere L-plan tower house may have been built by George Crichton of Cairns around 1440. It lacks little more than its parapet but is a neglected and overgrown shell.
Access: On farmland.

CAKEMUIR CASTLE, commandingly positioned two miles south-west of Fala Dam, is an eighteenth-century mansion with an austere L-plan tower house at one end. Attributed to Adam Wauchope of Cakemuir in the 1560s, the jamb (unusually) is semi-circular, as at Cramond.
Access: Private.

CARBERRY TOWER lies on a country estate a mile and a half south of Inveresk, off the A6124. Now largely a Victorian mansion in Scottish Baronial style, it preserves a modest tower house at one corner. An austere oblong, the tower comprises three storeys (the top and bottom ones vaulted) and rises to a parapet with thick, squat battlements for defence by artillery. This explains the absence of the usual attic but the innovation did not catch on. One corner supports an iron fire basket that was used as a beacon – a precious survival. The only large windows are later openings and the ground-floor entrance is now covered by a little porch. Hugh Rigg, an advocate who leased the lands from the abbot of Dunfermline, probably built the tower in the 1540s. Around 1600 the Riggs of Carberry added the adjoining west range, which is almost as high as the tower. It has been altered considerably but retains its ground-floor barrel vaulting and a four-storey jamb projecting at the far end. To the east, Queen Mary's Mount marks the spot where Mary Queen of Scots surrendered to the rebels at Carberry Hill in 1567.
Access: Now a hotel but open to non-residents.

COLINTON CASTLE is an elongated L-plan tower house in the grounds of Merchiston Castle School (which is not at the eponymous castle). This overgrown ruin, with a row of barrel-vaulted undercrofts and a tall jamb, was built by the Foulis family in the late sixteenth century.
Access: On private land.

CRAIGCROOK CASTLE lies off Craigcrook Road in the western suburbs of Edinburgh. It incorporates a Z-plan tower house, possibly as old as the 1540s, with round and square flanking towers (the latter now embedded in extensions). It was erected by the Adamsons of Craigcrook.
Access: Private.

CRAIGMILLAR CASTLE is the greatest of the castles now enveloped in the Edinburgh suburbs. It stands three miles south of Holyrood Palace, in a tenuous swathe of green off Craigmillar Castle Road. Bounded to the south by a low cliff, the castle consists of a tower house and a rare machicolated curtain wall. According to tradition, the tower house was erected by Sir Simon Preston, who purchased the lordship in 1374. If so it would be one of the oldest L-plan tower houses to survive (compare David's Tower at nearby Edinburgh Castle), but the fifteenth century is considered more likely. There is similar uncertainty about the surrounding curtain. It once bore the year 1427 above the entrance, but dates down to the early sixteenth century have been suggested. This curtain encloses a small quadrangle dominated by the tower house, which is placed at the back of the courtyard.

Cylindrical towers flank the four corners of the curtain. The north-eastern tower has keyhole gunports commanding the approach to the castle. If the curtain really dates from 1427 then they are the oldest in Scotland. A round-headed gate arch pierces the middle of the north side. It is surmounted by a panel displaying the arms of the Prestons of Craigmillar – a helmet with a unicorn crest above the tilted shield. Although the slim towers and simple gateway form an economical version of the quadrangular castles then prevalent in England, the continuous machicolated parapet is a rare conceit anywhere in Britain. It crowns all four corner towers as well, but has disappeared on the west owing to the later rebuilding on that side. In addition to the surviving east and west ranges, blocked windows show that buildings once stood against the north curtain too, reducing the courtyard to a narrow passage in front of the tower house.

The jamb is defensively placed at the back of the tower house, immediately above the cliff. It was therefore necessary to pass around the tower to reach the entrance – unwelcome visitors would have been caught in the narrow corridor between this tower and the south curtain. Another panel of the Preston arms surmounts the doorway in the jamb, flanked by the main block. A passage leads to the barrel-vaulted undercroft, originally divided into two by a wooden floor.

In the jamb a spiral staircase ascends to the hall, which did not form the high, vaulted chamber it now appears to be. An ornate row of corbels on either side shows that this space was also divided by a wooden floor. The upper stage in the vault can only have formed a dimly lit sleeping loft rather than the solar. A hooded fireplace occupies the dais end of the hall, its long lintel supported on shafted columns. At the opposite end, a mural chamber occupies one corner. A doorway leads to the so-called Queen Mary's Room in the jamb. Originally the kitchen, it was converted into a residential chamber when the new kitchen was built outside. Mary Queen of Scots is more likely to have occupied the east range on her two visits here. The spiral stair ascends to another room in the jamb, which presumably served as a small solar since the tower house lacks the further storey it craves. The stair merely continues to a gabled attic that was added later; there is no sign of an any attic over the main block. From the top there is a sweeping view over the city.

Originally the tower house was isolated from the rest, but passages were later cut through from both the undercroft and the hall to a wide spiral staircase just beyond. This serves an austere residential block, standing against the east curtain. It was built sometime after the Earl of Hertford's attack of 1544 during the Rough Wooing, when the castle was burnt despite the assurances given by the English when negotiating its surrender. Vaulted rooms at three levels include a new kitchen, superseding that in the tower house. The gabled attic stage served as a long gallery. In front of the castle extends an outer courtyard of sixteenth-century date. It is bounded by a low precinct wall of little defensive value, though the circular dovecote commanding the approach is pierced by shot holes. The only building to remain here is the roofless chapel, a simple gabled structure.

Its proximity to Edinburgh made the castle a frequent magnet for royal visits. In 1479 John Stewart, Earl of Mar and Garioch, was imprisoned here by his brother, James III, dying suspiciously soon afterwards. It was also here in 1566 that the Earl of Bothwell and his fellow conspirators made the 'Craigmillar Bond' to murder Lord Darnley. In 1660 the impoverished Prestons sold the castle to Sir John Gilmour, a distinguished judge. He largely rebuilt the hall block in the west range as a more up-to-date residence. This is also now roofless.

Access: Open daily (HES).
Reference: Guidebook by C. Tabraham.
Relations: Early L-plan tower houses at Dunnottar, Edinburgh and Neidpath. There is a similar towered enclosure at Threave. The Prestons' tower at Uttershill.

CRAMOND TOWER, within the site of a Roman fort, has been restored for occupation. This tall tower house was built by Bishop of Dunkeld towards the end of the fifteenth century. A curious variant of the L-plan, the little jamb is a semi-circular stair turret, as at Cakemuir.

Access: Private.

CRICHTON CASTLE is as impressive in its way as neighbouring Borthwick but the two are quite different in character. To begin with, Crichton is now a ruin, though a very substantial one. Moreover, whereas Borthwick is dominated by its great tower house, the Crichton family developed the castle from a more modest tower house into an intricate complex around a compact courtyard. Tall ranges occupy all four sides but no attempt was made to create a unified exterior with corner towers like nearby Craigmillar. It rises prominently above the River Tyne, two miles south of Pathhead off the B6367, and is reached by a track leading south from the collegiate church.

The oldest part is the ruinous tower house on the east side of the courtyard, beside the present entrance. This oblong structure was vaulted at two levels but two sides have collapsed, taking most of the vaulting with them. A wooden floor divided the lower stage into two levels. One corner is walled off to form

Crichton Castle, Midlothian

a pit prison, reached from above via the tiny kitchen. The upper stage formed a lofty hall, originally reached via an external stair. There may have been a further storey containing a solar, but nothing remains.

John de Crichton probably built the tower house before his death in 1406. His son, Sir William, became Lord Chancellor in 1439, during the minority of James II. The following year he engineered the murder of the young Black Douglas heirs at the Black Dinner in Edinburgh Castle, cynically entertaining them here *en route*. In 1445 the castle was sacked in a revenge attack by the Douglases, but William survived to expand it. On the south side of the courtyard stands his gatehouse, at right angles to the earlier tower house. It forms a massive oblong block with a heavy machicolated parapet. The entrance passage lies between two barrel-vaulted undercrofts but the outer gateway was later walled up. A staircase ascends from the courtyard to the floor above. This originally formed a lofty great hall, supplanting the older hall in the tower house, but it was later subdivided. Note the monumental fireplace, part of the original structure.

Chancellor Crichton's west range contained domestic offices, centred on a kitchen over a vaulted undercroft. Beside it, a passage leads to a narrow postern. South of the kitchen a square tower is the dominant feature of the castle skyline. It probably housed the castle's retainers but, unusually, none of its six storeys are vaulted. The Chancellor also built the cruciform collegiate church for the good of his soul. His son, another William, supported the Duke of Albany's seizure of power in 1482. As a result James III besieged the castle the following year. William fled to England and Crichton was granted to the Hepburns.

In 1559 the castle was ransacked by the Earl of Arran after James Hepburn, the notorious fourth Earl of Bothwell, intercepted an English subsidy intended for the Protestant Lords. Bothwell was forced into exile in 1567, following his disastrous marriage to Mary Queen of Scots. Francis Stewart inherited the title and provided the castle with its last and finest building. The courtyard front of his four-storey north range, against the older curtain wall, is a masterpiece of the Italian Renaissance in Scotland. Above the seven-arched loggia is a rusticated facade copied from a palazzo in Ferrara. A grand staircase ascends to the dining room on the first floor. Beyond it, a spacious withdrawing room occupies the tower-like projection at the north-east angle of the castle. This range was built following the earl's return from exile in Italy in 1581. Nevertheless the barrel-vaulted storerooms at ground level are typically Scottish. The windows looking outwards were barred by iron grilles, while the wide-mouthed gunports below the withdrawing room show that defence was not entirely neglected.

Francis also remodelled the older buildings. As at some other keep-gatehouses in Britain, the combination of entrance defences with a residence had proved inconvenient. He blocked the old gate passage, contriving a new gateway in the narrow gap between the gatehouse range and the tower house. Chancellor Crichton's great hall was divided into two floors of residential chambers and given larger windows. The gabled stable block just outside the castle is another of his additions. Despite his cultured tastes, Stewart was an unstable personality who terrorised his cousin, James VI. He was finally exiled in 1594, following his involvement in the Catholic Uprising. James' order to destroy the castle was not carried out but it was abandoned and sank into ruins.

Access: Open daily in summer (HES).
Reference: Guidebook by C. Tabraham and N. Scott.
Relations: Borthwick. Keep-gatehouses at Rothesay, Caerlaverock, Tantallon and Doune. Chancellor Crichton's brother's castle at Blackness.

DALHOUSIE CASTLE rises commandingly above the South Esk river. It is set in spacious grounds two miles south-east of Bonnyrigg, off the B704. Until 1860 it was the seat of the Ramsays of Dalhousie, a Norman family who received the lordship from David I. In 1400 Sir Alexander Ramsay held out against Sir Henry Percy (Hotspur) in a long siege, but the existing complex dates from the mid-fifteenth century. Its original layout – a tower house closely surrounded by a concentric curtain wall with a round tower at one corner – resembled nearby Borthwick Castle. Although the tower house is still complete, its original L-plan is obscured by later buildings that have filled most of the former courtyard. The conversion of the castle into a mansion began in 1618 under Sir George Ramsay. Then in 1825 the ninth Earl of Dalhousie commissioned the architect William Burn to transform the interiors in Gothic Revival style.

Much of the surrounding curtain survives but is difficult to disentangle from Burn's extensions. The east curtain retains a few arrow slits and a blocked gateway, while the canted south-east corner embodies the lower part of an oblong tower that overlooked the river. However, the west side of the castle is the show front. The circular tower at the north-west corner preserves its vaulted well chamber at ground level. Burn remodelled the two upper floors and provided the heavily projecting parapet. Immediately beside this tower is the most interesting feature of the original castle – the entrance gate, which resembles the one at Dirleton. Above the little archway, a panel bearing the Ramsay arms is flanked by twin recesses where the drawbridge beams rested. They are framed within a much taller arch, with machicolated round bartizans at the corners. From 1633 the first Earl of Dalhousie built up the remainder of the west front into a turreted residential range.

The gateway now leads directly into Burn's neo-Gothic entrance hall. Beyond is the tower house. Sir George Ramsay filled in the re-entrant angle with a grand staircase. Burn transformed the first-floor hall into the Long Room, while the two upper storeys have been partitioned. However, three pointed vaults still mark the ground floor of the main block, while a spiral stair descends to a gloomy pit prison in the base of the jamb.

Access: Now a hotel but open to non-residents.

Relations: Borthwick and Dirleton.

EDINBURGH CASTLE AND TOWN WALL Crowning the precipitous crag that dominates the city, Edinburgh is the most famous of all Scottish castles. It has played a central role in the turbulent history of Scotland, but only certain portions of the royal castle survive. Much of the existing complex is a Hanoverian fortress built to counter the Jacobite threat. Occupation was purely military by that time and the old palace on the summit suffered the indignity of conversion into barracks. Despite Victorian attempts to reinstate a castellated appearance more in keeping with its earlier history, much of Edinburgh Castle is still grimly utilitarian.

Castle Rock is the core of an extinct volcano – one of several dramatic outcrops in this 'Athens of the North'. The Northumbrians established a burgh or fortified town here. It emerges from obscurity in 1093, suffering the first of many sieges when the devout Queen Margaret resisted her usurping brother-in-law, Donald Bane. Tradition ascribes the tiny Romanesque chapel to her, though the rock was not yet a castle in the accepted sense. We can only surmise that it became so – a fortified royal residence rather than a communal stronghold – under Margaret's feudalising sons. By 1175 it was important enough to be one of the five Scottish castles ceded to Henry II after William the Lion's capture at Alnwick. Nothing is known about the thirteenth-century castle, though it is likely that Alexander II or III undertook some stone building here.

Edinburgh surrendered after a five-day siege when Edward I invaded in 1296 – a tougher resistance than he encountered anywhere else. However, in 1314 Thomas Randolph, Earl of Moray, found a way up the rock and surprised the English garrison in a night attack. Robert the Bruce levelled the castle to render it useless to the enemy. Only St Margaret's Chapel was spared. Nevertheless, the English reoccupied the site when Edward III invaded in support of Edward Balliol. They were driven out in 1341 by a band of Scots who entered the castle disguised as merchants.

Bruce's son David II refortified the summit from 1358, after his release from eleven years' captivity in England. His successor, Robert II, continued building. Between them they raised a strong screen wall against the cliff facing the Old Town, with a massive tower house (David's Tower) at one end. Only the lower half of David's Tower survives, buried within the later Half Moon Battery. In 1445 this castle fell to the Black Douglases after a nine-month siege. The attack was provoked by the murder of the young Earl of Douglas and his brother at the infamous Black Dinner in the castle five years earlier. In the fifteenth century the Stewart kings erected a palace quadrangle on the summit. Much of this survives in a mutilated state, notably James IV's great hall. The later Stewarts preferred to reside in Holyrood Palace; there were only occasional royal visits to offset the castle's normal role as a state fortress and arsenal.

One of these visits occurred in 1566, when Mary Queen of Scots gave birth to the future James VI. Following her flight into exile two years later the deposed queen's adherent, Sir William Kirkcaldy of Grange, provoked the longest of the castle's sieges, defying the town for an astonishing five years. It was finally battered into submission by English cannon in 1573 and Kirkcaldy was hanged. David II's screen wall was destroyed by the bombardment and the Earl of Morton, regent for the young James VI, had it rebuilt. Further lengthy sieges took place in 1640, when the castle fell to the Covenanters, and 1650, when it was taken and strengthened by Oliver Cromwell. Having surrendered to the forces of William and Mary in 1689, the castle successfully resisted both the Old and the Young Pretender. Its defences were largely rebuilt between these two great Jacobite risings.

The only easy approach is from the Royal Mile. In front of the castle is the Esplanade, a parade ground on the site of a sixteenth-century ravelin. A bridge crosses Cromwell's rock-cut ditch to the outer gatehouse, which dates entirely from 1887. The small forecourt within faces Regent Morton's massive screen wall of the 1570s, ending in the curved Half Moon Battery. High up to the left is the east wing of the palace quadrangle. A pathway, skirting the foot of the screen wall, ascends a natural ledge in the rock to the Portcullis Gate, with its Renaissance outer portal. This oblong gatehouse was also rebuilt by Morton but has a Victorian top floor. Just beyond, the steep Lang Stairs ascend directly to the summit.

Following the ledge the visitor ascends to the middle courtyard. Although it formed part of the medieval castle, the present defences are Georgian. General Wade, known for his military road network, built the enclosing wall with gun batteries in the 1730s. The buildings within are also Georgian, notably the handsome Governor's House and the enormous New Barracks. Foog's Gate, a survivor from an earlier spate of building under Charles II, leads to the upper courtyard on the summit of the rock.

The summit formed the inner courtyard of the original castle. To the east it is bounded by the parapet of Regent Morton's screen wall, with a row of later gun embrasures. It offers panoramic views of the city and the Firth of Forth. The Half Moon Battery encases the lower part of David's Tower, built in 1368–77. Its projecting jamb made it the first L-plan tower house in Scotland. Only the little St Margaret's Chapel is older. Although unlikely to be Queen Margaret's work, it is still one of the oldest church buildings in Scotland. First mentioned in 1130 during the reign of her son David I, the chevron ornament of the chancel arch and the semi-circular apse behind it are consistent with that date. For centuries it was abused as a powder magazine, being restored to something like its original appearance in 1851. Another feature of the summit is the famous cannon, Mons Meg, given to James II by the Duke of Burgundy in 1457. The pride of the royal siege train, it destroyed the walls of Norham Castle on the Tweed before the Battle of Flodden. This 'great iron murderer' (as Cromwell called it) finally burst in 1682 but has been restored.

Crown Square forms an inner quadrangle that originated as the palace of the Stewart monarchs. On the north side, Lorimer's National War Memorial (1924) occupies the site of a larger church erected by David II. The west wing was rebuilt in 1708 as the Queen Anne Barracks and is now a regimental museum, while the east wing originated as a residential annexe to David's Tower under James IV. It was remodelled by Mary Queen of Scots (the year 1566 is carved above the entrance) and again in anticipation of James VI's brief homecoming in 1617. A panelled room within marks his birthplace; above are the Scottish Regalia, including James IV's sword and James V's crown. They were hidden after the Act of Union to prevent them from being taken south, only to be rediscovered in 1817.

On the south side of the quadrangle is the great hall, overlooking the cliff. Despite a thorough Victorian restoration, this is still the hall that James IV built from 1496. Its open timber roof is largely original and a great rarity in Scotland, though the hammerbeams have been renewed. Beneath the hall and the rebuilt west wing are the cavernous Vaults, rough substructures built in the fifteenth century to provide a level base for the palace quadrangle on this sloping site. Graffiti attest the many French and American prisoners of war who were incarcerated here in the eighteenth and nineteenth centuries.

Edinburgh had one of Scotland's few town walls but only a few sections remain. Emerging as the Scottish capital in the fifteenth century, the medieval burgh was confined to the glacial ridge descending eastwards from the castle along the High Street. In 1450 James II granted a licence to build the original King's Wall, which protected the south and east sides of the Old Town but has vanished. No wall was built on the north – the valley here was flooded to create the Nor Loch (long since drained). Following the disaster at Flodden in 1513, the circuit was hurriedly extended further south to take in the suburb of Cowgate. Appropriately called the Flodden Wall, it did not prevent the town from being burnt to the ground by the English in 1544, though the castle held out. Strengthened for artillery during the Jacobite period, the town's defences were mostly pulled down from the 1760s, when Edinburgh expanded beyond the high tenement blocks of its old confines into the magnificent New Town.

From Grassmarket a staircase known as 'The Vennel' ascends to a squat, square tower with dumbbell gunports, in the shadow of the castle. It marks the south-west corner of the Flodden Wall. The long stretch with mock battlements running south from here is actually part of Telfer's Wall, a further short extension built as late as 1628 to enclose Heriot's Hospital. The Flodden Wall reappears a little further east, cutting through Greyfriars' Kirkyard and now covered with macabre monuments. Another length of plain walling, running along Drummond Street before turning into Pleasance, marks the south-east corner of the Flodden Wall.

Access: The castle precincts, chapel, palace buildings and Vaults are open daily (HES). The town wall remains are freely accessible (LA).
Reference: HES castle guidebook. *Edinburgh Castle* by I. MacIvor.
Relations: The castle-palaces of Falkland, Holyrood, Stirling and Linlithgow. Other royal work at Tarbert, Dundonald, Rothesay, Lochleven, Dumbarton, Dunbar, Tantallon, Blackness and Ravenscraig (Fife). The town walls at Peebles and Stirling.

HAWTHORNDEN CASTLE is perched above the North Esk river, a mile and a half north of Rosewell via a sideroad off the A6094. It crowns a promontory as audaciously as nearby Rosslyn Castle. A twisting drive leads to the narrow entrance gateway, placed between the ruined tower house and a wing of the later house. The Classical archway dates only from the 1630s but is still overlooked by shot holes and closed by an iron-studded door. Within, the castle forms a compact, triangular courtyard sloping down towards the cliff. The modest tower house at the south-east angle, probably built by the Douglases of Hawthornden in the fifteenth century, was a three-storey oblong. One wall, facing the courtyard, has collapsed above the level of the barrel-vaulted undercroft. An annexe contains a pit prison. Beside it, a stretch of curtain wall bounding the south side of the courtyard is pierced by window openings denoting the position of the vanished great hall. Near the apex is a rock-cut well.

Hawthornden was twice damaged during the English invasions of the 1540s. The picturesque range on the north-west, supplanting the older curtain, was erected by the poet Sir William Drummond, who entertained Ben Jonson here. A Latin inscription modestly records that he restored the house in 1638, but it has been much altered since. The cliffs below the castle are undercut by ancient caves, said like many to have sheltered Robert the Bruce at some point during his chequered early years fighting the English.

Access: Private (now a retreat).
Relations: Rosslyn.

HOLYROOD PALACE   This royal residence, officially called the Palace of Holyroodhouse, is overlooked by the volcanic outcrop of Salisbury Crags. It stands off Canongate at the eastern end of Edinburgh's Royal Mile. David I founded Holyrood Abbey for Augustinian canons in 1128. The abbey guesthouse developed into a royal palace under the Stewarts, who came to prefer it to their inconvenient residence in Edinburgh Castle at the upper end of the Royal Mile. It suffered the depredations of Hertford's troops in 1544 during the Rough Wooing. After the Reformation the abbey disappeared, only the imposing early Gothic nave being retained as the Chapel Royal of the palace. Even this has been roofless since 1768. Sir William Bruce erected the magnificent quadrangle forming the present palace for Charles II, who never visited. Its predecessor had mostly been destroyed during the Roundhead occupation. Of the older Stewart palace only the four-storey James IV Tower remains, at the north-west corner of the present complex. The matching south-western tower is entirely Bruce's, though it marks the fulfilment of James V's unfinished intentions.

James IV began the tower house bearing his name but left it incomplete when he fell at Flodden in 1513. His son, James V, resumed building after coming of age in 1529. John Ayton was the master mason. Its *bastille* plan with circular angle turrets is unusual for a Scottish tower house. There is no turret at the south-east corner because an earlier residential range abutted here. Nevertheless, the tower was conceived as a self-contained unit, housing the private royal quarters. In the original design it could only be entered at first-floor level via a drawbridge. The tower is capped by an embattled parapet projecting on corbels.

James V was involved in marriage negotiations when he completed the tower house, so the two main floors were intended as separate suites for the king and his prospective queen. Both are divided into an audience chamber and a bedroom, with alcoves in the western turrets. The third turret contains the spiral stair. When the new palace was built the tower house suffered a drastic internal remodelling. Bruce adjusted the floor levels, installing panelling and the sash windows. The coffered ceilings of the queen's rooms on the second floor are original but the heraldic panels are later insertions. This level is redolent with tragic memories of Mary Queen of Scots. In 1566 her husband Lord Darnley and his adherents burst into the pregnant queen's supper party in the north-west turret. Accusing David Riccio of adultery with the queen, they dragged the unfortunate secretary to the spiral staircase, where he was stabbed approximately fifty-seven times.

Access: The grounds, state rooms and James IV Tower are open regularly.
Reference: Guidebook by J. Richardson.
Relations: The castle-palaces of Falkland, Edinburgh, Stirling and Linlithgow. Other work of James IV and V at Tarbert, Rothesay, Dumbarton, Dunbar, Tantallon and Blackness.

LAURISTON CASTLE stands five miles north-west of central Edinburgh in wooded grounds overlooking the Firth of Forth. It is reached via a drive off Barnton Gardens. This tower house remains unspoilt externally, except for the insertion of some larger windows. Four storeys high including the gabled attic, the roof line is enlivened by round corner bartizans, dormer windows and a large chimney stack. Lauriston is a comparatively rare example of a T-plan tower house. The jamb projects centrally and is now embedded in the later house alongside. Its square upper floors rise over a semi-circular base, which contained the spiral staircase up to the hall. Sir Archibald Napier built the tower after purchasing the lands in 1587. His main residence was Merchiston Castle, Lauriston being occupied by one of his sons. In 1824 the architect William Burn built a little mansion onto the present tower house. The tower itself did not escape renovation, its first-floor hall being transformed into a comfortable dining room. Nevertheless, it preserves a narrow staircase ascending from one of the window embrasures to a mural chamber with a listening hole (laird's lug) overlooking the hall. Below are twin vaulted undercrofts.

Access: Grounds open daily (LA). There are periodic tours of the interior.
Relations: Merchiston. T-plan towers such as Castle Campbell, Drummond and Queen Mary's House.

LIBERTON TOWER stands off Liberton Drive in an Edinburgh suburb. This tower house is quite severe, sparsely fenestrated and vaulted at two levels. It was built by the Dalmahoys sometime in the fifteenth century and later abandoned for picturesque Liberton House nearby.

Access: Private (now a holiday let).

MERCHISTON CASTLE is another stronghold now enveloped by suburban Edinburgh, standing two miles south of Edinburgh Castle off Colinton Road. Now part of Napier University, this tower house is hemmed in by discordant glass and concrete. The tower follows the L-plan, its corbelled-out parapet rounding into tiny bartizans at the corners. Originally the tower was divided into five storeys – surprisingly none of them vaulted – plus a later attic that is recessed within the parapet. Unusually for an L-plan tower house, the original entrance is not in the re-entrant angle but in the opposite wall at second-floor level (the archway has been renewed). The tower was built by the Napiers of Merchiston, prominent burgesses of Edinburgh, probably soon after they acquired the lands in 1438. In 1572 Sir Archibald Napier resisted two attacks by supporters of Mary Queen of Scots, then holding out in Edinburgh Castle, including an attempt to smoke out the tower by lighting fires against its walls. His son John was a mathematician who invented logarithms.

Although the tower is unspoilt outside, the Napiers remodelled the interior after the Restoration, inserting a grand staircase at one end to replace the spiral stair in one corner. The transformed hall, on the second floor, is covered by a seventeenth-century plaster ceiling, while the chamber above (made loftier by combining two storeys into one) has a painted ceiling of allegorical and sometimes lewd figures dated 1581. This is not *in situ*, having come from a mansion near Musselburgh.

Access: Exterior only.
Relations: The Napier tower at Lauriston.

PINKIE HOUSE, in secluded grounds in the middle of Musselburgh, is a splendid mansion built by the first Earl of Dunfermline from 1613 onwards (compare his work at Fyvie). However, the east range incorporates a sixteenth-century L-plan tower house of the abbot of Dunfermline.

Access: Now Loretto School.

ROSSLYN CASTLE is reached by a pathway running down from the astonishing Rosslyn Chapel (the village itself is usually spelt 'Roslin'). The first castle may have been raised by Sir William Sinclair, one of the knights who died fighting the Moors in Andalucia *en route* to take Robert the Bruce's heart to Jerusalem. However, the earliest portions now surviving are probably the work of his descendant of the same name. This William Sinclair built Rosslyn Chapel as a magnificent family burial place. Created first Earl of Caithness in 1455, William relinquished his ancestral jarldom of Orkney, at that time still a Norwegian dependency. His northern power base was Castle Sinclair Girnigoe.

Only tantalising portions survive of William's castle. It occupies a spectacular promontory at the neck of a loop in the North Esk river, three miles south-west of Bonnyrigg, with sheer drops on all sides but one. The only level approach – from the north – is cut off by a deep ditch, crossed by a sixteenth-century bridge. It leads to the remains of the entrance gateway, flanked by a ruined square tower. An unusual stretch of curtain wall closes the north-west side of the roughly oblong courtyard. Its outer face is reinforced by a series of closely spaced triangular buttresses. Beyond is the one surviving corner of an oblong tower house, rising to a machicolated crown. This tower was slighted by the Earl of Hertford in 1544 during the Rough Wooing. Further damage was inflicted on the castle by General Monck in 1650 and by an Edinburgh mob in 1688.

Hertford's depredations were only made good half a century later with the construction of a new residential range on the south-east side of the castle in the 1590s. From the courtyard this gabled block appears to be just two storeys high. In fact the range is built against the cliff face and there are three more storeys below courtyard level, served by a grand staircase. Each lower level comprises four barrel-vaulted chambers linked by a corridor. Further rooms are located in the square jamb projecting at the south corner. Shot holes are placed beneath the windows, while more threatening gunports pierce the jamb low down. Only the north-eastern part of the range is still occupied, the rest surviving as an empty shell. The ruined great hall at courtyard level, later subdivided, has a fireplace bearing the year 1597 and the initials of William St Clair, Baron of Rosslyn. A plaster ceiling in the inhabited part shows that he was still embellishing the house in 1622.

Access: The ruined part is freely accessible but the residential block is private (now a holiday let). Uphill return.

Reference: Guidebook to chapel and castle by J. Thompson. *PSAS* (12).

Relations: The Castle of Mey, Castle Sinclair Girnigoe, Old Keiss and Ravenscraig (Fife) were other strongholds of the Sinclair earls.

SMEATON HOUSE stands in the grounds of Dalkeith Home Farm, just to the south-west of Whitecraig. It incorporates a length of curtain wall and two round corner towers, one now truncated. They were part of a fifteenth-century courtyard castle of the abbots of Dunfermline.

Access: On private land.

UTTERSHILL CASTLE (otherwise called Outtershill) is a prominently sited ruin just south of Penicuik, reached by a short footpath starting at a bend in the B6372. It began in the sixteenth century as a humble, two-storey stronghouse of the Penicuik family but was later remodelled and extended, perhaps after the Prestons of Craigmillar Castle acquired the land in 1604. The new section accommodated a kitchen at ground level and a solar above, in line with the hall in the older part. At least one further storey was added, converting the building into an elongated tower house, but only the two lower floors now remain. The undercroft vault has fallen in but its curve can still be seen against the side walls

Access: Freely accessible.
Reference: *PSAS* (128).
Relations: Craigmillar. The converted stronghouse at Littledean.

OTHER SITES *Dalkeith Palace* (grounds open), a Queen Anne mansion built from 1702, incorporates in its south wing the undercroft of a tower house of the Douglas earls of Morton. *Calder House* (at Mid Calder), *Crookston Old House* (near Fountainhall) and *Monkton House* (near Millerhill) have tower houses embedded in them, while the towers of *Cousland* (near Crossgatehall), *Hirendean* (near Waterheads) and *Lennox* (near Currie) are very ruinous. *Newton House* (near Dalkeith) retains a round flanking tower from the barmkin.

Some other sites are now in the suburbs of Edinburgh. *Craiglockhart Castle* (Glenlockhart Road) is the stump of a small tower house, while *Roseburn House* (off Roseburn Street) developed out of another tower. *Castle Gogar*, a handsome laird's house of 1625 by Edinburgh Airport, embodies an older tower. Another barmkin turret survives in the grounds of *Comiston House*. Castle Avenue marks the site of the quadrangular castle of *Corstorphine*, built by Sir Adam Forrester from 1374. Only a later dovecote has survived demolition. The port of *Leith* was fortified by the French in 1548 and resisted an attack by the English in 1560, after which the ramparts were demolished.

MORAY AND NAIRNSHIRE

These two adjoining counties on the Moray Firth have a variety of castles, though a few of particular interest are not usually accessible. Little Nairnshire possesses Cawdor Castle, an evocative complex of courtyards and residential buildings that has grown up around the original tower house of the Cawdor family. Kilravock also has a fine tower house, while Rait is an unusual hall house built during the Wars of Independence. Auldearn's royal motte now has a dovecote on top, while the little watch tower at Ardclach later became a bell tower.

Moray recalls the much larger province of Moravia that twelfth-century Scottish rulers battled to dominate. Duffus has the fine earthwork castle of a Flemish settler from that era, with an early tower house that proved too heavy for the artificial motte on which it sits. Lochindorb, a Red Comyn stronghold on a lonely island, is a good example of a castle of enclosure with round flanking towers and even a concentric outer wall. Spynie's massive tower house is just one element of an episcopal courtyard castle, while Darnaway – long the seat of the powerful earls of Moray – preserves its remarkable hall roof. Among later tower houses are stately Brodie and the excellent little Coxton Tower.

County reference: BoS *Aberdeenshire: North and Moray*; BoS *Highland and Islands* (for Nairnshire).

ARDCLACH BELL TOWER is a mile and a half south of Redburn, via a sideroad off the A939. 'Tower' is a generous appellation for this diminutive, two-storey structure, though it does stand high up overlooking the valley of the River Findhorn. It is reached from the road by a steep flight of steps. The yellow-harled exterior is very plain, with tiny windows and a few shot holes. In fact the vaulted ground floor has no windows and served as a grim prison cell, but the floor above is a modest residential chamber with a fireplace. One of the gables bears the rather late year 1655, so the tower is generally attributed to the Covenantor Alexander Brodie of Lethen, though he may just have refurbished an older structure. Evidently it was a simple watch tower commanding an extensive view. A bellcote was later added to one gable to serve Ardclach's parish church, beside the river two hairpin bends below.

Access: Freely accessible (HES – uphill walk).
Relations: Repentance Tower and Castle Varrich were other watch towers.

AULDEARN CASTLE An unusually large motte known as Dooket Hill overlooks the village and the A96, three miles east of Nairn. A low rampart bank surrounds the summit but there is no evidence of an accompanying bailey. The castle (originally called Eren) is attributed to King William the Lion, despite the proximity of vanished Nairn Castle. It is mentioned in a charter of 1188 but seems to have been abandoned before long. In 1645 the Marquis of Montrose raised his standard on the motte before defeating a superior Covenanter force at the Battle of Auldearn. The circular Boath Dovecote on the summit was erected later that century.
Access: Freely accessible (NTS).
Relations: The motte at Duffus. William the Lion built the first Red Castle.

BRODIE CASTLE stands in extensive grounds off the A96, four miles west of Forres. The Brodie family lived here from the twelfth century, but the present structure consists of a Z-plan tower house forming the south end of a rambling nineteenth-century mansion, the harling giving a deceptive unity to the whole. As seen from the approach, the tower house forms the left half of the facade. The main block is much altered, with enlarged windows and restored dormers rising from the attic, but the entrance still occupies the old position beside the south flanking tower. This square tower is the best-preserved part. It rises four storeys to an elaborately corbelled-out parapet with one round corner bartizan and cannon spouts. Wide-mouthed gunports command the base, while a slender stair turret projects in the re-entrant angle from the first-floor upwards. A gabled attic, recessed within the parapet, bears the year 1567. Alexander Brodie only regained his possessions the previous year, after losing them for his part in the fourth Earl of Huntly's revolt, so this would signify a very rapid construction unless building started beforehand. Another stone records John Russell as the master mason.

A later annexe on the south-west side has further confused the original layout of the tower house, filling up the re-entrant angle, though this extension is old enough to have gunports of its own. The ground-floor vaulting of the main block (with Romanesque-style columns) is only Victorian, but the intricate plaster decoration on the first-floor vault of the south tower dates from the 1630s. Brodie was sacked by the Royalists under the Marquis of Montrose during his lightning campaign of 1645. From 1824 the architect William Burn added the wing north-east of the tower house and large extensions behind, enveloping the square north flanking tower in the process. The tower house interior was transformed into a series of fine rooms, including the Red Drawing Room which is formed out of the first-floor hall.
Access: Open daily (NTS).
Reference: Guidebook by S. Blackden and C. Hartley.
Relations: Z-plan tower houses such as Ballindalloch and Carnousie.

BURGIE CASTLE Four miles east of Forres along the A96, a sideroad signposted 'Burgie Mains' runs in half a mile to this tall oblong tower, immediately behind a wall. It rises six storeys to a corbelled-out parapet with battlements and corner bartizans. The entrance into the vaulted ground floor is closed by a yett, while a rounded stair turret rises a little higher than the rest. The structure looks too slender to be a tower house proper and a closer inspection reveals fragments of attached walls. There is even a blocked-up fireplace embedded in the outer wall at first-floor level, bearing the year 1602 and the arms of the Dunbars of Burgie. It becomes apparent that it was the north-west flanking tower of a (probably) Z-plan tower house. The rest was destroyed in 1802 as a source of stone for nearby Burgie House, the tower being retained as an eye-catcher.

Access: Well seen from the road.
Relations: The similar tower at Gordon Castle.

CASTLE GRANT, originally called Freuchie Castle, occupies a large estate two miles north of Grantown-on-Spey. This chief seat of the Grant family has expanded into a mansion over the centuries but an L-plan tower house, attributed to James Grant around 1535, still forms its core.

Access: Private.

CAWDOR CASTLE, amid fine gardens six miles south-west of Nairn (via the B9090), has developed into a picturesque mansion of three courtyards surrounding a central tower house. It was originally known as Calder. The Shakespearean connection with Macbeth is spurious but the thanes of Cawdor were here by 1295. The tower house, or at least its lower part, may date from the time of William of Cawdor. An unusual strand of evidence supports this dating – the trunk of a holly tree still rising from the floor of the barrel-vaulted undercroft. Carbon dating suggests that the tree stopped growing around 1372. According to legend a donkey chose the castle's location by coming to a halt beneath this tree. If so it discerningly chose a site that is naturally defended at the back by a steep drop to the Cawdor Burn.

The tower house is a tall oblong, dominating the rest of the castle. Three main storeys surmount the undercroft, the topmost floor being covered by a pointed vault. Above that a gabled attic, added early in the seventeenth century, is recessed within the parapet. There are round corner bartizans with conical roofs. The original first-floor entrance has been converted into a window but another doorway leads directly into the undercroft. A box machicolation projects from the wall high above, though the ground-floor doorway is now sheltered within a later staircase annexe. In the undercroft is a mural prison, visible through a modern opening but once reached only from a trapdoor on the floor above. A straight mural staircase ascends to the first-floor hall, now called the 'Tower Room'. From here the upper floors are reached by a spiral

Cawdor Castle, Nairnshire

staircase in one corner. In contrast to the gaunt undercroft, the upper floors were modernised following a fire in 1819, while the windows are seventeenth-century enlargements. If the tower house already existed, then the licence to crenellate granted to another William Cawdor in 1454 would relate to expansion. The yett protecting the ground-floor doorway is said to have come from Lochindorb Castle, which William dismantled in 1456. It may be the second William who built the oblong walled enclosure around the tower house. Much of this curtain wall survives, fronted by a broad ditch.

The powerful Campbell dynasty contrived to add Cawdor to their feudal empire. In 1499 the Earl of Argyll kidnapped the infant Cawdor heiress, marrying her to his son, Sir John Campbell. A fireplace lintel in the later dining room commemorates this enforced union. In 1523 Sir John withstood a siege by the Cawdor family, who disputed his tenure. In 1683–43 another John Campbell of Cawdor largely rebuilt the residential buildings around the little courtyard to north of the tower house, against the older curtain. They were further remodelled by Sir Hugh Campbell from 1684. The original great hall in the north range was divided into two storeys: the drawing room below and a bedchamber adorned with Flemish tapestries above. The opulent interiors of these ranges reflect more recent centuries of continued habitation.

A small forecourt is contrived to the east, in front of the tower house. Here the curtain is pierced by an entrance gate that retains its drawbridge, once raised by the wooden beams that project above the gateway. Gateway and drawbridge date only from the 1640s but their archaic nature suggests a renewal of the original arrangement. Although the larger south courtyard is also part of the original enclosure, its surrounding buildings were mostly erected by the earls of Cawdor in Victorian times, in a style matching the rest.

Access: Open daily in summer (HHA).
Reference: Guidebook by the Earl of Cawdor.
Relations: Lochindorb. Early tower houses like Dundonald, Lochleven and Threave. Late courtyard castles such as Tolquhon, Edzell and Rowallan.

COXTON TOWER, three and a half miles east of Elgin off the B9103, stands in the grounds of a Victorian successor house. This classic little tower house, empty since 1867 but still intact, is something of an enigma. The thick walls and sturdy vaults do not seem to go with the year 1644 inscribed on a heraldic panel above the entrance. It has been argued that such a date must refer to repairs and that the tower was actually built somewhat earlier, after a predecessor went up in flames in 1584. The unusually thick walls suggest that Alexander Innes of Coxton, the laird at the time, was taking no chances on a second conflagration. The panel bears the arms and initials of Alexander's grandson of the same name.

The harled tower, rising from a square base, is unusual for being barrel vaulted at all four levels, including the gabled attic which is roofed externally with stone slabs. The vaults spring from alternate pairs of walls at each level. At diagonally opposite corners high up are round bartizans with conical roofs and shot holes; the other two corners sport square, embattled bartizans projecting on corbels. Iron grilles still bar some of the small windows. A later ground-floor doorway leads into a plain little undercroft with more shot holes. The only communication with the floor above is a hatch in the vault. The original entrance, still guarded by its yett, is on the floor above and is now reached by a staircase. Above one window in the spartan first-floor hall is another panel of the Innes arms. From here an unusual corner staircase curves upwards to the second floor and then again to the attic. Covered by a pointed vault in contrast to the others, the attic is the loftiest room and may have been divided into two levels by a wooden floor.

Access: On private land.
Relations: Smailholm Tower is also covered by a barrel vault.

DARNAWAY CASTLE, ancestral seat of the earls of Moray, lies on a large, wooded estate reached by a sideroad off the A96, four miles south-west of Forres. The castle was established by that great warrior Thomas Randolph, for whom the earldom was first created by his uncle, Robert the Bruce. It grew into a courtyard complex with a tower house. Sidelined in favour of Castle Stuart around 1625, the old castle decayed for two centuries. The tenth earl returned to Darnaway and built the present stately pile from 1810, sweeping away the remains apart from the so-called Randolph's Hall, which projects from the rear of the mansion. Unfortunately, this great hall was heavily remodelled when the new mansion was built, being harshly refaced and refenestrated, but the restorers at least had the good taste to leave the original pitched roof alone. This magnificent timber structure has only one Scottish counterpart – the hall roof of Edinburgh Castle – and while Darnaway's roof covers a smaller area, it is unquestionably finer, as well as being over a century older. Tree-ring analysis demonstrated that the beams were cut in 1387, putting its construction in the time of the fourth earl, John Dunbar. Two of the trusses are finely decorated and there are some comic little characters carved at the ends of the hammerbeams. The survival of such a treasure makes one shudder to realise the sheer amount that has perished.

Access: There are occasional open days.
Reference: *The Great Hall and Roof of Darnaway Castle, Moray* by G. Stell and M. Baillie.
Relations: Castle Stuart. Great halls at Edinburgh, Doune and Stirling.

DUFFUS CASTLE is a haunting ruin dominating the Moray plain, five miles north-west of Elgin via the B9012. The later masonry crowns one of the most impressive motte-and-bailey castles in Scotland. These earthworks were raised around 1151 by Hugh de Freskin, a Flemish settler who received lands in the rebellious province of Moravia under David I. His castle consists of a conical motte and a D-shaped bailey platform, the two being separated by a ditch.

Freskin was the ancestor of the powerful Moravia family but Duffus passed by marriage to Sir Reginald Cheyne. In 1305 Edward I granted him 200 oaks for building works, suggesting that the present castle was in the course of construction. A considerable portion of his curtain wall survives, built in straight sections along the curved edge of the bailey. It is a simple replacement for the earlier timber palisade, without flanking towers. Three small posterns pierce the curtain, but the main gateway has vanished.

Wing walls link the curtain with a large tower on the summit of the motte. This can be viewed either as a conservative oblong keep or as a progenitor of the Scottish tower house, though there were only two unvaulted storeys. The ground-floor doorway is unusual so early on – evidently the motte was considered a sufficient obstacle. It was barred by a portcullis and leads into the undercroft. A straight mural stair ascended to Sir Reginald's lofty hall on the floor above. Here a mural passage leads to a chamber from which the portcullis was operated. At either end of this passage doorways led onto the parapet of the curtain. The consequences of building a heavy tower on an artificial mound must have soon become apparent. Subsidence has led to

Duffus Castle, Moray

deep cracks in the structure, while one corner has split off completely and slid some way down the slope.

It is likely that the tower house's structural defects led to early abandonment. A domestic range occupies the north side of the bailey. This range is now very ruinous, but enough survives to show that it consisted of a great hall and three undercrofts in line. It was built by the Sutherlands of Duffus, sometime after they acquired the castle in 1350. In 1452 the Earl of Moray burnt the castle in his campaign against the Earl of Huntly. It was still occupied in 1689, when Bonnie Dundee lodged here during his Jacobite rebellion, but was abandoned soon afterwards.

Access: Freely accessible (HES).
Reference: Guide by W. D. Simpson. *PSAS* (92).
Relations: Motte-and-bailey earthworks such as the Bass of Inverurie and the Mote of Urr. Early tower houses at Drum, Hallforest, Lochleven and Torthorwald. The Sutherlands' work at Skelbo.

GORDON CASTLE stands on an estate just outside Fochabers. Alongside the surviving wing of a Georgian mansion rises a tall, square-plan tower built around 1540 by George Gordon, fourth Earl of Huntly, though much altered since. It may have been part of a courtyard complex.

Access: A functions venue. Visible *en route* to the nearby walled garden and open by appointment.

KILRAVOCK CASTLE   The chiefs of Clan Rose were lairds of Kilravock (pronounced 'Kilrock') from the thirteenth century until 2012. An imposing, oblong tower house dominates one end of a later mansion. It is the subject of a licence to crenellate, granted in 1461 to Hugh Rose by the MacDonald Lord of the Isles, who was then in control of the north. That same year the MacKintosh clan burnt Kilravock in a night attack and Hugh only regained possession with the Earl of Huntly's help. Externally his 'toure of fens' (to quote the licence) has changed little, with inhospitably small windows. Unassuming little round bartizans clasp the angles of the corbelled-out parapet. Three vaulted chambers at ground level are connected by a corridor. There are three main storeys above, including a first-floor hall. The gabled attic, recessed within the parapet, and a corner caphouse over the spiral staircase are sixteenth-century additions. The tower house is reputed to have been built by the master mason Thomas (or Robert) Cochrane, a shadowy favourite of James III. Mary Queen of Scots visited during her northern progress in 1562.

Early in the seventeenth century a gabled staircase jamb was added at one corner, though this is lower than the main block. It was onto this that the Roses appended a residential wing in 1665–67, still in the Scottish Baronial tradition with vaulted undercrofts and dormer windows (the courtyard front is a later remodelling). Bonnie Prince Charlie and the pursuing Duke of Cumberland lodged here on consecutive nights in 1746. At the back of the house, on the slope to the River Nairn, part of the sixteenth-century barmkin wall survives, along with a square flanking tower that doubled up as a dovecote. The mansion stands in spacious grounds off the B9091, three miles west of Cawdor.

Access: No longer open.
Relations: Auchindoun is also attributed to Cochrane.

LOCHINDORB CASTLE is a neglected ruin on an islet in Loch Indorb. A road runs three miles south-west of Dava to the nearest viewpoint, on the east shore of the loch. This is one of the earlier stone castles of Scotland. It is attributed to John Comyn, lord of Badenoch and Lochaber, in the late thirteenth century. His branch of the family was known as the Red Comyns to distinguish them from the Black Comyn earls of Buchan. The castle consists of an irregular quadrangle dictated by the confines of the islet. Round towers guarded the corners, as at his castle of Old Inverlochy in the Great Glen, but the enclosure here is larger and the towers are now more ruinous. Only the north-east tower, with fish-tail arrow slits, remains fairly complete. Large chunks have been torn out of two of the towers, while the south-eastern tower has collapsed. In contrast, the surrounding curtain wall rises largely to full height. As at Inverlochy, the entrance is a simple gate arch in the middle of the north curtain. Remains of a later, hall-like building oddly abut the outer face of the north curtain, its gable end flanking the gateway. From here begins an outer curtain running even closer to the loch shore. It turns to follow the east side of the castle before rejoining the inner curtain at the south-east corner tower.

John Comyn was one of the three main claimants to the vacant Scottish throne but Edward I adjudicated in favour of John Balliol in 1292. Edward stayed here for ten days during his campaign of 1303. The outer curtain is sometimes ascribed to Edward because of its concentric character but John Comyn was clearly familiar with Edwardian-style defensive principles. In 1306 Comyn's son of the same name was murdered by Robert the Bruce at Dumfries. Bruce's first act as self-appointed king was to launch the campaign that drove the Comyns into exile, although there is no record of any siege here.

Lochindorb did suffer a protracted siege in 1336, when it was attacked by Sir Andrew Murray, the Guardian of Scotland. The Countess of Atholl supported the English nominee, Edward Balliol, who was seeking to win his father's throne. She was relieved by Edward III in person. Robert II granted the castle to his son, Alexander Stewart, Earl of Buchan. Known as the Wolf of Badenoch, his brutal career culminated in the burning of Elgin Cathedral in 1390. The castle later passed into Douglas hands and, following the downfall of the Black Douglases in 1455, James II gave William Cawdor the task of slighting the castle. The yett at Cawdor Castle is said to have come from here. It seems that he did little more than throw down the battlements – a survey of 1793 shows the corner towers still intact at that time. Nevertheless, the castle was never reoccupied and so was spared later embellishment.

Access: Distantly visible from the loch shore near Lochindorb Lodge. Caution needed if you do get across.
Reference: *PSAS* (46).
Relations: Cawdor. John Comyn's castles at Old Inverlochy, Urquhart and Blair (Perthshire). The concentric outer wall at Macduff's Castle.

RAIT CASTLE stands three miles south of Nairn on a wooded hillside overlooking the B9101, from which it is approached via a public footpath. It was probably built around 1300 by Sir Gervase de Rait. He retained the constableship of vanished Nairn Castle under Edward I. This unusual hall house seems to have been inspired by contemporary fortified manor houses in England. It passed eventually to the Campbells of Cawdor but was left to decay.

Though now a ruin, the building has survived centuries of abandonment remarkably well. It remains intact to the wall-head except for the collapsed north-east end, while one portion of a corbelled-out parapet survives. The great hall stood at first-floor level over an unvaulted undercroft – the floor joists were carried on a ledge in the walls. Tiny openings lit the undercroft but the hall has large, pointed windows with Y-tracery that seem to invite assault. Nevertheless, they are balanced by defensive features. Near the north-east end is the pointed entrance doorway, formerly reached by an external stair. The arch was closed by a portcullis, as the surviving grooves reveal. Furthermore, the south corner of the hall block is flanked by a circular tower. It has another traceried window at hall level but, since there is no fireplace, it cannot have been very hospitable. The tower is covered by a stone dome, a feature of some Edwardian towers in Wales. A modest fireplace near the west end of the hall indicates the position of the dais. Presumably this was supplemented by an open hearth in the centre of the hall. A narrow latrine turret projects at the dais end. The hall house formed one side of a courtyard, as attested by a surviving chunk of curtain wall.

Access: Freely accessible.
Reference: *PSAS* (71 and 92).
Relations: There is a similar hall house at Old Tulliallan.

SPYNIE PALACE, the old fortress home of the bishops of Moray, stands two miles north-east of their ruined cathedral at Elgin, off the A941. It occupies a low cliff overlooking Loch Spynie, which once extended to the sea. A castle existed here by 1300, in the time of Bishop David de Moravia. Some of the original curtain wall survives but most of the present courtyard complex dates from the fifteenth century. David Stewart, bishop in 1462–76, added the mighty tower house after excommunicating the Earl of Huntly. The fourth Earl of Bothwell took refuge here in 1567 following the surrender of his wife, Mary Queen of Scots. He survived an assassination attempt by the bishop's illegitimate sons before fleeing to Norway. Alexander Lindsay failed to capture the palace in 1589 and the Royalists were similarly frustrated in 1645. Nevertheless, Spynie was already decaying, and it fell into ruins after the abolition of Scottish episcopacy in 1689.

A ruinous curtain surrounds the courtyard. The south and west sides, following an irregular course, survive from the original stronghold. Straight lengths of fifteenth-century curtain complete the quadrangle on the north and east. On the east side is the main entrance, a simple gateway overlooked by twin machicolations and triangular bartizans. The sculpted shield above the damaged entrance arch depicts the arms of Bishop John of Winchester (1435–60), so the curtain may be ascribed to him. On the north a walled passage descends to a postern, once providing access to the loch shore. Square mural towers clasp two corners of the enclosure. Half of the five-storey south-east tower has collapsed but the smaller north-west tower is virtually complete. Both towers were given wide-mouthed gunports by Bishop Patrick Hepburn (d.1573).

Only footings remain of the residential buildings that stood around the courtyard. The original hall lay against the west curtain, as shown by the tall windows that pierce it. This became a service wing when a new great hall was built on the north side in the fifteenth century. A chapel stood against the south curtain, as shown by the delicate piscina high up.

David's Tower dominates the palace at the south-west angle of the courtyard. It is one of the most ambitious fifteenth-century tower houses. In contrast to the ruined state of much of the palace, this oblong structure remains at its full height of five storeys below the parapet, though now a shell. The crowning vault proved too heavy for the east wall, weakened by mural chambers. Eventually the vault collapsed, taking the inner face of the east wall with it. The main entrance leads directly into the first-floor hall but another doorway opens into the two vaulted undercrofts below. One of them is circular, because it formed the base of a round flanking tower from the original castle. A mural passage leads to the square undercroft alongside, its wide-mouthed gunports also inserted by Bishop Hepburn. He added attic gables within the corbelled-out parapet, which rounds at the corners to support vanished bartizans. From here there is a panoramic view of the courtyard and the coastline beyond. Hepburn's arms can be seen on the south face of the tower house, alongside those of Bishop Stewart.

Access: Open regularly in summer (HES).
Reference: Guidebook by C. Tabraham. *The Palace of the Bishops of Moray at Spynie* by W. D. Simpson.
Relations: The large tower houses at Comlongon and Borthwick. An earlier Bishop of Moray's work at Loch an Eilean.

OTHER SITES   A natural motte known as Lady Hill in the cathedral burgh of *Elgin* marks the site of a royal castle where Edward I lodged in 1296. The featureless stump of what appears to be a later tower house of the earls of Moray is now overlooked by the Duke of Gordon's Monument. The original castle was destroyed by Robert the Bruce, along with the royal castles at *Forres* and *Nairn*. *Rothes Castle*, another early stronghold, is reduced to a length of plain thirteenth-century curtain wall overlooking the town. Mottes can be found at *Altyre* (near Rafford) and *Cantraydoune* (near Cantraywood).

There are several very ruined tower houses, such as *Asliesk Castle* (near Alves), *Dunphail Castle* and *Lethendry Castle* (near Cromdale). Z-plan *Inshoch Castle* (near Auldearn) has crumbled badly since it was sketched by MacGibbon and Ross. *Blervie Castle* (near Rafford) was a tall flanking tower, similar to nearby Burgie, but much of it collapsed in 2006. *Innes House* (near Lossiemouth) is a handsome laird's house of the 1640s, embodying an older tower.

ORKNEY

This archipelago north of Caithness is notable for its Neolithic sites. The Orkney Islands belonged to Norway until they were dowered to Scotland in 1468, on James III's marriage to Margaret of Norway, being formally annexed four years later. Their Norse heritage is recalled by two twelfth-century secular structures: Cubbie Roo's Castle, now just the stump of the oldest keep in Scotland, and the altered hall of the Bishop's Palace in Kirkwall. Otherwise, Orkney's few castles are late but notable. The Earl's Palace complexes at Kirkwall and Birsay are testimony to the ambition of the two Stewart earls of Orkney, Robert and Patrick, while Noltland on the remote island of Westray is an unusually formidable Z-plan tower house built by the islands' sheriff.

County reference: RCAHMS *Orkney and Shetland* (vol. 2). BoS *Highland and Islands*.

BIRSAY: EARL'S PALACE Overlooking Birsay Bay at the north-west extremity of Mainland are the ruins of the Earl's Palace, a fortified mansion recalling the two Stewart earls of Orkney. By all accounts Robert Stewart, an illegitimate son of James V, was surpassed in cruelty only by his son Patrick. Around 1574 Robert, at that time sheriff of Orkney, commenced a quadrangle here, comprising two-storey ranges with square flanking towers at the corners. Three of the towers survive in varying states of preservation but, of the surrounding buildings, only some of the west range stands to an appreciable height. The rest of Robert's quadrangle is marked by footings against the ruinous outer walls. Enough remains to show that the palace comprised a group of well-lit chambers over vaulted storerooms, the fireplaces discharging into a row of tall chimneys. The regular layout and the chimneys show a Tudor influence all the more surprising so far north. Wide-mouthed gunports pierce not only the outer walls but those facing the courtyard too, showing that defence was still a consideration here. The entrance ran through the middle of the south range.

Robert was created Earl of Orkney in 1581 and died in 1593. Earl Patrick added the gabled block on the north side, beyond the confines of the original courtyard. It contained the new great hall and solar above a ground-floor kitchen. This block projects in front of the older north-east tower, which consequently lost its flanking role, and extends over the site of the presumed north-west tower. Though well provided with gunports, again facing both outside and in, the provision of large windows (later blocked) even at ground level demonstrates a confidence evident in Patrick's other residences at Kirkwall and Scalloway. Following his execution in 1615 the palace reverted to the bishops of Orkney but soon fell into decay. Close by on the Brough of Birsay are the precious remains of a Norse settlement.

Access: Freely accessible (HES).

Relations: Kirkwall and Scalloway.

CUBBIE ROO'S CASTLE   Wyre, a small island south of Rousay, possesses what is probably the oldest stone castle in Scotland. It is named after its builder, Cubbie Roo (or Cobbie Row) being a corruption of Kolbein Hruga. According to the *Orkneyinga Saga*, this Norse settler built a stone castle on Wyre around 1145. It occupies the high ground at the centre of the island, half a mile from the quay. Unfortunately this small, square-plan tower has been reduced to its lower courses. The walls stand high enough to show that slit windows pierced two sides of the ground floor but there is no trace of a doorway, which must have been on the vanished floor above. Footings of an annexe suggest a Norman-style forebuilding protecting the entrance. This rudimentary keep stood within an oval enclosure surrounded by two ramparts with a ditch in between. Over half the circumference remains. Around the keep are the foundations of various lean-to structures of later date, joined up to form a simple protective cordon. The ruins of St Mary's Chapel nearby are believed to have been built by Kolbein's son. *King Haakon's Saga* relates that the steward of King Haakon IV of Norway defended the castle in 1231 against the kinsmen of the Earl of Caithness, who were seeking vengeance for his murder.

Access: Freely accessible (HES). Ferries to Wyre depart from Tingwall.

Relations: Early keeps at Hailes, Aberdour and (possibly) the Castle of Old Wick.

KIRKWALL PALACE   The royal burgh of Kirkwall, on Orkney's Mainland, is dominated by its astonishing Romanesque cathedral. This was begun in 1137 by the Norse Earl Rognvald as a shrine to his martyred uncle, St Magnus. Across Palace Road stand the contrasting ruins of the Bishop's and Earl's palaces. They are now separated by the road called Watergate but were once connected by other buildings to form a single large quadrangle, belonging first to the bishops and later to the earls of Orkney. It is likely that the long hall range forming the Bishop's Palace was originally built by the first Bishop of Orkney, William the Old. Only the undercroft survives from his time but it is a unique piece of twelfth-century domestic architecture in Scotland. Note the row of slit windows, constructed in bands of different-coloured stone. In the original hall King Haakon IV of Norway died in 1263, following his

Kirkwall Palace, Orkney

abortive attempt to reclaim the Hebrides. The present great hall and the storey above were erected by Bishop Robert Reid (1541–58). He fortified the block by building a powerful circular tower at the north-west corner. Bishop Reid's Tower rises four storeys to a corbelled-out parapet, with a gabled caphouse recessed within. Three shot holes pierce the vaulted ground floor, while the room above formed the bishop's solar. A second, square tower on the other side of the north gable has vanished.

Robert Stewart, initially sheriff and later Earl of Orkney, seized the Bishop's Palace after the Reformation. His son and successor Patrick added the Earl's Palace in 1600–07, downgrading the old hall range that faces it to form service accommodation. This Renaissance mansion is the masterpiece of his master mason, Andrew Crawford. It boasts a magnificent new hall and solar on the east side, with a long south range containing the kitchen and guest chambers. All the ground-floor storerooms are barrel-vaulted and linked by a corridor. The ornate doorway, surmounted by worn heraldic panels, occupies the time-honoured place in the angle between the two ranges. However, despite a number of shot holes the mansion can scarcely described as defensive, even towards the outside of the quadrangle where three enormous bay windows projected. There is a hint of the tower house theme in the shorter wing at the north-west corner of the complex. Here the shot holes are most concentrated, even emerging from the angles of the building, while a pair of oversized, round corner bartizans project on decorative corbelling at the top.

Patrick Stewart may have had refined architectural tastes but his reputation is that of a detested tyrant. He spent his last four years imprisoned in Dumbarton Castle and was eventually charged with treason. In a one-sided trial it was alleged that his buildings had been erected by forced labour, his victims' blood being used to thicken the mortar. His execution in 1615 had to be delayed for a week to allow him time to learn the Lord's Prayer (perhaps a ruse). Meanwhile, Patrick's illegitimate son had seized Kirkwall, forcing the Earl of Caithness to intervene. This episode resulted in the destruction of nearby Kirkwall Castle, which had been erected by one of the jarls of Orkney in the fourteenth century.

Access: Open daily in summer (HES).
Reference: Guidebook by W. D. Simpson and C. Tabraham.
Relations: The early masonry at Cubbie Roo's, Castle Sween and (possibly) the Castle of Old Wick. Earl Patrick's work at Birsay and Scalloway.

LANGSKAILL HOUSE lies by the shore on the island of Gairsay. Two purely domestic ranges are linked by a screen wall with a gateway and a line of gunports. It bears the initials of William Craigie of Gairsay and the year 1676, which, if correct, would be very late for such a fortification.

Access: There is no boat service to Gairsay.

NOLTLAND CASTLE, one of the most formidable of the Z-plan tower houses, rises just to the west of Pierowall at the north end of the scenic island of Westray. Its uncompromisingly defensive tone is unusual for its time. Sir Gilbert Balfour, sheriff of Orkney and one of Cardinal Beaton's assassins back in 1546, obtained Westray in 1560 and the castle rose over the ensuing decade. Gilbert himself was usually absent, playing his part in the troubled reign of Mary Queen of Scots, notably in the murder of Lord Darnley. Building came to an abrupt end after Mary's abdication. Gilbert was charged with treason for his efforts to reinstate the exiled queen. Robert Stewart, his successor as sheriff, took the opportunity to seize the unfinished building in 1572. Gilbert fled to Sweden, where further treasonable machinations led to his execution. Restored to Gilbert's son Archibald, it was seized again in 1592 by William Stewart, brother of the infamous Earl Patrick. The Balfours wisely sold up in 1606.

This massive oblong block has square towers at diagonally opposite corners. It appears low in relation to its length because much of the structure was not completed to the intended height. The east end of the main block rises to four storeys plus attic gables, while an extra floor was squeezed into the adjoining north-east tower. However, the rest of the main block and the south-western tower never rose above three storeys; they also lack the corbelled-out parapet and corner bartizans that crown the finished eastern parts. A small barmkin was added later, perhaps under William Stewart. It is surrounded by the foundations of lodgings, while the round-headed entrance arch has been reconstructed from the original stones.

Noltland is remarkable for its profusion of wide-mouthed gunports – more than seventy of them, even piercing the angles of the building. They are regularly spaced in three rows around the whole exterior, 'giving the castle the semblance of some ancient man o' war's hull', as Douglas Simpson remarks. On the sunless north side they are the only openings in an otherwise blank wall, but the south front (facing the barmkin) is a little more friendly. Here, windows make an appearance from hall level upwards, though they are high up enough to avoid compromising security.

The only doorway occupies the standard position in the side of the south-west tower, flanked by the main block. It opens onto a broad spiral staircase but even here is a nasty surprise in the form of a shot hole piercing the central newel. A passage on the right leads to the huge, barrel-vaulted undercroft of the main block, once divided into two levels by a wooden floor. The splayed gunports piercing the thick walls would have made both floors fighting galleries in times of siege. However, they served the usual peacetime purposes as well, hence the great arch of the kitchen fireplace at the west end. Openings in the vault allowed provisions and munitions to be hoisted up to the hall above. The guardroom at the top of the main staircase has more shot holes greeting the unwelcome visitor, but there is a hint of decoration in the carved capital crowning the newel. Gunports even pierce the walls of the spacious hall, the lighting being restricted to two windows flanking the fireplace. Beyond a gabled cross-wall is the solar, connecting with a suite of private chambers in the north-east tower.

Access: Open daily (HES). There are ferries to Rapness on Westray from Kirkwall.

Reference: Guidebook by W. D. Simpson.

Relations: Good Z-plan tower houses such as Claypotts, Drochil and Castle Menzies.

OTHER SITES *Cairston Castle*, on a farm near Stromness on Mainland, is the ramshackle ruin of a small quadrangle with a round corner turret. It dates from 1587 though a Norse origin has been claimed.

PEEBLESSHIRE

A sparsely populated southern upland county, Peeblesshire has a number of small towers of local lairds, such as Cardrona, but most are badly ruined. Traquair House shows the gradual development of one such tower into a mansion. More ambitious is the Hays' early L-plan tower house of Neidpath. Regent Morton's Drochil Castle is one of the most accomplished examples of a Z-plan tower house, despite its incomplete and ruined state, while Peebles preserves a rare stretch of town wall. Most of these fortifications overlook the River Tweed.

County reference: RCAHMS *Peeblesshire* (vol. 2). BoS *Borders*.

BARNS TOWER overlooks the River Tweed on the Barns House estate, a mile north-west of Kirkton Manor. This modest oblong tower house is gabled but has no parapet. It was built by the Burnets of Barns in the late sixteenth century and later remodelled as servant quarters.

Access: Private (now a holiday let).

CARDRONA TOWER   Perched on a hillside overlooking the River Tweed, this severe L-plan tower house ruin survives largely to full height apart from one fallen gable. It retains its ground floor vault, from which a spiral stair in the jamb led to the hall above. There were two further storeys, including the attic. A few corbels show that a parapet walk existed on at least one side, though there were none on the gable ends. Probably built by the Govans of Cardrona late in the sixteenth century, it was abandoned for Cardrona House below in the eighteenth. The tower lies amid dense vegetation in Cardrona Forest, a mile south-west of Cardrona village off the B7062. It is about a mile by footpath from the forest car park.

Access: Well seen from the adjacent footpath (uphill walk).

DROCHIL CASTLE is a sophisticated Z-plan tower house, now quite ruined and woefully neglected beside Castle Farm. Its layout is unusual because the large main block is almost square in plan and each of the three levels was meant to be divided into two by a central corridor. This ground-floor corridor is entered on the west side through a mutilated doorway that has broken into a pedimented window just above. Immediately inside, a broad spiral staircase ascended to the upper floors. Two rows of undercrofts flank the corridor, one of them a kitchen with remains of a huge fireplace. The corridor vault has lost its apex, while the vaults that covered the undercrofts have fallen in.

Further up there is a great disparity between the two halves of the tower house. The northern part still rises virtually to its full height of three storeys, plus attic gables. Three rooms at each level were meant to be entered from the central corridor but not from each other. However, the southern part was never completed and rises only to first-floor level, where a long hall was intended. Of the two circular flanking towers, the south-western is only a stump but its counterpart on the north-east stands complete. Its upper rooms are square internally and the tower is crowned by the remains of a gabled caphouse supported on corbelling. A rounded stair turret projects in one of the re-entrant angles. Both towers have shot holes commanding the walls of the main block but the large windows expose the building's defensive limitations, even if they were once barred by iron grilles.

The tower house stands by the River Lyne, four miles north-west of Lyne Station via the A72, then a short way up the B7509. A stone reset in the adjacent farm buildings bears the year 1578 and the inscription IDEOM. This stands for James Douglas, the much-detested fourth Earl of Morton, who also built the residential block at Aberdour and strengthened Edinburgh Castle while he was regent. He probably started Drochil in that year, after being forced out of the regency (he was residing at Lochleven Castle in the meantime). William Schaw, later the king's Master of Works, may have been master mason. Building ceased abruptly in 1581, when Regent Morton's many enemies engineered his execution for his role in the murder of Lord Darnley. He was beheaded by the Maiden, an early form of guillotine that he had introduced to Scotland. His successors occupied the north wing but lacked the resources to complete the rest. It was abandoned in the seventeenth century and became a local quarry.

Access: Exterior only.
Reference: PSAS (22).
Relations: Aberdour and Edinburgh. Good Z-plan tower houses such as Claypotts, Noltland and Castle Menzies.

NEIDPATH CASTLE sits on a hillside overlooking the River Tweed, beside the A72 a mile west of Peebles. It is attributed to Sir William Hay around 1400. That period would suit this impressive tower house, one of the earliest surviving examples of the L-plan. Its austerity is still apparent despite the insertion of some larger windows after the Restoration. They were part of a modernisation by John Hay, second Earl of Tweeddale, before he sold the castle in 1686. Some damage had been inflicted in 1650, during a lengthy bombardment by Cromwell's army. Externally the tower forms a parallelogram but the main rooms within are more correctly rectangular. The corners of the tower are rounded off, making them more difficult to hack away with a pick. A sixteenth-century barmkin lies to the east. Its ruinous front range incorporates the ornate gateway but one side is delimited by a much later row of cottages.

The jamb overlooks the river at the back of the tower house. Originally the entrance was located beside it, as usual in L-plan towers, but this rather inaccessible doorway was later replaced by a new one cut through the south wall. The doorway facing the barmkin was inserted by Earl of Tweeddale. It leads into a room crowned by a barrel vault. This originally formed a lower hall for retainers but it now serves as a chapel. Below is a plain undercroft, with a huge well cut roughly into the bedrock. Owing to the sloping site the older entrances are at this level. Within the jamb is a pit prison, once reached only from above via an opening in the vault.

As part of his remodelling, the Earl of Tweeddale hollowed out the south-east corner of the tower to provide a grand staircase, supplementing the older spiral stairs. It ascends to the second floor. This was originally the great hall, a lofty chamber culminating in a pointed vault. Its enormous fireplace still fills the dais end but the earl divided the space into two storeys, both partitioned into panelled rooms. At hall level, the jamb contained the kitchen, but from here upwards the jamb has been a ruin since one side collapsed in the eighteenth century. The Hays remodelled the upper storey of the tower house towards the end of the sixteenth century and added a gabled attic. However, the wall-head still has parapet walks on the longer sides, connected by a covered passage at the gable end. Evidently it was still necessary to keep watch in the insecure Southern Uplands.

Access: Formerly open but now primarily a functions venue with periodic open days.
Reference: Anonymous guidebook.
Relations: Early L-plan tower houses at Dunnottar and Craigmillar. The Hays' work at Yester.

PEEBLES TOWN WALL   The royal burgh of Peebles had an early castle, probably established by David I, on the promontory between the River Tweed and the Eddleston Water. Its site overlooks the old Tweed Bridge. The castle was no doubt destroyed during the Wars of Independence and nothing survives, but there are some remains of a rare Scottish town wall. The English sacked the town in 1549 but the wall was only begun in 1570 'to resist the invasioun of thevis'. It covered an oblong area, except for a dent on the north-west caused by the Eddleston Water, and had four gates. Only the north-east corner of the circuit survives. A plain, low stretch of wall bounds the Eastgate car park, then turns south along Venlaw Road, the angle being flanked by a small, round tower with wide-mouthed gunports. Presumably a ditch augmented these rather insubstantial defences.

Access: Freely accessible.
Relations: Remains of town walls at Edinburgh and Stirling.

TRAQUAIR HOUSE, a mile south of Innerleithen in extensive grounds near the Tweed, claims to be the oldest inhabited house in Scotland. It began as a royal hunting lodge under Alexander I but nothing in the fabric is that old. The present mansion originated as a simple oblong tower house typical of the district, now forming the north-west end of the main range. This is attributed to James Stewart, son of the Earl of Buchan, who became first laird of Traquair in 1492 but fell at Flodden.

James' grandson, Sir John Stewart, was appointed captain of the royal guard in 1565. He built a hall range alongside the tower, terminating in an entrance jamb at the opposite end to the tower house – a common layout in the sixteenth century. His brother Sir William added a kitchen wing beyond, extending the jamb into a broader projection in front of the main block. Round bartizans clasp the corners of the lengthened jamb, while a window bears his initials and the year 1599. Further work was done by the first Earl of Traquair around 1642 to unify the different roof levels into one long range, four storeys high, including the gabled attic. Regular rows of enlarged windows give the mansion a more domestic air, while the white harling of the outer walls obscures their complex history – hence, the original tower no longer stands out from the rest. Two low wings of the 1690s project in front, marking the limits of the barmkin.

The entrance was originally in the customary position on the side of the jamb, which contains the spiral staircase linking all floors. On the ground floor a typical row of barrel-vaulted undercrofts is connected by a corridor. The upper storeys were transformed internally in the eighteenth century, attesting the family's prosperity despite their Jacobite sympathies. On the first floor the former great hall (now the high drawing room) retains part of an original painted ceiling, while a sixteenth-century mural depicting a hunting scene has been exposed in the museum room on the second floor. Traquair contains many items associated with Mary Queen of Scots, who visited in 1566, including James VI's supposed cradle.

Access: Open daily in summer (HHA).
Reference: Guidebook (Jarrold Publishing).

OTHER SITES   *Tinnis Castle* was a walled enclosure on a ridge above Drumelzier, now reduced to the meagre ruin of a round corner tower. *Barony Castle* (now a hotel near Eddleston) incorporates a large L-plan tower house in its main block, but an eighteenth-century transformation has eradicated all original features. Among other tower houses, *Winkston Tower* (near Peebles) is much altered, while *Castlehill Tower*, *Horsburgh Castle* (near Cardrona), *Lee Tower* (near Innerleithen), *Nether Horsburgh Castle* (near Cardrona) and *Whitslade Tower* (near Broughton) are all very ruinous.

PERTHSHIRE

Perthshire is large and its castles are distributed far and wide. Although there is a concentration around Perth and the River Tay, a number of them are attractively scattered around the rugged terrain that makes up so much of the county. From before the Wars of Independence there is only the plain curtain wall of Kinclaven Castle, built by Alexander II, and what seems to be a hall house at Castle Cluggy. Two courtyard castles survive from the fourteenth century: the fragmentary Black Castle of Moulin and the textbook stronghold of the Duke of Albany at Doune. The latter is one of the most evocative Scottish castles, unusually centred on a gatehouse rather than the customary tower house. From the sixteenth century Balvaird and Drummond retain simple barmkin gatehouses, while Scone Palace preserves a stretch of fortified precinct wall.

Otherwise, this is a land of tower houses, of which there are many, though quite a number are tucked away on private estates. Various families are represented, branches of the Stewarts and Campbells being the most common. The earliest probably date from the fifteenth century: the tower house at Blair now forms the core of an aristocratic mansion, while Drummond overlooks magnificent Jacobean-style gardens. There is the unusual case of two adjacent tower houses at Huntingtower, positioned side by side and later united by a linking block. L-plan towers of the following century abound and can be appreciated at Balvaird, Innerpeffray, Kinnaird and Pitheavlis. There are nearly as many Z-plans, represented most handsomely by Castle Menzies. Elcho Castle is an unusually complex tower house with several projecting towers.

County reference: BoS *Perth and Kinross*; BoS *Stirling and Central Scotland* (for the part transferred to Stirlingshire).

ABERUCHILL CASTLE is set in a large estate two miles west of Comrie. This gleaming white, largely Victorian mansion incorporates a modernised L-plan tower house with corner bartizans in the middle of its south front. It was built by the Campbells of Lawers around 1602.

Access: Private.

ARDBLAIR CASTLE lies in its own grounds a mile west of Blairgowrie. One corner of a later courtyard mansion is formed by an L-plan tower house, modest in size but with a delicate Renaissance portal. It was built by the Blairs of Balthayock in the late sixteenth century.

Access: Visible from the road.

ASHINTULLY CASTLE stands on an estate three miles north-east of Kirkmichael. The existing mansion incorporates a gaunt L-plan tower house, bearing the year 1583 and the initials of Andro Spalding of Ashintully. It was extended into a longer range in the seventeenth century.

Access: Private.

BALMANNO CASTLE, on a farm two miles south of Bridge of Earn, is a tower house of the stepped L-plan. Attributed to George Auchinleck of Balmanno in the 1570s, it was restored by Robert Lorimer. The taller square tower in the re-entrant angle has a corbelled-out stair turret.

Access: Private.

BALTHAYOCK CASTLE is an embattled, oblong tower house built by the Blairs of Balthayock, probably early in the fifteenth century. A stone staircase now leads up to the first-floor entrance. It stands in the grounds of Balthayock House, a mile north-east of Kinfauns.

Access: On private land.

BALVAIRD CASTLE crowns a ridge overlooking the A912, two miles north of Gateside. Its main feature is the handsome tower house – a good example of the stepped L-plan, with a stair turret projecting in the re-entrant angle. This contains the round-headed entrance doorway, surmounted by three heraldic panels. One of them bears the eroded arms of Sir Andrew Murray of Tullibardine and his wife, Margaret Barclay. Their son David Murray received Balvaird in 1508 and the tower probably existed by then. Windows are few in number but reasonably large on the upper floors. Corbels support the embattled parapet, rounding into tiny bartizans at the corners. Recessed within is a gabled attic flanked by chimneys. The stair turret rises higher, to a caphouse with its own bartizaned parapet.

A wooden floor divided the barrel-vaulted undercroft into two levels, with a pit prison in one corner. On the ground floor of the jamb is the kitchen. The wide spiral staircase ascends to the hall. Its window recesses retain stone seats, while the fireplace has a lintel supported by carved columns. An aumbry is framed by a delicate Gothic arch, perhaps taken from a church after the Reformation. Only the joists that carried the hall ceiling survive, allowing a view up to the solar and attic. A modern roof protects the building.

The tower house occupies the north-west corner of a small, ruined barmkin. The best-preserved part is the adjoining gatehouse, which once bore the year 1567. This oblong block consists of a vaulted gate passage with flanking guard rooms and the remains of a chamber above. Along with the very ruined east range it served as a new dwelling, supplementing the accommodation in the tower house. Ancillary buildings around the other sides of the barmkin are reduced to footings, except for one gable end. A thinly walled enclosure to the north contained a garden. When a later David Murray became Viscount Stormont in 1658 he moved to Scone Palace, leaving Balvaird to decay under tenant farmers.

Access: The courtyard is freely accessible (HES). The tower house is open occasionally.
Reference: *PSAS* (122).
Relations: Branches of the Murrays at Comlongon and Elibank.

BLACK CASTLE OF MOULIN From the attractive village of Moulin, just outside Pitlochry, a footpath runs south-east across a field to the Black Castle (or Caisteal Dubh). This is the shattered ruin of a small, quadrangular enclosure – a type comparatively rare in Scotland. The low mound on which it stands is believed to have originated as an ancient crannog, an artificial islet once rising above the shallow water of a now-drained loch. A couple of sections of curtain wall rise precariously to a reasonable height but otherwise the castle is fragmentary. Of the four circular turrets that guarded the corners, only part of one survives. The castle is attributed to Robert the Bruce's nephew, Sir John Campbell, who became Earl of Atholl around 1320. According to tradition the castle was burnt by the villagers in 1512, after its garrison had been wiped out by plague. It was never reoccupied.

Access: Freely accessible with caution.
Relations: Earlier quadrangles such as Old Inverlochy and Lochindorb.

BLAIR CASTLE A long tree-lined approach from Blair Atholl leads to this ducal mansion in the Strath of Garry, its white-harled walls gleaming against the surrounding hills. It is first mentioned in 1269, when the Earl of Atholl returned from crusade to find John Comyn of Badenoch building a castle on his land. In 1457 James II granted the earldom of Atholl to his half-brother, Sir John Stewart, but the Murrays inherited the title in 1626. Roundhead troops captured the castle in 1652. Lord George Murray, retreating with the Jacobites in 1746, vainly attempted to oust a Hanoverian garrison from his ancestral home, making Blair the last castle in Britain to withstand a siege. His loyalist brother James Murray, second Duke of Atholl, transformed and expanded it in the following decade. From 1869 the seventh duke eradicated the Classical features, adding bartizans and gables to give the complex a Scottish Baronial profile, though the work is quite restrained in comparison with the Duke of Sutherland's revamp of Dunrobin Castle.

Despite its strategic location Blair was never a major stronghold, consisting simply of the original tower house and a hall range to the north-west. The latter was added in the 1530s by the third Stewart earl, another John. Although these buildings still form the core of the existing mansion, most of the old features have been eradicated in successive reconstructions. The twin-turreted gatehouse on the entrance front is entirely Victorian. Immediately to its right is a square tower fronting the hall range, part of the third earl's expansion. Set back just to the right is Cumming's Tower. Traditionally attributed to John Comyn, this L-plan tower house is more likely to have been built by Sir John Stewart, after he became first earl in 1457. It comprises four storeys including the gabled attic (rebuilt). The higher jamb projects at the back. Two vaulted undercrofts below the third earl's hall are the only appreciable reminders of the older architecture. The great hall itself was transformed by the second duke into the graceful dining room, surmounted by the majestic drawing room.

Access: Open daily in summer (HHA).
Reference: Guidebook by J. Jauncey.
Relations: The Atholls' castle at Balvenie.

CARDROSS HOUSE, on an estate just east of Dykehead, is a brightly harled, eighteenth-century mansion incorporating an L-plan tower house at one corner. A lintel bears the year 1598 and the initials of David Erskine of Cardross. There is a fine plaster ceiling of that period within.

Access: A functions venue.

CASTLE CLUGGY lies hidden in woods on a promontory jutting into the north side of Loch Monzievaird, two miles west of Crieff. It is reached by a footpath along the shore from a holiday complex at the west end of the loch, off the A85. This austere structure is now a shell, still almost complete apart from its parapet. It consisted of three unvaulted storeys. The east face has stone toothings at each end, showing that the building once extended further. It may have been an early hall house that was later truncated into a square-plan tower house, a thinner cross-wall thus becoming an exterior wall. Described as an 'ancient fortalice' in 1467, it belonged to the Red Comyns before being seized by Robert the Bruce. The Murrays of Tullibardine obtained the lands in 1542 after a long-running and sometimes violent dispute with the Drummonds.

Access: Exterior only. There are plans to consolidate and open the interior.
Reference: *The History of Castle Cluggy* by K. Murray-Hetherington.
Relations: The Red Comyn castles at Old Inverlochy and Urquhart.

CASTLE HUNTLY occupies a rock to the south-west of Longforgan, overlooking the Firth of Tay. The dominant feature is a massive, embattled L-plan tower house for which Andrew, Lord Gray of Fowlis, obtained a licence in 1452. It is flanked by two matching Georgian wings.

Access: Now an open prison.

CASTLE MENZIES (pronounced 'Mingis') is one of the largest of the Z-plan tower houses. It stands off the B846 two miles west of Aberfeldy, beyond the village of Weem. An earlier tower here was burnt by the laird of Garth Castle in 1502. Documentary evidence suggests that the present building was commenced in 1557. Above the original entrance a heraldic panel bears the year 1571, along with the initials of James Menzies and his wife, Barbara Stewart. One of the dormer windows is inscribed with 1577, probably commemoration the completion. The building was restored from dereliction by the Menzies Clan Society from 1972, later extensions being demolished except for an adjacent Victorian wing.

The elongated main body of the tower house allows the hall and solar to be placed side by side at first-floor level, as in older hall houses. At diagonally opposite corners are massive, square flanking towers. They project considerably more to the north and south than they do to the east and west. Round bartizans are corbelled out on the other two corners of the main block and at the outer angles of the flanking towers. They are capped by conical roofs. Dormer windows line the wall-head but, as a sign of the changing nature of defence in the late sixteenth century, there is no parapet. There are wide-mouthed gunports near ground level. Two of them command the original entrance, in the re-entrant angle of the south-west tower. This doorway preserves its sturdy yett. Although the first-floor windows have been lengthened, it is clear that the hall and solar were well lit from the outset. Castle Menzies thus shows rather illusory trappings of defence, even if these windows were originally barred by iron grilles.

Another doorway was later inserted in the middle of the south front. It leads to a chamber that has been transformed into an early Georgian entrance hall, but the rest of the ground floor retains its austere, barrel-vaulted form. To the right is the kitchen with an arched fireplace, while on the left are two storerooms. They are connected by a corridor leading to the spiral staircase, with two tiny guard rooms at the base. This stair occupies part of the south-west tower and rises the full height of the building. The hall now forms an elegant Georgian dining room but the solar beyond retains a seventeenth-century plaster ceiling. On the second floor we find another hall and solar, a parallel residence for James Menzies' wife or heir, but disguised by later panelling. The attic roofs retain many original timbers. Numerous guest and family chambers were provided in the five storeys of the flanking towers. Bonnie Prince Charlie occupied a room in the south-west tower on his way south in 1745.

Access: Open daily in summer.
Reference: Guidebook by A. D. Dewar.
Relations: Good Z-plan tower houses such as Claypotts, Noltland and Drochil.

CLUNIE CASTLE is a tall, ruined L-plan tower house on a wooded crannog in the Loch of Clunie, west of Craigie. First built around 1500 by George Brown, Bishop of Dunkeld, it was later remodelled by the Lord Advocate Robert Crichton. There is an older motte by the shore.
Access: The island is visible from the shore.

COMRIE CASTLE is not in the Perthshire village of that name. It stands near the River Lyon in the grounds of a house, a mile south-east of Coshieville. This ruined, late sixteenth-century L-plan tower with a prominent, gabled staircase jamb belonged to the Menzies of Comrie.
Access: Visible from the road.

DOUNE CASTLE occupies a knoll between the River Teith and the Ardoch Burn, a short distance south-east of the village. It was built by Robert Stewart, Earl of Fife and (from 1398) first Duke of Albany. He ruled Scotland as Guardian on behalf of his infirm brother, Robert III. (The two brothers did not actually share the same forename, as King Robert had been christened with the 'unlucky' regal name John.) Albany may have had designs on the succession. His nephew and rival, the Duke of Rothesay, died while in his custody at Falkland Palace in 1402. Fear of a similar fate may have prompted the king to send his other son (subsequently James I) to France. Unfortunately the ship was intercepted by pirates. James was imprisoned by the English just days before he inherited the throne.

Doune reflects both the aspirations and the financial limitations of its builder. Douglas Simpson described it as 'the highest achievement of perfected castellar construction'. Nevertheless, it is an unusual castle for its time in being centred upon a gatehouse rather than a conventional tower house. It shows a calculated economy in its construction, with much evidence of chopping and changing as construction progressed. The castle forms a quadrilateral enclosure, bounded on three sides by a plain curtain wall. Apart from the Kitchen Tower this curtain lacks flanking towers, though round bartizans project at intervals from the parapet. The main domestic buildings are boldly concentrated on the north, facing the approach. On this front the dominant feature is the gatehouse, an oblong block with a single half-round tower flanking one side of the gateway. Alongside is the great hall, which fills the rest of the north range.

The outer arch of the gatehouse preserves its original gates, in effect a double yett made from interleaving iron bars. A vaulted guard chamber flanks the long gate passage and the building has some of the characteristics of a keep-gatehouse. It takes the place of the more usual tower house and looks formidable enough outside the castle, but there was no serious attempt to isolate it from within. A staircase ascends from the courtyard to the Duke's Hall, occupying the level over the gate passage. This barrel-vaulted room preserves its unusual double-arched fireplace, though the panelling is Victorian. There was no drawbridge or portcullis gear to interfere with domestic comfort, but the window recess on the north side contains a murder hole poised over the outer gateway. There may have been another in the mural chamber opposite. A spiral stair ascends to the solar on the floor above. The large window recess here formed an oratory, as shown by the piscina and aumbry. Owing to the disappearance of the wooden ceiling you can look up into the top floor of the gatehouse, which was probably partitioned into bedchambers.

A doorway connects the Duke's Hall with the larger great hall to the west. Its pitched roof and the minstrels' gallery are Victorian, like all the wooden roofs and floors in the castle. A large window overlooking the courtyard lights the dais end, while a row of barrel-vaulted undercrofts lies beneath. Beyond the great hall is the oblong Kitchen Tower, projecting a little from the western curtain. This seems to have started as an older tower house. Three storeys and a later attic in height, it contains a lofty, vaulted kitchen with an enormous fireplace and two serving hatches at first-floor level. Mary Queen of Scots is said to have lodged in the chamber above, though there is no record of her visiting. The awkward void between the Kitchen Tower and the hall block was later filled by an annexe containing a series of small chambers.

On the western curtain a blocked postern is overlooked by a row of machicolations at parapet level. Large windows piercing the south curtain, along with the jagged toothings on the Kitchen Tower, show that stone residential ranges were intended to continue around the rest of the courtyard, making this compact enclosure even smaller. They were never built. Humbler ancillary buildings of timber were later put up against the curtain instead.

Albany continued to rule Scotland during James I's long imprisonment in the Tower of London, allegedly doing as little as he could to secure his nephew's release. He died an octogenarian in 1420. His son Murdoch succeeded as Guardian, but there was a heavy price to pay when James was finally ransomed four years later. Murdoch and his family were executed and Doune was seized by the Crown, the castle becoming a dower house for widowed Scottish queens. A short siege in 1570 wrested it from adherents of the exiled Queen Mary. James VI ordered substantial repairs in 1581 – the gabled attic of the gatehouse is characteristic of that time. Bonnie Prince Charlie captured the castle on his march south in 1745. Subsequent decay was halted by the fourteenth Earl of Moray, who undertook a sensitive restoration from 1883. As a result, the castle has come down to us in an exceptional state of preservation, lacking little more than its battlements.

Access: Open daily (HES).
Reference: Guidebook by N. Scott. *Doune Castle* by W. D. Simpson. *PSAS* (72).
Relations: Keep-gatehouses at Rothesay, Caerlaverock, Tantallon and Crichton. The great halls of Darnaway, Edinburgh and Stirling.

DRUMMOND CASTLE is reached via a tree-lined avenue through a magnificent park, off the A822 between Crieff and Muthill. The commanding T-plan tower house is built against an outcrop of rock. It is attributed to John, first Lord Drummond, who obtained the lands in 1487. James IV was a frequent visitor, having fallen in love with John's daughter. She and her two sisters died suddenly in 1502 – allegedly poisoned by scheming nobles who engineered the marriage alliance with Princess Margaret, daughter of Henry VII. A stone staircase ascends to the first-floor entrance, flanked by the shallow jamb that contains the spiral staircase. The two lower levels retain their barrel-vaulted austerity. On the second floor is the hall, remodelled with a Victorian fireplace and panelling. In the 1850s Lord Willoughby de Eresby rebuilt the storey above, so the authentic-looking corbelled-out parapet and gables are entirely his work.

Alongside the tower is an oblong gatehouse with a double yett guarding the outer archway. Guard rooms flank the barrel-vaulted gate passage. The chamber above is linked to the tower house by a doorway cut through the wall. Dormer windows bearing the years 1630 and 1636 commemorate the work of the fourth Earl of Perth, but it seems likely that he merely added an attic to a sixteenth-century gatehouse, resembling the one at Balvaird. Drummond was damaged during the Roundhead invasion of 1651, then slighted by the Duchess of Perth to prevent Hanoverian troops from occupying her home in 1745. Tower and gatehouse formed the west side of a barmkin, now an open space in front of Lord Willoughby's Victorian mansion. They overlook a magnificent recreation of a formal Jacobean garden.

Access: The gardens are open daily in summer (HHA).
Relations: Balvaird. Castle Campbell, Lauriston and Queen Mary's House are other T-plan tower houses. The Jacobean garden at Edzell.

EDINAMPLE CASTLE lies on an estate overlooking Loch Earn, two miles south-east of Lochearnhead. This restored Z-plan tower house with round flanking towers was built from 1584 by 'Black Duncan' Campbell of Glenorchy (compare his castles at Barcaldine and Finlarig).

Access: Visible from the road.

ELCHO CASTLE is an impressive tower house overlooking the River Tay, five miles south-east of Perth. There is a tradition of an older stronghold where Sir William Wallace found refuge, but the present structure is entirely the work of Sir John Wemyss, whose ancestral seat was Wemyss Castle. He died in 1572 and his 'fortalice' is first mentioned the following year. His descendant, another John, was created first Earl of Wemyss in 1633. Despite intermittent occupation by the earls well into the eighteenth century, the main block is remarkably unspoilt. Decay was halted by a surprisingly sensitive restoration in the 1830s. By contrast, the barmkin gradually vanished. Only a round corner turret with shot holes survives.

Elcho is quite an elongated tower house. As seen from the south it appears to follow the Z-plan, with diagonally opposite corner towers. However, the north front facing the river shows a more elaborate layout with three flanking towers. A square tower projects at the north-west corner, slightly askew to the main block. The north-east tower is round with a square caphouse, while a semi-circular stair tower protrudes between them. Nevertheless, the largest tower is another square one, projecting boldly at the south-west corner. Its crowning parapet (the only part of the complex to have one) makes it look like an older tower house, adapted to form an entrance tower when the rest was built. Nevertheless, an examination of the masonry has shown that it is of one build with the rest. The fourth corner of the main block just has a round bartizan at the wall-head. Large windows from the first floor upwards show the concessions made to domestic comfort by this period, but they retain their original iron grilles. A more serious defensive purpose is demonstrated by the seventeen wide-mouthed gunports that pierce the walls and towers at ground level, covering every approach.

Two of the gunports command the only entrance in the south-west tower, flanked as usual by the main block. Within this tower two little guard chambers lie at the foot of the wide spiral staircase to the floor above. Three barrel-vault undercrofts, connected by a corridor, make up the ground floor of the main block. The first is the kitchen, its arched fireplace so deep that it forms a projection from the outside wall. Most of the first floor is occupied by the hall, with a smaller solar beyond. They are covered by original beamed ceilings with remains of a seventeenth-century plaster cornice. The floor above was originally partitioned into separate residential suites for members of the Wemyss family and their guests, each reached by its own spiral stair. Two of these stairs rise from the west end of the hall, while the third occupies the intermediate tower on the north wall. An attic (the intervening floor has gone) provides the usual gabled profile of the later Scottish tower house, with chimneys pointing skywards.

Access: Open daily in summer (HES).
Reference: Guidebook by A. MacSween.
Relations: Wemyss. Elongated tower houses at Castle Menzies, Ferniehirst and Duntarvie.

EVELICK CASTLE   From the village of Kilspindie a road twists and rises westwards for two miles until it reaches this battered tower house, standing at the roadside amid farm buildings. There is a commanding view of the Tay valley from here. The tower was built towards the end of the sixteenth century by the Lindsays of Evelick. It remains tolerably complete but is slowly decaying – the ruinous gable ends look precarious. The tower follows the L-plan: the jamb projects unevenly on two sides, while a rounded stair turret containing the entrance occupies the re-entrant angle. There were four storeys including the attic. Large windows denoting the first-floor hall show its defensive limitations, but the tower is unusually well provided with shot holes. A breach in one wall of the main block allows a glimpse into the wrecked interior. The undercroft vaults have fallen.

Access: Exterior only.
Relations: Lindsay branches at Ballinshoe, Edzell, Vayne and Dowhill.

FINGASK CASTLE, on an estate north of Rait, is a mansion of various periods. At one end it incorporates a gabled L-plan tower house with dormer windows. This is attributed to Patrick Bruce of Fingask, since a stone bearing the year 1194 would seem to be a corruption of 1594.

Access: A functions venue. The gardens are open by appointment.

FINLARIG CASTLE, just north of Killin, is reached from the A827 along Pier Road. This tower house stands on a wooded mound overlooking the head of Loch Tay. It probably followed the Z-plan but one of the flanking towers, if it existed, has completely disappeared. The other tower is a massive square, rising largely to its full height of four storeys, including the one surviving attic gable. The main block is quite ruinous and continues to decay, though part still stands high. Enough remains within to show that the ground floor consisted of a kitchen and two other compartments, one of which retains its barrel vault. A doorway in the side of the flanking tower led to a straight staircase ascending to the first-floor hall. High above the doorway a panel bears the royal arms and the year 1609. The Black Book of Taymouth relates that the tower house was one of several built by Sir Duncan Campbell of Glenorchy, known as Black Duncan. Close by is the nineteenth-century mausoleum of his descendants, the earls of Breadalbane.

Access: Freely accessible with caution.
Relations: Black Duncan's tower houses at Barcaldine and Edinample.

GARTARTAN CASTLE stands in the grounds of its successor, Gartmore House, to the north of Gartmore village. This ruined and overgrown Z-plan tower house has round flanking towers of different sizes. It is attributed to Malcolm MacFarlane of Gartavertane in the 1590s.

Access: On private land.

GARTH CASTLE occupies a crag overlooking the Keltney Burn, a mile north-west of Coshieville. It is attributed to Alexander Stewart, the ill-famed Wolf of Badenoch (d.1394). The austere, oblong tower house looks suitably early but was partly reconstructed in the 1880s.
Access: Private.

GRANTULLY CASTLE occupies an estate beside the Tay, two miles south-west of Grandtully village. One wing of this stately mansion is a fifteenth-century oblong tower house, later converted to the Z-plan by adding flanking towers. It was held by the Stewarts of Grantully.
Access: Private.

HUNTINGTOWER CASTLE, known originally as Ruthven Castle, is puzzling at first sight. It consists of two very close but separate tower houses that have subsequently been connected by a narrow linking building. Together they formed the south end of a vanished barmkin that had a great hall on the west side. The East Tower is the older of the two, but it began as a gatehouse. A blocked archway visible to one side of the tower is evidence of the gate passage, while a keyhole gunport shows that there must have been a clear

Huntingtower Castle, Perthshire

field of fire to the west when this gatehouse was built, probably in the fifteenth century by the Ruthvens.

Before the century was over the entrance was walled up and the gatehouse was converted into an oblong tower house. About the same time the West Tower was built alongside, with a taller jamb attached to it. There is no doorway in the angle between the jamb and the main block, which is unusual for an L-plan tower house. Instead the first-floor entrance, now approached up a flight of stone steps, was reached from the vanished great hall. In 1480 William, first Lord Ruthven, divided his lands with his son of the same name, who died at Flodden in 1513. It is likely that these twin towers were built to form separate residences for father and son. The corbelled-out parapets with small, round corner bartizans are identical. Perhaps the barmkin gateway was located in the gap between the towers. There are other instances of twin tower houses at Kellie and the Old Place of Mochrum, though in those cases the towers are of different periods.

In 1582 another William Ruthven, first Earl of Gowrie, lured the adolescent James VI here. Gowrie then ruled in his name until James finally escaped ten months later. Although initially pardoned for this Raid of Ruthven, Gowrie was later executed for treason. His two sons perished in 1600 during the Gowrie Conspiracy, an alleged attempt to assassinate James at Perth. Wishing to eradicate their name, the king ordered that the castle should henceforth be called Huntingtower. It was modernised later in the seventeenth century, probably by the fourth Earl of Tullibardine after 1663.

Both towers contain three main storeys plus later attics with crow-stepped gables. Although the West Tower and its jamb are still roofed, they have lost their intervening floors. On the south front the regular rows of sash windows were probably inserted by the Earl of Tullibardine. The East Tower avoided this transformation and preserves more of its original aspect. One large window lights the hall at first-floor level. A beamed ceiling over this hall was painted around 1540 and is probably the oldest surviving example of its kind. Abstract patterns adorn the plaster between the joists, while the figures on the main beams are charmingly crude. Both towers also retain patches of delicate wall paintings. The nine-foot gap between the towers, now filled by Tullibardine's connecting block, is known as the Maiden's Leap. According to tradition the first Earl of Gowrie's daughter leapt across the void to escape being caught in her lover's chamber. Huntingtower can be found off Castle Brae on the edge of Perth, three miles west of the city centre via the A85.

Access: Open daily in summer and regularly in winter (HES).
Reference: Guidebook by D. Pringle and C. Tabraham.
Relations: Work of the Ruthven earls at Scone and Dirleton. The twin towers at Kellie (Fife) and the Old Place of Mochrum. Painted ceilings at Delgatie, Earlshall and Crathes.

INNERPEFFRAY CASTLE   Innerpeffray, four miles south-east of Crieff via the B8062, is of interest for its chapel and adjoining library. The severe chantry chapel was built in 1507 by John, first Lord Drummond. The tower house of his descendants, the Drummonds of Innerpeffray, stands a short distance to the south, overlooking the River Earn. From the chapel a footpath skirts a field to reach the ruin. It is rather a plain structure following the stepped L-plan, with prominent crow-stepped gables and lofty chimneys. Four storeys high including the attics, the entrance is located as usual in the square stair turret. It leads to a corridor connecting a row of vaulted undercrofts, but the spiral stair to the upper floors has fallen. The tower was probably built around the middle of the sixteenth century, though the row of windows denoting the first-floor hall in the rear wall are seventeenth-century enlargements. A breach here permits a glimpse of the shattered interior.

Access: Exterior only.
Relations: The chief Drummond seat at Drummond Castle.

KINCLAVEN CASTLE   About a mile south of Meikleour, a sideroad leads south-west from the A93 to a bridge across the River Tay. Taking the path to the left beyond the bridge, you follow the river for a short distance until reaching a ridge opposite the confluence with the River Isla. The neglected remains on the tree-covered top are not terribly instructive, but this is an early castle of enclosure and a royal one at that. Tradition asserts it was built by Malcolm Canmore. However, the square, walled courtyard suggests the thirteenth century. There is good reason to believe that Alexander II built it after Perth Castle was destroyed by flooding in 1209. Garrisoned by the English after Edward I's invasion, the castle was reputedly retaken by William Wallace. Sir Andrew Murray, Guardian of Scotland, definitely recovered it in 1337 from another English garrison. From that time onwards it seems to have been abandoned, though not subjected to the usual level of destruction.

Much of the surrounding curtain wall still stands to a reasonable height, especially on the south and east. However, many of the facing stones having been robbed away, leaving featureless masses of rubble core. In places the plinth is still visible. At three of the four corners there are indications of flanking towers, probably little more than square turrets. A gap near the south end of the west wall denotes the position of the gateway. Wooden residential buildings no doubt stood against the curtain – three breaches in the east wall denote windows lighting the great hall. The most interesting feature is on the south curtain, where an opening leads to a mural passage ending in a small postern in the outer face of the wall. It appears to have been flanked by another tower. There is no evidence for any accompanying ditch.

Access: Freely accessible with caution.
Relations: Alexander II's curtain at Banff and other early curtains at Red Castle, Castle Sween and Castle Roy.

KINNAIRD CASTLE is a handsome tower house on a commanding knoll just north of the village, which is tucked away off the road between Rait and Ballingdean. The tower just about follows the L-plan, though the jamb is so narrow that it could be called a buttress. Rising four storeys to a corbelled-out parapet, with a rebuilt attic above, the ground-floor entrance archway is still closed by a yett. Steps rise to another doorway in the front of the jamb, which is conjectured to have been reached from the wall walk of a vanished barmkin wall. The undercroft is unusual for being only partly vaulted at each end and having a deep pit prison in the floor. Built by the Kinnairds around 1500, the tower has mostly small windows and gunports of the inverted keyhole and dumbbell types, a couple of them with cross-slits. A gabled kitchen building bearing the year 1610 stands adjacent at a lower level. The tower was restored for occupation from an empty shell in 1855. There is a motte (Barton Hill) near the village church.

Access: Well seen from the road.
Relations: Easily confused with Kinnaird Head in Aberdeenshire or Kinnairdy in Banffshire.

MEGGERNIE CASTLE occupies an estate two miles west of Bridge of Balgie. This gleaming white, Victorian mansion is dominated by an oblong tower house, built around 1585 by Colin Campbell of Glenlyon. Unusually large square corner bartizans are corbelled out high up.

Access: Private.

MEGGINCH CASTLE, on an estate two miles north of Errol, is a nineteenth-century mansion incorporating a T-plan tower house. The jamb is semi-circular with a square caphouse. A Latin inscription above one of the windows records that Peter Hay of Megginch erected it in 1575.

Access: The gardens are open occasionally.

METHVEN CASTLE is a curious edifice on an estate a mile east of Methven village. It appears to have begun as an early seventeenth-century E-plan tower house of Ludovic Stewart, Duke of Lennox. The central recess was filled in and round corner turrets added around 1664.

Access: Private (now a holiday let).

MONCUR CASTLE, on the Rossie Priory estate south of Baledgarno, was built by the Kinnairds of Inchture late in the sixteenth century. It is the overgrown ruin of a Z-plan tower house, though the round and square angle towers do not flank the main block very effectively.

Access: On farmland.

MURTHLY CASTLE occupies a large estate two miles west of Murthly village. Its oldest part is a modest oblong tower with a wing at right angles, both built by the Abercrombies of Murthy in the sixteenth century. They now form one corner of a largely seventeenth-century mansion.

Access: A functions venue.

NEWTON CASTLE occupies secluded grounds on the western edge of Blairgowrie. This unspoilt Z-plan tower house has one square and one round flanking tower (the latter crowned by a caphouse). It was built by the Drummonds of Newton, probably late in the sixteenth century.

Access: Private.

PITHEAVLIS CASTLE is now caught up in the suburbs of Perth. It rises in Pitheavlis Castle Gardens off Needless Road, a mile south-west of the city centre. This L-plan tower house is four storeys high, including the gabled attic. The wall-head is plain except for twin round bartizans corbelled out at the corners of the jamb. The entrance occupies the standard position in the side of the jamb. A semi-circular stair turret projects at the rear. Original features including gunports are concealed beneath the re-harled exterior, while the interior has been greatly altered through conversion into flats after a long period of dereliction. The tower was probably built after Robert Stewart of Braco Wester purchased the lands in 1586.

Access: Exterior only.
Relations: The Stewart branches at Blair, Doune, Grantully and Methven.

SCONE PALACE occupies a country estate to the west of Scone town. It stands close to the site of Scone Abbey, an important Augustinian monastery founded by Alexander I. This coronation place of Scottish monarchs harboured the royal regalia and the Stone of Scone, until Edward I made off with them in 1296. Its destruction by a Protestant mob in 1559 heralded the Scottish Reformation and barely a stone now remains. William Ruthven, first Earl of Gowrie, turned the abbot's palace into a secular residence before his execution for treason in 1600. This in turn has been completely replaced by the present neo-Gothic mansion, built by the third Earl of Mansfield in 1803–08. However, north-east of the house is a section of the abbey's precinct wall, which must have enclosed a sizeable area. The actual wall is reduced to its lower courses but a round flanking tower and a gate arch flanked by half-round turrets remain to nearly their full height. These probably date from William Ruthven's tenure: all three towers have wide-mouthed gunports and there are three armorial panels over the gateway. The gateway itself – the Archway of Scone – had to be reassembled after a van crashed into it in 2010.

Access: Open daily in summer (HHA).
Reference: Guidebook by J. Jauncey.
Relations: Work of the Ruthven earls at Huntingtower and Dirleton.

STOBHALL CASTLE lies off the A93, two miles north of Guildtown. Though strongly positioned above the Tay, this seat of the Drummonds of Stobhall is a picturesque jumble of domestic buildings. The oldest is a chapel dated 1578 with a tower-like priests' house attached.

Access: Private.

TALLA CASTLE lies concealed on wooded Inchtalla in the Lake of Menteith. This small courtyard complex, quite domestic in character, has decayed badly since MacGibbon and Ross drew it. It was built by John Graham, sixth Earl of Menteith, late in the sixteenth century.

Access: The island is visible from neighbouring Inchmahome, which has a boat service from Port of Menteith to its priory.

WHITEFIELD CASTLE   From the village of Kirkmichael on the A924, the public footpath to Glenshee heads north across open pasture towards this prominently sited ruin, which is over a mile from the road. Said to occupy the site of a hunting lodge of Malcolm Canmore, the squat L-plan tower house once bore the year 1577. Like Ashintully Castle, just half a mile away, it belonged to the Spalding family and the two towers are of similar dimensions. However, Whitefield only seems to have comprised two storeys and a vanished attic. The doorway is in the customary place in the side of the jamb, which projects unequally in two directions. The ground floor of the main block is divided into two barrel-vaulted compartments with wide-mouthed gunports. One of them was the kitchen. The jamb has the remains of a staircase to the first-floor hall. The rear of the tower is more ruinous than the front and the whole continues to decay.

Access: Freely accessible with caution.

Relations: Ashintully.

OTHER SITES   *Perth*'s early royal castle was washed away by flooding in 1209 and replaced by Kinclaven Castle. The site, now occupied by Perth Museum, is near the bridge across the River Tay. During their occupation the English constructed a town wall but this was destroyed after Robert the Bruce recaptured the town in 1313. *Inchbervis Castle* (near Stanley) preserves the stump of a round flanking tower from a walled courtyard. There is a motte beside the Tay at *Cargill*.

Loch Dochart has the ruin of an island tower house raised by 'Black Duncan' Campbell (see Finlarig). *Bamff House* (near Gauldswell), *Belmont Castle* (at Meigle) and *Braco Castle* (gardens open) are mansions incorporating tower houses. Those at *Carnbane* (near Fortingall), *Castle Rednock* (near Port of Menteith), *Glasclune* (near Blairgowrie) and *Gleneagles* are shattered ruins. *Glendevon Castle* is a mutilated Z-plan tower house.

RENFREWSHIRE

Positioned on the south bank of the Firth of Clyde, this county has long been scarred by industry and several of its castles now have an urban setting. Much the best is the delightful Renaissance mansion of Newark Castle beside the Clyde, which grew from an older tower house and gatehouse. Mearns has a good fifteenth-century tower house with machicolations, while other towers include Barr, Johnstone and Castle Levan.

County reference: BoS *Lanarkshire and Renfrewshire. The Castles of Glasgow and the Clyde* by G. W. Mason.

ARDGOWAN CASTLE is reached along a drive starting at Inverkip. This shell of a small oblong tower house, built by the Stewarts of Ardgowan around 1500, stands on a cliff's edge in the grounds of Ardgowan House. The embattled parapet is carried on rows of corbelling.

Access: A functions venue. Group tours of the estate can be arranged.

BARR CASTLE stands in a field close to the A760, half a mile south of Lochwinnoch. This austere oblong tower house was built by the Glens of Barr, probably early in the sixteenth century. It rises complete to the rows of continuous corbelling – a south-western trait – that supported the vanished parapet, rounding at the corners to support bartizans. When MacGibbon and Ross drew the tower this parapet remained intact, along with the attic gables recessed within (part of one remains). There was also one side of a barmkin wall that has since disappeared. The tower is now an empty shell with blocked windows in all four storeys, connected by a spiral staircase at one corner. There are two vaulted compartments (one of them the kitchen) at ground level. The ground-floor entrance is covered by a shallow porch with a triangular pediment, added in the seventeenth century.

Access: Well seen from the road.
Relations: There is another Barr Castle in Ayrshire.

CALDWELL TOWER, a mile west of Uplawmoor, is a tall, embattled oblong with a jarring modern annexe of wood. Built by the Mures of Caldwell in the sixteenth century, it looks a little too slender for a conventional tower house and may have been part of a courtyard complex.

Access: Visible from the road.

CASTLE LEVAN now lies at the end of Stirling Drive in the suburb of the same name, two miles south-west of Gourock. It overlooks the Firth of Clyde and, more immediately, a steep drop to the Levan Burn. This pink-harled tower house appears unusually squat but rises three storeys to an elaborate corbel table, rounding at the corners in the usual way. The parapet and gabled attic were renewed, along with part of the jamb, when the building was restored from a ruinous state for occupation in the 1980s. This is an extreme variant of the L-plan where the jamb forms nearly a separate structure, joined only to the main block at one corner. In fact, the jamb is believed to be a fifteenth-century tower of the Mortons of Levan – rather small for a conventional tower house – onto which a larger main block was appended after it was acquired by the second Lord Sempill in 1547. The entrance, flanked by the jamb, leads into barrel-vaulted cellars. A spiral staircase in the linking corner connects the transformed storeys above in both wings.

Access: Well seen from the road (now a guesthouse).
Relations: Dalcross has a similar layout.

JOHNSTONE CASTLE is an unlikely sight in a housing estate to the south of Johnstone town centre, off Tower Road. This is a genuine L-plan tower house that has been subjected to some later eccentricities. The main block of four storeys, including the attic, is unspoiled except for some window enlargements. A round bartizan is corbelled out high up at one corner. The jamb, which projects unequally on two sides, preserves the original entrance in the side wall. However, it has been given neo-Gothic windows that are out of character with the rest. The tower house was built in the sixteenth century by the Cochrane family and was originally known as Easter Cochrane. The Houstons of Johnstone changed the name and embellished the jamb after they purchased it in 1733. Fragments of attached walling show that the tower in fact became the core of an extensive mansion, now demolished. It is still occupied.

Access: Exterior only.

MEARNS CASTLE is to be found a mile east of Newton Mearns town centre. From Waterfoot Road, beside Mearns Castle High School, a drive leads to this oblong tower house, standing forlornly on a knoll. Beside it is a jarring 1970s parish church of corrugated iron, occupying the site of the barmkin. Mearns is a good example of the earlier type of tower house, distinguished by a row of boldly projecting corbels at the wall-head. They supported a machicolated parapet that has otherwise disappeared. The ashlar walls are severe and the windows are mostly small. A pair of corbels high up near one corner denote an overhanging latrine. The original entrance is a round-headed doorway at first-floor level. It was later supplanted by a new entrance immediately below, leading into the vaulted undercroft. A straight mural staircase ascends from here to the lofty, barrel-vaulted hall above. From there a spiral stair ascends to a passage overlooking the hall (the so-called minstrels' gallery) and on to the solar, which is covered by a modern roof. A mural chamber here led to the latrine observed outside. There is no evidence for any later attic. The tower was built by Herbert, Lord Maxwell, who received a licence to crenellate in 1449.

Access: Exterior only.

Relations: Work of the lords Maxwell at Caerlaverock and Buittle.

NEWARK CASTLE is stranded in the post-industrial surroundings of Port Glasgow, overlooking the Firth of Clyde off Castle Road. Long occupied by a cadet branch of the powerful Maxwell family, this splendidly compact Renaissance mansion – the grandest of the four Newark castles in Scotland – incorporates parts of an older stronghold. George Maxwell's 'new werk' is first mentioned in 1484. His tower house and gatehouse form the extremities of the later mansion. The tower house is a relatively modest oblong but survives intact. Now entered from the east wing of the house, its barrel-vaulted lower stage was once divided into two storeys. A spiral staircase ascends to the hall, heated by a large fireplace, and on to the solar, which has lost its wooden floor.

The simple gate tower has a barrel-vaulted guard room to one side of the entrance passage, with early gunports of the dumbbell and inverted keyhole types. There are two upper floors but the parapet has given way to a gabled roof. Presumably the tower house and the gatehouse were linked by a barmkin wall, now vanished. A round angle turret behind the tower house, doubling up as a beehive dovecote, survives from an outer enclosure.

Around a century later the tower house and gatehouse were linked by the new mansion, comprising two ranges at right angles. It is distinguished by a row of windows with pediments marking the principal floor, while dormer windows light the attic. The focal point is the great hall on the first floor of the north range, with a large fireplace of Classical inspiration. Above is the long gallery, a new amenity catching on from England, which runs the full length of the range (the wider middle part above the hall was originally partitioned into bedchambers). Below is the usual row of barrel-vaulted undercrofts, linked by a corridor. One of them is the kitchen, with the customary arched fireplace. The shorter east range has another corridor leading past a vaulted bakehouse to the older tower house. A bedchamber on the first floor of this range preserves its original panelling, as well as a fold-down bed in a cupboard. Although defence was not a serious consideration by this time, the windows facing the outside world were covered by iron grilles, while the crow-stepped gables are flanked by round corner bartizans with shot holes. The main entrance is placed beside the re-entrant angle between the two ranges in the traditional manner. New windows matching the rest of the mansion were inserted in the tower house, while its plain parapet was remodelled with ornamental openings above the corbels. Unusually, no attic appears to have been added.

A pediment above the main entrance bears the year 1597 and the entwined initials of Sir Patrick Maxwell of Newark and his wife Margaret Crawford. It also holds an inscription, 'The blissingis of God be heirin'. Pious sentiments from a cultured laird who nevertheless indulged in murderous feuds with his neighbours and became an incessant wife-beater. Poor Margaret finally escaped his clutches after forty-four years of misery. The Maxwells sold Newark in 1694 and the impoverished tenants who followed have preserved the complex in a remarkably unspoilt state.

Access: Open regularly in summer (HES).
Reference: Guidebook by A. Cox and C. Tabraham.
Relations: The three other Newark castles in Ayrshire, Fife and Selkirkshire. Stanely was another tower of the Maxwells of Newark. The great hall fireplace is virtually identical to the one in Spedlins Tower.

STANELY CASTLE, two miles south of Paisley, is the austere ruin of an L-plan tower house, built early in fifteenth century by the Maxwells of Newark Castle. Complete except for its parapet and one deep breach, the tower now rises serenely from the water of Stanely Reservoir.

Access: Visible from the shoreline.

OTHER SITES *Renfrew's* early castle survived the Wars of Independence as a stronghold of the Stewart kings. Castlehill Gardens marks the site, but nothing remains. Thirteenth-century *Duchal Castle*, stormed by James IV during the Earl of Lennox's revolt in 1489, is reduced to a few chunks of masonry on a rocky promontory near Milton. *Polnoon Castle* (near Eaglesham) is a motte bearing some masonry fragments. *Dargavel House* (on a Ministry of Defence site near Bishopton) incorporates a much-altered Z-plan tower house, while *Elliston Castle* (near Howwood) and *Ranfurly Castles* (at Bridge of Weir) are very ruined towers.

ROSS

Early royal castles raised to control the unruly north have long since perished. Ross is huge but much of it is inhospitable terrain, resulting in a relative dearth of castles. There are several late tower houses in the eastern parts of the county, on the Black Isle and the Fearn Peninsula. Castle Craig, Fairburn and Kinkell can be sought out, though much the best is Castle Leod further inland. The west coast with its many sea lochs boasts fragmentary (but beautifully sited) Strome Castle and the romantic Eilean Donan, which would be nearly as meagre but for its twentieth-century reconstruction. The latter belonged to the MacKenzies, who were the dominant clan in the county.

County reference: BoS *Highland and Islands*.

BALLONE CASTLE stands near the edge of a cliff overlooking the Moray Firth, a mile north-east of Rockfield on the Fearn Peninsula. This restored Z-plan tower house, with one round and one square flanking tower, was built by the Dunbars of Tarbat in the late sixteenth century.

Access: Visible from the road.

CADBOLL CASTLE lies among the outbuildings of Glenmorangie House to the north-east of Hilton of Cadboll. This squat ruin is a sixteenth-century L-plan tower house with a round flanking tower at one corner. It was a grange of nearby Fearn Abbey until the Reformation.

Access: On private land.

CASTLE CRAIG is a lonely sentinel on the north shore of the Black Isle, overlooking Cromarty Firth. From the B9163, four miles north-east of Culbokie, take the sideroad to Craigton. Where it peters out a rough track (signposted) descends north-west towards the shore. From the approach it looks complete: a modest tower house of four storeys, including the gabled attic that still appears to be roofed. On the gable end only there is a fine stretch of corbelling to support a vanished parapet with round corner bartizans. Reaching the far side, it becomes clear that the other end has collapsed entirely, but this allows an unhindered view of the decaying interior with remains of barrel vaulting at all levels, including the attic. In fact this was merely the jamb of a large L-plan tower house to which it was joined at one corner. A low stretch of barmkin wall is perched on the edge of the cliff overlooking the firth. The tower was probably built by the Urquhart sheriffs of Cromarty sometime in the sixteenth century.

Access: Freely accessible with caution.

Relations: There is also a Craig Castle in Aberdeenshire and a Craig House in Angus.

CASTLE LEOD   A tree-lined drive leads to this striking tower house, set on a country estate off the A834, a mile north of Strathpeffer. It has been held by the chiefs of Clan MacKenzie since 1513, apart from a period of forfeiture in 1746–84 after the last Jacobite rising, and remains the seat of the earls of Cromartie. Roderick MacKenzie inherited in 1608 and the tower used to be attributed to him. The year 1616 is carved on a dormer window high up, along with his initials and those of his wife, Margaret MacLeod. However, there is good reason to regard the main part as an older structure. Despite some Victorian restoration and the addition of a lower extension at the rear, this remains one of the best tower houses in the far north.

The tower follows the L-plan, with the jamb projecting in two directions as was customary in later examples. There are five storeys in all, including the attic. Wide-mouthed gunports pierce the walls low down and some of the original windows still have their iron grilles. Round bartizans clasp the corners high up. Along the gable ends and on the front of the jamb are lengths of parapet projecting on elaborate rows of corbelling. Their presence suggests that the tower is a generation or so older than the early seventeenth century. The frontal projection of the jamb is unusually shallow now but that is because most of the re-entrant angle has been filled by a later extension, rising to a wall-head punctuated by two dormer windows and another corner bartizan. It is likely that this extension is Roderick MacKenzie's contribution.

The entrance is placed in the traditional position, flanked by the jamb, with a row of weathered heraldic panels above. It leads to a staircase ascending in short, straight flights to the first-floor hall, with a big fireplace at one end. Above it, the extension is given over to bedchambers supplementing the rooms in the main block and the jamb. The two upper storeys of the tower house, reached by twin spiral staircases in the thickness of the wall, are empty and have lost their dividing floor. On the ground floor is the customary row of barrel-vaulted storerooms and a kitchen with a large fireplace in the jamb.

Access: Limited opening times in summer (HHA).

Relations: MacKenzie branches at Eilean Donan, Fairburn, Kilcoy and Kinkell.

EILEAN DONAN CASTLE is one of the most photogenic of Scottish castles, but much of it is a twentieth-century reconstruction. Occupying a rocky islet off the north shore of Loch Duich, facing Dornie on the A87, the setting is as

Eilean Donan Castle, Ross

stunning as it was strategically important. According to tradition the castle was first established by the Mathesons at the behest of Alexander II as a bulwark against the Norse. It enters recorded history in 1331, when the severed heads of fifty local rebels 'decorated' the battlements. By that time the castle was held by the MacKenzies of Kintail. In 1509 they entrusted it to the MacRaes, who became its hereditary captains. Thirty years later Duncan MacRae repulsed an attack by Donald Gorm of Sleat, personally firing the arrow that felled this notorious Skye chieftain. The castle met its end in the brief Jacobite rising of 1719. Garrisoned by a Spanish expeditionary force, it was blown up following a bombardment by three Hanoverian frigates. In 1912 John MacRae-Gilstrap, a descendant of the captains, began a reconstruction that took twenty years to complete. It is not especially faithful to the original, which is known in some detail from a military survey of 1714.

The roughly square enclosure was surrounded by a simple, towerless curtain wall, possibly dating from the thirteenth century. However, this curtain has almost entirely been rebuilt on the original foundations, while the machicolated gateway is pure invention. An oblong tower house was added on a knoll at the northern corner of the rocky courtyard in the late fourteenth century. Convincingly restored with a parapet and gabled attic, in fact only the wall facing the courtyard is largely original. A stone staircase on this side ascends to the first-floor entrance, closed by a yett recovered from the castle well. It leads into the reconstructed hall, deliberately spartan. Even the vault of the gloomy undercroft is a reproduction.

More genuine masonry can be seen in the additions the MacRaes made after 1509. The oblong tower projecting at the south corner of the enclosure is original in its lower parts, as the change in masonry demonstrates. It formed the MacRaes' own dwelling, the tower house being reserved for MacKenzie visits. Most complete in terms of the original structure is the tapering salient that guards the approach from the mainland. It terminates in the hexagonal well tower, intended as an artillery platform. Buried foundations show that an outer curtain originally enclosed the rest of the islet. The graceful bridge connecting to the mainland at Dornie is one modern convenience the castle did not previously possess.

Access: Open daily.

Reference: Guidebook (Conchra Charitable Trust). *The Mediaeval Castles of Skye and Lochalsh* by R. Miket and D. L. Roberts.

Relations: MacKenzie clan strongholds at Castle Leod, Fairburn, Kilcoy and Kinkell. The restorations of Duart and Kisimul.

FAIRBURN TOWER From Marybank, on the A832, a zigzag of roads leads to this lofty, re-harled tower house, nearly two miles to the south-west. Murdoch MacKenzie, who had been in the service of James V, received the lands in 1542. He built a handsome, four-storey oblong with a profusion of shot holes and wide-mouthed gunports low down. Unusually for this period, the entrance was placed at first-floor level for greater security. The modest hall at this level has a latrine passage and a straight staircase to the barrel-vaulted undercroft below. A spiral staircase ascended in one corner to the upper floors. Early in the seventeenth century another MacKenzie of Fairburn added the gabled attic, no doubt replacing an older parapet, with round bartizans at two corners of the wall-head. He also converted the tower to the L-plan by adding the slender jamb, which contains a new spiral stair all the way up to the gabled caphouse. The jamb covers the original entrance; a new ground-floor doorway was provided in the jamb, though – unusually – not in the re-entrant angle. The tower was abandoned around 1800 for nearby Fairburn House. It fell into an appalling state, with deep cracks threatening the structure, but the Landmark Trust restored it to a habitable condition in 2021.

Access: Well seen from the road (now a holiday let). There are occasional open days.

Relations: Strongholds of the MacKenzies at Castle Leod, Eilean Donan, Kilcoy and Kinkell.

KILCOY CASTLE lies in its own grounds two miles south-west of Tore. This well-restored Z-plan tower house has twin round flanking towers of unequal size. It is quite a late example, having been built by Alexander MacKenzie of Kilcoy who acquired the lands in 1618.

Access: The gardens are open occasionally.

KINKELL CASTLE is a variant of the Z-plan tower house theme: the main block has one round flanking tower and, at the corner diagonally opposite, a round stair turret corbelled out from the first floor upwards. This modest, re-harled structure is four storeys high, including the gabled attic. There is no parapet. Wide-mouthed gunports near the base of the walls command all approaches. The entrance is in the side of the flanking tower. Two vaulted chambers, one a kitchen, occupy the ground floor, while in the hall on the floor above is a fireplace bearing the year 1594. The tower would thus have been built by John MacKenzie of Gairloch. A seventeenth-century extension has been demolished. Tradition has it that Bonnie Prince Charlie initially went into hiding here after the Battle of Culloden. It was restored from dereliction by the artist Gerald Laing from 1969. The tower stands at a bend in a sideroad off the A835, a mile south-east of Conon Bridge on the Black Isle.

Access: Well seen from the road.
Reference: *Kinkell: The Reconstruction of a Scottish Castle* by G. Laing.
Relations: MacKenzie clan seats at Castle Leod, Eilean Donan, Fairburn and Kilcoy.

ROCKFIELD CASTLE was formerly known as Little Tarrel. A mile south of Portmahomack, a track runs south from the B9165 and leads in half a mile to Rockfield Farm. This modest, harled building is really an L-plan laird's house as opposed to a tower house proper, but it is well equipped with wide-mouthed gunports. Just three storeys high including gabled attic, the entrance is flanked by the jamb as usual. A reset inscription gives a year in the 1550s (the last digit is missing), along with the initials of Alexander Ross and his wife Elizabeth. The house was restored for occupation in the 1980s.

Access: Well seen from the footpath.

STROME CASTLE, now very much a ruin, is strongly situated on a knoll jutting into Loch Carron, overlooking the former ferry crossing to Stromeferry. It can be found three miles south-west of Lochcarron village, off the road that follows the loch shore. Sections of wall with robbed window openings suggest the lower floor of an oblong hall house. A grass-covered pile of rubble at the landward end denotes a fallen tower house. An early origin is claimed but the castle is first mentioned in 1472, when it belonged to John MacDonald, Lord of the Isles. It was captured by the third Earl of Huntly in 1503 as part of James IV's ongoing vendetta against the MacDonalds. Strome passed to their kinsmen, the MacDonells of Glengarry, who feuded with their MacKenzie neighbours. Kenneth MacKenzie, Lord Kintail, laid siege in 1602. On this occasion it is said that the garrison held out staunchly until their barrels of gunpowder were accidentally drenched by a maidservant bringing water from the well. A MacKenzie prisoner escaped with the news and the defenders surrendered. It was blown up by the victors, the MacDonells retiring to their new stronghold at Invergarry.

Access: Freely accessible (NTS).
Relations: Invergarry. Ardtornish and Castle Sween were other strongholds of the lords of the Isles.

OTHER SITES William the Lion established a royal castle at *Dingwall*. It survived recapture from the English during the Wars of Independence but is reduced to a few chunks of masonry in the grounds of Castle House. William is also credited with vanished *Ormond Castle*, on a hilltop near Avoch. His brother David erected the first *Redcastle*, overlooking the Beauly Firth near Milton, though the present structure is the much-altered shell of a late sixteenth-century L-plan block. *Cromarty*'s large fifteenth-century tower house has also disappeared. *Tulloch Castle* (now a hotel near Dingwall) incorporates a largely rebuilt tower house, while the small tower of *Newmore Castle* (near Achnagarron) is reduced to a stump.

ROXBURGHSHIRE

Rolling Roxburghshire equates to the wild Middle March of the Scottish Border, which had its own warden organising defence like his eastern and western neighbours. The motte at Hawick recalls Norman penetration. Until its destruction in 1460, Roxburgh Castle was an English outpost in Scotland and the most important fortification in the county, but it is now a series of grassy mounds and battered fragments. Tower houses begin here with one of the largest and strangest: the great mass of Hermitage Castle, successively a stronghold of the Black and Red Douglases, with its yawning arches linking the corner towers. The fifteenth century has bequeathed a mighty ruined tower house at Cessford and a very striking one at Smailholm. From the following century there survive two rare examples of tower houses built in pre-existing towns: Queen Mary's House in Jedburgh and Drumlanrig's Tower at Hawick. Littledean's D-shaped gun tower is unique. Buckholm is a typical example of the simple later tower houses of the county; others are badly ruined or privately occupied. Branxholme and Ferniehirst are late tower houses following elongated Z-plans, the latter now much the finer of the two. These strongholds were the lairs of various reiving families, of whom the most notorious were the Kerrs.

County reference: RCAHMS *Roxburghshire* (2 vols). BoS *Borders*.

BRANXHOLME CASTLE occupies a wooded estate overlooking the A7 and the River Teviot, four miles south-west of Hawick. It developed into a mansion of the dukes of Buccleuch, descendants of the original builders. An older tower here suffered several English attacks before being blown up by the Earl of Sussex during his invasion of 1570. Sir Walter Scott of Branxholme began rebuilding immediately, his wife Margaret Douglas continuing the work following his death in 1574. Her contribution is commemorated on two heraldic panels, now reset in a later extension.

An elongated Z-plan tower house originally formed the south side of a walled courtyard. The main block was greatly altered in 1837 by the architect William Burn, who added the bay windows overlooking the river. However, the ground floor retains the usual row of vaulted undercrofts linked by a corridor. At the south-west angle is the Nesbie Tower, a five-storey projection of squarish plan. This is the dominant feature of the castle but its wide-mouthed gunports are now blocked and the corbelled-out attic stage has been rebuilt. The corridor runs to the smaller north-eastern tower, containing a broad staircase. This is now embedded within a later extension dating from 1790 onwards. It runs northwards to the vaulted stump of the square Tentyfoot Tower, which guarded the north-east corner of the barmkin.

Access: A functions venue but well seen from the road.

Relations: Ferniehirst follows a similar layout. Branches of the Scotts at Goldielands, Aikwood and Dryhope.

BUCKHOLM TOWER occupies a lonely upland position about a mile north-west of Galashiels. It is best reached from the A7, taking the sideroad signposted to Buckholm. Beyond Buckholm Farm a footpath leads south in half a mile to the shell of this plain L-plan tower house with a later wing attached. Three storeys high plus the attic gables, the tower has a vaulted ground floor that did not communicate with the rest. The gabled jamb is just a shallow projection that contained the spiral stair. One side of the barmkin wall also survives, including the finely moulded gate arch. The tower was built by John Pringle or Hoppringle of Tynnis – a stone once bore the year 1582. Occupied until the early twentieth century, it is now in a dangerous condition.

Access: Exterior only.

Relations: Pringle branches at Smailholm, Torwoodlee and Whytbank. Barmkin gateways at Burleigh, Redhouse and Midhope.

CESSFORD CASTLE, stands at the roadside, two miles south-west of Morebattle. It is a ruined tower house overlooking the Kale Water. This massive L-plan structure was probably built by Andrew Kerr after he obtained Cessford in 1446. Despite long abandonment it rises almost to full height, though the parapet has perished and there is an ominous crack running through the masonry. A ground-floor doorway, immediately flanked by the large jamb, leads through the thick wall into the undercroft, once divided into two storeys by a wooden floor. Its vault has fallen. The hall above is a lofty chamber with several narrow windows and mural chambers in the corners. A spiral stair in the re-entrant angle ascended to it, but there is also an outside entrance (once reached by a wooden stair) into the jamb higher up. At this level the jamb contains a vaulted kitchen with a serving hatch facing the hall. Tiny chambers and a pit prison occupy the lower part of the jamb. Presumably the austere chamber over the kitchen formed the solar, there being no higher storey in the main block. Around the tower is a roughly square earthwork with a couple of pieces of barmkin wall remaining.

Already sacked by the English in 1519, Lord Dacre laid siege in 1523. This time the Kerrs of Cessford put up a stout if brief resistance. Dacre's cannon blasted a breach in the tower house and his men tried to fill the undercroft with gun powder, but the defenders set fire to it before the vault could be blown. The English despaired of taking the castle but its owner, another Sir Andrew Kerr, returned to negotiate an honourable surrender. In 1544, during the Rough Wooing, the Earl of Hertford captured and burnt the tower more easily. The walls of the tower house had to be patched up after these attacks and the jamb was heightened in much thinner masonry, but this addition is now fragmentary. The first Earl of Roxburghe abandoned Cessford early in the seventeenth century, his descendants ultimately settling at Floors Castle.

Access: Exterior only (LA).

Relations: Other Kerr branches at Corbet, Ferniehirst, Littledean and Queen Mary's House.

COLMSLIE TOWER stands on Colmslie Farm at Langshaw, four miles north-east of Galashiels and close to Hillslap Tower. This oblong tower is ruined and overgrown, with a deep breach in one wall. It may have been built by Melrose Abbey shortly before the Reformation.

Access: On farmland.

CORBET PEEL TOWER, a mile south-east of Morebattle, is a curious oblong structure with gunports, now in the grounds of Corbet Tower, a Victorian mansion. Rather small to be a conventional tower house, it belonged to the Kerrs of Corbet and bears the year 1575.

Access: The gardens are open occasionally.

DARNICK TOWER is set in its own grounds within the village. This rare example of the T-plan has a corbelled-out parapet and a jamb crowned by a gabled caphouse. A plaque bears the initials of Andrew Heiton of Darnick and the year 1569. There is a ruined stronghouse close by.

Access: Visible from the road.

DRUMLANRIG'S TOWER stands in the middle of Hawick. It can be found at the south end of the High Street, beside the Slitrig Water before it flows into the River Teviot. The little burgh already existed when the tower was built, so it is a rare example of the sort of urban tower house that was once a common sight in sixteenth-century Scottish towns (compare Queen Mary's House in Jedburgh). Facing the street is the long range of a late seventeenth-century residence of the Duchess of Buccleuch, which was later converted into a coaching inn. One segment of it (refaced to match the rest) is actually the jamb of an L-plan tower house, which projects intact at the back of this range. The harled tower rises three storeys to a plain parapet with cannon spouts; a gabled attic is recessed within. The interior has been much altered and adapted for use as a museum. However, the ground floor retains its barrel vault and the spiral stair survives in the re-entrant angle, which is now embedded in the later extension. Hawick was burnt by its own inhabitants in 1570 to prevent occupation by the invading English but the 'castle called Davlamoryke' escaped, so it is possible that the existing tower was built not long beforehand. It belonged to the Douglases of Drumlanrig in Dumfriesshire, hence the name.

Access: Open regularly as the Borders Textile Towerhouse (LA).

Relations: Queen Mary's House. Hawick Mote is nearby.

FATLIPS CASTLE, or Minto Tower, rises majestically on the edge of Minto Crags. The unflattering name is of relatively recent origin. At first sight it appears to be one of the most evocative of the Border tower houses but little more than the barrel-vaulted undercroft (once divided into two by a wooden floor) is original. The tower was built by the lawless Turnbulls of Minto to replace a predecessor burnt by the Earl of Hertford in 1545. The three storeys above the undercroft, including the gabled attic and the heavily corbelled-out parapet with corner bartizans, mostly belong to an imaginative reconstruction carried out around 1857 by the Earl of Minto for use as a shooting lodge. Nevertheless, the panoramic view from the top, reached by a corner spiral stair, rewards the steep and often muddy ascent to the tower. From 2012 it was restored from dereliction, omitting the intervening floors. The tower stands two miles north-east of Denholm, taking the sideroad to the right of the B6405 after crossing the River Teviot.

Access: Exterior at any time (uphill walk). There is a key keeper in Denholm.

FERNIEHIRST CASTLE is a picturesque pile in spacious grounds overlooking the Jed Water, two miles south of Jedburgh off the A68. Its position, nine miles from the Border at Carter Bar, was a perilous one and explains its stormy history. The original castle of the powerful Kerr family, dating from the 1470s, was captured by Lord Dacre in 1523. In 1548 Scottish and French troops massacred the English garrison but the Earl of Sussex burnt it in a retaliatory raid in 1570. James VI demolished the castle 1593, during his showdown with the fifth Earl of Bothwell, but rebuilding must have started straight after. Replica plaques above the main entrance bear the arms and initials of Sir Andrew Kerr of Ferniehirst (later first Lord Jedburgh) and the year 1598. After long used as a farmhouse it was comprehensively restored in the 1890s by the ninth Marquess of Lothian and again in the 1980s by Lord Lothian.

Ferniehirst is an unusually elongated variant of the tower house theme. Even in this frontier location the rebuilding concentrated more on appearance than defence, anticipating the union of the two crowns that took place in 1603. There is no parapet but a liberal supply of shot holes, while the windows are mostly later enlargements. The main range is three storeys high to the wall-head but, unusually, the attic is not utilised for extra accommodation and only chimneys rise above the roof line. The building is almost a Z-plan, having a round tower with a conical roof at the east corner and a taller jamb projecting from the far end of the north-west front. A low kitchen projection opposite this jamb was an afterthought. Most of the first floor is occupied by the great hall, renovated in 1898. Even the two fireplaces were renewed. Beneath is a row of six barrel-vaulted undercrofts. They are said to be survivals from the original castle and, if so, dictated the layout of the present structure.

The dominant feature of the tower house is the jamb, which rises to five storeys including the gabled attic. At the summit are round corner bartizans with more conical roofs. The doorway, placed as usual in the side of the jamb, leads to a staircase ascending in straight flights to hall level. After that the jamb contains bedchambers and the stair transfers to a graceful, rounded turret corbelled out in the re-entrant angle. This staircase rises anti-clockwise, which is unusual though by no means unique. It supports the belief that the Kerrs were prone to being left-handed, or rather trained their men to wield weapons in their left hands to befuddle their opponents. Evidently the existing range formed the south-east side of a quadrangular barmkin that has otherwise vanished. An outlying stronghouse (now the visitor centre) was adapted as a Catholic chapel in 1621.

Access: Limited opening times in summer.
Reference: Guidebook by R. Lawson.
Relations: The similar layout of Branxholme. Queen Mary's House belonged to the Kerrs of Ferniehirst and there were other Kerr branches at Cessford, Corbet and Littledean.

GOLDIELANDS TOWER, three miles south-west of Hawick, stands beside a farmhouse. This gaunt, oblong shell lacks little more than its parapet. It was built by Walter Scott of Goldielands, one of the party who rescued the reiver Kinmont Willie from Carlisle Castle in 1596.

Access: On farmland.

HAWICK MOTE   From Drumlanrig's Tower (see above) the visitor should cross the Slitrig Water and ascend in a south-westerly direction along the streets known as Howegate and Loan to reach this motte. It rises in Moat Park and provides a commanding view over the old burgh of Hawick (pronounced 'Hoyk') and its surrounding hills. A modern flight of steps provides easy access to the summit. Although not large, this is a classic motte of conical shape with steep sides and a flat top, doubtless once supporting a wooden tower. There is no trace of the ditch that presumably surrounded it or, indeed, of any bailey. David I granted Hawick to Henry Lovel, a Norman settler from Castle Cary in Somerset, and the motte is ascribed to him or one of his successors. The Lovels forfeited their Scottish lands during the Wars of Independence.

Access: Freely accessible (LA).
Reference: *PSAS* (48).
Relations: Drumlanrig's Tower is nearby.

HERMITAGE CASTLE This brooding Border stronghold stands at the head of Liddesdale. It is six miles north of Newcastleton, on a lonely road off the B6399. The existing castle is set within an older rampart and ditch, raised around 1240 by Nicholas de Soules to replace the earthwork at Liddel. Here, in 1342, Sir William Douglas starved to death his rival, Sir Alexander Ramsay of Dalhousie. William's widow married Hugh Dacre, a Cumbrian lord, but Hermitage was back in Douglas hands by 1371. Over the following decades they converted the Dacres' manor house into an unusually complex tower house. Construction probably began in the time of William, first Earl of Douglas, who also built Tantallon Castle. It passed to his illegitimate son George, first Earl of Angus, the ancestor of the Red Douglas line. By the time he died in 1402 the castle was probably complete.

Hermitage developed in several stages. It began as an unusual manor house built by Hugh Dacre, with twin ranges on either side of a narrow yard. This was built up by the first Earl of Douglas into an oblong block with a small entrance jamb at the south-west corner. Square towers were then added at the other three corners in a *bastille* arrangement, while the original jamb was replaced by a longer wing – the Douglas Tower – at right angles to the main block. Finally, the whole complex received its uniform, corbelled-out parapet. Below the parapet, a regular series of square putlog holes is testimony to a

Hermitage Castle, Roxburghshire

wooden hoarding that ran all the way around the wall-head. The castle derives its distinctive profile from the tall arches that connect the corner towers on the east and west fronts. They look like monumental gateways but their purpose was to support a continuous surface for the hoarding on these sides. There is a similar arrangement at Bunratty Castle in Ireland.

A modest doorway on the south side of the main block was actually the entrance to Hugh Dacre's manor house. The footings of this house can still be seen in the undercroft, with a spiral staircase at the rear. Internally the tower house is now an empty shell, later alterations having obscured the original arrangement on the three upper floors. No doubt the great hall filled the main block at first-floor level. A kitchen occupied the ground floor of the Douglas Tower, while a passage leads to a well in the south-east tower. At the base of the north-east tower is a sinister pit prison, accessible only from above.

In 1492 a suspicious James IV ordered Archibald Douglas, the fifth earl, to give Hermitage to the Hepburns in exchange for Bothwell Castle. James V seized the castle for himself. The menacing, wide-mouthed gunports may have been inserted during his reign, while the earthwork ravelin to the west probably followed soon after. They show some regard for Border defence, though the castle saw surprisingly little action in the turbulent times that followed. In 1566 Mary Queen of Scots undertook a long day's ride from Jedburgh and back to visit James Hepburn, the fourth Earl of Bothwell. Her future husband was recovering from wounds sustained in a skirmish with a Border reiver. A long period of decay ended in the 1820s with a restoration by the fifth Duke of Buccleuch. He rebuilt parts of the parapet and the arch between the eastern corner towers, so the exterior perfection of the castle is not entirely authentic. Sir Walter Scott observed at the time that 'its ruins are still regarded by the peasants with peculiar aversion and terror'.

Access: Open daily in summer (HES).
Reference: Guidebook by C. Tabraham.
Relations: Tantallon and the other Black Douglas castles at Old Tulliallan, Threave, Bothwell and Newark (Selkirkshire). The *bastille* plans of Thirlestane, Crookston and Holyrood.

HILLSLAP TOWER stands five miles north-east of Galashiels, near Langshaw and close to Colmslie Tower. This gabled L-plan structure has a re-entrant stair turret, unusually supported by an arch. Over the entrance doorway are the initials of Nicholas Cairncross and the year 1585.

Access: Private.

LITTLEDEAN TOWER Nearly a mile east of Maxton, on the A699, a sideroad is signposted 'Ploughlands'. Where the road ends, a footpath at the edge of a field runs north-east towards this unusual ruin. It is perched with steep falls to the River Tweed and the Littledean Burn on two sides. Guarding the approach is a squat, semi-circular tower – a forbidding battery with two rows of wide-mouthed gunports, though now with a menacing crack running through it. A steep gable end, recessed within the fallen parapet, follows the curvature of the wall. The entrance, a mural passage surmounted by a little guard chamber, is at the rear, flanked by a bits of wall representing a narrower range that stood behind. This range was a humble stronghouse rather than a tower house but it managed to resist an attack during the Earl of Hertford's invasion of 1544. Marcus Kerr of Littledean probably added the gun tower soon afterwards as a precaution against future incursions. It is an unusually serious piece of defensive work for the period, though its five storeys (including two in the attic) provided extra accommodation.

Access: Freely accessible with caution.
Relations: Other Kerr branches at Cessford, Corbet, Ferniehirst and Queen Mary's House.

QUEEN MARY'S HOUSE   The royal burgh of Jedburgh has lost its once-important castle but is still dominated by the ruins of a great medieval abbey. Another relic of interest is this T-plan structure on Queen Street. The main block, just three storeys high including the attic, is supplemented by a taller jamb of four storeys. Both portions are crowned by crow-stepped gables with chimneys at the apex. The entrance, in the side of the jamb, leads to a broad staircase spiralling up to the first-floor hall. From here the stair transfers to a narrow spiral in a turret corbelled out in the re-entrant angle. There is the usual barrel-vaulted ground floor, including a kitchen. An unusual feature is the gate passage running through one end of the main block to the former barmkin (now a garden) behind. Though often dismissed as a stronghouse rather than a tower house proper, this town house of the Kerrs of Ferniehirst is more sophisticated that the rustic farmhouses to which that label is usually applied. It was one of half a dozen fortified houses in the town and stands comparison with Drumlanrig's Tower in Hawick.

The house now forms the Mary Queen of Scots' Visitor Centre and is a shrine to that tragic monarch. It is stuffed with many precious artefacts associated with her, including the death mask made following her grisly execution at Fotheringhay Castle in 1587. Mary rented a property from Lady Kerr when she stayed in Jedburgh for a few weeks in 1566, lying seriously ill after her long day trip to Hermitage Castle to visit the Earl of Bothwell. Disappointingly, the present structure is almost certainly a decade or two later in date.

Access: Open daily except in winter (LA).
Reference: LA guidebook.
Relations: Drumlanrig's Tower and Hermitage Castle. Ferniehirst also belonged to the Kerrs of Ferniehirst.

ROXBURGH CASTLE   Two miles west of Kelso, overlooking the A699, stood one of the most important Border castles. Established by David I, it is first mentioned in 1128. Along with Berwick, Edinburgh, Stirling and Jedburgh, this was one of the five castles handed over to Henry II of England as pledges for William the Lion's release from captivity, then sold back by Richard I to raise money for his crusade. Falling to Edward I without resistance in 1296, Robert the Bruce's sister Mary was imprisoned here for four years, allegedly in a cage suspended from the battlements (the Countess of Buchan suffered a similar fate at Berwick). Its surprise recapture by Sir James Douglas in 1313 was achieved by the Scots approaching the walls at nightfall. If we can believe John Barbour's poem *The Brus*, they were dressed in dark cloaks, were mistaken for cattle by the guard, and had scaled the walls by the time the deception was realised. Most of the garrison was carousing in the great hall and put up little resistance, the remainder holding out in the keep for a day longer.

Following recapture in 1333 during Edward III's campaign in support of Edward Balliol, Roxburgh was for long an English royal outpost in Scotland. The renowned master mason John Lewyn was contracted to build here in 1378 but its deplorable state is attested in a survey of 1416. After an unsuccessful Scottish attack the following year some repairs were carried out. James I tried to capture the castle again in 1436, but abandoned the siege after two weeks when a relieving force arrived. James II took advantage of civil war in England to besiege the castle in 1460. He took too close an interest in his cannon and was struck dead when a bolt flew out of one. His widow, Mary of Gueldres, persevered with the siege and destroyed the castle on its eventual surrender. The English raised one of their artillery forts on the site in 1547, but this too was demolished under the terms of the Treaty of Boulogne three years later.

Originally known as Marchmount Castle, it occupied a long, tapering ridge between the rivers Tweed and Teviot. A vanished royal burgh lay below at their confluence (the present village of Roxburgh is two miles away). Today the castle is reduced to sorry fragments of masonry but the earthworks are still quite impressive, including the ditch on the west at the foot of the ridge. A complex of earthworks – modified in 1547 – guards the more gentle approach at the south end, along with some footings of a gate tower. More ditches divide the lengthy summit into successive enclosures, while a motte-like mound marks the buried base of an oblong keep. Chunks of curtain wall cling precariously to the steep slope above the Teviot. At the narrow northern apex of the ridge are the stump of a half-round tower and the footings of a barbican. Although the thirteenth-century castle probably had stone defences, the surviving vestiges date from the English occupation. The summit provides a panorama of the two rivers and of eighteenth-century Floors Castle nearby.

Access: Freely accessible with caution, though a difficult ascent.

Reference: Scottish Historical Review (22). The History of the King's Works (vols 2 and 4).
Relations: Lochmaben and vanished Jedburgh were other English outposts.

SMAILHOLM TOWER is one of the most evocative of the smaller Border strongholds, rising on a rocky knoll two miles south-west of Smailholm village. Its narrow enclosure is naturally defended by cliffs. Only on the west is there a gentler approach, closed by the remains of a barmkin wall. A simple oblong tower house dominates the summit. This was probably built by George Pringle of Smailholm, a squire of the Earl of Douglas, or his son Robert who succeeded in 1459. The windows are small and the re-floored interior evokes the insecurities of Border life. A doorway leads to a barrel-vaulted undercroft, once divided into two storeys as the surviving corbels show. In one corner a spiral stair ascends to the lofty hall. Carved corbels supporting the fireplace lintel are the only trace of ornament in the tower. Above is the solar, with a mural latrine in one corner. As the external stonework shows, this was originally the top floor.

During Henry VIII's Rough Wooing, Northumbrian reivers were unleashed on the Borders. Raids compelled John Pringle to become an 'assured Scot'

Smailholm Tower, Roxburghshire

(compliant to the English) in 1548 and an attic storey was added soon after. This has the gabled profile characteristic of so many later tower houses, but Smailholm is unusual because this top level is crowned by a barrel vault. Lengths of parapet were provided on the longer sides of the tower, a stone seat showing some consideration for the guard. In 1635 the tower was sold to the Scotts of Harden, ancestors of Sir Walter Scott, whose childhood visits here stoked his passion for Scottish history.

Access: Open daily in summer (HES).
Reference: Guidebook by C. Tabraham.
Relations: Coxton Tower is also covered by a barrel vault. Pringle branches at Buckholm, Torwoodlee and Whytbank.

OTHER SITES *Jedburgh*'s hilltop royal castle was first raised by David I. It was one of the five important castles ceded to England by William the Lion. Having survived several sieges during the Wars of Independence, it was finally demolished in 1409 after its recapture from the English. Castle Jail (open, on Castle Gate) was built on the site in 1823. *Bedrule Castle*, a thirteenth-century towered enclosure of the Comyns, has also vanished. Nearby is the Norman motte of *Fast Castle*, while the motte at *Riddell* is crowned by the General's Tower of 1885. Another, distinctly triangular motte – *Liddel Castle* near Castleton – was the forerunner of Hermitage Castle.

As usual, some tower houses are very ruined, much altered or considerably rebuilt:

Allanmouth Tower (ruin, near Teviothead)
Barnhills Tower (ruin, near Newton)
Burnhead Tower (near Burnfoot)
Cavers House (ruin, near Hawick)
Fulton Tower (ruin, near Bedrule)
Ladhope Tower (ruin, near Galashiels)
Langshaw Tower (ruin, near Galashiels)
Lanton Tower
Timpendean Tower (ruin, near Jedburgh)
Wallace's Tower (ruin, at Roxburgh)
Whitton Tower (ruin, near Morebattle)

SELKIRKSHIRE

Though sheltered from England by Roxburghshire, this is still Border territory. In the heart of the pastoral Southern Uplands, it is a land of simple tower houses, not numerous and in some cases badly ruined. Newark Castle is the earliest and grandest, a fifteenth-century seat of the Black Douglases accompanied by a later barmkin wall. The Scotts emerged as the dominant family in the county, notorious for reiving. Aikwood is a well-restored example of their work, embellished at the end of the sixteenth century with gables and caphouses, whereas Dryhope is now a gaunt shell.
  County reference: RCAHMS *Selkirkshire*. BoS *Borders*.

AIKWOOD TOWER, five miles south-west of Selkirk off the B7009, overlooks Ettrick Water. It is secluded from the road by a screen of trees. This oblong tower house rises to four storeys, including the attic. Michael Scott of Harden received a charter confirming his possession in 1517 and may have been the builder. The original ground-floor entrance retains its iron-studded door. It leads into a barrel-vaulted undercroft with a couple of shot holes showing some regard for defence. A cross-wall divides the lower three floors into chambers of unequal size. All floors are reached by a spiral staircase in one corner. The first-floor hall has a massive fireplace, its lintel supported on corbels. A reset stone above one of the windows bears the year 1602 and the initials of Robert Scott of Aikwood. That would go well with the addition of the attic, no doubt supplanting an older parapet. Chimneys surmount the crow-stepped gables while restored dormer windows interrupt the wall-head. Little gabled caphouses are corbelled out at diagonally opposite corners – a Selkirkshire trait. From 1990 the politician Sir David Steel contrived a modern home out of what had been a roofless shell, reviving the Scots name Aikwood in place of the anglicised Oakwood.
  Access: A functions venue with occasional open days.
  Relations: Branches of the Scotts at Dryhope, Kirkhope and Branxholme.

DRYHOPE TOWER   This austere oblong tower house has long been a ruin but rises mostly to full height. The ground-floor entrance arch is closed by a yett-like gate that is not the original. It leads into the customary undercroft, which has lost its vault and is pierced by blocked gunports. The space above was originally divided into hall and solar by a wooden floor. The modest hall has robbed window apertures and the remains of a large fireplace. The tower is crowned by a barrel vault. In the corner cavity once occupied by the original staircase a steel replacement spirals up to the wall-head on top of the vault, providing a commanding view of the Yarrow valley. The tower's austerity suggests that Dryhope dates from the early sixteenth century – one of several built in Selkirkshire by branches of the dominant Scott family. It survived an order for destruction in 1592, following Richard Scott of Dryhope's involvement in a plot against James VI. A stone bearing the year 1613 and the initials of Philip and Mary Scott, now in a nearby farm building, may commemorate vanished wall-head embellishments. The tower stands in a field overlooking the Dryhope Burn and the Southern Upland Way. It is two miles north-east of Cappercleuch, off the A708.

Access: Freely accessible (LA).
Relations: Branches of the Scotts at Aikwood, Kirkhope and Branxholme.

ELIBANK CASTLE is concealed in woodland on a hillside high above the River Tweed. Taking the road that follows the south bank of the river from Walkerburn, you proceed three miles eastwards to Elibank House. A short way beyond a path ascends to the remains, which only come into sight when quite close. The dominant feature of this neglected ruin appears to be a typical Border tower, oblong and still largely complete to the wall-head. It rises to four storeys and is vaulted over the undercroft and at the summit. Tall windows pierce the walls. It has been suggested that this may have been built in response to a charter of James IV ordering the construction of a house (as opposed to a licence to crenellate). However, this structure just formed the solar end of a longer block that has largely disappeared, though the toothings of masonry show that it originally rose to the same height and had walls of the same thickness. There is no clear join between the two parts, so it was probably all built as one in the late sixteenth century, perhaps after Sir Gideon Murray acquired the property from the Liddells in 1594. The barrel-vaulted undercrofts of this range are buried beneath a grassy mound of rubble. At the far end was a projecting jamb of which only one gable end stands high, so the building in fact formed an elongated L-plan tower house. There was a small courtyard in front and terraced gardens beyond. The Murrays of Elibank later abandoned the building, which was in ruins by 1722.

Access: Freely accessible with caution (uphill walk).
Relations: Branches of the Murrays at Comlongon and Balvaird.

KIRKHOPE TOWER stands sentinel on a lonely hillside, a mile north-west of Ettrickbridge. This well-restored oblong tower house has a corbelled-out parapet and twin gabled caphouses at alternate corners. It was probably built by the Scotts of Harden late in the sixteenth century.

Access: Private.

NEWARK CASTLE is one of the most impressive of the Border tower houses. This massive oblong block is now an empty shell. It was probably begun by Archibald, fourth Earl of Douglas, who also completed Bothwell Castle. He lost an eye at the battle of Homildon Hill in 1402 and spent some years in English captivity. Archibald's 'new work' is first recorded in 1423 as a hunting lodge in Ettrick Forest. He was killed in Normandy the following year, fighting the English at the Battle of Verneuil, and the tower may have been left incomplete. It appears that the two storeys above the hall were added later, perhaps after the downfall of the Black Douglases in 1455. Sir Thomas Joffray was building here in 1467 but soon afterwards James III granted Newark to his queen, Margaret of Denmark. A panel on the west wall depicts the royal arms.

A wooden stair must have provided access to the arched doorway at hall level, now inaccessible. Another entrance directly below connects with a mural passage leading to the corner staircase. Ahead is the barrel-vaulted undercroft, once divided into two levels by a wooden floor. The hall above is lit by the ragged apertures of windows that are later enlargements. A cross-wall was later inserted to create a kitchen at one end. The upper storeys are now bereft of their wooden floors. Before 1600 attic gables were added within the corbelled-out parapet, giving six storeys in all. Little caphouses at diagonally opposite corners, marking the tops of the spiral stairs, date from the same period.

Lord Grey failed to capture the castle during the English invasion of 1547 but he returned to burn it the following year. The ruinous barmkin wall was probably erected after those attacks. Much remains of this concentric defence around the tower except on the north, where there is a steep drop to the Yarrow Water. The wall is well provided with wide-mouthed gunports, while two square turrets flank the south and east sides. In 1645 more than 100 Royalist prisoners were executed here after their defeat by General David Leslie at nearby Philiphaugh. Newark stands five miles west of Selkirk off the A708, within the country estate surrounding Bowhill, the late Georgian mansion of the dukes of Buccleuch.

Access: Exterior only.
Reference: *PSAS* (16).
Relations: The Black Douglas castles at Tantallon, Threave, Bothwell and Hermitage. Scotland has three other Newark castles in Ayrshire, Fife and Renfrewshire.

TORWOODLEE TOWER is an attractive and well-maintained ruin on a hillside two miles north-west of Galashiels. It is reached by a sideroad ascending to Torwoodlee Mains from the A72. An earlier house here was burnt by the Elliots during a feud in 1568. A date stone once bore the initials of George Pringle of Torwoodlee and the year 1601. That would be about right for this structure, which (despite the name) is the principal range of a semi-defensive courtyard house as opposed to a tower house proper. The most prominent feature is a semi-circular stair turret projecting from the facade, squared off into a two-storey caphouse high up. The ground floor of the main block was divided into a series of barrel-vaulted compartments, now gone but attested by the imprint on the side walls. The first floor of the shattered interior would have been divided into a great hall and solar, presumably with a vanished attic above. A little is left of the barmkin wall on the terraced ground in front. It was abandoned for nearby Torwoodlee House in 1763.

Access: Freely accessible.
Relations: Pringle branches at Whytbank, Buckholm and Smailholm.

WHYTBANK TOWER, the seat of the Pringles of Whytbank, is a mile north-west of Clovenfords. The oblong tower house was largely rebuilt for reoccupation in the 1980s but there is a ruined row of sixteenth-century undercrofts from the residential buildings of the barmkin.

Access: Private.

OTHER SITES *Selkirk* has a denuded motte-and-bailey earthwork (Peel Hill) off Castle Street. It is mentioned as early as 1119 and was occupied during Edward I's invasion. *Howden Motte* crowns a hill nearby. The austere tower houses of *Blackhouse* (near Gordon Arms), *Gamescleugh*, *Thirlestane* (both near Ettrick) and *Windydoors* (near Blackhaugh) are all very ruinous.

SHETLAND

Like Orkney, the distant Shetland Islands belonged to Norway until their formal acquisition by James III in 1472. Though renowned for ancient sites such as Jarlshof and Mousa Broch, this impoverished archipelago was virtually castle-free throughout the Middle Ages. Only at the end of the sixteenth century were two fine tower houses built: L-plan Scalloway, a seat of the infamous Patrick Stewart, Earl of Orkney, and his uncle's Z-plan retreat at Muness on the remote island of Unst.

County reference: RCAHMS *Orkney and Shetland* (vol. 3). BoS *Highland and Islands*.

MUNESS CASTLE has the distinction of being the most northerly British castle by a long chalk. On the island of Unst, the northernmost of the Shetland archipelago, it stands three miles east of Uyeasound. This roofless Z-plan block is unusually low, consisting of just two storeys and an attic. Only battered gable ends attest the attic but the rest stands intact to the wall-head. Round towers project at diagonally opposite corners, while the other two angles have round bartizans elaborately corbelled out near the top. The windows of the principal floor are quite small, with ornate shot holes beneath. Lower down the walls are pierced by gunports – some wide-mouthed, others of the inverted keyhole and dumbbell types that were old-fashioned by the time Muness was built. Above the entrance, which is near but not right beside one of the flanking towers, a worn but still legible plaque tells us the builder and the probable year of completion:

> List ye to knaw yis building quha began
> Laurence the Bruce he was that worthy man
> Quha ernestly his airis and ofspring prayis
> To help and not to hurt this vark aluayis
> The yeir of God 1598

Instead of the spiral stairs still common at that time, the entrance doorway leads to the foot of a grand staircase rising in straight flights to the first floor, as at Scalloway. A ground-floor corridor runs past the usual barrel-vaulted undercrofts to the kitchen, with remains of a large fireplace. The main floor above is divided into three rooms by cross-walls, the largest being the modest hall flanked by private chambers.

Laurence Bruce of Cultmalindie was appointed sheriff of Shetland by his half-brother Robert Stewart, Earl of Orkney. They seem to have competed in ruthlessness towards their island populations. Growing tensions with Robert's notorious successor Patrick may explain why it was built, though architectural details similar to Scalloway Castle suggest he employed the earl's master mason, Andrew Crawford. Bruce later testified against Earl Patrick at his trial. Despite the inscribed entreaty, the castle was burnt by French pirates in 1627 and abandoned before the end of that century.

Access: Open daily (HES). Ferries connect Unst to Mainland via the island of Yell.
Reference: Scottish Historical Review (38).
Relations: Scalloway. Z-plan tower houses such as Claypotts, Noltland and Castle Menzies.

SCALLOWAY CASTLE is a striking tower house on the waterfront, dominating a picturesque harbour village on the west coast of Mainland. Though long an abandoned shell, its tall, gabled profile survives intact. It was built by Patrick Stewart, Earl of Orkney, from 1599 onwards to consolidate his hold on Shetland and rival his uncle's new castle at Muness. As in some other late L-plan tower houses, the jamb projects unequally on two sides. The diagonally opposite angle of the tower house has a round stair turret corbelled out from the first floor upwards. Round bartizans project from the wall-head at the other corners. As usual with tower houses of this period, there is no parapet. The entrance doorway, surmounted by three heraldic panels (two now empty), occupies the traditional place in the side of the jamb. It leads to a vaulted staircase in the jamb, not the usual spiral but ascending in short, straight flights to the first-floor hall. This spacious room has two fireplaces and was well lit. A spiral staircase in the corner turret ascended to the floor above and then the attic, which are now open to the sky. There is another spiral stair in a corbelled-out turret occupying the re-entrant angle, from the hall to the next floor only. At ground level the main body of the tower contains two vaulted rooms linked by a corridor. One was the kitchen, as the wide fireplace demonstrates.

Andrew Crawford, master mason of Earl Patrick's splendid new palace at Kirkwall, was probably responsible for this refined tower as well. Despite some shot holes its defensive capabilities are modest, even some ground-floor windows being invitingly large. Though originally barred by iron grilles, they attest the confidence of a supposed tyrant who treated the islanders as a source of free labour for his building projects. Having evaded previous attempts to bring him to justice, Patrick was imprisoned and ultimately executed for treason in 1615 following his son's attempt to seize the Orkneys. The tower later received a Roundhead garrison but drifted into decay in the eighteenth century, when Lerwick replaced Scalloway as Shetland's administrative centre.

Access: Exterior at any time (HES). The key is available at the adjacent Scalloway Museum.

Reference: Guidebook by B. H. St John O'Neil.

Relations: Earl Patrick's work at Birsay and Kirkwall.

OTHER SITES A small fragment of *Castle Holm* occupies a tidal islet in the Loch of Strom, near Whiteness on Mainland. It may possibly represent a keep of the Norse period.

SKYE

The Isle of Skye – now linked to the mainland by the modern Skye Bridge – and its smaller neighbours form the northern half of the Inner Hebrides, were once part of the Norse Kingdom of the Isles. Historically, they were attached to Inverness-shire, though long the seat of fiercely independent clans. The few castles scattered around the dramatic coastline of Skye are stunningly located but mostly very ruined, like Duntulm and Caisteal Maol. Dunvegan is the one castle that has not crumbled but it has undergone later transformation into a fine residence. It is still the seat of the MacLeod chieftains who dominated the island.

County reference: RCAHMS *Outer Hebrides, Skye and the Small Isles*. BoS *Highland and Islands*. *The Mediaeval Castles of Skye and Lochalsh* by R. Miket and D. L. Roberts.

BROCHEL CASTLE crowns a precipitous rock overlooking the east coast of Raasay, a long island extending between Skye and the mainland. A road snakes its way north for eight miles from the Clachan jetty to reach the remains. This crumbling ruin was described as 'ane strange little casteil' in 1549, and it remains so. An oblong tower house on the summit is reduced to a corner fragment. More substantial is the triangular bastion that projects at a lower level, extending to the tip of the rock like the prow of a ship. Otherwise there is just a finger of masonry attesting vanished residential buildings, which rose against the cliff face on this side. According to tradition, the castle was built around 1500 by Calum, the first MacLeod laird of Raasay, but the bastion is a later sixteenth-century addition for artillery defence.

Access: Well seen from a public footpath. Raasay is reached by ferry from Sconser on Skye.

Relations: MacLeod clan castles at Dunscaith, Duntulm, Dunvegan and Ardvreck.

CAISTEAL MAOL, or Castle Moil (the 'bare castle'), guards the entrance to Loch Alsh, overlooking Kyleakin. The rock on which it stands is steep on all sides, though it is possible to ascend the side facing Kyleakin for panoramic views. Only one leaning wall and an isolated corner of this oblong tower house still rise high, but it is a dramatic ruin when seen from the Skye Bridge.

The tower was probably built by the MacKinnons in the fifteenth century. According to tradition, they levied a toll on ships passing through the narrow strait between Skye and the mainland. Clan chieftains assembled here in an abortive attempt to restore the lordship of the Isles following James IV's death at Flodden.

Access: Freely accessible at low tide, though a difficult ascent.

DUNSCAITH CASTLE, otherwise known as Dun Sgathaich, occupies a promontory at the mouth of Loch Eishort, just west of Tokavaig on Skye's Sleat peninsula. The rock-cut ditch – facing the only landward approach from the east – is spanned by a single-arched bridge with a chasm at the apex that must have been crossed by a drawbridge. Without it, the void is hazardous to cross. Beyond, a flight of steps ascends to a simple gateway piercing the straight east curtain wall, which though quite ruinous is the best-preserved part of the castle. Other fragments of wall cling to the edge of the cliffs and there are vestiges of courtyard buildings, though no evidence of a tower house. This simple enclosure may have been built by the MacLeods of Dunvegan sometime in the fourteenth century. In 1515 the MacLeods and MacLeans were pardoned for having seized the castle, which was then in royal hands.

Access: Well seen from the bridge.

Relations: Duntulm and Dunvegan were other strongholds of the MacLeod chiefs.

DUNTULM CASTLE can be found nine miles north of Uig at the end of the Trotternish peninsula on Skye. This picturesque but desolate ruin crowns a promontory overlooking Duntulm Bay. It was long a bone of contention between the MacLeod and MacDonald clans. Although there are sheer drops to the sea on three sides, the MacLeods of Dunvegan left nothing to chance in the fifteenth century by raising a curtain wall all around the headland, fronted by a ditch on the landward side. This wall is now fragmentary, though there are vestiges of a sea gate and a round corner tower at the rear. A hall range closed the only landward approach from the south, now represented only by the barrel-vaulted undercroft of an oblong tower house that stood to the west. One corner of this tower rose high until it fell in a gale in 1990. Behind the tower, the simple shell of a gabled house runs to the cliff's edge. This later addition is now the most prominent feature, raised by Sir Donald MacDonald of Sleat in 1617 after the Privy Council ordered him to build a 'civile and comlie house' here.

Access: Well seen from the adjacent footpath.

Relations: The MacLeod chiefs also held Dunscaith and Dunvegan.

DUNVEGAN CASTLE crowns a rock overlooking Loch Dunvegan, in a wooded estate a mile beyond the village in the far north-west of Skye. Despite sweeping later alterations this is one of the most evocative castles in the Hebrides. No doubt it occupies an older defensive site, as the 'dun' prefix implies. Still occupied by the chiefs of Clan MacLeod, the castle exhibits work from most centuries since the thirteenth. The clan traces its origins to Leod, a shadowy son of King Olaf of Man, who controlled much of the northern Hebrides by the time he died around 1280. Leod is believed to have raised the simple curtain wall around the compact summit, forming a revetment around the rock. Owing to the later residential buildings on the landward side, it is only towards the loch that the curtain can still be appreciated. Even here it has been reduced in height to provide an unimpeded view of the loch, then crowned with mock battlements.

Towards the land on the east the castle is cut off by a deep rock-cut ditch, now partly filled to provide a terrace in front of the entrance. The landward front now looks like a castellated sham due to successive attempts between 1790 and 1850 to give the older residential buildings an air of unity. Regular rows of sash windows pierce the walls and the dour, grey harling conceals a complex building history. The neo-Gothic porch with its flanking turrets is a Victorian addition – originally there was no entrance on this side. Behind it, the main range embodies a hall of 1623, itself probably incorporating an older structure. To the south the range ends with the four-storey Fairy Tower, added by Alasdair MacLeod around 1500. Its corbelled-out parapet ends abruptly halfway along the crow-stepped gable.

To the north of the main block is the old tower house, rising at an angle to the rest. This four-storey oblong is attributed to Malcolm MacLeod around 1360. An added jamb projects off-centre, making the tower house a comparatively rare example of the T-plan type. Since the jamb rises from the rock outside the castle, the entrance to the tower house is not placed here but faces the courtyard (it is now covered by a much later corridor). When Dr Johnson visited in 1773 the tower house was an abandoned shell, but it was restored soon afterwards by Norman MacLeod. He enlarged the windows and added corner bartizans to match the later buildings alongside, while the jamb was heightened to dominate the rest of the castle.

Internally the state rooms reflect the transformation wrought in the nineteenth century. The first floor of the tower house now forms an elegant drawing room. Behind protective glass here is the Fairy Flag, a tattered scrap of ancient cloth revered by the clan. At this level the vaulted chamber in the jamb retains its original character, an opening in the floor providing the only access to a grim pit prison beneath. The barrel-vaulted ground floor of the tower house, later converted into a kitchen, is similarly austere. The courtyard front of the residential buildings is now as uniform as its outer face. Rock-cut steps descend past the well to a sea gate through the curtain, originally the only

Dunvegan Castle, Skye

entrance to the castle. It was reduced to a narrow postern in the seventeenth century and is still closed by a yett.
   Access: Open daily in summer (HHA).
   Reference: Guidebook by H. MacLeod.
   Relations: The MacLeods of Dunvegan also held Dunscaith and Duntulm. Castle Campbell, Lauriston and Drummond are other T-plan towers.

OTHER SITES   On the Sleat peninsula of Skye, *Knock Castle* is a fifteenth-century hall house reduced to little more than one wall. *Caisteal Uisdean* (Hugh's Castle) is the stump of a small tower house on Skye's Trotternish peninsula (near Uig). *Coroghan Castle* is a curious little gun battery perched inaccessibly high up on a boss of rock near the eastern tip of Canna. All three occupy dramatic coastal settings.

STIRLINGSHIRE

Stirlingshire, stretching from the Firth of Forth to Loch Lomond, contains the battlefields of Stirling Bridge, Falkirk and Bannockburn. The great royal castle of Stirling stands comparison with Edinburgh for its dramatic history, its commanding setting on a volcanic rock and its palace complex. The great hall and the palace block vividly evoke the era of the Stewart monarchs. On a humbler scale, the remains of a fifteenth-century quadrangle can be seen at Mugdock. Airth Castle has developed from a tower house into a mansion, while Torwood is an elongated tower house of some distinction. Otherwise, the county has towers such as Almond and Plane, while Sir John de Graham's Castle is a striking earthwork.

County reference: RCAHMS *Stirlingshire* (2 vols). BoS *Stirling and Central Scotland*.

AIRTH CASTLE crowns a steep bank overlooking the Pow Burn, two miles west of Kincardine Bridge off the A905. According to tradition William Wallace rescued his uncle, the priest of Dunipace, from an older stronghold here. In 1488 James III's troops, defeated by the rebels at nearby Sauchieburn, sacked Airth. The new king, James IV, gave Robert Bruce of Airth 100 pounds' compensation for 'the byggin of his place that was byrnt'. Bruce no doubt spent the money on the oblong tower house that forms the oldest part, at the south-west angle of the present triangular complex. Known as Wallace's Tower, it rises three storeys to an embattled parapet.

A hall range over barrel-vaulted undercrofts was added on the east soon after. It is almost as high as the modest tower. Alexander Bruce then appended a gabled east wing, with a panel bearing the year 1581. A jamb – with a wide spiral staircase and tall corner bartizans – occupies the angle between the two ranges. Alexander also enlarged the windows of the older parts and added an attic with crow-stepped gables behind the parapet of the older tower. The southern facade above the burn thus appears to be a uniform composition. In 1807 Thomas Graham-Stirling added the castellated north-west front that stretches awkwardly between the tower house and the east wing, obscuring the courtyard facades of the older buildings. The interiors were also transformed during this neo-Gothic phase.

Access: Now part of a hotel complex.

Relations: Other branches of the Bruce family at Clackmannan, Earlshall, Fingask and Muness.

ALMOND CASTLE stands neglected and forlorn midway between Polmont and Linlithgow. From Vellore Road, off the A801, a signposted turning leads to Muiravonside Church; where the road comes to an end, take the footpath north alongside the Union Canal, then eastwards through the waste ground of a demolished industrial estate. The tower house stands amid the trees. A fifteenth-century L-plan structure, it is unusual for retaining the archaic arrangement of an entrance at first-floor level rather than in the re-entrant angle. A spiral stair rose upwards from the entrance, serving both the main block and the jamb, but the ground floor could only be reached via a hatch in the jamb. The tower stands virtually to its full height of four storeys and has barrel vaults crowning both the undercroft and the top of the tower. However, this ruin is in a hazardous condition with many loose stones and a gaping hole in the undercroft vault. It was built by the Crawfords of Haining, traditionally in the reign of James III, and was called Haining until its owner became Lord Almond in 1633. A fragment of a later annexe clings to the fabric and there is a scrap of barmkin wall.

Access: Well seen from the footpath.

BARDOWIE CASTLE overlooks Bardowie Loch in secluded grounds north of the village. This handsome, oblong tower house is attributed to John Hamilton of Bardowie around 1530. The timber roof of the gabled attic is largely original. An added wing of 1713 is almost as tall.

Access: Private.

CASTLECARY CASTLE, or Castle Cary, lies to the south of Castlecary but is separated from it by the M80 motorway. This oblong tower house with battlements is attributed to Henry Livingstone of Middlebinning around 1480. There is a seventeenth-century wing alongside.

Access: Private.

CULCREUCH CASTLE, in extensive grounds just outside Fintry, consists of a modest tower house and an eighteenth-century block alongside. The oblong tower, raised around 1500 by the Galbraiths of Culcreuch, rises to a double row of corbels supporting the rebuilt parapet.

Access: Formerly a hotel but now private.

DUCHRAY CASTLE occupies a large estate three miles west of Aberfoyle. This oblong tower house has a round corner turret containing the spiral stair. Built by William Graham of Duchray after 1569, the tower was extended and refenestrated in neo-Gothic style in the 1820s.

Access: Private (now a holiday let).

DUNTREATH CASTLE, on an estate two miles north-west of Blanefield, is a striking oblong tower house with a corbelled-out parapet. Built by the Edmonstones of Duntreath late in the fifteenth century, it stands beside a Victorian mansion that supplanted a substantial barmkin.

Access: A functions venue. The gardens are open occasionally.

MUGDOCK CASTLE is one of the attractions of Mugdock Country Park, two miles north of Milngavie off Mugdock Road. It overlooks the little Mugdock Loch, which once came up to its walls. Sir Patrick Graham of Mugdock witnessed a charter here in 1372 and the castle was probably rising at that time. The dominant feature now is a slender, square tower, rising complete to a plain parapet. The upper half is strangely corbelled out on three sides like a former parapet heightened. Above the vaulted undercroft three storeys of chambers, one covered by a ribbed vault, are linked by a spiral stair. Ruined lengths of curtain wall extend from it to north and east. The northward curtain contains a narrow gateway with a portcullis groove, immediately beside the tower. It runs to a vaulted basement – all that remains of a second angle tower. So Mugdock was a rare example of the quadrangular type of castle with towers of equal status at all four corners, though they did not project beyond the curtain. The remainder was levelled in 1875 to make way for a new house, the ruins of which complicate the site.

An outer courtyard was added to the west in the fifteenth century, perhaps by another Patrick Graham who became first Lord Mugdock in 1458. It is entered through another simple gate arch positioned at the foot of the surviving tower, which thus commanded both the inner and outer entrances. The surviving stretch of outer curtain is pierced by wide-mouthed gunports and has the shell of a later outbuilding backing on to it.

James Graham, the celebrated Marquis of Montrose, may have been born in the castle in 1612. Already imprisoned for his Royalist sympathies, the castle suffered partial destruction in 1641 by order of parliament. It sustained further damage in an attack by the Covenanters three years later, while Montrose was leading the Royalist army. Nearby Craigend Castle was built as a castellated mansion in 1816 but has also succumbed to ruin.

Access: Branches of the Grahams at Duchray, Knockdolian and Mains (Angus).

OLD SAUCHIE HOUSE is on an estate two miles west of Auchenbowie. This restored L-plan tower house has prominent gables but no skyline adornments. Built by the Erskines of Little Sauchie late in the sixteenth century, it has a lower seventeenth-century wing alongside.

Access: Private.

PLANE CASTLE is about a mile east of Plean but they are separated by the M9 motorway. From the village it is necessary to take a roundabout route involving the A9, the B9124 and an unsignposted road running south from the latter. The simple oblong tower house is authentic for the three storeys up to the corbelled-out parapet, with the bases of bartizans at three corners. It was built by the Somervilles of Plean late in the fifteenth century. The ungainly top storey was added in 1908. A residential range adjoins the tower at one corner and ends in a projecting jamb. It bears the year 1539 on a dormer window but was largely rebuilt from ruin in the 1990s. The tower was also restored for occupation at that time.

Access: Well seen from the road (now a holiday let).

SIR JOHN DE GRAHAM'S CASTLE, otherwise called Dundaff Castle, is an unusual earthwork in a prominent position. It consists of a square courtyard surrounded by a deep ditch. The courtyard does not rise any higher than the outer lip of the ditch so it would be an exaggeration to call it a motte. Surprisingly, it even lacks a rampart bank. It is named after Sir John de Graham, Lord of Dundaff, who fought the English at Stirling Bridge in 1297 and fell at the Battle of Falkirk the following year. The earthwork may in fact have been raised by one of his predecessors. The defences and residential buildings would have been entirely of timber, though there are fragments of a later building outside. The site lies in a clearing in forest terrain. It is just off the B818, four miles west of Muirmill, now overlooking the west end of the Carron Valley Reservoir.

Access: Freely accessible.

STIRLING CASTLE, MAR'S WARK AND TOWN WALL Stirling vies with Edinburgh as the grandest of Scottish castles. They have much in common, from the volcanic outcrops on which they stand to the Renaissance palaces on their summits. As a royal palace, this 'Windsor of the Stewarts' lasted longer than Edinburgh, and has survived more in its original form. Although it too degenerated into a Hanoverian fortress guarding against the Jacobite threat, its buildings have regained their majesty through careful restoration. Guarding the lowest crossing of the River Forth and the route to the Highlands, Stirling was famously the 'key to Scotland'. This strategic importance is reflected in the two great battles fought within sight of its walls during the Wars of Independence.

The site may have been occupied from ancient times but Stirling only enters recorded history under Alexander I, who died here in 1124. In 1175 it was one of the five castles handed over to Henry II of England. They were the price paid for William the Lion's release following his capture at Alnwick. Richard I sold them back to William to raise money for his crusade.

Stirling Castle, Stirlingshire

Stirling was much fought over during the Wars of Independence. Succumbing without resistance to Edward I during his invasion of 1296, the castle surrendered on terms the following year after the stunning victory of Andrew Moray and William Wallace at nearby Stirling Bridge. Changing hands twice more, the castle again yielded to Edward in 1304 following a long siege. The 'Hammer of the Scots' wouldn't accept the garrison's surrender until he had tried out a new and formidable siege engine, the War Wolf, on its walls. By 1314 the wheel had turned and Stirling was holding out as one of the last English strongholds left in Scotland. Its Scottish governor agreed to surrender to Edward Bruce if the castle was not relieved by Midsummer's Day. Edward II and his army, hurrying to raise the siege, spectacularly foundered at Bannockburn just two miles away. After the battle Robert the Bruce followed his usual strategy of destroying the fortifications to deny their use by the enemy. The English nevertheless re-garrisoned the site during their invasion of 1333. They resisted an attempt to dislodge them four years later but were starved into surrender in 1342.

A royal castle of this importance probably had some stone buildings in the thirteenth century but nothing survives. There is documentary evidence of activity under Robert II, the first Stewart king, but the only relic is part of the North Gate. Ambitious rebuilding under successive Jameses swept away the older works. The mutilated Forework facing the city, along with the two palace quadrangles within, are their creation. James VI was brought up here and the castle remained his favourite seat until 1603. After his departure to England there were only occasional royal visits. Stirling fell quickly to the Roundhead army under General Monck in 1651. During the Jacobite period the palace was converted into barracks and the outer defences were rebuilt. Though criticised at the time for their inadequacy, they were strong enough to repulse the retreating Jacobites in 1746.

Castle Rock forms a long promontory with a sheer drop to the west, steep falls on the east and a relatively gentle ascent from the city to the south. It is on this side that the main defences are concentrated. The first obstacle is a stone-lined rampart for artillery, built by the engineer Theodore Dury in 1708–14. A projecting spur containing the gate passage replaced an older ravelin raised by Queen Mary of Guise in 1559. To the right, the flanking bastion known as the French Spur incorporates much of her masonry.

Beyond these outer defences we are confronted with James IV's Forework, built in 1500–09. This screen wall is one of the grandest castle fronts in Scotland. Admittedly, it is defensively inadequate for this period, lacking the thickness required for the emerging power of cannon, and must therefore be as much for show as for defence. In the middle is the gatehouse, an oblong block with circular towers projecting boldly at the outer corners. They have dumbbell gunports at all three surviving levels, but the gatehouse was deprived of its upper floors during the Hanoverian remodelling. Pedestrian archways flank the main portal. To the west an embattled stretch of curtain wall, overlooked by the ornate facade of James V's palace block, leads to the oblong Prince's Tower on the edge of the cliff. This resembles contemporary tower houses, with three main storeys and a gabled attic above the corbelled-out parapet. The curtain to the east of the gatehouse ends at the Elphinstone Tower, once matching the Prince's Tower but truncated during the military occupation to form a gun emplacement.

Beyond the gate passage we reach the Outer Close. Ahead rises the tall gable end of the great hall, while to the left is the enchanting east facade of James V's palace block. A gateway between them leads into the quadrangle known as the Inner Close. Like Crown Square in Edinburgh Castle, this was laid out by the Stewarts from the late fifteenth century. On the east is the magnificent great hall, re-harled in 'royal gold'. Supposedly begun by James III before his murder, it is more likely to be entirely the work of his son, James IV. It was completed in 1503 and resembles his hall at Edinburgh Castle. The hammerbeam roof is a modern reconstruction, based on the one at Edinburgh, but in other respects this hall is more authentic. Having avoided a heavy Victorian renovation, it was freed of later subdivisions after military occupation finally ceased in 1964. The vast space was heated by no fewer than five fireplaces. A spiral stair halfway along ascended to a gallery, while twin bay windows project at the dais end.

On the north side of the Inner Close is the Chapel Royal. Mary Queen of Scots was crowned in its collegiate predecessor. Her son James VI rebuilt the chapel, with its Classical portal, in 1594, while the restored wall paintings date from 1628. Opposite the great hall is the King's Old Building. According to tradition this is where the eighth Earl of Douglas was murdered in 1452. He was stabbed to death by James II and his supporters, then thrown out of a window. However, the existing structure was only built in the 1490s, during James IV's reign, and it was transformed during the military occupation. Overlooking the precipitous western edge of the castle rock, it now houses a regimental museum.

To the south, the Inner Close is bounded by another of the splendid facades of James V's palace block. This smaller quadrangle was erected in the last few years of James V, who died, still young, in 1542. His Master of Works was Sir James Hamilton of Finnart, whose reward was execution on a trumped-up charge of treason. Financed by the king's exactions from the Church and aristocracy, it shows the influence of Francis I's palaces and French craftsmen were employed. The exterior is notable for its Renaissance sculpture. Between the large windows with their protective grilles, there are niches with spiral columns supporting statues of the Planetary gods – the king among them. Its principal floor housed matching suites for James and Mary of Guise on the north and south, culminating in connecting bedchambers in the shorter east wing. The colourful decor is an ingenious modern attempt to evoke their original splendour. There are storage undercrofts below and an attic storey above, the latter displaying an array of carved wooden medallions from the original ceilings. Tradition asserts that James' pet lion roamed the austere courtyard, known as the Lion's Den.

A low gun battery of Queen Anne's reign bounds the east side of the main courtyard, crowning a revetment against the rock face. It commands a dramatic view across the Forth to the Wallace Monument and the Ochil Hills beyond. Changing direction at the North Gate, the wall continues to the western cliff as a conventional curtain with a parapet walk, though this section was rebuilt as late as 1583. Beside the North Gate steps descend to the surviving parts of the kitchen complex of 1542, with reconstructed vaults. The gabled North Gate was remodelled around the same time as a twisting entrance passage with rough vaulting, but the outer archway is the oldest masonry in the castle, dating from 1381. It descends to the uneven Nether Bailey, really just a back yard filling the northern apex of the promontory and containing a row of nineteenth-century powder magazines.

Like Edinburgh, the royal burgh of Stirling developed on a glacial ridge sloping downwards from Castle Rock. The descent down Castle Wynd passes Argyll's Lodging and Mar's Wark, two contrasting town mansions of the later

Stuart nobility. Mar's Wark shows all the trappings of defence without any serious credibility. The two-storey facade has wide-mouthed gunports low down but a row of large windows, admittedly once covered by iron grilles, lighting the upper floor. Below them are vaulted undercrofts believed to have served as shops, with individual doorways giving access from the street. Heraldic panels and cannon spouts enliven the facade. Two polygonal turrets are set together to flank the entrance gateway in time-honoured fashion. Once through the gate passage it becomes clear that the inner wall has vanished above undercroft level. The surviving range was meant to be part of a grand courtyard mansion, begun in 1570 by John Erskine, first Earl of Mar and subsequently regent. It was left incomplete on his death just two years later. The house was damaged during Bonnie Prince Charlie's retreat and has remained a ruin ever since.

Just beyond is Holy Rude Church, a striking Gothic building where the infant James VI was crowned. Behind the adjacent Cowane's Hospital, a pathway known as the Back Walk follows the course of Stirling's old town wall. Only the south-western part of the circuit remains, descending steeply towards the city centre, but it is the longest stretch of town wall remaining in Scotland. It is mostly a plain wall of roughly hewn boulders, some huge, and there are a few gaps. One stretch with wide-mouthed gunports rises from an outcrop of rock. A round bastion here was later converted into a dovecote, as the beehive top demonstrates. Beyond Corn Exchange Road the wall culminates in a well-preserved section with unusually large gunports. An isolated survivor from the eastern part of the circuit is another bastion, now located in a viewing chamber in The Thistles shopping centre off Port Street. Although older defences (probably of earth and timber) are recorded, the existing stone wall was begun after the English victory at Pinkie in 1547. It is thus a reaction to military disaster, like Edinburgh's Flodden Wall.

Access: The castle precincts, kitchens and palace buildings are open daily (HES). Mar's Wark (HES) and the town wall remains (LA) are freely accessible.

Reference: Guidebook to the castle and Mar's Wark by P. Yeoman and K. Owen. *Stirling Castle* by R. Fawcett.

Relations: The castle-palaces of Falkland, Edinburgh, Holyrood and Linlithgow. Other royal work at Tarbert, Dundonald, Rothesay, Lochleven, Dumbarton, Dunbar, Tantallon, Blackness and Ravenscraig (Fife). The town walls at Edinburgh and Peebles.

TORWOOD CASTLE   Torwood village is two miles north-west of Larbert. From Glen Road a public footpath runs south for half a mile to this brooding ruin in an open field. Its walls stand virtually to full height and their decay is being halted by gradual consolidation work. A stone bearing the year 1566 was discovered nearby, implying that this fortified mansion was built by

Sir Alexander Forrester of Garden, keeper of the royal forest of Torwood. Architectural similarities suggest the same team of masons who went on to build Carnasserie Castle in Argyll. It is otherwise known as Torwoodhead.

The building may be described as an elongated tower house but it is just three storeys high, including an attic that is now attested only by crow-stepped gables. It follows the stepped L-plan, the jamb being a little higher than the rest. A doorway in the side of the jamb is surmounted by an armorial panel. It leads to a broad spiral staircase ascending to the first floor, which is divided into a hall and a smaller solar. The windows are large, though the sockets for iron grilles are prominent and there is a liberal supply of shot holes. Two of the hall windows start higher up than the others, presumably to accommodate a large dresser beneath. A smaller stair in the re-entrant stair turret led up to the attic but also down to the ground floor, where a long corridor links three barrel-vaulted cellars and a vaulted kitchen with a huge fireplace. There are thus two adjacent staircases from the ground to the first floor, along with a third from the wine cellar. The upper part of the jamb contained chambers at three levels. A barmkin was surrounded by further residential buildings, as attested by the short stretch of wall running from the jamb.

Access: Exterior only.

Relations: Carnasserie. Elongated tower houses at Castle Menzies, Elcho and Ferniehirst.

TOUCH HOUSE occupies an estate a mile west of Cambusbarron. This mansion was the home of the Setons of Touch. A splendid William Adam facade fronts an older range, projecting from one end of which is an oblong tower house of the sixteenth century with an embattled parapet.

Access: Private.

OTHER SITES Stately *Callendar House* (LA – open), in a large park just outside Falkirk, grew from a tower house that is still embedded unrecognisably in the facade right of the porch. Another is incorporated in *Gargunnock House*, while *Blairlogie Castle* (or The Blair) is a modest hillside tower. *Bruce's Castle* (near Plean), *Elphinstone Tower* (near Dunmore) and *Woodhead House* (near Lennoxtown) are shattered tower houses. There are mottes at *Fintry* and the *Keir Knowe of Drum* (near Kippen).

SUTHERLAND

Considering its size, Sutherland has surprisingly few castles, their paucity reflecting the emptiness of this vast expanse of hill and moorland even before the Highland Clearances. The main castles are concentrated in the east around the Dornoch Firth. Skelbo, with its early curtain wall and fourteenth-century hall house, is the oldest. Trapped within the rambling mansion of Dunrobin Castle is the old tower house of the earls of Sutherland, who were also responsible for the sixteenth-century block that forms Dornoch Castle. Ardvreck and Castle Varrich are striking towers in solitary locations in the west and north.

County reference: RCAHMS *Sutherland*. BoS *Highland and Islands*.

ARDVRECK CASTLE is a picturesque ruin on a promontory jutting into Loch Assynt, a mile north of Inchnadamph off the A837. It is the only castle in western Sutherland. This oblong tower house was built by the MacLeods of Assynt, probably early in the sixteenth century. Only the south wall still stands to its full height of four storeys. The other end has collapsed, though the twin barrel-vaulted undercrofts remain complete. Later in the century the tower was remodelled with a curious turret at one angle. Its circular lower part contained the spiral staircase, but halfway up the turret is corbelled out into a square caphouse projecting diagonally from the corner of the tower house. In 1650 the Marquis of Montrose, whose attempt to rekindle the Royalist cause ended in defeat at Carbisdale, took refuge in the tower but was betrayed to the Covenanters. He was hanged at Edinburgh. Ardvreck was sacked by the MacKenzies as late as 1672 in a dispute with the MacLeods over a bad debt. It was abandoned for by nearby Calda House, which is also now a ruin.

Access: Freely accessible with caution.
Relations: MacLeod castles at Brochel, Dunscaith, Duntulm and Dunvegan.

CASTLE VARRICH, or Caisteal Bharraich, is a prominent landmark offering a commanding view over the sea loch known as the Kyle of Tongue. From the village of Tongue a footpath winds up for about a mile to the rocky summit on which it is placed. After the exhilarating climb, the structure turns out to be quite a diminutive effort – a small oblong tower, never higher than the two remaining storeys – and now quite ruined, though well maintained. A

Norse origin has been claimed for it, akin to Cubbie Roo's Castle, but this is unsubstantiated. It is more likely to date from the sixteenth century, built by either a bishop of Caithness or, after the Reformation, by the MacKays. Too small and inconvenient for a conventional tower house, it evidently served as a look-out post.

Access: Freely accessible (LA – uphill walk).
Relations: Cubbie Roo's. Ardclach and Repentance Tower were other watch towers.

DORNOCH CASTLE originated as the seat of the bishops of Caithness and is still sometimes called the Bishop's Palace. It faces the charming little cathedral built by Bishop Gilbert de Moravia early in the thirteenth century, though much restored since. After the Reformation the earls of Sutherland became hereditary constables. In 1570 the cathedral and the burgh surrounding it were burnt during a skirmish between supporters of the twelfth earl, Alexander Gordon, and his bitter rival, the Earl of Caithness. The palace surrendered after a week's siege by the latter's son, the Master of Caithness, and was then razed. Alexander or his son John presumably built the present L-plan tower house as a replacement once peace had returned; it is possible that some of the older fabric is incorporated. With the expansion of Dunrobin Castle in the seventeenth century it fell into decay. It was restored in 1813 to house the county assizes, though soon supplanted by the new courthouse and jail next door. The restoration, along with further adaptations since, have robbed the structure of most of its original features.

The tower house, facing Castle Street, formed one side of a quadrangle that has otherwise disappeared. The main block has been much altered but preserves a mutilated kitchen fireplace in the unvaulted undercroft (now a bar). It has three upper storeys, including the attic. The five-storey jamb is taller and more authentic externally, apart from enlarged windows. Several shot holes (the only overt signs of defence) can be seen low down, while round bartizans project between the crow-stepped gables. In the re-entrant angle a rounded turret contains the entrance and a spiral staircase to the upper floors. A second stair turret projects out of the main block. The lower tower at the other end was added during the restoration.

Access: Now a hotel but open to non-residents.
Relations: The earls' castle at Dunrobin.

DUNROBIN CASTLE is perched above the Dornoch Firth two miles north-east of Golspie, just off the A9. It is the rambling stately home of the dukes of Sutherland. No doubt an older fortification occupied this rock, as the 'dun' prefix implies. The dukes' ancestors have probably been here since William the Lion granted much of Sutherland to Hugh de Moravia, grandson of the Flemish settler Hugh de Freskin. However, the memorable south-east show front, a French-style chateau punctuated by slender turrets on a cliff overlooking fine gardens, dates mainly from the nineteenth century.

A castle here is first mentioned in 1401. The oblong tower house forming its core may have been new at that time, making its builder Robert Sutherland, the sixth Earl of Sutherland. Four storeys high with later vaults inserted at each level, this simple structure reflects the limited resources of the earls. A yett is preserved beside the later ground-floor entrance. The present parapet, with tiny corner bartizans, dates from a later remodelling. In 1641 the fourteenth earl, John Gordon, commenced a residential range to the west of the tower, only connected by the round stair turret he added to serve both. In the eighteenth century it was expanded to form a small courtyard on the site of the original barmkin.

This merely forms the west wing of the present mansion. In 1844 the second Duke of Sutherland commissioned the architect Sir Charles Barry to expand Dunrobin in full-blown Scottish Baronial style. As a result, the original tower house now stands inconspicuously between two courtyards. Only the modest first-floor room, at the level of the grandiose state rooms, is on show to visitors and its exterior is visible only from the windows overlooking the two courtyards. The dominant feature now is the massive Victorian entrance tower overlooking the landward front.

Access: Open daily in summer (HHA).
Reference: Guidebook (Heritage House).
Relations: Dornoch was another castle of the earls of Sutherland.

SKELBO CASTLE rises above Loch Fleet, four miles north of Dornoch and reached by a sideroad off the A9. This forlorn ruin is dominated by a shattered hall house on an older motte, marking the north angle of a roughly triangular enclosure. From the hall a stretch of plain wall descends the motte slope towards the Skelbo Burn – the chief relic of the curtain that once enclosed the bailey, though other fragments are discernible elsewhere. This curtain is attributed to Gilbert de Moravia, Bishop of Caithness. He obtained Skelbo in 1211, so it may be one of the oldest stone curtains in Scotland. The castle certainly existed by 1290. Here, in that year, the commissioners coming to greet the child queen, Margaret of Norway, learnt that she had died in Orkney following her stormy voyage across the North Sea. Robert the Bruce captured the castle during his 1308 campaign against the Comyns.

The oblong hall house dates from the late fourteenth century, when the Sutherlands of Duffus held the castle. The hall stood above an unvaulted undercroft and its position on a motte was probably inspired by the tower house of their castle at Duffus. It seems to have suffered the same subsidence problems on this artificial mound – it is now reduced to the ruinous north wall and one other corner. Two gaping holes mark the position of the hall windows. A gabled house with a barrel-vaulted undercroft, now a shell, was built on the perimeter of the bailey around 1600. The castle is reached by following a track that leaves the road at the foot of the motte, then doubles back uphill. Skelbo should not be confused with nearby Skibo Castle, a Victorian mansion.

Access: Freely accessible with caution.

Relations: Duffus.

OTHER SITES *Proncy Castle* (near Evelix) is a low motte bearing the grassy foundations of a possibly Norse keep. *Borve Castle* is little more than the site of another early stronghold, on a dramatic coastal headland near Farr.

WESTERN ISLES

The Western Isles or Outer Hebrides belonged to Norway before their purchase by Alexander III in 1266. Historically, Lewis formed part of Ross, while the others were attached to Inverness-shire. There are important ancient sites like Callanish and Dun Carloway but castles are few and fragmentary, mostly located near the south end of this long chain of islands. Kisimul Castle is the one notable stronghold – an evocative little fifteenth-century complex of tower house and walled barmkin on an islet off the coast of Barra. It was the power base of the dominant MacNeil clan. (There are ferries to the Western Isles from Oban, Ullapool and Uig on Skye.)

County reference: RCAHMS *Outer Hebrides, Skye and the Small Isles*. BoS *Highland and Islands*.

BORVE CASTLE In a field a mile west of Lionacleit on Benbecula are the shattered remains of an oblong tower house. Just two jagged sides remain. Attributed to Ami MacRuari, estranged wife of the Lord of the Isles, in the 1340s, it was later held by the MacDonalds of Benbecula.

Access: Visible from the road.

CALVAY CASTLE is a very ruined fifteenth-century enclosure with the remains of a square corner tower. It was similar in layout to Kisimul Castle and also belonged to the MacNeils of Barra. The castle lies on a rocky islet off Calbhaigh island, at the entrance to Loch Boisdale.

Access: Visible from the Oban-Lochboisdale ferry.

KISIMUL CASTLE is otherwise called Kiessimul or, in Gaelic, Caisteal Chiosmuil. It rises romantically on an islet off Castlebay, Barra's harbour village. At high tide the sea comes almost to the walls. For most of its history this was the chief seat of Clan MacNeil, who claimed descent from an Irish king. Early dates have been suggested for this austere little stronghold. The tower house has been likened to a Norman keep and the curtain wall even attributed to the first MacNeil of Barra, who arrived according to tradition in 1030. However, austerity is no sure proof of antiquity in the Hebrides and the castle does not feature in John of Fordun's fourteenth-century list of island castles. In fact, it was probably built by Gilleonan MacNeil after he obtained Barra from the MacDonald Lord of the Isles in 1427. He may even have employed the masons who built Old Breachacha Castle on Coll. There are shadowy tales of feuds and sieges. In 1840 the MacNeils were forced to sell up but, almost a century later, the decaying castle was purchased by a descendant – the architect Robert MacNeil – who had prospered in America. He began a slow and gruelling restoration, in parts amounting to rebuilding, that was finally completed in 1970.

The castle consists of a square-plan tower house, projecting diagonally at the south-east angle of a compact walled enclosure tailored to the rock. A narrow doorway – overlooked by a simple box machicolation – forms the entrance, immediately flanked by the tower house. In its present form this entrance is part of a sixteenth-century remodelling. Curiously, the parapet was heightened all round but the stone wall walk was not raised in step with it. Instead a timber sentry platform was provided, supported by putlog holes that have been reused for the current parapet walkway.

Some simple residential buildings around the barmkin were rehabilitated by Robert MacNeil. Proceeding clockwise from the tower house is the kitchen, followed by the Tanist House which formed the cramped residence of the MacNeil heir. Against the relatively long north-west stretch of curtain is the hall block, later partitioned into a two-storey house but now one big room again. On the north-east another range is believed to have been the chapel. The courtyard fronts of these internal buildings have largely been rebuilt, while the wooden storey over the chapel is out of harmony with the rest.

Dominating all is the tower house, which rises from a tall plinth. A stone staircase ascends to the parapet of the curtain, from which a wooden bridge – replicating the original arrangement – crosses the void to a mural lobby in the tower house. This lobby is placed between floors, straight staircases leading up and down in the thickness of the wall to the adjacent levels. The top chamber has a few narrow windows but no fireplace, so the main accommodation must always have been in the barmkin buildings. Below is a dimly lit guard room, while the ground floor is a dank undercroft. None of these storeys are vaulted but the tower house was re-floored during the restoration.

Access: Open daily in summer (HES). A boat service runs from Castlebay (weather permitting).
Reference: Guide by S. Farrar. *Castle in the Sea* by R. MacNeil. *PSAS* (146).
Relations: Old Breachacha. The MacNeils also built Calvay. Other restorations at Duart and Eilean Donan.

OTHER SITES A castle of the MacLeods overlooking *Stornoway* harbour on Lewis was destroyed by Roundhead troops in 1654 (nearby Lews Castle is a Victorian sham). The stumps of two diminutive towers occupy islets in small lochs: *Castle Sinclair* (near Castlebay on Barra) and *Caisteal Bheagram* (near Tobha Mor on South Uist).

WEST LOTHIAN

First and foremost in this small county comes the defensible royal palace at Linlithgow, still a magnificent quadrangle though now an empty shell. It was begun by James I and embellished by most of his namesake successors. Blackness Castle is another fifteenth-century complex, jutting into the Firth of Forth and interesting for successive adaptations to changing military requirements. Otherwise, there is the usual group of tower houses. Kinneil and Niddry are impressive fifteenth-century examples, while Midhope is a picturesque example of the later type and Duntarvie Castle is an elongated structure of some elegance.

County reference: RCAHMS *Midlothian and West Lothian*. BoS *Lothian*; BoS *Stirling and Central Scotland* (for the part transferred to Falkirk).

BLACKNESS CASTLE protrudes into the Firth of Forth midway between Abercorn and Bo'ness. The adjacent bay had long been an important harbour, but the castle is first mentioned in 1449. It was probably newly built at that time by Sir George Crichton, Chancellor Crichton's brother and briefly Earl of Caithness. In 1454 he was imprisoned here by his disinherited son, only being released when James II besieged the castle. Henceforth, it was a royal stronghold, serving as a state prison and supply base for nearby Linlithgow Palace. In 1537 James V sent his Master of Works, Sir James Hamilton of Finnart, to remodel the castle for defence against artillery (compare his own castle at Craignethan). Building continued after Hamilton's execution for alleged treason in 1540.

Blackness remained steadfastly loyal to Mary Queen of Scots following her abdication. Despite a blockade it held out – like Edinburgh Castle – until 1573. The castle fell again following a day-long bombardment by Oliver Cromwell in 1650. It was restored from ruin in 1667 to house a garrison. In 1870 the castle was drastically converted into an ammunition depot but was abandoned after the First World War. Long military service has bequeathed a rather grim demeanour but most of the Victorian disfigurements have been swept away, including the concrete roof that covered the entire courtyard. The embattled parapets are a modern attempt to restore a more castellar appearance.

George Crichton served as Lord High Admiral and his castle, by accident or design, resembles a stone ship stranded on the rocks. The narrow, walled enclosure tapers to a triangular tower forming the 'prow' at the north-eastern extremity, while the slender, free-standing tower house within is the 'mast'. Sir James Hamilton thickened the more vulnerable south-east curtain wall to withstand cannon, blocking the original entrance gateway that can now only be seen externally. Cromwell's naval artillery severely damaged the slighter north-west curtain, which was largely rebuilt in 1667.

Hamilton built up the narrow landward end of the castle into the three-storey South Tower, though the original battlements of the curtain are still discernible in the masonry halfway up. This tower, irregular in plan because it follows the line of the older curtain, is provided low down with an intimidating row of wide-mouthed gunports, emanating from the vaulted chambers within. The gaping hole filled with lighter stones is a relic of Cromwell's bombardment. A great hall, with a much restored timber roof, fills most of the upper floor of the tower. Alongside is an oblong gun battery, added during the minority of Mary Queen of Scots but remodelled in 1693. It contains the entrance passage to the castle, running parallel with the curtain before reaching a gateway into the courtyard.

In the middle of the courtyard rises the slender tower house of oblong plan. Appropriately known as the Prison Tower, its most famous inmate was Cardinal Beaton in 1543. Nevertheless, it formed Sir George Crichton's original dwelling. Three residential storeys (now deprived of their wooden floors) surmount a barrel-vaulted undercroft, which contains the entrance. Hamilton added the crowning vault to provide a platform for cannon (hence no attic), while the round corner turret containing the spiral staircase dates only from the 1667 remodelling.

Access: Open daily (HES).
Reference: Guidebook by C. Tabraham and A. Burnet.
Relations: Craignethan and Sir James' other castle at Cadzow. James V's work at Dunbar, Tantallon, Falkland, Edinburgh, Holyrood, Stirling and Linlithgow. Broughty was also converted into a coastal fort.

BRIDGE CASTLE rises on an estate two miles north of Armadale. This Victorian mansion incorporates a sixteenth-century L-plan tower house of the Stewarts of Brighouse. It is curious for the slightly detached jamb, linked to the parapet of the main block by a single-arched bridge.

Access: Private.

DUNDAS CASTLE occupies an estate south-west of South Queensferry. The present complex is a neo-Gothic mansion incorporating an L-plan tower house for which James Dundas obtained a licence to crenellate in 1424. A tower of unusual rhomboid plan projects from one corner.

Access: A functions venue.

DUNTARVIE CASTLE, off the B8020 a mile north of Winchburgh, is a familiar sight from the M9 motorway. It is a tower house of the comparatively rare elongated type, probably built by James Durham some time after he acquired the lands in 1588. Abandoned in the nineteenth century, the building has been the object of a protracted restoration that began in 1994 and has continued despite a number of setbacks.

The main block is four storeys high, including the gabled attic. Rows of windows, particularly large at first-floor level, pierce the south facade. They show the defensive limitations of the building, even if this side enjoyed some modest protection from a vanished barmkin. By contrast, the north front is quite martial in appearance, with few windows and a tall, square tower of five storeys at either end, forming an E-plan layout. These towers project in two directions, though the re-entrant angle on the west was later filled in with a small extension. The north-east tower collapsed in a gale in 1995 and has been rebuilt in modern brick. In the two northern re-entrant angles rounded stair turrets are corbelled out from the first floor upwards. A ground-floor doorway in the middle of the south front leads into the usual group of barrel-vaulted undercrofts, one of them the kitchen. Facing the doorway a straight staircase ascends to the first floor, which was divided into the hall and solar. The upper floors are reached by the turret stairs.

Access: A functions venue but well seen from the road.

Relations: E-plan layouts such as Craigston, Castle Stuart and Castle Kennedy.

KINNEIL HOUSE Just off the A904, on an estate that is now a country park a mile west of Bo'ness, stands the gaunt mass of a tower house that developed into a mansion but was abandoned in 1828. This narrow oblong block has two contrasting facades. The west side, overlooking a ravine, preserves a severe aspect with two rows of wide-mouthed gunports near the bottom. James, Lord Hamilton, received a licence to crenellate in 1473 but the gunports were inserted by a later James Hamilton, the second Earl of Arran. Made Duke of Chatelherault by the French king, he became regent in 1542 following James V's early death. His support for the exiled Mary Queen of Scots led to the tower being slighted by the Earl of Morton in 1570. The Duchess of Hamilton restored it as a residence from 1677. She transformed the east front into a Classical ensemble with five rows of sash windows, a balustraded parapet and turrets at either end. Internally the tower house is now a gutted shell, though protected by a modern roof.

Connected to the eastern turret is a purely residential block that Chatelherault built shortly before relinquishing the regency in 1554. It contains two storeys of chambers over the usual barrel-vaulted undercrofts. Two first-floor rooms preserve the finest Renaissance wall paintings in Scotland, rediscovered in

1936. The Parable Room, with its six large depictions of the Good Samaritan parable, complements the Old Testament roundels in the vaulted Arbour Room.
Access: Exterior at any time (HES). The residential block has limited opening times.
Reference: HES guide.
Relations: Brodick, Cadzow and Craignethan were other castles of the Hamilton earls. The wall paintings at Huntingtower and in the Chapel Royal at Stirling.

LINLITHGOW PALACE   The majestic ruin of this royal palace overlooks Linlithgow Loch. David I built a manor house here and founded the royal burgh. James of St George, Edward I's renowned military engineer, fortified the site in 1301 during the Wars of Independence. His Peel of Linlithgow was a simple enclosure of earth and timber – a stark contrast with the mighty castles James had designed in North Wales. In 1313 it was captured by a band of Scots who, according to John Barbour's poem *The Brus*, entered on the pretext of delivering hay and blocked the portcullis with their cart. Nothing survives from that period and the existing palace is entirely the work of the Stewart monarchs following a devastating fire in 1424. Located midway between the castles of Edinburgh and Stirling, it was a popular retreat for Scottish queens. James V and Mary Queen of Scots were both born here. The palace was as capable of defence as most castles of its era, even if later hostilities passed it by.

James I began the present palace in 1425, on return from his long captivity in England. A large quadrangle may have been intended from the outset but less than half had been built when he was assassinated in 1437. The main survival from his time is the east range, containing the original entrance and the great hall. He also erected the eastern half of the south range. The west range and the rest of the south range are James III's – building is recorded here in 1469. From 1491 James IV erected a less durable north range that later collapsed. He also remodelled the great hall, converted the eastern part of the south range into a chapel and contrived square towers (which do not project at all) at the western corners. In the 1530s James V created a new entrance from the town on the south side and modernised the interiors. When James VI visited his homeland in 1617, he ordered the rebuilding of the north range, which had fallen ten years earlier. Linlithgow saw few later visits from its absent monarchs and the palace fell into decay. In 1746 the Duke of Cumberland's advancing troops spent a winter's night here. They accidentally started a fire in the north range and the ensuing conflagration engulfed the whole palace.

Although the palace is now a roofless shell it is virtually complete. It is concealed from the town behind the splendid parish church of St Michael, built with royal assistance in the fifteenth century. Beside the church tower is James V's squat outer gatehouse, with flanking turrets and heraldic panels

Linlithgow Palace, West Lothian

on the parapet. Beyond rises the south front of the palace but to follow the building sequence it is better to start with James I's east front. In the middle is the original gateway, crowned by a heraldic panel displaying the royal arms. Two narrow recesses held the drawbridge beams when raised. Flanking them are tall niches with delicate canopies but, otherwise, the facade is quite severe. To the right of the gateway the footings of three round turrets are connected to the wall by flying buttresses, a curious arrangement reinforcing what must have proved to be an unstable section of wall.

We can now return to the south front. East of James V's squat porch, five lancet windows denote James IV's chapel. James III's west range is the plainest of all, despite the enlarged windows lighting the royal quarters. The Jacobean north range has far more windows, showing that defence was no longer a consideration when it was rebuilt in 1618–20. Owing to the sloping site, this tall range is higher than the east range, which was given a recessed caphouse at the north-east corner to compensate. An oriel window in the north-west tower (originally one of a trio) denotes the position of the king's oratory.

James V's porch leads into the courtyard. In the middle is the elaborate, triple-tier King's Fountain of 1538. It is a riot of Renaissance sculpture with many carved figures. The courtyard fronts of the surrounding ranges differ considerably. James I's east range is pierced by the original gate passage, with a pit prison beneath. Above the archway three ornate niches are surmounted by soaring angels and a decorative canopy. Beside it is the first-floor doorway to the great hall, once reached by a flight of steps. James IV added six clerestory windows higher up. He also added the tall stair turrets at each corner of the courtyard and the corridors against the south range. Rows of mullioned windows here show a rare Tudor influence in Scotland, no doubt a result of his marriage to Margaret Tudor. James VI had the windows in the west range enlarged, while his five-storey north range is a Classical contrast with its central stair turret and the five regular rows of large windows crowned by ornate pediments.

The ground floors of each range are divided into the usual series of barrel-vaulted storerooms. Taking the spiral staircase in the north-east corner, we ascend to the upper kitchen in the north-east corner of the quadrangle. Beyond the stone screen is James I's great hall, known as the Lyon Chamber, which occupies most of the east range above the undercrofts. Beneath James IV's clerestory is a wall passage from which the portcullis of the inner gateway was operated. A magnificent fireplace runs the full width of the dais end, its long lintel supported by four shafted columns with carved capitals. This end of the hall is covered by a barrel vault.

James IV's vaulted corridors – an unusual feature for their time – connect the rooms in the south range. His tall chapel has delicate niches between the lancet windows. The other main chamber in the south range at first-floor level served as a guardroom, controlling access to the king's residential suite beyond. James III's west range, as remodelled by James V, contained the king's private hall and presence chamber, with his bedchamber in the north-west tower. A matching suite on the floor above was presumably for Queen Mary of Guise. A mural stairway descends to the wine cellar on the ground floor of the north-west tower. Its ribbed vault is much finer than the other vaults in the palace, the corbels depicting merry servants drinking from large flagons. Indeed, the palace is rich in sculptural decoration, much of it sadly mutilated.

Access: Open daily (HES).

Reference: Guidebook by A. Cox and C. Tabraham. *PSAS* (126).

Relations: The castle-palaces of Falkland, Edinburgh, Holyrood and Stirling. Other royal work at Tarbert, Dundonald, Rothesay, Lochleven, Dumbarton, Dunbar, Tantallon, Blackness and Ravenscraig (Fife).

MIDHOPE CASTLE stands beside a farm, half a mile south-west of Abercorn. The original oblong tower house is a modest but handsome structure of six storeys, including a low, vaulted basement and the gabled attic. A caphouse marks the top of the spiral staircase in one corner, while the other three corners have tall, round bartizans corbelled out near the top. A stone beside the outer gateway displays the year 1582, along with the initials of

Alexander Drummond of Midhope and his wife, Marjorie Bruce. Alongside the tower is a residential block just one storey lower, added around 1600 but extended later in the century. It too has a vaulted ground floor, containing the kitchen. The Renaissance doorway into the tower was inserted by the third Earl of Linlithgow in the 1660s. As a rare bonus much of the barmkin wall is preserved, enclosing an oblong courtyard with the tower and range on the north. It is clearly of little defensive value but retains a fine gate arch in ashlar masonry on the east, with a blank armorial panel above. The earls of Hopetoun went on to build Hopetoun House as a successor mansion and the tower was left to estate workers. After some restoration it appears intact externally. A painted ceiling from the tower is now relocated in the old house called Abbey Strand on Canongate in Edinburgh.

Access: The exterior is regularly accessible.

Relations: Other Drummond branches at Drummond, Innerpeffray and Newton.

NIDDRY CASTLE, just the south-east of Winchburgh, occupies a crag overlooks the Niddry Burn. It is an excellent example of the sturdier type of L-plan tower house, rising austerely to five storeys below parapet level. Small windows accentuate the impression of solidity. The entrance, immediately flanked by the jamb, involves a right-angled turn towards the spiral staircase and then another into the barrel-vaulted ground floor, which was once divided into two by a wooden floor. The stair is in the thickness of the wall, so the jamb contains small chambers at each level. At the base it formed a pit prison, originally only accessible from above. There is a large fireplace in the hall at the next level, with a kitchen in the jamb. The two upper floors have several mural chambers, while a row of corbels at the wall-head supported a vanished parapet with corner bartizans. The tower was closely surrounded by a light barmkin wall with round angle turrets, two sides of which have been excavated and exposed.

The tower is attributed to George, fourth Lord Seton, who inherited in 1478. His son fell at Flodden in 1513. Mary Queen of Scots stayed overnight in 1568, after escaping from Lochleven Castle, *en route* to defeat at the Battle of Langside and exile. Niddry was attacked twice during the struggles that followed. Some time afterwards two further storeys were added, recessed within the parapet. These less substantial walls did not survive the long period of abandonment so well and a modern attic utilises the surviving stumps as gable ends. Having fallen into decay, the tower was restored as a residence from 1986.

Access: Well seen from the adjacent golf course.

Reference: *PSAS* (127).

OTHER SITES On the country estate of majestic Hopetoun House is the site of *Abercorn Castle*. This Black Douglas stronghold endured a month-long bombardment from James II during their rebellion in 1455. James also destroyed their newly built *Inveravon Castle* (near Grangemouth), which at least preserves part of a round flanking tower. The gun battery on *Inchgarvie*, an islet in the Forth overawed by the Forth Railway Bridge, incorporates fragments of a castle built by James IV for coastal defence. *Barnbougle Castle* (near Cramond) and *Carriden House* (near Bo'ness) incorporate much-altered tower houses, while the little tower of *Murieston Castle* (near West Calder) was transformed into a Gothic folly in 1824. Of *Staneyhill Tower* (also on the Hopetoun estate), only the undercroft vault and the handsome re-entrant stair turret still stand.

WIGTOWNSHIRE

Wigtownshire, ending in the hammerhead of the Rhins of Galloway, is the relatively remote western half of once fiercely independent Galloway. Its castles are mainly concentrated in the benign coastal areas around Stranraer and the Machars peninsula. Druchtag Motte is the most eloquent earthwork from the age of Norman colonisation. After that there is little until the sixteenth century, when the usual group of tower houses sprang up as the bases of truculent lairds. Many are now in a sorry state, but the Castle of Park, the Castle of St John, Dunskey and Sorbie are good examples of the L-plan. Castle Kennedy goes further with two jambs, while the Old Place of Mochrum, not content with a single tower house, sprouted a second.

County reference: RCAHMS *Galloway* (vol. 1). BoS *Dumfries and Galloway*.

CASTLE KENNEDY now serves as a landscape feature in the splendid Castle Kennedy Gardens, part of the Lochinch Castle estate. They are located off the A75, three miles east of Stranraer and just to the north of Castle Kennedy village. The tower house originally occupied an islet in a loch, but landscaping has reduced it to two smaller ones (White and Black) on either side. It has been an empty shell since it was gutted by fire in 1716. At that time the tower was little more than 100 years old, as its construction was underway in 1607. The name recalls its builder, John Kennedy, fifth Earl of Cassillis, whose main power base was in Ayrshire.

The tower house is one of several late examples following the so-called 'E-plan'. Twin square towers project from the corners of the principal east facade, as at Castle Stuart and Craigston. Symmetry is thus preferred to the more practical Z-plan, while the large windows from the first floor upwards show the casual attitude to defence that is to be expected at this late date. The towers project in two directions; square turrets, rising a little higher than the rest, protrude in the rear re-entrant angles. One of them contained the spiral staircase. The main block rises to five storeys, including the attic gables. The entrance is in the facade, closely flanked by the left-hand tower. It led to a passage running the full length of the main block but the dividing wall and the undercroft vault have fallen, along with the gable at the rear of the main block. Ruinous later wings adjoin the tower house on two sides.

Access: The gardens are open daily in summer (exterior only of the tower).
Relations: Cassillis, Craigneil, Dunure and Maybole were other castles of the Kennedy earls. Other E-plan layouts at Craigston, Castle Stuart and Borthwick.

CASTLE OF PARK   Half a mile west of Glenluce, a drive off the Old Military Road leads to this grey-harled L-plan tower house overlooking the Water of Luce. Above the entrance is the re-gilded inscription: 'Blissit be the name of the Lord. This verk vas begun the first day of March 1590 be Thomas Hay of Park and Ionet Mak Dovel [Janet MacDowell] his spous.' Thomas Hay was the son of the commendator of nearby Glenluce Abbey, which he is said to have used as a quarry for building. It was restored to a habitable condition by the Landmark Trust in the 1990s.

The tower is five storeys high including the attic but, apart from crow-stepped gables, the roofline is unadorned and there is no parapet. The windows in the main block have been enlarged. The entrance, in the usual position in the side of the jamb, is guarded by a shot hole. The ground floor contains three barrel-vaulted cellars, linked by a corridor. One of them is the kitchen with an arched fireplace. The jamb contains a generous spiral staircase to the third floor, from which a much narrower stair in a corbelled-out turret ascends to a chamber at the top of the jamb. There is also a spiral stair (renewed in wood) at the opposite corner of the tower from the first floor upwards. A mural chamber occupies one corner at each level. The first floor is still an open hall with a large fireplace but the upper floors have been partitioned into bedrooms. Much original timber survives in the attic roof.

Access: Formerly in state care but now a holiday let.

CASTLE OF ST JOHN   This tower house now stands on Castle Street in the middle of Stranraer. Ninian Adair of Kinhilt erected it around 1510, though the little port was not established until 1595. It takes its name from a chapel that stood close by. From 1678 John Graham of Claverhouse used it as a base for persecuting the Covenanters of Galloway during the so-called 'Killing Time' – the future hero of Killiecrankie was known locally as Bluidy Clavers rather than Bonnie Dundee. Covenantors were incarcerated here and the tower is unusual for its conversion into the town jail in 1821. Despite lax jailers and many prisoners escaping, it remained in use for nearly a century.

The tower is unspoilt externally. It may be called an L-plan structure, though the jamb is just a shallow staircase projection surmounted by a mutilated caphouse. The plain parapet is supported on continuous corbelling. Sometime after 1608 a branch of the Kennedy family added a fourth storey, partly recessed within the parapet. Its attic was supplanted by the present embattled parapet during the jail period, when the flat roof was used as an exercise yard. The tall bellcote is an addition of that time. A wide-mouthed gunport commands the approach to the ground-floor entrance. It leads into twin vaulted undercrofts for storage, one of them preserving the imprint of the wooden frame used in the construction of the vault. Off the spiral stair a mural chamber provided a strongroom for valuables. The stair ascends to the hall, later adapted to serve as the jailer's quarters. Surprisingly, the barrel vault was only inserted at that time. The old fireplace was reduced in size and two of the original windows were blocked. Behind the fireplace is a pit prison, reached from a mural chamber above. The two upper floors are partitioned into cells with iron doors, evoking the grim spirit of the nineteenth-century penal system.

Access: Open regularly in summer (LA).
Reference: LA guidebook.
Relations: Ninian probably also built Dunskey Castle.

CRAIGCAFFIE TOWER, in secluded grounds a mile north-east of Innermessan, is a handsome oblong with corner bartizans and lengths of parapet on the gable ends. The tower bears the year 1570 on one gable, along with the initials of John Neilson of Craigcaffie.

Access: Private (now a holiday let).

DRUCHTAG MOTTE   Overlooking Main Street just to the north-east of Mochrum village is a classic castle mound. It is conical with a flat top, surrounded by a ditch with some remains of a rampart beyond, but there is no trace of any accompanying bailey. A rope has been provided to help the visitor clamber up the steep slope and to ease their descent. No excavations have been undertaken but no stone defences ever replaced the wooden keep and stockade that presumably crowned the summit. Its history is quite obscure: it may have been raised by a Norman or Flemish settler in the twelfth century or by a local lord following the Galloway rising of 1174, when the newcomers were temporarily ousted.

Access: Freely accessible (HES).
Relations: Mottes such as Dalmellington, Dinvin and the Mote of Urr.

DUNSKEY CASTLE is reached by a short walk along an exhilarating coastal footpath from picturesque Portpatrick, on the Rhins of Galloway. It is spectacularly sited, closing the neck of a promontory with sheer drops to Castle Bay and the Irish Sea. Immediately in front is a broad ditch that may be a relic of an older stronghold, burnt by the McCullochs in a tit-for-tat raid in 1496. The existing ruin consists of a tower house of the stepped L-plan type and an adjoining range to the west. The tower may have been erected early in the sixteenth century by Ninian Adair of Kinhilt, but, if so, it was remodelled by his grandson William Adair in the 1580s. It comprises four storeys including the attic, the prominent gables of which rise straight from the walls. The jamb faces the promontory and there is a stair turret in the re-entrant angle.

Three barrel-vaulted storerooms occupy the ground floor of the main block, while a spacious hall filled the floor above. The adjoining range may not have been added until Hugh, Viscount Montgomery, acquired the lands in 1608. It contained a long gallery over a row of vaulted cellars – one near the middle of the front forming a gate passage into the barmkin on the promontory.

William Adair is said to have tortured the commendator of vanished Soulseat Abbey here to obtain the monastic lands – a story similar to that of the Earl of Cassillis at Dunure Castle. The castle was soon abandoned for a predecessor of nearby Dunskey House and was already falling into ruins in 1684. Its reasonably complete state is all the more surprising in this exposed position, though most of the door and window openings have been robbed into ragged holes and the masonry looks precarious in places.

Access: Exterior only (uphill walk).
Relations: Dunure. Ninian Adair also erected the Castle of St John.

GALDENOCH CASTLE can be found on the Rhins of Galloway. A mile south-east of Knocknain, a rough track runs from the B738 to this small L-plan tower house, standing beside a farm. It rises mostly to full height though still a decaying ruin. The tower is four storeys tall including the attic, with its pronounced crow-step gables. The entrance, in the side of the jamb, leads to the vaulted ground floor. A spiral stair in the jamb ascended to the hall and the floor above, from which a stair turret in the re-entrant angle led to the attic. The collapse of this turret has left the only breach in the tower's walls. There is also a round bartizan corbelled out high up at the rear. The hall windows are larger than the rest but have largely been robbed off their dressed stones. A panel on the jamb bears the year 1547 and the initials of Gilbert Agnew of Lochnaw.

Access: Exterior only.
Relations: The Agnews also held Lochnaw Castle.

ISLE CASTLE overlooks the picturesque harbour in the Isle of Whithorn (a village but no longer an island). This small L-plan tower house off Main Street is as plain as they come, grey-harled with shallow bartizans clasping the corners. It consists of three storeys plus the usual gabled attic; the ground floor has the customary barrel vault. The tower belonged to the Houstons of Drummaston. A reset stone bearing the year 1674 suggests a very late origin but it is more likely that it refers to additions, the tower itself being somewhat older in character. The re-entrant angle is largely filled by an eighteenth-century stair block.

Access: Well seen from the road.
Relations: There is an Isle Tower in Dumfriesshire.

LOCHNAW CASTLE occupies an estate overlooking Lochnaw Loch, two miles west of Leswalt. This picturesque courtyard mansion of 1663 and later incorporates at one corner an embattled oblong tower house, built by the Agnews of Lochnaw in the fifteenth century.

Access: Private.

OLD PLACE OF MOCHRUM From Culshabbin, on the B7005, a side road runs two miles north past Mochrum Loch to this striking mansion, set in its own grounds. Alternatively known as Drumwalt Castle, it was the seat of the Dunbars of Mochrum until 1738. The present complex consists of an oblong courtyard dominated by twin tower houses that are set close together but at right angles to each other. They bound much of the south and west sides of the courtyard and are the only genuinely old parts. The lower north and east ranges, despite their authentic look, were built entirely by the fourth Marquess of Bute from 1900. They occupy the site of the original barmkin; the outer gate arch, positioned beside the western tower, stands on the foundations of the old. The two towers are linked by a lower structure (now the chapel) built by the third Marquess of Bute, John Crichton-Stuart, in the 1870s. He also rescued the two towers from ruin. The third marquess was a keen restorer of castles in Scotland, in addition to his more celebrated Welsh work at Cardiff and Castell Coch.

The presence of two adjacent tower houses is unusual but not unique. At Huntingtower the two are contemporary and are taken to be joint abodes for the lord and his heir. However, here the western or Old Tower was probably built late in the fifteenth century, the southern or Red Tower being added 100 years or so later. It therefore supplanted the original tower house, which may nevertheless have been taken over by the heir. The oblong Old Tower is original in its three storeys up to the wall-head, though the corner bartizans and the lengths of parapet along the gable ends required some renewal. Only the crowning attic with its dormer windows is a complete reconstruction. The T-plan Red Tower, which has a spiral staircase in the jamb, was more ruinous in its upper parts. It has been reconstructed with a curious double-storey attic, giving five storeys in all.

Access: A functions venue.

Relations: The twin tower houses at Huntingtower and Kellie (Fife). The Marquess of Bute also restored Rothesay, Sanquhar and Falkland.

SORBIE TOWER A turning off the B7052 leads to this L-plan tower house, a mile east of Sorbie village. Alternatively known as the Old Place of Sorbie, it was almost certainly raised by Alexander Hannay of Sorbie, who was laird from 1569 until his death around 1612. Hannay's descendants were impoverished by feuding with their neighbours and forced to sell up. The tower was abandoned around 1748. Although a ruin, this impressive structure still stands mostly to full height and in good condition following a long campaign of gradual consolidation by the Clan Hannay Society that began in 1965.

Similar in design to the Castle of Park, the tower rises to four storeys, including the attic gables. The entrance, in the side of the jamb, leads to a corridor connecting three barrel-vaulted undercrofts in the main block, one of them the kitchen with a large fireplace (restored). There is a probable prison cell in the base of the jamb. A staircase in straight flights ascends the jamb to the first-floor hall. The upper floors, which were both partitioned into two chambers, are now open to the sky. They were reached via a spiral stair in a turret corbelled out in the re-entrant angle, allowing three storeys of further accommodation in the jamb. Only the corbelling remains of round bartizans high up at three corners. Adjacent to the tower is a denuded motte, distinctly square in outline, which excavations have confirmed was raised in the twelfth century.

Access: Exterior at any time. There are periodic open days.
Relations: The Castle of Park.

OTHER SITES *Wigtown*'s early royal castle was successively captured by William Wallace and Robert the Bruce during the Wars of Independence and then destroyed. *Cruggleton Castle* (near Garlieston) suffered the same fate. This seat of the lords of Galloway, on a coastal promontory, is now marked only by the precarious fragment of a later vault. The mottes of *Ardwell*, *Balgreggan* (near Sandhead), *High Drummore* and *Innermessan* demonstrate Norman settlement in Galloway.

The county has the usual mishmash of very ruinous or much-altered tower houses:

Auchness Castle (near Ardwell)
Baldoon Castle (ruin)
Carscreugh Castle (ruin, near Glenluce)
Cassencarie House (ruin, near Creetown)
Castle Stewart (ruin, near Challoch)
Castlewigg (ruin, near Whithorn)
Corsewall Castle (ruin, at Barnhills)
Craighlaw Castle
Killumpha Tower (near Port Logan)
Myrton Castle (ruin, near Port William)
Ravenstone Castle (near Whithorn)
Sinniness Castle (ruin, near Stair Haven)

GLOSSARY

Arrow slits pierce the curtain walls and towers of some of the earlier stone castles, enabling archers to fire on the enemy without. Classic arrow slits are typically tall and narrow (just a few inches wide), as at *Kildrummy* and *Dirleton*. Occasionally there are cross-slits to allow lateral fire (*Skipness*) or fish tails at the base to cover the ground outside more effectively (*Lochindorb*). The embrasure behind the arrow slit had to be tall enough to accommodate an archer or crossbowman and wide enough for him to manoeuvre. No doubt there were more examples before the destruction of so many castles during the Wars of Independence and the later adaptation of others for defence by guns. The later curtain at *Threave* is unusually well provided with arrow slits, but tower houses of the fourteenth and fifteenth centuries generally display a sparing use of shorter slits, which were at least as important for providing a little light and ventilation. With the advent of firearms, arrow slits transitioned to the much more common gunports and shot holes.

Ashlar masonry refers to smooth, finely cut blocks of stone, carefully laid in straight courses. The majority of Scottish castles are built of rubble, but good early examples of ashlar can be found in the mural towers of *Kildrummy* and the keep at *Bothwell*. It also features in a number of later tower houses, notably *Borthwick*.

Attic   It is unusual for a complete Scottish tower house *not* to be surmounted by an attic. Most of the towers that survive intact have that characteristic gabled profile. If no attic now exists, it is more than likely that this relatively vulnerable projection above the wall-head has perished over the course of time. Where older towers are concerned, the attic is invariably an addition of the sixteenth or early seventeenth century, maximising the available space in the tower. Often the attic is recessed within the older parapet – even some new towers of the later sixteenth century followed this arrangement. However, as the use of firearms was making the parapet obsolete, it became common to eliminate it altogether and let the attic rise straight from the wall-head. With the development of the Scottish Baronial style, attics are often enlivened by corner bartizans, dormer windows and crow-stepped gables, as at *Craigievar* and *Crathes*. They provided perfunctory accommodation for servants or a small garrison.

Aumbry   A mural cupboard for storing valuables, often beside the hall fireplace. It is sometimes framed by a delicate Gothic canopy, as in the tower houses at *Borthwick* and *Comlongon*.

Bailey   The earthwork enclosure often accompanying mottes of the Anglo-Norman period and later. They are surrounded by a ditch and often by an earth rampart too, as at the *Mote of Urr*. The perimeter would have been defended by a wooden stockade. For other castle enclosures the term courtyard or barmkin is more generally used in Scotland.

Barbican   An outer extension to a gateway or gatehouse, increasing the number of barriers a besieger had to force his way through. They occur rarely in the relatively simple entrance arrangements of most Scottish castles, except for a handful of very ruinous examples. Long entrance passages with various obstacles were contrived in the sixteenth century at *Blackness* and *Dunnottar*.

Barmkin   The little courtyard that usually accompanied a tower house. It was surrounded by a wall and contained the necessary ancillary buildings. The tower house was situated either on its perimeter or within, thus creating a small-scale concentric defence. *Old Breachacha* and *Auchindoun* provide a good example of each type, with curtain walls that are strong enough to offer effective outer defence. As the tower house became less of a fortress and more of a residence, the barmkin too became more domestic in character, bounded by a series of buildings that doubled up as the curtain. There may be one or two flanking towers, as at *Tolquhon*, which is rare for the conceit of a twin-towered gatehouse rather than a simple gateway providing the way in.

The main characteristic of barmkin walls today is their low survival rate. They may be reduced to a stretch of curtain, an arched gateway or an isolated flanking tower, retained as a dovecote. Many have disappeared completely or been replaced by later buildings of a purely domestic nature. For the enclosures of more extensive castles *see* **Courtyard**.

Bartizans are the small turrets that are corbelled out at the wall-head. They are common at the corners of tower houses and are normally rounded, though square examples can also be found. They may be open to the sky or capped by conical roofs. Although their function is more aesthetic than defensive, they are sometimes pierced by menacing shot holes pointing downwards.

Bastion The term can be used to describe any type of flanking tower but is especially used for the low, angular flankers on artillery defences such as *Eyemouth*.

Battlements *see* **Parapet**.

Caisteal Gaelic for 'castle'. Currently, only a few castles in the Highlands and islands are primarily known by their Gaelic names.

Cannon From primitive beginnings, the science of artillery developed rapidly in the fifteenth century, with the manufacture of long gun barrels and the appearance of iron cannon balls. James II was a devotee of the new weapon and the great cannon Mons Meg, which he received as a gift from the Duke of Burgundy in 1457, can still be seen at *Edinburgh Castle*. James also led the way in beginning a castle at *Ravenscraig* (Fife) with extra-thick walling to withstand bombardment. Mons Meg went on to blast the walls of Norham Castle on the English side of the Tweed in 1513. James himself was felled by a bolt flying from one of these unstable devices at the siege of *Roxburgh* in 1460.

Since castles (in a watered-down form) continued to be built in Scotland throughout the sixteenth century and into the seventeenth, it is surprising how few of them paid much attention to the growing power of artillery. They might well be provided with gunports and shot holes for defence by firearms, but the lofty tower house was no match for the royal cannon. Nor was it intended to be, since the response to artillery required thicker walls and a squatter profile, as demonstrated by the Henrician coastal forts on the south coast of England. This was not conducive with lordly symbolism and there are just a handful of surviving artillery experiments. A massive gun battery was added at *Dunbar Castle* in 1515. *Blackness* and *Craignethan* have unusually thick screen walls, both designed by the king's Master of Works, Sir James Hamilton of Finnart, in the 1530s. The Half Moon Battery at *Edinburgh* is massively thick and with good reason, since its predecessor had been blasted down in the great siege of 1568–73. A few other strongholds, such as *Eilean Donan* and *Littledean*, have modest gun batteries.

Serious fortifications of the time, such as the forts raised by the English during their invasion of 1547, were garrison posts rather than residences. They adopted the new Italian system of thick earth ramparts to cushion the impact of enemy fire, with large arrow-head bastions providing gun emplacements. *Eyemouth Fort*, strengthened by the French in 1557, is the best survivor. The principles still applied when *Edinburgh*, *Stirling* and *Dumbarton* castles were converted into Hanoverian fortresses during the Jacobite period.

Cannon spouts, which appear on the roof line of many later tower houses, are like gargoyles insofar as they discharge water from the roof but are decoratively shaped like cannon.

Caphouse A small, usually gabled structure appearing above the parapet of many later tower houses, as at *Amisfield*. They are often placed at the top of the spiral staircase.

Captain *see* **Constable**.

Castle The term derives from the Latin *castellum*, meaning 'little fort'. Its restriction to private strongholds of the Middle Ages is a specialist definition, not embraced by most dictionaries. However, if a suitable word did not exist one would have to be invented. It is best to regard the castle as a fortified house, because the combination of residential and defensive roles is a feature common to most medieval fortifications but not usually to those of earlier and later periods. This does not imply that castles were constantly occupied or that they were intended to be impregnable in the event of siege. Our definition is flexible enough to include those later tower houses that are sometimes dismissed as castles because of their concessions to domestic comfort (though not to every turreted laird's house). Nor is there any size restriction. Castles range from vast complexes such as *Edinburgh* and *Stirling* to the many simple tower houses. Note that in Scotland the title 'castle' is often a modern elevation, supplanting 'tower' or even 'house'.

Chapel Most pre-Reformation castles would have had a chapel but well-preserved examples are few and far between. The little Romanesque chapel in *Edinburgh Castle* is much the oldest. Three lancet windows piercing the thirteenth-century curtain wall at *Kildrummy* suggest a chapel of some elegance, but most later castle chapels tend to be austere structures, sometimes surviving only in part. No doubt they were enlivened by carved woodwork, stained glass and wall paintings, all sadly perished. More sumptuous are the chapels in the residences of the Stewart monarchs: *Rothesay*'s is free-standing, while those at *Linlithgow* and *Falkland* form part of the quadrangle. Unlike some Norman keeps in England, full chapels found no room in the Scottish tower house, though sometimes there is an alcove oratory with a piscina, as at *Affleck*. Lack of space sometimes led to the chapel being built outside the walls, as at *Dunstaffnage*. The triumph of Calvinism in 1560 saw the destruction or secularisation of many private chapels, which explains the dearth of remains. Worship now centred on the parish kirk and other establishments were superfluous, except for James VI's Chapel Royal at *Stirling*. Catholics maintained their own discreet places of devotion.

Concentric castles are those having two parallel lines of defence, the outer wall closely surrounding the inner. In addition to providing a double obstacle against attackers, the inner curtain wall rises higher than the outer so that defenders could fire on the enemy from two levels simultaneously. Furthermore, besiegers who had forced their way into the outer courtyard would find themselves in a narrow space under fire from the parapets on either side. The idea, like so much else, originated in the East and came to western Europe through the Crusades. Scotland has nothing like the concentric castles of Wales, but there are partial concentric defences at *Lochindorb* and *Macduff*'s castles. Furthermore, in some instances the barmkin wall surrounds the tower house quite closely and produces a similar effect, as at *Auchindoun* and *Threave*.

Constable The official in charge of a castle during the owner's absence, often in Scotland styled the keeper or captain. The post tended to become a hereditary right, as with the MacRaes at *Eilean Donan*. Some castles, particularly royal ones, would be occupied by the constable and a small caretaker household for long periods. The constable generally had quarters distinct from the lord's – at *Dunstaffnage*, for example, he occupied the gatehouse.

Corbel A stone bracket projecting from a wall, carrying a roof support or machicolations. Many tower house parapets project over a row of corbels. This is often elaborated into two or three alternating rows. In the south-west there is the alternative of continuous corbelling, where there is no gap between the individual stones. A bartizan supported on successive rows of moulded stonework is described as being 'corbelled-out'.

Courtyard The area enclosed by the rampart or curtain wall, otherwise referred to as the bailey. It was impossible to condense all the necessary accommodation into the keep or tower house, so there was invariably an accompanying courtyard containing ancillary buildings. The modest size of most Scottish courtyards was dictated by their defensive locations on hills or islets, or merely by economic necessity. This compactness could provide a defensive advantage, because they only required a small garrison to defend them. The shape of the courtyard too is often dictated by the terrain. However, as early as the thirteenth century, builders recognised the advantages of a regular layout where possible. This is generally oblong, ideally with corner towers at as *Dunstaffnage* and *Old Inverlochy*, but there are curious circular and triangular plans at *Rothesay* and *Caerlaverock*. Walled courtyards are often empty now but there would have been little open space when they were filled by great hall and kitchen, workshops and stables. This is still evident where these buildings do survive, as at *Craigmillar* and *Crichton*. For the modest walled enclosures accompanying later tower houses, *see* **Barmkin**.

Crenellations Kings gave their approval for private castle building by means of a 'licence to crenellate'. This was a charter permitting a subject to crenellate or fortify his house. Surviving Scottish licences are few compared with England, and they do not always tie in with the probable date of existing buildings (the earliest known is for *Kindrochit* in 1390). On the whole, they seem to have been an unsolicited reward for loyal service rather than a response to an application. *See also* **Parapet**.

Crow steps (or corbie steps) are the little steps forming the edges of gables on later Scottish tower houses and other residential buildings.

Curtain The wall surrounding a courtyard, normally surmounted by a parapet walk. Curtain walls had to be thick enough (generally eight to ten feet) to withstand the pounding of siege engines and high enough (up to thirty feet) to frustrate attempts at scaling them. Early examples were towerless (*Castle Sween*, *Castle Roy*) but, as the thirteenth century progressed, mural towers were often provided to flank vulnerable stretches of wall. In the more advanced castles of the period, such as *Kildrummy* and *Dunstaffnage*, they provided comprehensive fire power along each stretch. Owing to the threat of undermining the curtain was most vulnerable at its base, so the wall often rises from a projecting plinth. Sometimes the curtain and its towers are pierced by arrow slits. There may be windows too, if domestic buildings backed onto the curtain, but this was ill-advised from a defensive point of view unless that particular stretch was inaccessible from outside owing to steep falls.

Curtains raised after the Wars of Independence could still be formidable, particularly where there is only one vulnerable side to defend, as at *Tantallon* and *Stirling*. However, most castles henceforth were tower house dominated, with the curtain very much an outer line of defence. This is particularly true of the barmkin walls attached to later tower houses, which were usually quite modest in height, inadequately flanked by one or two turrets and entered through a simple gateway. Despite the frequent use of shot holes and gunports, there were only sporadic attempts to make curtains resistant to the increasing power of artillery (*Ravenscraig* in Fife, *Craignethan*). This demonstrates the defensive limitations of most later Scottish castles.

Dais The dais end of the great hall is the end where the lord's table was situated. It is often where the fireplace is located.

Ditch *see* **Moat**.

Dovecote The dovecote (or doocot) is a common sight in Scotland and quite a number are in or close to a castle. Many are of the classic beehive type, like *Dirleton* and *Dunure*. Where a barmkin flanking tower has survived it is generally because it doubled up as a dovecote.

Drawbridge The drawbridge was an ingenious device, alternating as bridge and barrier. In the thirteenth century the most common variety was the turning bridge, which pivoted half in and half out of the gate passage. When the outer part was raised, the inner part sank into a deep pit, as at *Kildrummy*. This would present a further obstacle to assailants if they succeeded in smashing their way through. A later method involved a pair of wooden beams above the gateway, which raised the drawbridge when their inner halves were lowered. Recesses for these beams are still visible at *Linlithgow* and elsewhere, while *Cawdor* has a late but still surviving example. A drawbridge was never long enough to span the full width of the ditch or moat, so its outer end would have connected with an abutment from the far side.

Doune had no drawbridge but merely a double yett, presumably to avoid the inconvenience of raising equipment cluttering the lord's hall above the gate passage. Such iron gates became the standard defence in later barmkins, though a little drawbridge sometimes barred the way into the tower house. At *Borthwick* it crossed the chasm between the portal and the parapet of the curtain wall.

Dun Generic term for an ancient fortification, such as a hillfort or broch. Some castles occupy older sites and the prefix 'dun' is a common one – as at *Dundonald*.

Ecclesiastical fortifications Despite the wars that often resulted in abbeys and cathedrals being pillaged, Scotland had few fortified churches or monasteries. The cathedral monastery at *St Andrews* is surrounded by a towered precinct wall longer than some town walls. *Arbroath* and *Crossraguel* abbeys have both a tower house and a defensible gatehouse, the latter also a feature at *Pittenweem Priory*. A defensive bell tower is attached to *Dysart Old Church*. Episcopal castles such as *Carnasserie*, *Spynie* and *St Andrews* are indistinguishable from those of secular lords.

Edwardian Where castles are concerned this term refers to the reign of Edward I of England (1272–1307). It represents the apogee of medieval military architecture in Britain, when castles are distinguished by their high, thick curtain walls, round flanking towers and twin-towered gatehouses. Edward and his barons erected some splendid examples of the style to overawe conquered Wales. Ironically, the cost of the Welsh building programme drained the royal coffers, so by the time Edward marched north he could only construct forts of earth and timber. In any case, Scotland was never sufficiently subdued to create the conditions necessary for undisturbed construction, though baronial castles such as *Old Inverlochy* and *Lochindorb* show a familiarity with Edwardian principles.

Embrasure   An opening through a wall; i.e. the recess behind a window or arrow slit.

E-plan refers to a tower house with projecting jambs at either end of one side.

Fireplaces increasingly abounded in tower houses and domestic buildings, as attested by chimneys rising above the wall-head where they survive. Sometimes there are impressive rows as at *Birsay* and *Muchalls*, attesting the many individual fireplaces within. The huge, segmental arch of the kitchen fireplace is a common sight, as is the long lintel of the hall fireplace (most spectacularly at *Linlithgow*). In courtyard halls the central hearth with a 'louvre' in the roof long persisted, though *Stirling*'s massive great hall has five fireplaces to heat it!

Garden   A garden was a common amenity beyond the barmkin, though the only significant survivor is the ornamental garden wall at *Edzell*. A formal Jacobean garden has been recreated here and there is another on a grander scale at *Drummond*.

Garrison   It is a misconception to imagine castles as filled permanently with armed retainers. In times of peace a large garrison would be an unnecessary and costly conceit. Even in wartime, too large a garrison could be a liability, consuming provisions without contributing effectively to defence. This is particularly true of the many tower houses. A castle required enough men – mostly archers – to maintain a healthy resistance from the wall-head and arrow slits. In later times that translated to gunners and gunports. Records are sketchy and we know more about the English garrisons that were ousted during the Wars of Independence and later. Fighting men formed just part of a castle's complement. We should remember the stewards, blacksmiths, administrators, stablers, carpenters and watchmen who were vital members of the establishment.

During the Jacobite period there were more regular garrisons of professional soldiers. The Earl of Breadalbane built barracks at *Kilchurn* to house his private army. *Edinburgh*, *Stirling* and *Dumbarton* castles all became Hanoverian fortresses, with outposts in the adapted tower houses of *Braemar* and *Corgarff*. Coastal defence brought military occupation to *Blackness* and *Broughty*, while *Stirling* remained a barracks until 1964.

Gatehouse   The most vulnerable parts of any fortification are its entrances. The earlier walled enclosures of Scotland, such as *Castle Sween* and *Old Inverlochy*, have simple gateways through the curtain wall. As the thirteenth century neared its end Scotland adopted the 'B-plan' gatehouses that had recently come to maturity in England and Wales, where a pair of round-fronted towers flank a long entrance passage containing portcullises and draw-barred doors. Hence, the gatehouse did not so much evolve in Scotland as arrive at its apogee. *Caerlaverock* and *Urquhart* are the two best-preserved examples, though both were much rebuilt to their original design later on. *Kildrummy* must have been one of the finest but has been reduced to its base. Fragments of others can be found at *Bothwell*, *Buittle*, *Dundonald* and *Morton*. This sophisticated type of gatehouse almost died out after the Wars of Independence. There were occasional revivals in the sixteenth century, more for aesthetic appeal than defensive strength, at *Stirling*, *Falkland*, *Fyvie*, *Tolquhon* and *Dudhope*. A few gatehouses are oblong blocks with a single flanking tower, akin to L-plan tower houses, as at *Doune* and *Sanquhar*.

The other standard type of gatehouse, a single tower with a gate passage running through its lowest storey, is not much better represented. There are thirteenth-century prototypes at *Rothesay* and *Ardrossan*. *Tantallon* and *St Andrews* have fine gate towers of the fourteenth century. *Crichton*'s fifteenth-century gatehouse is a massive oblong block, while James IV's new gatehouse at *Rothesay* is conspicuous for its extended gate passage. At three of the examples cited the gate arches were later blocked to create standard tower houses unencumbered with winding gear, a new and simple entrance gateway being inserted through the curtain close by. Later gatehouses tend to be simple oblongs, as at *Drummond* or the Portcullis Gate in *Edinburgh Castle*.

Scotland on the whole is conspicuous for its shortage of true gatehouses. After the Wars of Independence, with the barmkin of secondary importance to the tower house, the simple gateway made a comeback, often enjoying some protective cover from overhead machicolations or nearby flanking towers, as at *Threave* and *Burleigh*. Where there is a residential range against the barmkin wall, the gate passage runs through it, as at *Balvenie*, *Edzell* and even *Linlithgow*. The age of the drawbridge and portcullis had come to an end and these gateways were typically closed by double yetts, still surviving at *Balvenie* and *Doune*.

For gatehouses fulfilling some of the functions of a keep, *see* **Keep-gatehouse**.

Gunports first appear in English fortifications in the late fourteenth century; they filtered through to Scotland during the fifteenth. The earliest examples are probably at *Craigmillar* and *Threave*. These early gunports resemble an inverted keyhole, consisting of a small, circular opening for the gun and a slit for sighting above. Sometimes there is a second opening at the top for better sighting, giving a dumbbell shape. The lower opening is just above floor level because early cannon had no mountings. The guns of the era were not very powerful weapons and their range was extremely limited. Wide-mouthed (or letterbox) gunports, permitting a broader range of fire, first appeared on the new gun battery at *Dunbar* in 1515 and are a common sight thereafter, often being inserted through older masonry. They are generally used sparingly, to guard the approaches and the vulnerable entrance, but there are unusual concentrations at *Claypotts*, *Elcho* and, above all, *Noltland*. Firing primitive cannon in the confined space of a vaulted guardroom must have been a very unpleasant experience and hazardous as well! *See also* **Shot holes**.

Hall The hall was the centre of medieval domestic life. Lordly houses typically consisted of a 'great' or main hall, flanked on one side by the owner's private chamber (solar) and on the other by a group of service rooms, notably the kitchen. This plan might be elaborated with additional private rooms and a chapel beyond the solar. This standard layout was not always strictly adhered to, particularly in a castle where defensive considerations might modify the plan. The components of the manor house were often up-ended into a keep or tower house, with the hall usually at first-floor level. Most surviving Scottish halls are actually within tower houses, though in the smaller examples they are unassuming little spaces. In some tower houses the hall level is higher than the others and crowned by a barrel vault, creating a surprisingly noble chamber, whether at *Dean* in the fourteenth century, *Borthwick* in the fifteenth or *Craigievar* in the sixteenth. In other cases, however, rows of corbels or joist holes show that what looks like a lofty chamber today was once divided into two by a wooden floor. The hall also tended to be better lit than the other floors. Sometimes the undercroft below is interpreted as a lower or 'laigh' hall for retainers.

In many cases the hall inside the tower remained the great hall, because the tower house remained the principal accommodation. However, greater lords often sought to move to more spacious accommodation. When residential buildings did escape into the courtyard, they were placed against the curtain wall where the castle is least vulnerable – the side overlooking a river or a steep drop if possible. Windows could then be cut through the curtain with less loss of security. The hall itself was the largest of the castle's domestic buildings. It was the centre of administration and justice, as well as being the chief dining area. The lord and his personal household occupied a platform (dais) at the solar end of the hall, while the rank and file sat on benches below. Many retainers actually slept in the hall. Heating was increasingly provided by means of fireplaces, though the traditional hearth in the middle of the floor was sometimes preferred, smoke escaping through a hole or 'louvre' in the roof. The main entrance to the hall was located at the service end. Draughts were kept at bay to some extent by a long wooden screen. Most courtyard halls in Scotland are integrated with other domestic buildings, standing above the kitchen and other vaulted undercrofts.

The courtyard buildings were as much a part of a castle as the fortifications but, in many cases, they have vanished or are fragmentary, leaving only a defensive shell. Needless to say, the outer walls were stouter and therefore more likely to last. Furthermore, it is clear that many domestic buildings were of timber, and these have never survived. Nevertheless, some fine courtyard halls still remain. Much the grandest are the royal halls at *Edinburgh*, *Stirling* and *Linlithgow*, but there are good Baronial examples at *Doune*, *Bothwell*, *Castle Campbell* and *Newark* (Renfrewshire). The oldest is the twelfth century hall undercroft at *Kirkwall*, followed by the mysterious, subterranean Goblin Hall at *Yester*. The halls at *Edinburgh* and *Darnaway* preserve their hammerbeam roofs. In castles that have matured into later mansions, such as *Blair* (Perthshire), the hall often remains the principal room, though transformed by later fashion and rebranded the dining room or drawing room.

Hall house   An early form of Scottish castle was a strongly built hall raised over an undercroft. A number of these hall houses in the west probably date from the thirteenth century. They are mostly badly ruined, though *Lochranza* remains a good example. *Rait* and *Old Tulliallan* are more sophisticated fourteenth-century versions of the theme, while tower houses such as *Dundonald* and *Craignethan* are more akin to hall houses in the emphasis they give to the hall. Some other tower houses demonstrate at least a pause in building above the hall, implying that they were in effect hall houses until their upper storeys were added, as at *Alloa*.

Harling is a rough-cast wall finish. The re-harling of many towers in recent times is authentic and protective, but can look jarringly new. Bright colouring is not to everyone's taste but may be preferable to iron grey.

Hoarding   A covered wooden gallery was sometimes positioned in front of the battlements, with holes in the floor through which assailants could be observed and fired upon. Putlog holes can sometimes be seen in the masonry for the beams that supported these hoardings, as at *Threave* and *Hermitage*. Inevitably, such structures were vulnerable to fire, so the hoarding was sometimes superseded by stone machicolations.

Inscriptions   From the late sixteenth century we are often enlightened by a heraldic panel above the entrance to the tower house or barmkin, giving the initials of the laird and his lady and a year that may signify the beginning or completion of work. Years are often inscribed on dormer windows too. However, caution is required as they may commemorate repairs or a year of particular significance to the family. Occasionally the builder is more forthcoming, supplying names and specific dates as at *Muchalls* and *Tolquhon*, while the laird of *Muness* turns to verse. At *Huntly Castle* the Marquis of Huntly shouts from the rooftops with a big inscription at the wall-head. Family mottos and religious admonitions are also encountered.

Islands in lochs or off the coast provide a natural defence for some castles. Island strongholds such as *Eilean Donan*, *Castle Stalker* and *Kisimul* are among the most photogenic. Other important castles occupying islets include *Lochindorb*, *Lochleven*, *Innis Chonnell* and *Threave*. *Kilchurn* and *Rosyth* used to be on islands before land reclamation. *Loch Doon Castle* was moved stone by stone in 1935 when its islet site was threatened. Few castles have been proved to stand on those ancient, artificial islets known as crannogs.

Jamb   The projecting wing of an L-plan or T-plan tower house.

Keep   Many castles have one tower dominating the rest. Depending on the size of the castle it may be the only tower, or the chief tower of many. This is the keep, donjon or great tower. Usage has long labelled as tower houses the many Scottish 'keeps' built in the centuries after the Wars of Independence, so they have a separate entry, but pre-war keeps are covered here.

Scotland has very few of the square-plan or oblong-plan keeps so common in Norman England, and certainly nothing on a grand scale. Those Norman keeps date mainly from the twelfth century, when castle masonry is scarce in Scotland. The only exception is in the far north, where *Cubbie Roo's Castle* in the Orkneys has at its base a small tower built by a Norse settler. The *Castle of Old Wick* in Caithness may be another. They are only keeps in a rudimentary sense. Moving into the early thirteenth century, there are keep-like towers at *Aberdour* and *Hailes*, both now very ruinous. By the time we reach *Drum* and *Duffus* early in the fourteenth century we are seeing the birth of the tower house.

The thirteenth century saw a small group of cylindrical keeps, their shape dictated by the same reasons that produced round or round-fronted flanking towers. A few of them – such as *Dunstaffnage* and *Old Inverlochy* – are only deemed to be keeps insofar as they are a bit larger than the other towers, while *Dirleton*'s D-shaped 'keep' is merely the largest tower still surviving there. *Kildrummy* would have had the tallest of the group but is sadly reduced to its base. That leaves *Bothwell*, which is still impressive despite half of it being torn down during the Wars of Independence. Other castles followed the thirteenth-century trend of being totally keep-less, with either no towers or towers of equal size, though some (such as *Loch Doon*) are so small that they might be regarded as an English-style shell keep.

Keep-gatehouse   The entrance to a castle is often situated beside the commanding presence of a keep or tower house. It was a logical step to combine these two structures, enabling the lord or his deputy to maintain control over the gateway in times of danger. In Scotland the gatehouse was an English import of the late thirteenth century, during which time there was a short-lived enthusiasm (mostly in Wales) for keep-gatehouses. A characteristic of the fully developed keep-gatehouse is that the inner gates were barred from the gate passage, not the courtyard, so that the building could be isolated from the rest of the castle if the need arose. The living accommodation lay on the upper storeys, though the floor immediately above the gate passage would be inconvenienced by the portcullis and drawbridge mechanisms. *Caerlaverock* employs some of the principles, while the gatehouse at *Kildrummy* would be a prime example were it not reduced to its footings. Because of the domestic inconvenience, keep-gatehouses never became popular, but elements of the theme later re-appeared from time to time, as at *Tantallon, Doune, Crichton, Rothesay* and *Falkland*.

Kitchens, with their huge arched fireplaces, can be impressive in their own right. In England, the kitchen was usually placed at a safe distance from the great hall to minimise the risk of fire spreading. In Scotland, the ubiquitous barrel vault was trusted to contain the fire, so in courtyard castles the kitchen is generally one of the undercrofts beneath the hall. Occasionally the kitchen occupies a mural tower, as at *Doune* and *Linlithgow*. In tower houses there is no standard position. They often fill the ground floor of smaller towers, while in larger ones they occupy one of the undercrofts linked by a corridor. Where the hall is on the second floor, the kitchen may be on the floor below, as at *Lochleven* and *Threave*. However, sometimes the kitchen is more conveniently placed at the level of the hall, either partitioned off at one end or in the jamb of an L-plan tower house. There are occasional 'kitchenettes' squeezed into mural chambers. Serving hatches for the quick delivery of food are common.

Lairds' houses, which are characteristic of the late sixteenth and seventeenth centuries, are not within the scope of this book but there is no absolute distinction between them and tower houses. They employ a lot of the same Scottish Baronial features but are generally lower and more domestic in nature. They are included if they are particularly well provided with shot holes, like the *House of Schivas*.

Lancet A narrow window with a pointed head. Though more typical of early Gothic architecture, in Scotland they are often employed later, as in the chapel at *Linlithgow*.

Latrines in castles are often called 'garderobes', though that term literally means a wardrobe. Castles are surprisingly well equipped with latrines. Often the seat and shaft have disappeared but any wall passage coming to a dead end is likely to have been one. Unless the chute could be positioned directly over a river, it discharged into the ditch or a cesspit, which would have to be cleaned out from time to time!

L-plan refers to a tower house with a projecting jamb on one side.

Machicolations feature on some Scottish castles. They are a reworking in stone of the wooden hoardings described above. The parapet projects out from the wall face on corbels and in the gap between each corbel is a hole through which objects could be dropped onto the enemy. Sometimes only the corbels survive. At *Craigmillar* the entire curtain wall and its corner towers are machicolated, but that is a unique extravagance. Some whole towers (*Borthwick*, *Comlongon*, *Mearns* and the Laigh Tower at *Dean*), along with the gatehouses of *Caerlaverock* and *Crichton*, have similar machicolated crowns. They influenced the many towers that have parapets projecting on corbels but are not in fact machicolated. More common is the single box machicolation that appears high up over many a gateway and tower house entrance.

Master mason   The role of master mason is synonymous with that of the modern-day architect. Often we do not know who the architect was, as even in later times the records are scanty. Alexander III's master mason Richard Cementarius may have built the early tower house at *Drum*. The Savoyard master James of St George, renowned for his Welsh castles, worked on the wooden fort at *Linlithgow* (which must have been something of a come-down for him). Henri Merlzioun, who designed the revolutionary castle at *Ravenscraig* in Fife for James II, was French. A whole legend has been woven around Thomas (or Robert) Cochrane, the master mason who supposedly became a friend of James III and was hanged (along with other low-born favourites) in 1482. By the sixteenth century we know more names: Thomas Leiper and several members of the Bell family were active in the north-east, while Andrew Crawford built the handful of castles in the Northern Isles. A silent witness to the master masons and their teams are the masons' marks they have left on many a block of stone, identifying (back then) the mason responsible. Where these marks are consistent throughout, as they are in the tower house at *Borthwick*, they suggest a single, uninterrupted building campaign.

Mines were dug to undermine castle walls and counter-mines were dug to intercept them. Both mine and counter-mine can be explored at *St Andrews Castle*, a reminder of the great siege of 1546–47 (*see* **Sieges**).

Moat   The moat surrounding a castle was as vital for defence as the curtain wall or rampart bank. Indeed, it is the combination of the two that made defence credible. A wall is vulnerable on its own because, without a moat in front, there is little to prevent attackers and their siege engines getting close. It should be emphasised that moats do not have to be wet and most Scottish castles, being situated on elevated ground, made do with a dry ditch on the side or sides that were not protected naturally by steep falls. A ditch with steep sides is just as effective a barrier. In Scotland the only moats still water-filled are at the low-lying castles of *Caerlaverock* and *Rothesay*. There are also the natural moats protecting castles on islets in lochs (*see* **Islands**).

Mote *see* **Motte**.

Motte   The flat-topped mound forming the citadel of many earthwork castles. Mottes are not as common in Scotland as they are in England but, since they were the staple fortification of the Norman and Flemish settlers invited to Scotland by David I, a number survive. They are particularly concentrated in the areas they settled most: the south-west (where they are called 'motes') and, to a lesser extent, the north-east. Local rulers such as the lords of Galloway responded quickly with mottes of their own. They were relatively cheap and easy to construct – especially with a force of pressed labour – but it is wrong to imagine them as the product of a few days' work. Excavations have shown how mottes were gradually built up, layer upon layer, and sometimes heightened at a later date. They have also demonstrated that, in Scotland, mottes continued to be raised well into the thirteenth century. Scotland's rugged terrain often provided a ready-made mound that just required scarping and shaping. An extreme is *Dumbarton*, with two unequal peaks that might be regarded as a natural motte-and-bailey castle on a gigantic scale! However, appearances can be deceptive: the supposed Motte of Tillydrone in Old Aberdeen proved on excavation to be an ancient burial mound.

Many of these earthworks moulder away on farmland or are camouflaged by dense foliage. Nevertheless, some good examples are readily accessible. The classic motte is tall and conical, as demonstrated at the *Bass of Inverurie* and the *Mote of Urr*. However, many mottes were never raised to such a height, resulting in a lower mound with a relatively large summit. Nor are they all circular or oval in plan – several in Scotland have a distinctly square outline. The motte was invariably surrounded by a ditch or a wet moat. It was the earthwork counterpart of the stone keep – on its summit would typically be a palisade and a wooden tower. In England there were invariably one or more accompanying baileys, the narrow confines of the motte top being insufficient to accommodate a garrison and horses. However, some Scottish examples curiously exhibit no trace of any outer enclosure.

Unlike England, few of Scotland's stone castles occupy motte-and-bailey sites. Sometimes there is an older motte nearby. Stone keeps could not safely be erected on top of artificial mounds because of their immense weight, as demonstrated at *Duffus* where the later tower house has gradually subsided. The relatively low motte at *Buittle* carries fragments of a later curtain wall, while *Huntly Castle* eschews the motte but occupies the adjacent bailey.

Murder holes are openings in a vaulted roof through which unpleasant surprises could be dropped on the heads of assailants. Blocks of stone would have been the most likely weapon, not the boiling oil of popular imagination. They are found in the vault of a gate passage or a tower house entrance.

Oriel   A delicate, projecting window, as at *Huntly Castle* and *Linlithgow*.

Parapet   The wall shielding defenders on the wall walk. In a medieval fortification defence was conducted primarily from the wall-head, so battlements (or crenellations) were a feature of the earliest stone castles. Battlements are divided into two parts: the solid bits (merlons) shielding the defenders and the gaps (crenels) from which they could fire at the enemy. Since they are inevitably the weakest part of the wall, battlements rapidly succumb to decay. Often they have disappeared or been rebuilt – the earliest examples are the walled-up ones visible at *Rothesay*, followed by the well-preserved tower house parapet at *Drum*. While a number of tower houses are crowned by embattled parapets, it is curious to note that some (even *Borthwick*) have plain parapets *without* crenels.

The parapet of many tower houses projects out on one or more rows of corbels and rounds into bartizans at the corners. In a few cases these corbels support machicolations. By the sixteenth century there was invariably an attic at the top of the tower, either recessed within the parapet or eliminating the parapet entirely, since wall-head defence had largely given way to gunports near ground level.

Pele house   *see* **Stronghouses**.

Plinth   A sloping projection at the base of a wall. This is a common feature giving greater stability, but in fortifications it strengthened the base against undermining. Furthermore, objects thrown from the battlements could ricochet dangerously onto a besieging force.

Portcullis   One of the standard defensive features of an entrance, the portcullis was a grille that could be lowered to block the entrance passage. Usually, it was made of wood but reinforced with metal strips. Raising and lowering was accomplished by means of a windlass located in the chamber above the gate passage. You can often see the grooves into which the portcullis slotted. This applies not only to gateways and gatehouses but to keep and tower house entrances too (as at *Bothwell* and *Duffus*). In later castles the portcullis was usually supplanted by the less awkward yett.

Postern In addition to the gatehouse, castles were often provided with one or more subsidiary entrances. The postern (or sallyport) takes the form of a small gateway through the curtain wall or a flanking tower. Convenience of access may have been a factor, but their defensive purpose was to act as outlets for counter-attacking the enemy. We can discern a typical dilemma in the provision of posterns, for while they were ideal for aggressive defence, they also presented the besieger with a comparatively easy way in.

Prisons are much more common in Scottish than in English castles, reflecting the greater life-and-death jurisdiction exercised by Scottish lairds. But they were temporarily holding places for prisoners pending trial, not the 'oubliettes' of popular imagination. There is a tendency to misrepresent any dimly lit undercroft as a dungeon when it was really just a storeroom. In earlier castles the base of a mural tower formed a convenient prison, as at *Kildrummy*. *Hailes* has the first example of a pit prison, reached only from above through a hatch. Pit prisons are common in tower houses, whether forming small mural chambers reached from a passage above or in the base of the jamb of an L-plan tower. *Threave* has an unusually large one. High-ranking prisoners would have enjoyed somewhat better conditions, such as Mary Queen of Scots at *Lochleven*. The Vaults at *Edinburgh Castle* were later used to house prisoners of war, while the *Castle of St John* became the local jail.

Putlog holes are sometimes visible in the masonry. They received the ends of wooden beams that supported scaffolding during initial construction, or (if just below the parapet) a hoarding.

Quadrangular castles On the whole, Scottish courtyard castles are laid out irregularly to follow the terrain. However, in the thirteenth century castle builders began to recognise the advantages of a simple, roughly oblong layout, in which the curtain wall could be effectively flanked by a minimal number of towers (generally one at each corner). This is demonstrated at *Lochindorb*, *Old Inverlochy* and in the curious triangular variant at *Caerlaverock*. After 1300 the majority of new English castles were distinguished by their quadrangular plans with corner towers of equal status. In Scotland, even when the layout is roughly quadrangular, the dominant tower house and the sparing use of mural towers leads to a more irregular effect, as at *Crichton*. *Craigmillar* with its corner turrets is an exception and there are later quadrangles on the English model at *Boyne* and *Fyvie*. *Linlithgow* is a royal palace quadrangle with a defensive glower to the outside world; those at *Edinburgh* and *Stirling* are securely positioned well inside the outer walls.

Rampart A wall of earth, originally with a palisade on top. Earthwork castles usually have a rampart immediately behind the ditch.

Re-entrant angle   The internal angle between the main block of an L-plan tower house and its jamb. In later examples, it is often occupied by a stair turret.

Roof   Original wooden roofs cover tower houses such as *Alloa* and *Claypotts*, but they are uncommon in Scotland's challenging climate. Only two hall roofs still retain many of their original timbers, at *Edinburgh* and *Darnaway*. They are fine hammerbeam structures, showing that Scotland did not lag behind in skilled carpentry. Not many original wooden ceilings have survived but several tower houses (such as *Delgatie*, *Crathes* and *Huntingtower*) preserve painted beamed ceilings of the late sixteenth century. The artistic standard may not be high but the effect is very colourful and the cartoon-like depictions of mythological or allegorical figures are charming. Conversely, there is no doubting the artistry of a generation later in the plaster ceilings of *Craigievar*, *Glamis*, *Muchalls* and *Thirlestane*. See also **Vaults**.

Royal castles   Some of the early castles destroyed during the Wars of Independence were royal strongholds. The only two to preserve any standing masonry are the simple walled enclosures at *Banff* and *Kinclaven*. In ensuing centuries, Scottish monarchs had direct control over fewer castles than their English counterparts (who garrisoned *Roxburgh Castle* as an English outpost for over a century). The list of royal castles varies over time, but the most important – where the monarch was likely to be when not on progress, out campaigning, a prisoner in England or an exile in France – were *Edinburgh*, *Stirling* and *Linlithgow*. These are all central Scottish locations that were as much palaces as castles. Successive Stewart rulers contributed to their fabric. James IV and V created new palaces with residual defensive features at *Falkland* and *Holyrood*.

The other castles actually built by Scottish kings are modest in comparison but sometimes innovative for their time. Robert the Bruce himself added the outer courtyard at *Tarbert*. Early tower houses at *Lochleven* and *Dundonald* are attributed to David II and Robert II. James II began the early artillery fortification at *Ravenscraig* in Fife, while James IV contributed to older castles at *Dumbarton*, *Dunbar* and *Rothesay*. Another artillery defence was attempted by James V at *Blackness*. In some cases their purpose was primarily military, though they could accommodate the royal retinue when required. Several of these castles are in the west, reflecting the royal preoccupation with bringing island clans to heel.

Scottish Baronial is the term – coined much later on – for the architectural style that developed out of French antecedents in the sixteenth century. It features crow-stepped gables, corbelled-out parapets, bartizans with conical roofs, caphouses and dormer windows. They give later Scottish tower houses and contemporary domestic buildings their distinctive and unique profile. The style was revived with even greater intensity in Victorian times.

Shot holes In addition to gunports, small shot holes for handguns are a common feature of later Scottish castles, though their distribution varies from just a couple covering the entrance to more concentrated displays. They most often appear near ground level and high up in bartizans, angled downwards. Sometimes they are placed just below windows, enabling the handler at some personal risk to see what he was shooting at. Shot holes that are triple externally, as at *Tolquhon* and *Muchalls*, allowed a wider field of fire. The ornamental appearance of some shot holes shows a late tendency to embellish even the most utilitarian feature.

Sieges The earliest recorded siege of a Scottish castle is the successful assault on *Rothesay* in 1230, when the Norse invaders hacked through the 'soft' curtain wall with axes. Only *Edinburgh* put up any resistance when Edward I invaded in 1296, but most of the early castles suffered at least one siege during the ensuing Wars of Independence. Some were attacked multiple times: many did not survive this cataclysmic period, as they were destroyed by the Scots themselves to deny their use by the English. This scorched earth policy acknowledged that no fortification was impregnable against an enemy well equipped with manpower and siege engines.

Both English invaders and Scottish opponents had two basic options – direct assault or a slow containment. A blockade would inevitably be successful, sooner or later, if the besieger was strong enough to enforce it. In 1314 the Scots recovered *Stirling Castle* after the English army sent to relieve it was crushed at Bannockburn. However, since a blockade was so time-consuming, direct assaults were often attempted first. Sometimes besiegers would be fortunate enough to succeed without serious fighting – the Scots in particular showed great resourcefulness and cunning against a better-equipped enemy. In 1313 they recaptured *Roxburgh* and *Linlithgow* in stealth attacks that took the garrisons by surprise. Otherwise, the besieger's aim was to penetrate a castle's defences, whether by climbing over, breaking through or undermining. Most methods of attack could not begin until the assailants had reached the base of the wall. This meant that the ditch or moat must first be crossed by erecting a causeway of earth or rocks – a difficult enterprise while being showered with arrows and stones from the battlements and flanking towers.

It was then possible to reach the parapet by means of scaling ladders or siege towers. A forbidding siege tower called the Belfry is mentioned at the English siege of *Bothwell* in 1301, while Sir Andrew Murray employed another to recapture the same castle in 1337. Castle walls at that time could be battered only by rams and catapults. The battering ram, suspended from its protective 'cat', was an effective weapon if it could be sustained for long enough. Catapults had the advantage of being operable from a distance. The arm was pulled back by means of a windlass, then suddenly released to dispatch a boulder with force. A giant sling known as the *trebuchet* had also been perfected by this time. It is likely that the War Wolf brought up to *Stirling* in 1304 was one. Edward I was so determined to try out his new toy that he battered the walls even though the garrison had already offered to surrender.

If other methods failed, the besieger was left with the option of undermining. This entailed digging a tunnel towards the castle walls and excavating a wide hollow beneath the foundations. Tunnel and hollow were supported by wooden props that were then set alight, resulting in the collapse of the wall above. Undermining offered a high chance of success, but it was a difficult process demanding skilled personnel. *St Andrews* preserves the remarkable mine cut out of the rock by the besiegers in 1546, along with the successful counter-mine dug by the defenders to intercept it.

By that time cannon had come along to batter walls more effectively, though castles such as *Threave* (1455), *Roxburgh* (1460) and *Tantallon* (1491) put up a stout resistance against the primitive new weapon. Even as late as 1528 James V's artillery was unable to 'ding doun Tantalloun' (Tantallon), while diehard supporters of Mary Queen of Scots held out in *Edinburgh Castle* for an astonishing five years (1568–73). Nevertheless, by the time of the Civil Wars, Scottish castles were obsolete as fortifications. Only *Huntly Castle* (1647) and *Dunnottar* (1651) emulated the heroic defiance offered by so many English and Welsh castles. They often surrendered after a token bombardment by the Roundheads, as at *Borthwick* (1650). Nor did they distinguish themselves during the successive Jacobite convulsions of 1689–1746, though an abortive attack on *Blair* (Perthshire) by the retreating Jacobite army in 1746 makes it the last British castle to have suffered a siege.

Later tower houses were not intended to withstand anything more formidable than hostile neighbours and bands of marauders. They were only likely to be assailed by an army if they happened to be in the way, as at *Fa'side* in 1547. While many towers never suffered attack, as far as we know, others were remodelled or rebuilt after a predecessor was damaged or destroyed in feuding. The standard method of attack was to light fires against the outer walls to 'smoke out' the occupants. *Merchiston* withstood such an attempt in 1572.

Slighting The process of rendering a fortification untenable to prevent its use by an enemy. This was achieved by breaching walls and undermining towers, or (later) by blowing them up with gunpowder. During the Wars of Independence, Robert the Bruce deliberately razed many castles in the south and centre. The destruction generally seems to have been quite thorough, judging from the paucity of early remains. Border tensions resulted in later demolitions at *Roxburgh* and *Dunbar*. Unlike England, slightings do not figure large in the Civil Wars but some castles, such as *Eilean Donan* and *Inverness*, were blown up during the Jacobite uprisings.

Solar The solar, great chamber or laird's room was the chief or even the only private room of the medieval house, to which the lord and his immediate family could escape from the bustle of the great hall. In the classic manor house plan it was located beyond the dais end of the hall. This layout is normally adhered to in castles with residential buildings in the courtyard, such as *Dirleton* and *Tolquhon*. Sometimes the tower house is in effect a chamber block attached to the hall, as at *Carnasserie* and *Melgund*. In hall houses and elongated tower houses the hall and solar are placed next to each other, the arrangement sometimes being duplicated on the floor above to provide a separate household for the lady of the house or the lord's heir (*Castle Menzies*, *Huntly Castle*). In L-plan towers there was the possibility of keeping the solar at the same level as the hall by placing it in the jamb, especially if there was no higher storey. However, the most common arrangement in tower houses was to locate the solar on the floor above the hall, thus up-ending the standard domestic plan. In larger towers such as *Borthwick* this upper floor might be divided into a solar and another residential chamber. Depending on the height of the tower, there could be one of more storeys of bedchambers above.

Stairs communicate between the different levels of towers or provide access from the courtyard to the wall walk. Straight stairs are often found in the thickness of the wall but the spiral staircase (in Scotland called a turnpike stair) was more practical in towers. It occupies a hollow cylinder, usually positioned at one corner. Each step radiates from a central post or newel. Spiral stairs are often steep and narrow to the point of hazardousness but in larger tower houses they can be quite spacious. Typically, in later L-plan and Z-plan tower houses there is a generous staircase in the jamb up to the first-floor hall, then a narrower stair to the upper floors in a turret corbelled out in the re-entrant angle. From the late sixteenth century there was the alternative of 'scale and platt' stairs ascending in short, straight flights (as at *Scalloway*). Often the steps have long gone, leaving only the empty stair well.

Most spiral stairs in Scotland ascend clockwise. There is a colourful theory that this was a defensive ploy, since attackers fighting their way up the stair would find their sword arms impeded by the newel, whereas defenders could swing theirs freely. On the whole it would be better to keep intruders out, rather than duelling on the stairs, but no doubt there were instances of desperate defence. A more prosaic explanation is that the right-handed majority find it more comfortable to have the newel on the right when ascending.

Stronghouses or pele houses are the equivalent of the bastles on the English side of the Border. These rustic, thick-walled farmhouses are excluded because they can only be classed as defensive in the most rudimentary sense. Anything grander should be considered a tower house, though there is inevitable confusion between the two types, especially with badly ruined buildings. *Littledean* and *Uttershill* are examples of stronghouses that were later upgraded into towers.

Tower house   For keeps built before the Wars of Independence, *see* **Keep**. Later Scottish keeps are usually called tower houses, though there is no fundamental difference in their role. Most Scottish castles built between the fourteenth and seventeenth centuries are first and foremost tower houses, varying greatly in size depending on the resources and accommodation needs of the lord and his retinue. Although most of them had a walled barmkin outside, the outer defences were in most cases decidedly subordinate. Tower houses show a high degree of consistency from the English Border to the Northern Isles but their nature changed radically over this long period. Most were continually occupied and earlier towers often underwent drastic modification later on. Architectural investigations often conclude that supposedly later towers are in fact remodellings of earlier ones, the general principle of builders being 'waste not, want not'. Until the late sixteenth century it is rare to have definitive evidence for the builder. The architectural severity of most tower houses before this period results in a large margin of error and huge disagreement when trying to assign a date.

With these reservations in mind, it seems that *Drum*, *Duffus* and *Hallforest* set the standard early in the fourteenth century. *Lochleven*, *Dean*, *Dundonald*, *Hermitage* and *Threave* are among the most striking from the latter half of that century. These early tower houses are mighty, thick-walled stone boxes with absolutely no frills externally. The windows are often very small (except perhaps for the hall) and the entrance, placed at first or even second-floor level, had to be reached by a removable wooden stair or possibly just a ladder. Only *Dundonald* had a staircase annexe resembling the forebuildings of Norman keeps in England. Nevertheless, these forbidding exteriors conceal some quite handsome living quarters within. Internal arrangements vary considerably, but the manor house was basically up-ended into tower form, with storage on the ground floor, the hall above that and the solar and bedchambers on top. The ground floor was invariably barrel vaulted and there were frequently one or more vaults at higher levels too. Such towers were crowned by a parapet, though in some cases it is a plain wall without crenellations.

Tower houses that probably date from the fifteenth century are four times as numerous and almost as severe. *Borthwick* followed by *Comlongon* are the most impressive, both of these towers being distinguished by machicolated crowns. The sixteenth century saw a gradual mellowing towards the picturesque, turreted, gabled variety, built or remodelled in their hundreds in the last few decades. The advent of firearms saw defence move away from the parapet to gunports or shot holes at ground level. An attic stage was invariably added, either recessed within the parapet or supplanting it completely. The skyline embellishments – corbelled-out parapets, corner bartizans, dormer windows, caphouses and crow-stepped gables – are purely for aesthetic effect and are hallmarks of the Scottish Baronial style, exemplified in such soaring examples as *Amisfield*, *Craigievar* and *Crathes*. Walls got thinner and windows became larger, though barred by iron grilles. By now the entrance was invariably placed at ground level for greater convenience. Vaulting was still common, particularly on the ground floor, primarily to prevent the spread of fire.

Such domestic refinements bring into question the defensive nature of these later tower houses. Despite the presence of wide-mouthed gunports (notably at *Noltland*) they were no match for the growing power of artillery. They can at best be regarded as strong enough to deter bands of marauders and hostile rivals. As the seventeenth century progressed far fewer new buildings can be regarded as genuine tower houses. Admittedly, there is no absolute distinction, but the tower house gradually mellowed into the picturesque but more homely laird's house. Nevertheless, a few undeniable tower houses, such as *Braemar* and *Castle Stuart*, were erected in troubled spots in the 1620s – probably for show or out of deference to tradition. By the time we reach the strange case of *Leslie* in the 1660s, it is starting to look more like revival than survival.

The oblong box without any projections remained a popular type of tower house even in the sixteenth century. However, from the beginning there were permutations to provide more accommodation and improve security. Most common is the L-plan tower house, which has a short wing or 'jamb' projecting from one side of the main block. The first appears to have been the now-buried David's Tower at *Edinburgh Castle*, begun in 1358, but others such as *Dunnottar* and *Neidpath* followed by the end of the century. It became the norm to place the entrance at ground level in the side wing of the jamb, where it could be flanked by the main block, on in the main block where it could be flanked by the jamb. Investigations sometimes show the jamb to be an addition to an older oblong tower. The jamb itself can vary from being a small adjunct containing the spiral stair (*Affleck*) to a large projection as big as the main block itself (*Clackmannan*). From the sixteenth century there is often a stair turret in the re-entrant angle between the main block and the jamb, forming a stepped L-plan (*Craigievar*, *Glamis*). In some cases another tower projects from one of the rear corners of the main block (*Dunderave*, *Killochan*). Occasionally the jamb is semi-circular, at least lower down, as at *Cramond*. Increasingly, in later examples, the jamb flanks two sides of the main block and thus constitutes half a Z-plan (see below). *Castle Levan* and *Dalcross* are extreme examples where the two blocks only connect at adjacent corners. Occasionally the jamb projects from the middle of the main block, giving a T-plan. *Borthwick* pioneered the so-called 'E-plan' (with the middle bar removed), having a jamb at each end of the facade and a recess in between. This form was revived in a handful of late tower houses, such as *Craigston*, *Castle Kennedy* and *Castle Stuart*.

From the mid-sixteenth century there appeared tower houses with projecting towers at diagonally opposite corners, forming the Z-plan. It was a logical evolution from L-plan tower houses with jambs flanking two sides of the main block. The earliest example is possibly *Craigcrook* in the 1540s. The majority of the Z-plan tower houses are to be found in the north-eastern counties. The flanking towers can be round or square, or there may be one of each (sometimes they are of different sizes). The entrance is still invariably flanked by one of the towers. Occasionally a Z-plan was created by adding flanking towers to an oblong tower house, as at *Castle Fraser*. The use of only two flanking towers may suggest economy but is actually more efficient than towers at all corners in an age of firearms, since otherwise gunners would be peppering their own walls. Nevertheless, there are a few examples from the pre-artillery era of the *bastille* plan, with towers at all four corners (*Crookston*, *Hermitage*), while *Elcho* has several projecting towers. The cylindrical keep, popular in the thirteenth century, did not enjoy a revival later on. The only round tower house to survive is that at *Orchardton*, though *Littledean Tower* has a semi-circular gun battery.

While the tower house is typically taller than it is long, there are exceptions at all periods where special prominence is given to the great hall (*Dundonald*, *Craignethan*). From the fifteenth century some tower houses sprouted an adjoining range containing more extensive accommodation, while in the sixteenth century the tower was sometimes built from scratch as the solar wing of an adjoining hall block (*Carnasserie*, *Melgund*). As accommodation requirements grew more ambitious, it was a logical step to build a range of the same height throughout, resulting in some tower houses that are more elongated than the norm. Such structures still tend to be L-plan, with an entrance jamb at one end (*Ferniehirst*), or Z-plan with twin flanking towers (*Castle Menzies*). *Traquair House* has evolved from a simple tower into such a block. Occasionally we find the oddity of two adjacent tower houses, as at *Huntingtower* and the *Old Place of Mochrum*, implying duality in the lordship (laird and heir).

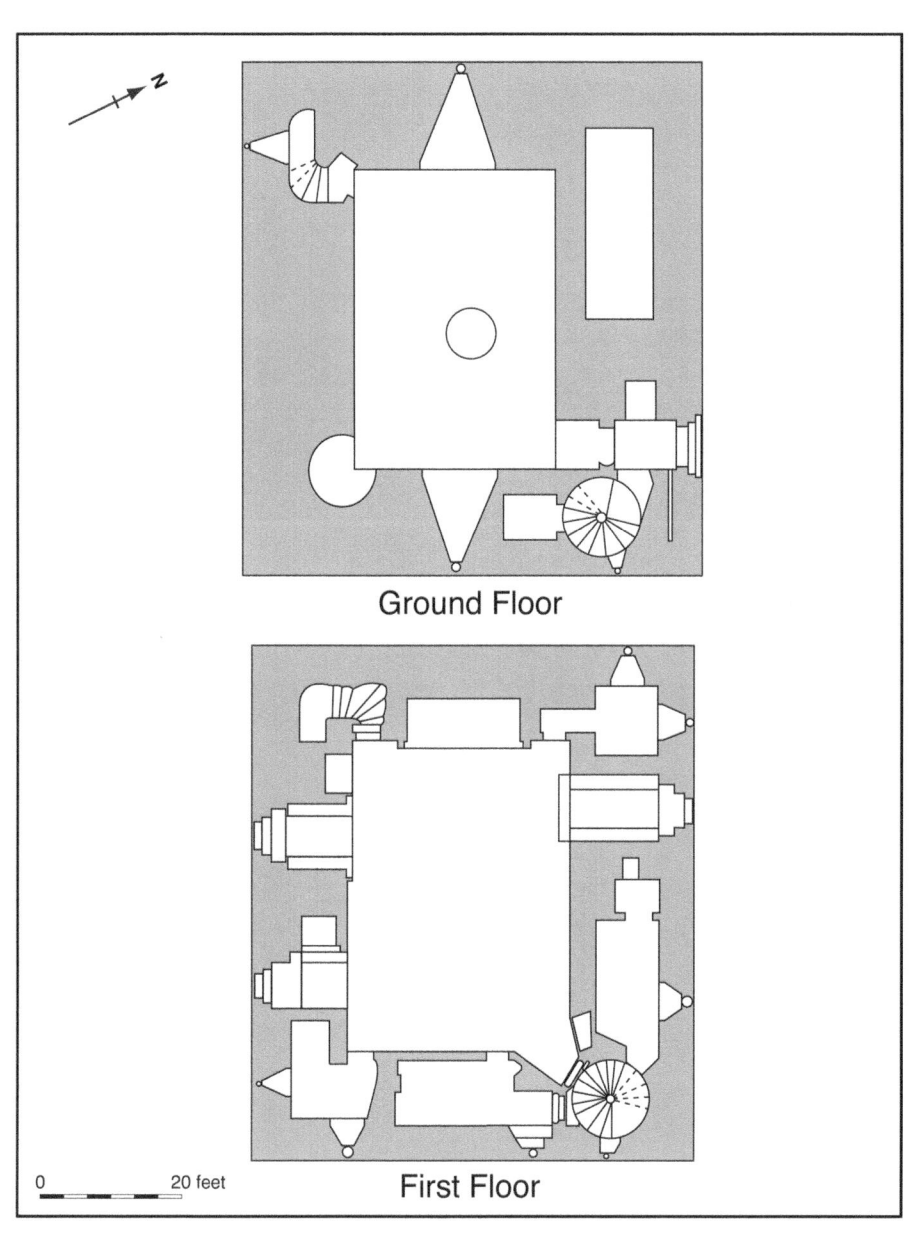

An oblong tower house: Comlongon

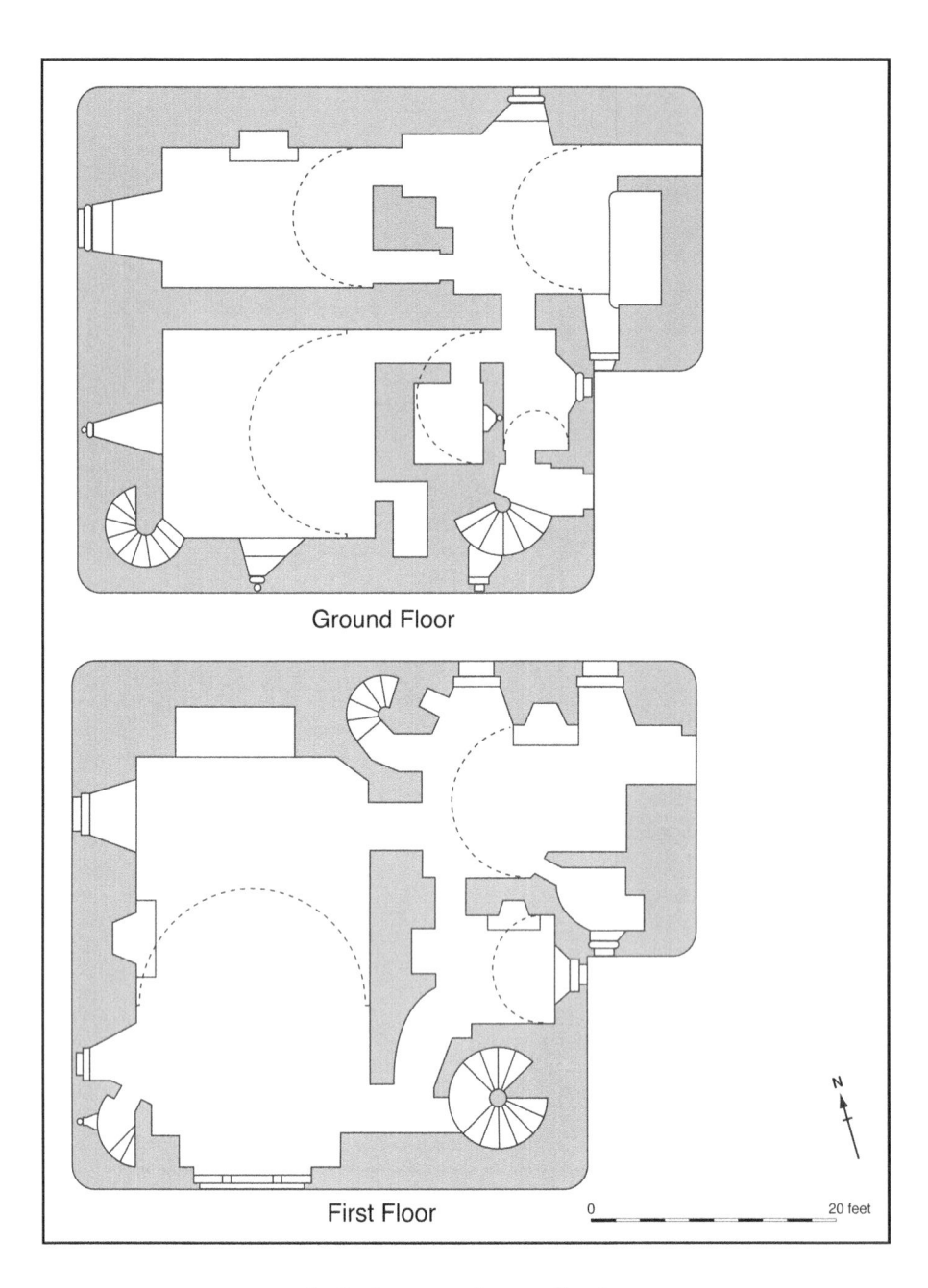

An L-plan tower house: Crathes

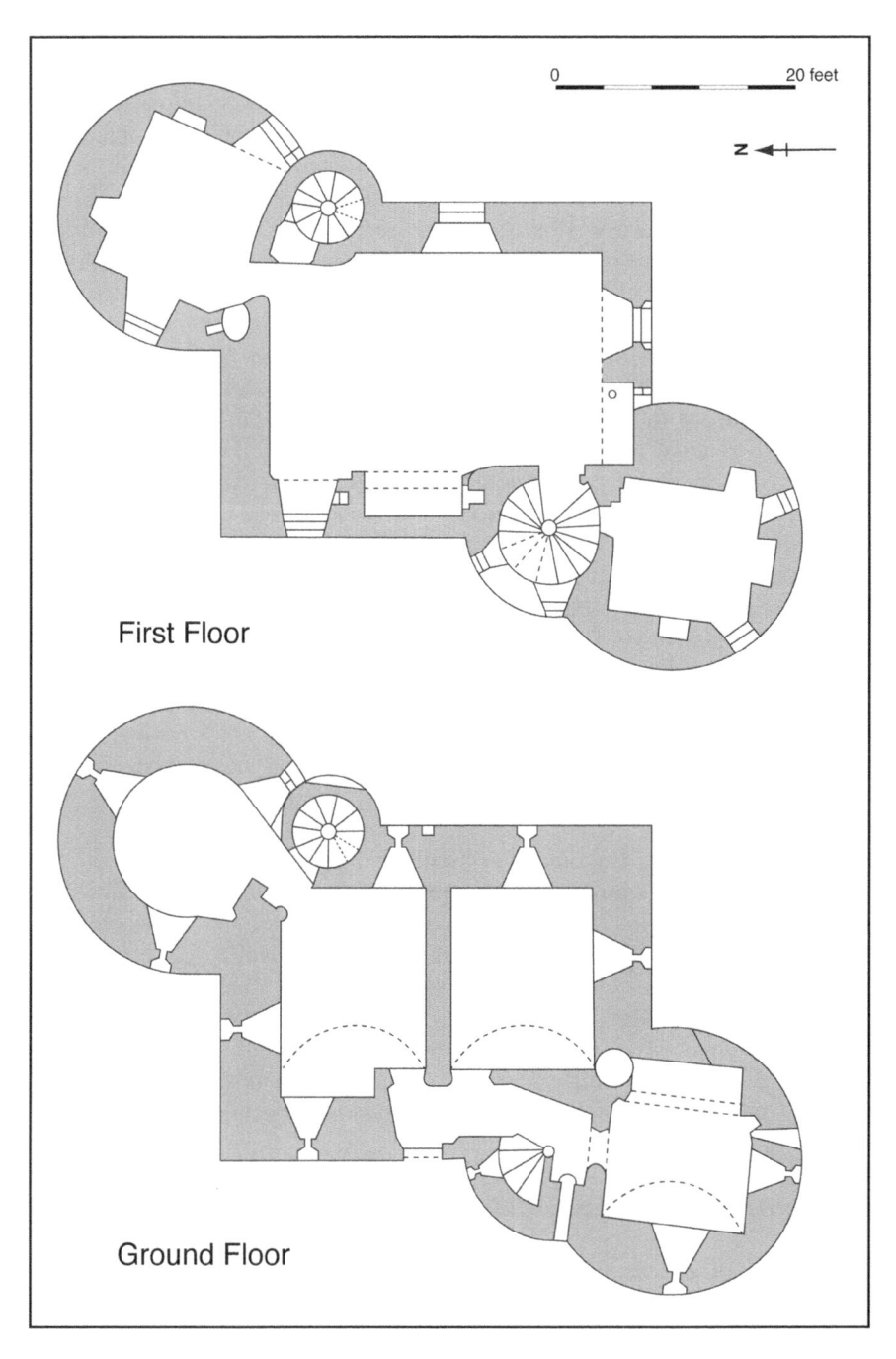

A Z-plan tower house: Claypotts

Towers Mural towers appear from the mid-thirteenth century as a direct import from England, the earliest examples probably being at *Dirleton*. In some cases, as at *Kildrummy* and *Rothesay*, they were early additions to older curtain walls. This was the heyday of the round or semi-circular flanking tower with no vulnerable corners to pick at or undermine. Such towers were placed to flank a curtain comprehensively and provide enfilading fire from the battlements and arrow slits. A regular enclosure – roughly square like *Lochindorb* and *Old Inverlochy*, or even triangular as at *Caerlaverock* – helped minimise the number of towers required. Their interiors also provided some rather spartan accommodation for castle functionaries.

Mural towers were still a feature of courtyard castles such as *Bothwell* and *Tantallon* in the fourteenth century, while slighter versions (with early gunports) guarded the angles of the curtain at *Craigmillar* and *Threave* in the fifteenth century. However, with the subordination of the barmkin to the tower house, they figure rather less in later Scottish castles. It is significant that when *Dirleton* was rebuilt after the Wars of Independence, the flanking towers that had been destroyed were not replaced. Where a barmkin wall survives there is often just one tower at a salient angle, as at *Lochleven* and *Old Breachacha*. *Tolquhon* has two at diagonally opposite corners, no doubt inspired by Z-plan tower houses. The tower house itself rarely doubles up as a flanking tower on the perimeter, being either inside the enclosure or flush with the barmkin wall. Barmkin towers sometimes survive in isolation owing to later use as a dovecote. The majority of these later mural towers are round in plan but, since circular rooms have never been popular, the chambers inside are often tailored to square.

Town walls Unlike England, few Scottish burghs were ever walled in stone. This reflects the poverty of most towns, along with Robert the Bruce's policy of destroying fortifications that could be captured and garrisoned by the English. There are portions of sixteenth-century walled circuits, with occasional flanking turrets, at *Stirling*, *Edinburgh* and *Peebles*. The former has some large gunports, but none are distinguished by their thickness or height. Dundee's town wall is reduced to a single gate arch, while those at *Dunbar* and Perth have vanished entirely. Other towns merely barred the roads leading in with isolated gates, so their value must have been largely symbolic. The only survivor is the West Port at *St Andrews*.

T-plan refers to a tower house with a projecting jamb in the middle.

Undercroft The lowest storey of a tower house was usually barrel vaulted and used as a storeroom or kitchen. In larger towers, and residential buildings generally, there is a row of vaulted undercrofts linked by a corridor. Particularly lofty undercrofts, like those at *Dundonald* and *Threave*, were divided originally into two storeys by wooden floors. Note that undercrofts are usually at ground level, though if the site is sloping they may be partially underground, as at *Craignethan* and *Huntly Castle*.

Vault   An arched ceiling of stone that served to prevent the spread of fire. Their use is much more widespread in Scottish domestic architecture than in English, partly because of the surprising shortage of timber at the time. Unvaulted tower houses like *Merchiston* and *Invergarry* are rare exceptions. Most ground floors of towers and domestic buildings are vaulted and sometimes one or more of the upper floors as well. *Borthwick* is divided into three vaulted stages, two of them subdivided by a wooden floor. Even on the upper storeys, most are plain barrel (or tunnel) vaults of continuous semi-circular section or, less commonly, pointed. More elaborate ribbed vaults can be found at *Old Tulliallan*, *Yester*, *Delgatie* and in the wine cellar at *Linlithgow*, along with the springers for fallen vaults as at *Auchindoun* and *Dundonald*.

Watch towers   Several free-standing towers are rather small to be regarded as fully fledged tower houses and appear to have served as lookout posts, such as *Ardclach* and *Repentance* towers.

Wells   Every castle needed a reliable supply of drinking water, so there was sure to be a well. It might be necessary to dig a long way to reach an underground source of water, so wells can be major engineering achievements in their own right. The well in the courtyard at *Tantallon* extends 100 feet deep. Wells are most often to be found in the undercrofts of mural towers and tower houses. That at *Neidpath* is exceptionally wide, while the wells at *Alloa* and *Lennoxlove* are carried in a shaft up to hall level. Some 'wells' are actually cisterns to collect rainwater, as at *Dunnottar*.

Windows   The provision of windows could seriously weaken a castle, but some were inevitable in a complex that was residential as well as defensive. Even in the thirteenth century, *Bothwell*'s keep was permitted windows to light the great hall and solar, while three chapel lancets compromised the curtain wall at *Kildrummy*. Curtains backing onto domestic buildings were often pierced by window openings, especially if facing inaccessible terrain. For two centuries after the Wars of Independence, tower houses are characterised by slits lower down and plain window openings higher up that do not occupy a very large proportion of the external wall space (as at *Borthwick*). Internally such windows are set in deep embrasures that help the light circulate, often with seats along the sides. Only from the sixteenth century did windows become larger. The original fenestration of many towers is obscured by the later enlargement of windows for greater comfort. Even if they were barred by iron grilles, as at *Elcho*, they demonstrate the limited defensive capabilities of these later tower houses. Most window openings remained simple oblongs, but the arrival of the Renaissance is heralded by architectural frills such as pediments and the dormer windows that enliven many an attic.

Yett   A strong gate resembling a portcullis insofar as it takes the form of an iron grille with interleaving bars. Yetts protected the entrances to tower houses and a number of examples survive *in situ*. There was usually a stout wooden door in front. Increasingly a single or double yett took the place of a portcullis at the entrance to the barmkin – good pairs survive at *Balvenie* and *Doune*.

Z-plan refers to a tower house with flanking towers at diagonally opposite corners.

BIBLIOGRAPHY

The references in the text are intended to provide the best sources of further information, but they are seldom the only ones. They are given below the county introduction where they cover some or all of the castles featured. Sources devoted to an individual castle are shown beneath that entry. Individual guidebooks, ranging from scholarly handbooks to glossy brochures, are available for many of the castles that are open to the public. Historic Environment Scotland has a well-illustrated series.

An important overall source is the *Royal Commission on Ancient and Historical Monuments in Scotland* (RCAHMS in the text). Unfortunately, this survey is far from complete, the level of detail varies tremendously from county to county and some of the volumes are showing their age. The more recent *Buildings of Scotland* series (BoS) covers the whole country but is chiefly architectural in scope. Articles on individual castles appear in various academic periodicals, notably the *Proceedings of the Society of Antiquaries of Scotland* (PSAS). The remarkable five-volume survey of Scottish castles by the Victorian architects MacGibbon and Ross remains a good source for many Scottish castles. More recent gazetteers by Tranter and Salter show the changes – for better and for worse – that have taken place since.

The following list is restricted to the more important works out of the many published. It includes some useful regional guides.

BOOKS

Armitage E. S., *Early Norman Castles of the British Isles* (London, 1912)
Bradbury J., *The Medieval Siege* (Woodbridge, 1992)
Brennan-Inglis J., *Scotland's Castles: Rescued, Rebuilt and Reoccupied* (Stroud, 2014)
Caldwell D. H. (ed), *Scottish Weapons and Fortifications* (Edinburgh, 1981)
Coulson C., *Castles in Medieval Society* (Oxford, 2003)
Coventry M., *Castles of the Clans* (Musselburgh, 2008)
—, *The Castles of Scotland*, 5th edn (Musselburgh, 2015)
Cruden S., *The Scottish Castle*, 3rd edn (Edinburgh, 1981)
Dargie, R., *Scottish Castles & Fortifications* (Thatcham, 2009)
Drahony P. & D., *Angus Castle Trails* (Finavon, 2000)
Fawcett R., *Castles of Fife* (Glenrothes, 1993)
Fenwick H., *Scotland's Castles* (London, 1976)
Fry P. S., *Castles of the British Isles*, 2nd edn (Newton Abbot, 1990)

Grimble I., *Castles of Scotland* (London, 1987)
Hill O., *Scottish Castles of the Sixteenth and Seventeenth Centuries* (London, 1953)
Lindsay M., *The Castles of Scotland* (London, 1986)
MacGibbon D. & Ross T., *The Castellated and Domestic Architecture of Scotland* (Edinburgh, 1887–94) 5 vols
MacKenzie W. M., *The Medieval Castle in Scotland* (Edinburgh, 1927)
Mason G. W., *The Castles of Glasgow and the Clyde*, 2nd edn (Musselburgh, 2013)
Maxwell-Irving A. M. T., *The Border Towers of Scotland: The West March* (Blairlogie, 2000)
McKean C., *The Scottish Chateau: The Country House of Renaissance Scotland* (Stroud, 2004)
Miket R. & Roberts D. L., *The Mediaeval Castles of Skye and Lochalsh* (Portree, 1990)
Morris M., *Castle: A History of the Buildings that Shaped Medieval Britain* (London, 2003)
Reid S., *Castles and Tower Houses of the Scottish Clans* (Oxford, 2006)
Renn D. F., *Norman Castles in Britain*, 2nd edn (London, 1973)
Ross S., *Scottish Castles* (Moffat, 1990)
Salter M., *Castles of Grampian and Angus* (Malvern, 1995)
—, *Castles of Lothian and the Borders* (Malvern, 1994)
—, *Castles of South-West Scotland*, 2nd edn (Malvern, 2006)
—, *Castles of the Heartland of Scotland*, 2nd edn (Malvern, 2007)
—, *Castles of Western and Northern Scotland* (Malvern, 1995)
—, *Discovering Scottish Castles* (Princes Risborough, 1985)
Simpson W. D., *The Ancient Stones of Scotland*, 2nd edn (Edinburgh, 1968)
—, *Castles in Britain* (London, 1966)
—, *Scottish Castles: An Introduction to the Castles of Scotland* (Edinburgh, 1959)
Sorrell A., *British Castles* (London, 1973)
Stell G., 'Castles and Towers in South-Western Scotland', *Transactions of the Dumfriesshire and Galloway Natural History and Antiquarian Society*, vol. 57 (Dumfries, 1982)
Tabraham C. J., *Scotland's Castles* (Edinburgh, 1997)
—, *Scottish Castles and Fortifications* (Edinburgh, 1986)
—, *Scottish Castles: Scotland's Most Dramatic Castles and Strongholds* (London, 2017)
Tabraham C. J. & Grove D., *Fortress Scotland and the Jacobites* (London, 1995)
Toy S., *The Castles of Great Britain*, 4th edn (London, 1966)
Tranter N., *The Fortified House in Scotland* (Edinburgh, 1962–66) 5 vols

WEBSITES

Ancient and Scheduled Monuments: *ancientmonuments.uk*
British Listed Buildings: *britishlistedbuildings.co.uk*
Canmore: National Record of the Historic Environment: *canmore.org.uk*
The Castle Guide: *thecastleguide.co.uk*
Historic Environment Scotland Portal: *portal.historicenvironment.scot*
The Scottish Castles Association: *www.scottishcastlesassociation.com*
Stravaiging Around Scotland: *www.stravaiging.com*

INDEX OF SITES

Main entries in the text are highlighted by an asterisk. Ordnance Survey references are given for all sites. Where the current administrative area differs from the historical county it is shown in brackets.

Abbot Hunter's Tower – *see* Mauchline
Abbot's Tower, Kirkcudbrightshire (Galloway)   NX 972 666
Abercorn Castle, West Lothian   NT 083 794
Aberdeen Castle, Aberdeenshire (Aberdeen)   NJ 944 063
*Aberdour Castle, Fife   NT 193 854
*Abergeldie Castle, Aberdeenshire   NO 287 953
*Aberuchill Castle, Perthshire   NN 744 212
*Abington Motte, Lanarkshire (South)   NS 932 250
Aboyne Castle, Aberdeenshire   NO 526 995
Achadun – *see* Achanduin
Achadunan Motte, Argyll: Mainland   NN 201 136
Achallader Castle, Argyll: Mainland   NN 322 442
*Achanduin Castle, Lismore, Argyll: Islands   NM 804 392
*Ackergill Tower, Caithness (Highland)   ND 352 547
*Affleck Castle, Angus   NO 495 388
*Aiket Castle, Ayrshire (East)   NS 388 488
*Aikwood Tower, Selkirkshire (Borders)   NT 420 260
*Ailsa Castle, Ayrshire (South)   NX 023 995
Aird Toranais – *see* Ardtornish

*Airlie Castle, Angus   NO 293 522
*Airth Castle, Stirlingshire (Falkirk)   NS 900 868
*Aldie Castle, Kinross-shire   NT 050 978
Allanmouth Tower, Roxburghshire (Borders)   NT 455 102
*Allardice Castle, Kincardineshire (Aberdeenshire)   NO 818 739
*Alloa Tower, Clackmannanshire   NS 889 925
*Almond Castle, Stirlingshire (Falkirk)   NS 956 773
Altyre Castle, Moray   NJ 035 553
Am Barra Calltainn – *see* Barcaldine
*Amisfield Tower, Dumfriesshire   NX 992 838
An Camas – *see* Kames
An Tairbeart – *see* Tarbert
*Arbroath Abbey, Angus   NO 644 414
*Ardblair Castle, Perthshire   NO 164 446
Ardchonnell – *see* Innis Chonnell
*Ardclach Bell Tower, Nairnshire (Highland)   NH 953 453
*Ardgowan Castle, Renfrewshire (Inverclyde)   NS 205 728
Ardmaddy Castle, Argyll: Mainland   NM 785 164
Ardross Castle, Fife   NO 508 007
*Ardrossan Castle, Ayrshire (North)   NS 233 424
Ardstinchar Castle, Ayrshire (South)   NX 086 824

*Ardtornish Castle, Argyll: Mainland (Highland)   NM 692 426
*Ardvreck Castle, Sutherland (Highland)   NC 240 236
Ardwell Mote, Wigtownshire (Galloway)   NX 103 455
*Arnage Castle, Aberdeenshire   NJ 936 370
Arnot Tower, Kinross-shire   NO 207 016
*Aros Castle, Mull, Argyll: Islands   NM 563 450
*Ashintully Castle, Perthshire   NO 101 613
Asliesk Castle, Moray   NJ 108 598
Asloun Castle, Aberdeenshire   NJ 542 149
*Auchanachie Castle, Aberdeenshire   NJ 498 469
Auchen – see Auchencass
*Auchencass, Dumfriesshire   NT 063 035
Auchenharvie Castle, Ayrshire (East)   NS 363 443
Auchenskeoch Castle, Kirkcudbrightshire (Galloway)   NX 917 588
Auchindoir Motte, Aberdeenshire   NJ 478 245
*Auchindoun Castle, Banffshire (Moray)   NJ 348 374
Auchinleck, Angus – see Affleck
Auchinleck Castle, Ayrshire (East)   NS 499 232
Auchness Castle, Wigtownshire (Galloway)   NX 106 447
Auchterhouse Castle, Angus   NO 332 373
*Auldearn Castle, Nairnshire (Highland)   NH 917 556
Auld Hill – see Portencross
Auld Petty Motte – see Castle Stuart
Auldton Mote, Dumfriesshire   NT 094 058
Avondale – see Strathaven
Ayr Castle, Ayrshire (South)   NS 333 224

Baile Bhoid – see Rothesay
*Balbegno Castle, Kincardineshire (Aberdeenshire)   NO 639 730
*Balcomie Castle, Fife   NO 626 099
Baldoon Castle, Wigtownshire (Galloway) NK 426 536
*Balfluig Castle, Aberdeenshire   NJ 593 153
*Balfour Castle, Angus   NO 337 546
*Balgonie Castle, Fife   NO 313 007
Balgreggan Mote, Wigtownshire (Galloway)   NX 095 505
Ballencrieff Castle, East Lothian   NT 487 783
*Ballinbreich Castle, Fife   NO 272 205
*Ballindalloch Castle, Banffshire (Moray)   NJ 178 365
*Ballinshoe Castle, Angus   NO 417 532
Ballogie – see Midmar
*Ballone Castle, Ross (Highland)   NH 929 837
*Ballumbie Castle, Angus   NO 445 344
Balmaclellan Mote, Kirkcudbrightshire (Galloway)   NX 652 793
Balmangan Tower, Kirkcudbrightshire (Galloway)   NX 651 456
*Balmanno Castle, Perthshire   NO 144 156
Balmbreich – see Ballinbreich
Balmoral Castle, Aberdeenshire   NO 255 952
*Balmuto Tower, Fife   NT 221 898
Balquhain Castle, Aberdeenshire   NJ 732 236
*Baltersan Castle, Ayrshire (South)   NS 282 087
*Balthayock Castle, Perthshire   NO 175 230
*Balvaird Castle, Perthshire   NO 170 115
*Balvenie Castle, Banffshire (Moray)   NJ 326 408
Balwearie Castle, Fife   NT 252 904
Bamff House, Perthshire   NO 222 515
Bandon Tower, Fife   NO 277 043
*Banff Castle, Banffshire (Aberdeenshire)   NJ 689 643

INDEX OF SITES

Bannachra Castle, Dunbartonshire
 (Argyll)   NS 343 843
*Barcaldine Castle, Argyll: Mainland
 NM 907 405
*Bardowie Castle, Stirlingshire (East
 Dunbartonshire)   NS 580 739
*Barholm Castle, Kirkcudbrightshire
 (Galloway)   NX 521 529
*Barjarg Tower, Dumfriesshire
 NX 876 901
Barmagachan Mote, Kirkcudbrightshire
 (Galloway)   NX 614 494
Barnbougle Castle, West Lothian
 (Edinburgh)   NT 169 785
*Barncluith Tower, Lanarkshire (South)
 NS 730 545
*Barnes Castle, East Lothian
 NT 528 766
Barnhills Tower, Roxburghshire
 (Borders)   NT 589 212
*Barns Tower, Peeblesshire (Borders)
 NT 215 391
Barntalloch Castle, Dumfriesshire
 NY 353 878
Barony Castle, Peeblesshire (Borders)
 NT 236 472
Barra Castle, Aberdeenshire
 NJ 792 258
*Barr Castle, Ayrshire (East)
 NS 502 365
*Barr Castle, Renfrewshire
 NS 347 582
Barrogill – *see* Castle of Mey
Barton Hill – *see* Kinnaird, Perthshire
*Bass Castle, East Lothian
 NT 601 873
*Bass of Inverurie, Aberdeenshire
 NJ 782 206
*Bavelaw Castle, Midlothian
 (Edinburgh)   NT 168 628
*Bedlay Castle, Lanarkshire (North)
 NS 692 700
Bedrule Castle, Roxburghshire
 (Borders)   NT 598 180
*Beldorney Castle, Aberdeenshire
 NJ 424 369
Bellabeg – *see* Doune of Invernochty

Belmont Castle, Perthshire
 NO 287 439
*Bemersyde House, Berwickshire
 (Borders)   NT 592 334
*Benholm Castle, Kincardineshire
 (Aberdeenshire)   NO 804 705
Benholm's Lodge – *see* Wallace Tower
Berriedale Castle, Caithness (Highland)
 ND 122 224
Bharraich – *see* Castle Varrich
Bhuirgh – *see* Borve, Western Isles
Biel House, East Lothian   NT 634 759
*Birsay: Earl's Palace, Mainland,
 Orkney HY246 280
Birse Castle, Aberdeenshire
 NO 520 905
*Black Castle of Moulin, Perthshire
 NN 946 589
Blacket Tower, Dumfriesshire
 NY 243 743
Blackhouse Tower, Selkirkshire
 (Borders)   NT 281 273
*Blackness Castle, West Lothian
 (Falkirk)   NT 055 803
Blair Castle, Ayrshire (North)
 NS 305 480
*Blair Castle, Perthshire   NN 866 662
*Blairfindy Castle, Banffshire (Moray)
 NJ 199 286
Blairlogie Castle, Stirlingshire
 NS 827 969
Blanerne Castle, Berwickshire (Borders)
 NT 832 564
Blervie Castle, Moray   NJ 071 573
Boddam Castle, Aberdeenshire
 NK 124 419
Boghall Castle, Lanarkshire (South)
 NT 041 370
Bonkyll Castle, Berwickshire (Borders)
 NT 805 596
*Bonshaw Tower, Dumfriesshire
 NY 243 721
Bordie Tower, Fife   NS 956 869
Boreland Mote, Kirkcudbrightshire
 (Galloway)   NX 585 551
*Borthwick Castle, Midlothian
 NT 370 597

Borve Castle, Sutherland (Highland)
   NC 725 642
*Borve Castle, Western Isles
   NF 774 506
Botel – *see* Buittle
*Bothwell Castle, Lanarkshire (South)
   NS 688 593
*Boyne Castle, Banffshire
   (Aberdeenshire)   NJ 612 657
*Braal Castle, Caithness (Highland)
   ND 139 601
Braco Castle, Perthshire   NN 823 113
Braemar – *see* Kindrochit
*Braemar Castle, Aberdeenshire
   NO 156 924
*Braidwood Castle, Lanarkshire (South)
   NS 839 471
*Braikie Castle, Angus   NO 628 509
*Branxholme Castle, Roxburghshire
   (Borders)   NT 464 116
Brathwell – *see* Braal
Breacachadh – *see* Old Breachacha
Breachacha – *see* Old Breachacha
Brechin Castle, Angus   NO 597 599
Breconside Tower, Dumfriesshire
   NX 841 889
*Bridge Castle, West Lothian
   NS 944 709
*Brims Castle, Caithness (Highland)
   ND 043 710
*Brochel Castle, Raasay, off Skye
   (Highland) NG 584 463
*Brodick Castle, Arran, Bute County
   (North Ayrshire)   NS 016 378
*Brodie Castle, Moray   NH 980 578
*Broughty Castle, Angus (Dundee)
   NO 465 304
Bruce's Castle, Stirlingshire
   NS 867 878
*Brunstane Castle, Midlothian
   NT 201 582
Brunston – *see* Brunstane
*Bucholie Castle, Caithness (Highland)
   ND 383 658
Bucholly – *see* Bucholie
*Buckholm Tower, Roxburghshire
   (Borders)   NT 482 378

*Buittle Castle, Kirkcudbrightshire
   (Galloway)   NX 819 616
*Burgie Castle, Moray   NJ 094 593
*Burleigh Castle, Kinross-shire
   NO 130 047
Burnhead Tower, Roxburghshire
   (Borders)   NT 514 166
Burntisland – *see* Rossend
Busby: The Peel, Lanarkshire (South)
   NS 594 561

*Cadboll Castle, Ross (Highland)
   NH 679 776
*Cadzow Castle, Lanarkshire (South)
   NS 734 537
*Caerlaverock Castle and Old Castle,
   Dumfriesshire   NY 026 656
*Cairnbulg Castle, Aberdeenshire
   NK 016 640
Cairnburgh Castle, Treshnish, Argyll:
   Islands   NM 308 445
*Cairns Castle, Midlothian (West
   Lothian)   NT 091 604
Cairston Castle, Mainland, Orkney
   HY 273 096
Caisteal Bheagram, South Uist, Western
   Isles   NF 761 371
*Caisteal Maol, Skye (Highland)
   NG 758 264
Caisteal na Nighinn Ruaidhe, Argyll:
   Mainland   NM 916 137
Caisteal Uisdean, Skye (Highland)
   NG 381 583
*Cakemuir Castle, Midlothian
   NT 413 591
Calbhaigh – *see* Calvay
Calder, Nairnshire – *see* Cawdor
Calder House, Midlothian (West
   Lothian)   NT 072 672
*Caldwell Tower, Renfrewshire (East)
   NS 422 551
Callendar House, Stirlingshire (Falkirk)
   NS 898 794
*Calvay Castle, South Uist, Western
   Isles   NF 817 182
Campbell – *see* Castle Campbell

INDEX OF SITES

Cantraydoune Motte, Nairnshire
 (Highland)   NH 789 461
Caprington Castle, Ayrshire (East)
 NS 407 363
*Carberry Tower, Midlothian (East
 Lothian)   NT 364 697
*Cardoness Castle, Kirkcudbrightshire
 (Galloway)   NX 591 553
*Cardrona Tower, Peeblesshire
 (Borders)   NT 300 378
*Cardross House, Perthshire
 (Stirlingshire)   NS 605 976
Careston Castle, Angus   NO 530 599
Carfrae Bastle, Berwickshire (Borders)
 NT 506 551
Cargill Castle, Perthshire   NO 157 374
*Carleton Castle and Little Carleton
 Motte, Ayrshire (South)
 NX 143 895
*Carnasserie Castle, Argyll: Mainland
 NM 838 009
Carnbane Castle, Perthshire
 NN 677 480
*Carnell House, Ayrshire (East)
 NS 467 322
*Carnousie Castle, Banffshire
 (Aberdeenshire)   NJ 670 504
*Carnwath Motte, Lanarkshire (South)
 NS 975 466
Carraig – *see* Carrick
*Carrick Castle, Argyll: Mainland
 NS 194 944
Carriden House, West Lothian
 NT 026 808
Carscreugh Castle, Wigtownshire
 (Galloway)   NX 223 599
*Carsluith Castle, Kirkcudbrightshire
 (Galloway)   NX 495 542
Cary – *see* Castlecary
Cassencarie House, Wigtownshire
 (Galloway)   NX 476 577
*Cassillis House, Ayrshire (East)
 NS 340 128
Castlebay – *see* Kisimul
*Castle Campbell, Clackmannanshire
 NS 961 993

*Castlecary Castle, Stirlingshire
 (Falkirk)   NS 786 775
*Castle Cluggy, Perthshire
 NN 840 234
*Castle Coeffin, Argyll: Islands
 NM 853 437
*Castle Craig, Ross (Highland)
 NH 632 638
*Castle Fraser, Aberdeenshire
 NJ 723 126
Castle Gogar, Midlothian (Edinburgh)
 NT 165 730
*Castle Grant, Moray (Highland)
 NJ 041 302
Castlehill Tower, Peeblesshire (Borders)
 NT 214 354
Castle Holm, Mainland, Shetland
 HU 395 475
*Castle Huntly, Perthshire
 NO 301 292
*Castle Kennedy, Wigtownshire
 (Galloway)   NX 111 609
*Castle Leod, Ross (Highland)
 NH 485 593
*Castle Levan, Renfrewshire
 (Inverclyde)   NS 216 764
*Castle Menzies, Perthshire
 NN 837 496
*Castle of Fiddes, Kincardineshire
 (Aberdeenshire)   NO 805 813
Castle of King Edward, Aberdeenshire
 NJ 722 562
*Castle of Mey, Caithness (Highland)
 ND 290 739
*Castle of Old Wick, Caithness
 (Highland)   ND 369 489
Castle of Park, Banffshire
 (Aberdeenshire)   NJ 587 571
*Castle of Park, Wigtownshire
 (Galloway)   NX 189 571
*Castle of Pittulie, Aberdeenshire
 NJ 945 671
Castle of Rattray, Aberdeenshire
 NK 088 079
*Castle of St John, Wigtownshire
 (Galloway)   NX 061 608

Castle Rednock, Perthshire
(Stirlingshire) NN 600 022
*Castle Roy, Inverness-shire (Highland)
NJ 007 219
Castle Shuna, Argyll: Mainland
NM 915 482
Castle Sinclair, Barra, Western Isles
NL 648 996
*Castle Sinclair Girnigoe, Caithness
(Highland) ND 379 549
*Castle Stalker, Argyll: Mainland
NM 920 473
Castle Stewart, Wigtownshire
(Galloway) NX 379 690
*Castle Stuart and Auld Petty Motte,
Inverness-shire (Highland)
NH 741 498
*Castle Sween, Argyll: Mainland
NR 713 788
*Castle Tioram, Inverness-shire
(Highland) NM 883 725
*Castle Varrich, Sutherland (Highland)
NC 581 567
Castlewigg, Wigtownshire (Galloway)
NX 428 432
Cathcart Castle, Lanarkshire (Glasgow)
NS 586 599
Cavers House, Roxburghshire (Borders)
NT 540 154
*Cawdor Castle, Nairnshire (Highland)
NH 847 499
Ceann Loch Alainn – see Kinlochaline
*Cessford Castle, Roxburghshire
(Borders) NT 738 238
*Cessnock Castle, Ayrshire (East)
NS 511 355
Chiosmuil – see Kisimul
Chonnell – see Innis Chonnell
Cille Mhartainn – see Kilmartin
*Clackmannan Tower,
Clackmannanshire NN 906 919
Claig Castle, Jura, Argyll: Islands
NR 472 627
*Claypotts Castle, Angus (Dundee)
NO 453 318
*Cleish Castle, Kinross-shire
NT 083 978

Cloncaird Castle, Ayrshire (South)
NS 359 075
*Closeburn Castle, Dumfriesshire
NX 907 921
Cluggy – see Castle Cluggy
*Clunie Castle and Motte, Perthshire
NO 114 440
Cluny Castle, Aberdeenshire
NJ 688 128
*Cluny Crichton Castle, Kincardineshire
(Aberdeenshire) NO 686 997
Cobbie Row's Castle – see Cubbie
Roo's Castle
Cockburnspath Tower, Berwickshire
(Borders) NT 785 699
Coeffin – see Castle Coeffin
*Colinton Castle, Midlothian
(Edinburgh) NT 216 694
*Collairnie Castle, Fife NO 307 170
*Colliston Castle, Angus NO 612 464
Colmonell – see Kirkhill
*Colmslie Tower, Roxburghshire
(Borders) NT 513 396
Colquhonnie Castle, Aberdeenshire
NJ 365 126
Comiston House, Midlothian
(Edinburgh) NT 240 686
*Comlongon Castle, Dumfriesshire
NY 079 690
*Comrie Castle, Perthshire NN 787 487
*Corbet Peel Tower, Roxburghshire
(Borders) NT 776 239
Corehouse – see Corra
*Corgarff Castle, Aberdeenshire
NJ 255 086
Coroghan Castle, Canna, off Skye
(Highland) NG 279 055
Corra Castle, Kirkcudbrightshire
(Galloway) NS 882 414
*Corra Castle, Lanarkshire (South)
NS 882 414
Corsbie Tower, Berwickshire (Borders)
NT 607 438
*Corse Castle, Aberdeenshire
NJ 548 074
Corsewall Castle, Wigtownshire
(Galloway) NX 991 715

INDEX OF SITES

Corsindae House, Aberdeenshire
 NJ 686 088
Corston Tower, Fife   NO 208 098
Corstorphine Castle, Midlothian
 (Edinburgh)   NT 199 723
*Cortachy Castle, Angus   NO 400 594
*Coull Castle, Aberdeenshire
 NJ 513 023
*Coulter Motte Hill, Lanarkshire
 (South)   NT 019 363
Cousland Castle, Midlothian
 NT 377 681
Couston Castle, Fife   NT 168 851
*Covington Tower, Lanarkshire (South)
 NS 975 399
*Cowdenknowes House, Berwickshire
 (Borders)   NT 579 371
*Coxton Tower, Moray   NJ 262 607
*Craigcaffie Tower, Wigtownshire
 (Galloway)   NX 089 641
*Craig Castle, Aberdeenshire
 NJ 471 248
*Craigcrook Castle, Midlothian
 (Edinburgh)   NT 211 743
Craighlaw Castle, Wigtownshire
 (Galloway)   NX 305 61
*Craig House, Angus   NO 704 563
*Craigie Castle, Ayrshire (South)
 NS 409 318
*Craigievar Castle, Aberdeenshire
 NJ 566 095
Craiglockhart Castle, Midlothian
 (Edinburgh)   NT 226 703
*Craigmillar Castle, Midlothian
 (Edinburgh)   NT 285 710
*Craigneil Castle, Ayrshire (South)
 NX 147 854
*Craignethan Castle, Lanarkshire
 (South)   NS 815 463
Craignish Castle, Argyll:
 Mainland   NM 771 016
Craig of Inverugie – *see* Ravenscraig,
 Aberdeenshire
Craig, Ross – *see* Castle Craig
*Craigston Castle, Aberdeenshire
 NJ 762 550
Crail Castle, Fife   NO 614 075

*Cramond Tower, Midlothian
 (Edinburgh)   NT 191 769
*Cranshaws Castle, Berwickshire
 (Borders)   NT 681 619
*Crathes Castle, Kincardineshire
 (Aberdeenshire)   NO 734 968
*Craufurdland Castle, Ayrshire (East)
 NS 456 408
Crawford Castle, Lanarkshire (South)
 NS 954 213
*Creich Castle, Fife   NO 329 212
*Crichton Castle, Midlothian
 NT 380 612
Cromarty Castle, Ross (Highland)
 NH 792 671
*Crombie Castle, Banffshire (Moray)
 NJ 591 522
*Crookston Castle, Lanarkshire
 (Glasgow)   NS 525 627
Crookston Old House, Midlothian
 (Borders)   NT 425 522
*Crossbasket Castle, Lanarkshire
 (South)   NS 666 559
*Crossraguel Abbey, Ayrshire (South)
 NS 275 083
Cruggleton Castle, Wigtownshire
 (Galloway)   NX 484 428
*Cruivie Castle, Fife   NO 419 229
*Cubbie Roo's Castle, Wyre, Orkney
 HY 442 264
*Culcreuch Castle, Stirlingshire
 NS 620 876
Cullen House, Banffshire (Moray)
 NS 232 102
Culzean Castle, Ayrshire (South)
 NJ 732 236
Cumaradh Beag – *see* Little Cumbrae
Cumbrae – *see* Little Cumbrae
Cumstoun Castle, Kirkcudbrightshire
 (Galloway)   NX 683 533
Cunningar Motte – *see* Midmar

Dairsie Castle, Fife   NO 414 160
*Dalcross Castle, Inverness-shire
 (Highland)   NH 779 483
*Dalhousie Castle, Midlothian
 NT 320 636

Dalkeith Palace, Midlothian
NT 333 679
*Dalmellington Motte, Ayrshire (East)
NS 482 058
*Dalquharran Old Castle, Ayrshire
(South)   NS 273 019
Dalry Mote, Kirkcudbrightshire
(Galloway)   NX 619 813
Dalswinton Old House, Dumfriesshire
NX 945 841
*Dalzell House, Lanarkshire (North)
NS 756 550
Dargavel House, Renfrewshire
NS 433 693
*Darnaway Castle, Moray
NH 994 550
*Darnick Tower, Roxburghshire
(Borders)   NT 532 343
Davlamoryke – see Drumlanrig's Tower
*Dean Castle, Ayrshire (East)
NS 437 394
*Delgatie Castle, Aberdeenshire
NJ 755 506
*Denmylne Castle, Fife   NO 249 175
Dhubhairt – see Duart
Dingwall Castle, Ross (Highland)
NH 553 589
Dinning Mote, Dumfriesshire
NX 892 901
*Dinvin Motte, Ayrshire (South)
NX 200 932
*Dirleton Castle, East Lothian
NT 516 839
Donan – see Eilean Donan
Doon – see Loch Doon
Doonfoot – see Greenan
*Dornoch Castle, Sutherland (Highland)
NH 797 897
Douglas Castle, Lanarkshire (South)
NS 843 318
*Doune Castle, Perthshire (Stirlingshire)
NN 728 011
*Doune of Invernochty, Aberdeenshire
NJ 351 129
*Dounreay Castle, Caithness (Highland)
NC 983 669

*Dowhill Castle, Kinross-shire
NT 118 973
*Drochil Castle, Peeblesshire (Borders)
NT 162 434
*Druchtag Motte, Wigtownshire
(Galloway)   NX 349 446
*Drum Castle, Aberdeenshire
NJ 796 005
*Drumcoltran Tower,
Kirkcudbrightshire (Galloway)
NX 869 683
*Drumin Castle, Banffshire (Moray)
NJ 184 303
*Druminnor Castle, Aberdeenshire
NJ 513 264
Drumlanrig Castle, Dumfriesshire
NX 851 992
*Drumlanrig's Tower, Roxburghshire
(Borders)   NT 502 144
*Drummond Castle, Perthshire
NN 844 181
Drumwalt – see Old Place of Mochrum
*Dryhope Tower, Selkirkshire (Borders)
NT 267 247
*Duart Castle, Mull, Argyll: Islands
NM 749 354
Dubh - see Black Castle of Moulin
Duchal Castle, Renfrewshire
(Inverclyde)   NS 334 685
*Duchray Castle, Stirlingshire   NS 480 998
*Dudhope Castle, Angus (Dundee)
NO 394 307
*Duffus Castle, Moray   NJ 189 673
*Dumbarton Castle, Dunbartonshire
(West)   NS 401 744
Dumfries Castle, Dumfriesshire
NX 970 764
Dunaverty Castle, Argyll: Mainland
NR 688 074
*Dunbar Castle and Town Wall, East
Lothian   NT 678 793
*Dunbeath Castle, Caithness (Highland)
ND 158 282
Dun Bheagan – see Dunvegan
Dun Breatann – see Dumbarton

Dundaff – *see* Sir John de Graham's Castle
Dundarg Castle, Aberdeenshire NJ 895 649
*Dundas Castle, West Lothian (Edinburgh) NT 116 767
Dundee Castle and Town Wall, Angus (Dundee) NO 405 302
*Dunderave Castle, Argyll: Mainland NN 143 096
*Dundonald Castle, Ayrshire (South) NS 363 345
Dunduff Castle, Ayrshire (South) NS 272 164
*Dunglass Castle, Dunbartonshire (West) NS 435 735
*Dunnideer Castle, Aberdeenshire NJ 613 282
*Dunnottar Castle, Kincardineshire (Aberdeenshire) NO 882 839
Dun Olla – *see* Dunollie
*Dunollie Castle, Argyll: Mainland NM 852 314
Dunoon Castle, Argyll: Mainland NS 175 764
Dunphail Castle, Moray NJ 007 481
*Dunrobin Castle, Sutherland (Highland) NC 850 008
*Dunscaith Castle, Skye (Highland) NG 595 121
Duns Castle, Berwickshire (Borders) NS 175 764
Dun Sgathaich – *see* Dunscaith
*Dunskey Castle, Wigtownshire (Galloway) NX 004 534
*Dunstaffnage Castle, Argyll: Mainland NM 883 345
Dun Staidhinis – *see* Dunstaffnage
*Duntarvie Castle, West Lothian NT 091 765
*Duntreath Castle, Stirlingshire NS 536 811
Duntroon – *see* Duntrune
*Duntrune Castle, Argyll: Mainland NR 794 956
Dun Tuilm – *see* Duntulm

*Duntulm Castle, Skye (Highland) NG 410 743
*Dunure Castle, Ayrshire (South) NS 253 158
*Dunvegan Castle, Skye (Highland) NG 247 481
Dunyvaig Castle, Islay, Argyll: Islands NR 406 455
*Durris House and Castle, Kincardineshire (Aberdeenshire) NO 798 968
*Dysart Old Church, Fife NT 303 930

Earl's Palace – *see* Birsay; Kirkwall
*Earlshall Castle, Fife NO 465 211
*Earlstoun Castle, Kirkcudbrightshire (Galloway) NX 613 840
Eastend House, Lanarkshire (South) NS 949 375
Easter Cochrane – *see* Johnstone
East Wemyss – *see* Macduff's Castle
*Eden Castle, Banffshire (Aberdeenshire) NJ 698 588
*Edinample Castle, Perthshire (Stirlingshire) NN 601 226
*Edinburgh Castle and Town Wall, Midlothian (Edinburgh) NT 252 736
Edingham Castle, Kirkcudbrightshire (Galloway) NX 839 626
*Edzell Castle and Motte, Angus NO 585 691
*Eilean Donan Castle, Ross (Highland) NG 881 259
Eilean Donnain – *see* Eilean Donan
Eilein – *see* Loch an Eilein
*Elcho Castle, Perthshire NO 164 211
Elgin Castle, Moray NJ 212 629
*Elibank Castle, Selkirkshire (Borders) NT 397 363
Elliston Castle, Renfrewshire NS 392 598
Ellon Castle, Aberdeenshire NJ 959 307
Elphinstone Tower, East Lothian NT 391 698

INDEX OF SITES

Elphinstone Tower, Stirlingshire
   (Falkirk)   NS 890 889
*Elshieshields Tower, Dumfriesshire
   NY 069 850
*Erchless Castle, Inverness-shire
   (Highland)   NH 410 408
Eren – *see* Auldearn
*Esslemont Castle, Aberdeenshire
   NJ 932 298
*Ethie Castle, Angus   NO 688 468
*Evelaw Tower, Berwickshire (Borders)
   NT 661 526
*Evelick Castle, Perthshire   NO 205 259
*Eyemouth Fort, Berwickshire
   (Borders)   NT 943 648

*Fairburn Tower, Ross (Highland)
   NH 469 523
*Fairlie Castle, Ayrshire (North)
   NS 213 549
*Falkland Palace, Fife   NO 254 075
Falside – *see* Fa'side
*Farnell Castle, Angus   NO 624 555
*Fa'side Castle, East Lothian
   NT 378 710
*Fast Castle, Berwickshire (Borders)
   NT 862 710
Fast Castle, Roxburghshire (Borders)
   NT 595 182
*Fatlips Castle, Roxburghshire
   (Borders)   NT 582 209
Fedderate Castle, Aberdeenshire
   NJ 897 498
*Fenton Tower, East Lothian
   NT 543 822
*Fernie Castle, Fife   NO 306 147
*Ferniehirst Castle, Roxburghshire
   (Borders)   NT 652 179
Fiddes – *see* Castle of Fiddes
*Finavon Old Castle, Angus
   NO 497 566
Fincharn Castle, Argyll: Mainland
   NM 898 043
*Findlater Castle, Banffshire
   (Aberdeenshire)   NJ 542 673

*Findochty Castle, Banffshire (Moray)
   NJ 455 673
*Fingask Castle, Perthshire
   NO 228 275
*Finlarig Castle, Perthshire
   (Stirlingshire)   NN 575 338
Fintry, Angus – *see* Mains, Angus
Fintry Motte, Stirlingshire   NS 611 866
Flemington Castle, Angus   NO 527 556
*Fordell Castle, Fife   NT 147 854
*Fordyce Castle, Banffshire
   (Aberdeenshire)   NJ 556 638
Forfar Castle, Angus   NO 456 508
Formantine – *see* Gight
Forres Castle, Moray   NJ 034 587
Forse Castle, Caithness (Highland)
   ND 224 338
*Forter Castle, Angus   NO 183 646
*Fourmerkland Tower, Dumfriesshire
   NX 909 807
*Fowlis Castle, Angus   NO 321 334
Fraoch Eilean Castle, Argyll: Mainland
   NN 108 252
Fraser – *see* Castle Fraser
Fraserburgh – *see* Kinnaird Head
French Camp, East Lothian
   NT 763 717
*Frenchland Tower, Dumfriesshire
   NT 102 054
*Freswick Castle, Caithness (Highland)
   ND 378 671
Freuchie – *see* Castle Grant
Fulton Tower, Roxburghshire (Borders)
   NT 605 158
*Fyvie Castle, Aberdeenshire
   NJ 764 393

*Galdenoch Castle, Wigtownshire
   (Galloway)   NZ 974 633
Galston – *see* Barr, Ayrshire
Gamescleuch Tower, Selkirkshire
   (Borders)   NT 284 147
*Gardyne Castle, Angus   NO 574 488
Gargunnock House, Stirlingshire
   NS 715 945
*Garleton Castle, East Lothian
   NT 509 767

Garlies Castle, Kirkcudbrightshire
(Galloway)   NX 422 692
Garrion Tower, Lanarkshire (South)
NS 797 512
*Gartartan Castle, Perthshire
(Stirlingshire)   NS 530 978
*Garth Castle, Perthshire   NN 764 504
Gauldwell Castle, Banffshire (Moray)
NJ 311 451
*Gight Castle, Aberdeenshire
NJ 827 392
*Gilbertfield Castle, Lanarkshire
(South)   NS 653 588
Gillespie Moat, Lanarkshire (South)
NT 039 377
*Gilnockie Tower, Dumfriesshire
NY 383 787
Gimehlean – see Gylen
Girnigoe – see Castle Sinclair Girnigoe
*Glamis Castle, Angus   NO 387 481
Glasclune Castle, Perthshire
NO 154 470
Glasgow Castle, Lanarkshire (Glasgow)
NS 603 656
Glenbervie House, Kincardineshire
(Aberdeenshire)   NO 769 805
*Glenbuchat Castle, Aberdeenshire
NJ 398 149
Glendevon Castle, Perthshire
NN 976 055
Gleneagles Castle, Perthshire
NN 929 093
*Glengarnock Castle, Ayrshire (North)
NS 311 574
Glenmorangie – see Cadboll
*Glensanda Castle, Argyll: Mainland
(Highland)   NM 824 469
Gloom – see Castle Campbell
*Goldielands Tower, Roxburghshire
(Borders)   NT 635 226
*Gordon Castle, Moray   NJ 350 596
Gourock – see Castle Levan
Graham's Castle – see Sir John de
Graham's Castle
Grandtully – see Grantully
Grant – see Castle Grant

*Grantully Castle, Perthshire
NN 891 513
*Greenan Castle, Ayrshire (South)
NS 312 193
*Greenknowe Tower, Berwickshire
(Borders)   NT 639 428
Gunn's Castle, Caithness (Highland)
ND 307 385
*Guthrie Castle, Angus   NO 563 505
*Gylen Castle, Argyll: Mainland
NM 805 265

Haddington Town Defences, East
Lothian   NT 510 730
*Haggs Castle, Lanarkshire (Glasgow)
NS 560 626
*Hailes Castle, East Lothian
NT 575 758
Haining – see Almond
Hallbar – see Braidwood
*Hallforest Castle, Aberdeenshire
NJ 777 154
Hallgreen Castle, Kincardineshire
(Aberdeenshire)   NO 832 721
*Harthill Castle, Aberdeenshire
NJ 687 252
*Hatton Castle, Angus   NO 302 411
Hawick – see Drumlanrig's Tower
*Hawick Mote, Roxburghshire
(Borders)   NT 499 140
*Hawthornden Castle, Midlothian
NT 287 637
*Hermitage Castle, Roxburghshire
(Borders)   NY 497 961
High Drummore Mote, Wigtownshire
(Galloway)   NX 130 359
*Hillslap Tower, Roxburghshire
(Borders)   NT 513 394
*Hills Tower, Kirkcudbrightshire
(Galloway)   NX 912 726
Hirendean Castle, Midlothian
NT 298 512
*Hoddom Castle, Dumfriesshire
NY 157 730
Hollows – see Gilnockie
*Holyrood Palace, Midlothian
(Edinburgh)   NT 269 739

Holyroodhouse – see Holyrood
Horsburgh Castle, Peeblesshire
   (Borders)   NT 285 391
*House of Schivas, Aberdeenshire
   NJ 898 368
Howden Motte, Selkirkshire (Borders)
   NT 458 269
Hume Castle, Berwickshire (Borders)
   NT 704 414
*Hunterston Castle, Ayrshire (North)
   NS 193 515
*Huntingtower Castle, Perthshire
   NO 084 252
Huntly, Perthshire – see Castle Huntly
*Huntly Castle, Aberdeenshire
   NJ 532 407
*Hutton Castle, Berwickshire (Borders)
   NT 887 548
Hynd Castle, Angus   NO 505 416

Inaltrie Castle, Banffshire (Moray)
   NJ 518 631
Inbhir Dhubhghlais – see Inveruglas
Inbhir Gharadh – see Invergarry
Inbhir Lochaidh – see Inverlochy
Inchbervis Castle, Perthshire
   NO 123 329
*Inchdrewer Castle, Banffshire
   (Aberdeenshire)   NJ 656 607
Inchgalbraith Castle, Dunbartonshire
   (Argyll)   NS 369 904
Inchgall – see Lochore
Inchgarvie Castle, West Lothian
   (Edinburgh)   NT 137 795
Ingleston Mote, Kirkcudbrightshire
   (Galloway)   NX 775 580
*Inglismaldie Castle, Kincardineshire
   (Aberdeenshire)   NO 644 669
Innermessan Mote, Wigtownshire
   (Galloway)   NX 084 633
*Innerpeffray Castle, Perthshire
   NN 905 179
*Innerwick Castle, East Lothian
   NT 735 737
Innes House, Moray   NJ 278 649
Innis Chonaill – see Innis Chonnell

*Innis Chonnell Castle, Argyll:
   Mainland   NM 976 119
Inshes House, Inverness-shire
   (Highland)   NH 695 437
Inshoch Castle, Nairnshire (Highland)
   NH 936 567
*Inverallochy Castle, Aberdeenshire
   NK 041 629
Inveraray Castle, Argyll: Mainland
   NN 096 093
Inveravon Castle, West Lothian
   (Falkirk)   NS 953 798
*Invergarry Castle, Inverness-shire
   (Highland)   NM 315 006
Inverkip – see Ardgowan
Inverlochy – see Old Inverlochy
*Invermark Castle, Angus
   NO 443 804
Inverness Castle, Inverness-shire
   (Highland)   NH 666 451
Invernochty – see Doune of Invernochty
*Inverquharity Castle, Angus
   NO 411 579
*Inverugie Castle and Motte,
   Aberdeenshire   NK 102 484
*Inveruglas Castle, Dunbartonshire
   (Argyll)   NN 323 096
Inverurie – see Bass of Inverurie
Irvine – see Seagate
*Isle Castle, Wigtownshire (Galloway)
   NX 466 366
Isle Tower, Dumfriesshire (near
   Bankend)   NY 028 689
*Isle Tower, Dumfriesshire (near
   Holywood)   NX 955 825

Jedburgh – see Queen Mary's House
Jedburgh Castle, Roxburghshire
   (Borders)   NT 647 202
*Johnstone Castle, Renfrewshire
   NS 43 0622

Kaim of Mathers, Kincardineshire
   (Aberdeenshire)   NO 763 649
*Kames Castle, Bute, Bute County
   NS 064 676
Karlaverock – see Caerlaverock

Keir Knowe of Drum, Stirlingshire
    NS 636 953
Keiss – *see* Old Keiss
Keith, Banffshire – *see* Milton
*Kelburn Castle, Ayrshire (North)
    NS 217 567
*Kellie Castle, Fife   NO 520 052
*Kelly Castle, Angus   NO 608 402
*Kenmure Castle, Kirkcudbrightshire
    (Galloway)   NX 635 764
Kennedy – *see* Castle Kennedy
Kerelaw Castle, Ayrshire (North)
    NS 269 428
Kiessimul - *see* Kisimul
*Kilbirnie House, Ayrshire (North)
    NS 304 541
*Kilchurn Castle, Argyll: Mainland
    NN 133 276
Kilconquhar Castle, Fife   NO 494 027
*Kilcoy Castle, Ross (Highland)
    NH 576 512
Kildonan Castle, Arran, Bute County
    (North Ayrshire)   NS 037 210
*Kildrummy Castle, Aberdeenshire
    NJ 455 164
*Kilhenzie Castle, Ayrshire (South)
    NS 308 082
Kilkerran Castle, Ayrshire (South)
    NS 293 005
*Killochan Castle, Ayrshire (South)
    NS 227 004
Killumpha Tower, Wigtownshire
    (Galloway)   NX 113 407
Kilmahew Castle, Dunbartonshire
    (Argyll)   NS 352 787
Kilmarnock – *see* Dean
*Kilmaronock Castle, Dunbartonshire
    (West)   NS 446 877
*Kilmartin Castle, Argyll: Mainland
    NR 836 991
Kilnmaichlie House, Banffshire (Moray)
    NJ 181 321
*Kilravock Castle, Nairnshire
    (Highland)   NH 814 493
Kincardine Castle, Kincardineshire
    (Aberdeenshire)   NO 671 751

*Kinclaven Castle, Perthshire
    NO 158 376
*Kindrochit Castle, Aberdeenshire
    NO 152 913
Kingencleugh Castle, Ayrshire (East)
    NS 503 257
Kingston – *see* Fenton
*Kininvie House, Banffshire (Moray)
    NJ 319 441
*Kinkell Castle, Ross (Highland)
    NH 554 543
*Kinlochaline Castle, Argyll: Mainland
    (Highland)   NM 697 476
Kinnaird Castle, Angus   NO 634 571
*Kinnaird Castle and Barton Hill,
    Perthshire   NO 242 290
*Kinnaird Head Castle, Aberdeenshire
    NK 999 677
*Kinnairdy Castle, Banffshire
    (Aberdeenshire)   NJ 609 498
*Kinneil House, West Lothian (Falkirk)
    NS 983 806
Kirkclaugh Mote, Kirkcudbrightshire
    (Galloway)   NX 534 521
*Kirkconnell House, Kirkcudbrightshire
    (Galloway)   NX 979 697
Kirkcudbright – *see* MacLellan's Castle
Kirkcudbright Castle,
    Kirkcudbrightshire (Galloway)
    NX 677 508
*Kirkhill Castle, Ayrshire (South)
    NX 146 859
*Kirkhope Tower, Selkirkshire
    (Borders)   NT 379 250
*Kirkwall Palace and Castle, Mainland,
    Orkney   HY 447 108
*Kisimul Castle, Barra, Western Isles
    NL 665 979
*Knock Castle, Aberdeenshire
    NO 352 952
Knock Castle, Skye (Highland)
    NG 672 087
*Knockdolian Castle, Ayrshire (South)
    NX 123 854
Knock Old Castle, Ayrshire (North)
    NS 194 631

*Knockhall Castle, Aberdeenshire
   NJ 992 265

Lachlan – *see* Old Castle Lachlan
Ladhope Tower, Roxburghshire
   (Borders)   NT 494 366
Lag Tower, Dumfriesshire
   NX 880 862
Lamington Tower, Lanarkshire (South)
   NS 980 320
Lanark Castle, Lanarkshire (South)
   NS 879 433
Langshaw Tower, Roxburghshire
   (Borders)   NT 516 397
*Langskaill House, Gairsay, Orkney
   HY 434 220
Lanton Tower, Roxburghshire (Borders)
   NT 618 215
Largo Tower, Fife   NO 418 034
Lauder – *see* Thirlestane Castle
Lauriston Castle, Kincardineshire
   (Aberdeenshire)   NO 759 666
*Lauriston Castle, Midlothian
   (Edinburgh)   NT 204 762
*Law Castle, Ayrshire (North)
   NS 211 484
Lee Tower, Peeblesshire (Borders)
   NT 328 396
Leith Town Defences, Midlothian
   (Edinburgh)   NT 260 760
Leitholm Peel, Berwickshire (Borders)
   NT 784 438
Lennox Castle, Dunbartonshire (West)
   NS 373 863
*Lennoxlove House, East Lothian
   NT 515 721
Lennox Tower, Midlothian (Edinburgh)
   NT 174 671
Leod – *see* Castle Leod
*Leslie Castle, Aberdeenshire
   NJ 599 248
Lethendry Castle, Moray (Highland)
   NJ 084 274
Lethington – *see* Lennoxlove
Leuchars Castle, Fife   NO 454 219
Levan – *see* Castle Levan
Leven – *see* Lochleven

*Liberton Tower, Midlothian
   (Edinburgh)   NT 265 697
*Lickleyhead Castle, Aberdeenshire
   NJ 627 237
Liddel Castle, Roxburghshire (Borders)
   NT 633 313
Lincluden Mote, Kirkcudbrightshire
   (Galloway)   NX 966 678
*Linlithgow Palace, West Lothian
   NT 003 774
Little Carleton Motte – *see* Carleton
*Little Cumbrae Castle, Bute County
   (North Ayrshire)   NS 153 514
*Littledean Tower, Roxburghshire
   (Borders)   NT 633 314
Little Tarrel – *see* Rockfield
*Loch an Eilein Castle, Inverness-shire
   (Highland)   NH 899 079
Lochbuie – *see* Moy
Loch Dochart Castle, Perthshire
   (Stirlingshire)   NN 407 257
*Loch Doon Castle, Ayrshire (East)
   NX 484 950
*Lochhouse Tower, Dumfriesshire
   NT 082 034
*Lochindorb Castle, Moray (Highland)
   NH 974 364
*Lochleven Castle, Kinross-shire
   NO 138 018
*Lochmaben Castle and Old Castle,
   Dumfriesshire   NY 089 812
*Lochnaw Castle, Wigtownshire
   (Galloway)   NW 991 628
*Lochore Castle, Fife   NT 175 959
*Lochranza Castle, Arran, Bute County
   (North Ayrshire)   NR 934 507
Loch Raonasa – *see* Lochranza
Lochwood Tower, Dumfriesshire
   NY 085 968
Lockhart's Tower – *see* Barr, Ayrshire
*Lordscairnie Castle, Fife   NO 348 178
Loudoun Castle, Ayrshire (East)
   NS 506 378
Lower Ingleston Mote, Dumfriesshire
   NX 799 900
*Luffness Castle, East Lothian
   NT 475 804

Lumphanan – *see* Peel Ring of Lumphanan
Lunan - *see* Red Castle, Angus
Lundin Tower, Fife   NO 399 029

*Macduff's Castle, Fife   NT 344 972
*MacLellan's Castle, Kirkcudbrightshire (Galloway)   NX 683 511
Maiden Castle, Fife   NO 349 015
*Mains Castle, Angus (Dundee)   NO 401 330
Mains Castle, Dunbartonshire – *see* Kilmaronock
*Mains Castle, Lanarkshire (South)   NS 627 560
Malcolm Canmore's Tower, Fife   NT 087 873
Maol – *see* Caisteal Maol
Mar – *see* Braemar
Marchmount – *see* Roxburgh
Markle Castle, East Lothian   NT 579 775
Mar's Wark – *see* Stirling
Mary Queen of Scots' House – *see* Queen Mary's House
*Mauchline Castle, Ayrshire (East)   NS 496 273
*Maybole Castle, Ayrshire (South)   NS 301 100
Mearnaig – *see* Glensanda
*Mearns Castle, Renfrewshire (East)   NS 552 553
*Meggernie Castle, Perthshire   NN 554 460
*Megginch Castle, Perthshire   NO 242 246
*Melgund Castle, Angus   NO 546 564
*Menstrie Castle, Clackmannanshire   NS 852 968
Menzies – *see* Castle Menzies
*Merchiston Castle, Midlothian (Edinburgh)   NT 243 717
*Methven Castle, Perthshire   NO 042 261
Mey – *see* Castle of Mey

*Midhope Castle, West Lothian   NT 073 787
*Midmar Castle and Cunningar Motte, Aberdeenshire   NJ 704 053
*Milton Tower, Banffshire (Moray)   NJ 429 512
*Mingary Castle, Argyll: Mainland (Highland)   NM 502 631
Minnigaff Mote, Kirkcudbrightshire (Galloway)   NX 410 665
Minto – *see* Fatlips
Miogharraidh – *see* Mingary
Mochrum – *see* Druchtag; Old Place of Mochrum
Moil – *see* Caisteal Maol
*Moncur Castle, Perthshire   NO 284 295
Moniack Castle, Inverness-shire (Highland)   NH 552 436
Monikie – *see* Affleck
*Monimail Tower, Fife   NO 299 141
Monkton House, Midlothian (East Lothian)   NT 349 717
Montfode Castle, Ayrshire (North)   NS 226 441
Montrose Castle, Angus   NO 710 574
*Monymusk House, Aberdeenshire   NJ 688 155
Mortlach – *see* Balvenie
*Morton Castle, Dumfriesshire   NX 891 992
Mote of Annan, Dumfriesshire   NY 192 667
*Mote of Urr, Kirkcudbrightshire (Galloway)   NX 815 647
Moulin – *see* Black Castle of Moulin
*Mountquhanie Castle, Fife   NO 347 212
Mouswald Tower, Dumfriesshire   NY 051 739
*Moy Castle, Mull, Argyll: Islands   NM 616 247
Muchall-in-Mar – *see* Castle Fraser
*Muchalls Castle, Kincardineshire (Aberdeenshire)   NO 892 918
*Muckrach Castle, Inverness-shire (Highland)   NH 986 251

*Mugdock Castle, Stirlingshire
    NS 549 772
*Muness Castle, Unst, Shetland
    HP 629 013
Murieston Castle, West Lothian
    NT 050 636
*Murroes House, Angus   NO 461 350
*Murthly Castle, Perthshire
    NO 070 399
*Myres Castle, Fife   NO 242 110
Myrton Castle, Wigtownshire
    (Galloway)   NX 360 432

Nairn Castle, Nairnshire (Highland)
    NH 885 566
*Neidpath Castle, Peeblesshire
    (Borders)   NT 236 404
Nether Abington – see Abington
Nether Horsburgh Castle, Peeblesshire
    (Borders)   NT 304 396
*Newark Castle, Ayrshire (South)
    NS 324 173
*Newark Castle, Fife   NO 518 012
*Newark Castle, Renfrewshire
    (Inverclyde)   NS 329 744
*Newark Castle, Selkirkshire (Borders)
    NT 421 294
*Newmilns Tower, Ayrshire (East)
    NS 536 374
Newmore Castle, Ross (Highland)
    NH 680 719
*Newton Castle, Perthshire
    NO 172 453
Newton House, Midlothian
    NT 332 699
Newtyle – see Hatton
*Niddry Castle, West Lothian
    NT 097 743
*Nisbet House, Berwickshire (Borders)
    NT 795 512
*Noltland Castle, Westray, Orkney
    HY 429 488
*Nunraw Tower, East Lothian
    NT 597 706

Oakwood – see Aikwood
Old Aberdeen – see Wallace Tower

*Old Breachacha Castle, Coll, Argyll:
    Islands   NM 159 539
Old Buittle – see Buittle
*Old Castle Lachlan, Argyll: Mainland
    NS 006 954
*Old Inverlochy Castle, Inverness-shire
    (Highland)   NN 121 755
*Old Keiss Castle, Caithness (Highland)
    ND 357 616
*Old Place of Mochrum, Wigtownshire
    (Galloway)   NX 308 541
Old Place of Sorbie – see Sorbie
*Old Sauchie House, Stirlingshire
    NS 779 883
Old Slains Castle, Aberdeenshire
    NK 052 301
Old Thirlestane Castle, Berwickshire
    (Borders)   NT 564 474
*Old Tulliallan Castle, Fife   NS 927 888
Old Wick – see Castle of Old Wick
Oliphant – see Milton
*Orchardton Tower, Kirkcudbrightshire
    (Galloway)   NX 817 551
Ormond Castle, Ross (Highland)
    NH 696 536
Outtershill – see Uttershill

Palace of Holyroodhouse – see
    Holyrood
Panmure Castle, Angus   NO 545 376
Park – see Castle of Park
*Peebles Town Wall and Castle,
    Peeblesshire (Borders)
    NT 249 403
Peel of Fichlie, Aberdeenshire
    NJ 459 149
*Peel Ring of Lumphanan,
    Aberdeenshire   NJ 576 937
*Penkill Castle, Ayrshire (South)
    NX 232 985
Perth Castle and Town Wall, Perthshire
    NO 119 238
Philorth – see Cairnbulg
*Pinkie House, Midlothian (East
    Lothian)   NT 350 727

INDEX OF SITES

*Pinwherry Castle, Ayrshire (South)
   NX 198 867
Pitcairlie House, Fife   NO 236 148
*Pitcaple Castle, Aberdeenshire
   NJ 726 261
*Pitcruvie Castle, Fife   NO 413 046
*Pitcullo Castle, Fife   NO 413 196
*Pitcur Castle, Angus (Perthshire)
   NO 252 370
*Piteadie Castle, Fife   NT 257 891
*Pitfichie Castle, Aberdeenshire
   NJ 677 168
*Pitfirrane Castle, Fife   NT 060 863
*Pitheavlis Castle, Perthshire
   NO 097 222
Pitlurg Castle, Banffshire (Moray)
   NJ 436 455
*Pitreavie Castle, Fife   NT 117 847
*Pitsligo Castle, Aberdeenshire
   NJ 928 669
*Pittarthie Castle, Fife   NO 522 091
*Pittenweem Priory, Fife   NO 549 025
Pittulie – see Castle of Pittulie
*Plane Castle, Stirlingshire   NS 849 869
Plean - see Plane
*Plunton Castle, Kirkcudbrightshire
   (Galloway)   NX 605 507
Polnoon Castle, Renfrewshire (East)
   NS 586 513
*Portencross Castle and Auld Hill,
   Ayrshire (North)   NS 176 488
Port Glasgow – see Newark,
   Renfrewshire
*Powrie Castle, Angus (Dundee)
   NO 421 346
*Preston Tower, East Lothian
   NT 393 742
Proncy Castle, Sutherland (Highland)
   NB 772 926
*Provan Hall, Lanarkshire (Glasgow)
   NS 667 663

*Queen Mary's House, Roxburghshire
   (Borders)   NT 651 206

*Rait Castle, Nairnshire (Highland)
   NH 894 525

Ranfurly Castle, Renfrewshire
   NS 384 652
*Ravenscraig Castle, Aberdeenshire
   NK 095 488
*Ravenscraig Castle, Fife   NT 921 925
Ravenstone Castle, Wigtownshire
   (Galloway)   NX 409 441
*Red Castle, Angus   NO 700 512
Redcastle, Ross (Highland)
   NH 584 495
*Redhouse Castle, East Lothian
   NT 463 771
Renfrew Castle, Renfrewshire
   NS 508 678
*Repentance Tower, Dumfriesshire
   NY 155 723
Rhymer's Tower, Berwickshire
   (Borders)   NT 572 383
Riddell Motte, Roxburghshire (Borders)
   NT 520 248
Roberton Mote, Kirkcudbrightshire
   (Galloway)   NX 604 456
Roberton Motte, Lanarkshire (South)
   NS 940 270
Robgill Tower, Dumfriesshire
   NY 248 716
*Rockfield Castle, Ross (Highland)
   NH 911 819
Rockhall Mote, Dumfriesshire
   NY 055 766
Roseburn House, Midlothian
   (Edinburgh)   NT 226 731
Roslin – see Rosslyn
Rossdhu Castle, Dunbartonshire
   (Argyll)   NS 361 896
*Rossend Castle, Fife   NT 225 859
*Rosslyn Castle, Midlothian
   NT 274 628
*Rosyth Castle, Fife   NT 115 820
*Rothesay Castle, Bute, Bute County
   NS 088 646
Rothes Castle, Moray   NJ 277 490
*Rowallan Old Castle, Ayrshire (East)
   NS 435 424
*Roxburgh Castle, Roxburghshire
   (Borders)   NT 713 337
Roy – see Castle Roy

*Rusco Tower, Kirkcudbrightshire (Galloway)   NX 584 605
Rutherglen Castle, Lanarkshire (South)   NS 614 618
Ruthven, Perthshire – see Huntingtower
Ruthven Castle, Angus   NO 302 479
Ruthven Castle, Inverness-shire (Highland)   NN 765 997

*Saddell Castle, Argyll: Mainland   NR 789 315
Saghadal – see Saddell
*St Andrews Castle, Precinct Wall and Town Defences, Fife   NO 513 169
St John – see Castle of St John
*Saltcoats Castle, East Lothian   NT 486 819
*Sanquhar Castle, Dumfriesshire   NS 795 093
Sauchie, Stirlingshire – see Old Sauchie
*Sauchie Tower, Clackmannanshire   NS 896 957
*Scalloway Castle, Mainland, Shetland   HU 405 393
Schivas – see House of Schivas
*Scone Palace, Perthshire   NO 114 265
*Scotstarvit Tower, Fife   NO 370 113
*Seafield Tower, Fife   NT 280 885
*Seagate Castle, Ayrshire (North)   NS 319 391
Selkirk Castle, Selkirkshire (Borders)   NT 470 280
Sgibnis – see Skipness
Shieldhill Castle, Lanarkshire (South)   NT 007 404
Sinclair – see Castle Sinclair Girnigoe
Sinniness Castle, Wigtownshire (Galloway)   NX 205 531
*Sir John de Graham's Castle, Stirlingshire   NS 662 858
*Skelbo Castle, Sutherland (Highland)   NH 792 952
*Skelmorlie Castle, Ayrshire (North)   NS 195 658
Skene House, Aberdeenshire   NJ 768 097

*Skipness Castle, Argyll: Mainland   NR 907 577
Slains Castle, Aberdeenshire   NK 101 361
*Smailholm Tower, Roxburghshire (Borders)   NT 638 347
*Smeaton House, Midlothian (East Lothian)   NT 347 699
*Sorbie Castle, Wigtownshire (Galloway)   NX 451 471
*Sorn Castle, Ayrshire (East)   NS 548 269
Southwick Mote, Kirkcudbrightshire (Galloway)   NX 936 570
*Spedlins Tower, Dumfriesshire   NY 098 877
*Spynie Palace, Moray   NJ 231 658
Stalker – see Castle Stalker
Stane Castle, Ayrshire (North)   NS 338 399
*Stanely Castle, Renfrewshire   NS 464 616
Staneyhill Tower, West Lothian   NT 092 784
*Stapleton Tower, Dumfriesshire   NY 234 688
*Stirling Castle, Mar's Wark and Town Wall, Stirlingshire   NS 790 941
*Stobhall Castle, Perthshire   NO 133 344
*Stoneypath Tower, East Lothian   NT 596 714
Stornoway Castle, Lewis, Western Isles   NB 423 327
Stranraer – see Castle of St John
*Strathaven Castle, Lanarkshire (South)   NS 703 444
Strathbogie – see Huntly, Aberdeenshire
*Strathendry Castle, Fife   NO 226 020
*Strome Castle, Ross (Highland)   NG 862 354
Struthers Castle, Fife   NO 377 097
Stuart – see Castle Stuart
Suibhne – see Castle Sween
Sundrum Castle, Ayrshire (South)   NS 410 213
Sween – see Castle Sween

INDEX OF SITES

*Talla Castle, Perthshire (Stirlingshire)
   NN 572 004
*Tantallon Castle, East Lothian
   NT 596 850
*Tarbert Castle, Argyll: Mainland
   NR 867 687
Tarbolton Motte, Ayrshire (South)
   NS 432 273
Tarvit – see Scotstarvit
*Terpersie Castle, Aberdeenshire
   NJ 547 202
Terringzean Castle, Ayrshire (East)
   NS 556 205
*Thirlestane Castle, Berwickshire
   (Borders)   NT 534 479
Thirlestane Tower, Selkirkshire
   (Borders)   NT 281 154
*Thomaston Castle, Ayrshire (South)
   NS 240 096
*Thornton Castle, Kincardineshire
   (Aberdeenshire)   NO 688 718
*Threave Castle, Kirkcudbrightshire
   (Galloway)   NX 739 623
Thurso Castle, Caithness (Highland)
   ND 124 689
Tibbers Castle, Dumfriesshire
   NX 863 983
*Tillycairn Castle, Aberdeenshire
   NJ 664 114
*Tilquhillie Castle, Kincardineshire
   (Aberdeenshire)   NO 722 740
Timpendean Tower, Roxburghshire
   (Borders)   NT 636 226
Tinnis Castle, Peeblesshire (Borders)
   NT 141 344
Tioram – see Castle Tioram
Tollard – see Toward
*Tolquhon Castle, Aberdeenshire
   NJ 874 286
*Torrance House, Lanarkshire (South)
   NS 654 526
*Torthorwald Castle, Dumfriesshire
   NY 033 783
*Torwood Castle, Stirlingshire (Falkirk)
   NS 836 844
Torwoodhead – see Torwood

*Torwoodlee Tower, Selkirkshire
   (Borders)   NT 467 378
*Touch House, Stirlingshire
   NS 753 928
*Toward Castle, Argyll: Mainland
   NS 119 678
Tower of Hallbar – see Braidwood
*Towie Barclay Castle, Aberdeenshire
   NJ 744 439
Traigh a Chaisteal – see Brodick
Tranent Tower, East Lothian
   NT 404 729
*Traquair House, Peeblesshire (Borders)
   NT 330 354
Tulliallan – see Old Tulliallan
*Tullibole Castle, Kinross-shire
   NO 053 006
Tulloch Castle, Ross (Highland)
   NH 547 605
Turnberry Castle, Ayrshire (South)
   NS 196 073

*Udny Castle, Aberdeenshire
   NJ 882 268
*Urquhart Castle, Inverness-shire
   (Highland)   NH 531 286
Urr – see Mote of Urr
*Uttershill Castle, Midlothian
   NT 238 594

Varrich – see Castle Varrich
*Vayne Castle, Angus   NO 493 599
Vow Castle, Dunbartonshire (Argyll)
   NN 331 127

Wallace's Tower, Roxburghshire
   (Borders)   NT 700 304
*Wallace Tower, Aberdeenshire
   (Aberdeen)   NJ 936 089
Wamphray Mote, Dumfriesshire
   NY 128 965
Waughton Castle, East Lothian
   NT 567 809
*Waygateshaw House, Lanarkshire
   (South)   NS 825 484
*Wedderlie House, Berwickshire
   (Borders)   NT 640 515

*Wemyss Castle, Fife   NT 329 951
Wester Braikie – *see* Braikie
Wester Kames Castle, Bute, Bute County   NS 062 681
*Westhall Castle, Aberdeenshire   NJ 673 266
West Kilbride – *see* Law
*Whitefield Castle, Perthshire   NO 089 617
Whitekirk Tower, East Lothian   NT 595 816
Whitslade Tower, Peeblesshire (Borders)   NT 112 350
Whitslaid Tower, Berwickshire (Borders)   NT 557 446
*Whittingehame Tower, East Lothian   NT 602 733
Whitton Tower, Roxburghshire (Borders)   NT 759 222

*Whytbank Tower, Selkirkshire (Borders)   NT 442 377
Wick – *see* Castle of Old Wick
Wigtown Castle, Wigtownshire (Galloway)   NX 437 550
Windydoors Tower, Selkirkshire (Borders)   NT 432 398
Wine Tower – *see* Kinnaird Head
Winkston Tower, Peeblesshire (Borders)   NT 245 430
Woodhall House, East Lothian   NT 433 680
Woodhead House, Stirlingshire (East Dunbartonshire)   NS 606 783
Woodhouse Tower, Dumfriesshire   NY 251 715
Wyre – *see* Cubbie Roo's Castle

*Yester Castle, East Lothian   NT 556 667